"Paul Cho highlights an important but understudied phenomenon in the Hebrew Bible: the willingness to die. He carefully, but engagingly, distinguishes between suicide, martyrdom, and other ways that the motif appears in ancient texts. Just as importantly, he keeps a keen eye upon the theological implications of the attitudes to death in the Hebrew Bible in order to develop a fuller picture of how death affects life on both the human and divine planes for people of faith today."

— **James D. Nogalski**
Baylor University

"Although martyrdom and a willingness to sacrifice one's life for the sake of others is often assumed to be a distinctive New Testament or Christian theme, Paul Cho's *Willingness to Die and the Gift of Life* argues that the theme is deeply embedded already in the Hebrew Bible / Old Testament. Cho expertly portrays how a wide array of protagonists in the Hebrew Bible exemplify the theme in different ways. Some actually give up their lives; others contemplate it and come dangerously close. Examples include Samson, Saul, Job, Judah, Moses, and Esther. Two Old Testament figures are genuine martyrs in the fullest sense: the Suffering Servant of Isaiah 40–55 and the persecuted members of the 'Wise' who were killed for their faith and promised a resurrection from the dead in Daniel 11. The book concludes with a provocative reflection on whether the God of the Hebrew Bible could conceivably ever die or be portrayed as willing to die."

— **Dennis T. Olson**
Princeton Theological Seminary

"Paul Cho has written a fresh and richly suggestive book. He shows that by a focus on a fresh interpretive question, texts are illuminated in new configurations that generate new possibilities for meaning and significance. Cho's work is marked in two important ways. On the one hand he attends carefully to the biblical text; on the other hand he has read widely and has mobilized fresh secondary material for his study. This book is welcome now in a culture of violence where life is precarious and widely under threat. It is only because of the inexplicable gift of life that we may think with freedom about death. In this study, Cho features those who thought courageously about death."

— **Walter Brueggemann**
Columbia Theological Seminary

"Paul Cho has produced an important and relevant work on the monumental subject matter of death in the Hebrew Bible as risked death, suicide, and martyrdom. Each chapter is a highly developed, self-contained exposition engaging theological, social, and ethical issues on death so that life may be furthered for those that continue to live in the here and now. From kings and heroes like Moses, Job, and Samson, to Queen Esther, the Suffering Servant, and Daniel and his three friends, Cho has provided an invaluable and fresh work with exceptional literary exposition. The work is timely and provocative."

— John Ahn
Howard University School of Divinity

"In this splendidly argued, creative, learned, and readable volume, one of the preeminent biblical scholars of the younger generation offers striking new insights into no less momentous an issue than that of death and life in the Hebrew Bible. Buckle your seat belt: this book is likely to change your views on that issue and on a multitude of biblical texts in the process. Enthusiastically recommended!"

— Jon D. Levenson
Harvard Divinity School

Willingness to Die and the Gift of Life

*Suicide and Martyrdom
in the Hebrew Bible*

Paul K.-K. Cho

William B. Eerdmans Publishing Company
Grand Rapids, Michigan

Wm. B. Eerdmans Publishing Co.
4035 Park East Court SE, Grand Rapids, Michigan 49546
www.eerdmans.com

© 2022 Paul K.-K. Cho
All rights reserved
Published 2022
Printed in the United States of America

28 27 26 25 24 23 22   2 3 4 5 6 7

ISBN 978-0-8028-7541-9

Library of Congress Cataloging-in-Publication Data

A catalog record for this book is available from the Library of Congress.

For Eunice,
Proverbs 18:22

Reader, I found her.

CONTENTS

	Preface	ix
	Acknowledgments	xiii
	List of Abbreviations	xv
1.	Kings and Hero Men and Suicide in the Deuteronomistic History	1
2.	Job and the Problem of Suicide	28
3.	Was Samson a Suicide Terrorist?	60
4.	The Other Samsons	100
5.	Judah's Scepter	131
6.	Moses from the Breach to the Cleft	155
7.	Queen Esther's Gambit	172
8.	From Suicide to Martyrdom	199
9.	The Suffering Servant Exalted and Lifted Up and Very High	224
10.	The Wise Shall Live Again	254
	Epilogue	263
	Selected Bibliography	271

CONTENTS

Index of Names and Subjects — 283

Index of Scripture and Other Ancient Texts — 292

PREFACE

He was either someone close to birth or death.

Graham Greene[1]

THE PRESENT BOOK IS A STUDY of figures in the Hebrew Bible who express a willingness to die or indeed die willingly. It examines how the Hebrew Bible conceptualizes the relationship between alloforms of voluntary death and life. As such, the book examines a diverse selection of biblical texts from a range of historical periods through several methodological lenses. Specifically, the book examines figures who commit or are thought to commit suicide in the Deuteronomistic History (Deuteronomy–2 Kings), Job as a person who exhibits suicide ideation, Samson as potentially a suicide terrorist, Judah, Esther and Moses as leaders who risk death for the benefit of Israel, and the Suffering Servant and the Wise as martyrs. The wide range of subjects and methodologies makes summation and a global thesis difficult. By design, therefore, each chapter provides an in-depth and relatively self-contained discussion.

Nevertheless, each chapter focuses on the relationship between death and life that obtains when a living person is willing to die. This overarching focus holds various discussions and analytical insights together, and the

---

1. Graham Greene, *The Power and the Glory* (London: Penguin Books, 1940), 123.

cumulative effect is a clearer understanding of the prestige and charism that attach to the willing embrace of death. While aspects of ancient Near Eastern culture, so different from our modern Western cultural attitudes especially toward voluntary death, can explain certain conclusions of the book—for example, the idea that a suicide might die to protect his honor—other conclusions represent genuine innovations concerning how we understand the way biblical traditions come to valorize voluntary death, in particular death that is embraced for the sake of the group or in faithful commitment to Yhwh. Death willingly embraced can unlock immense power, endowing the willing with the charism necessary to lead, sanctifying death into vicarious suffering and transforming it into a portal to a new and more glorious life.

Outline of Chapters

Chapters 1 and 2 treat suicide in the Deuteronomistic History and the book of Job. We tend to think of suicide as an intensely private event and as the unfortunate outcome of the desperate decision of a solitary individual. However, we have known at least since the French sociologist Émile Durkheim's landmark study *Suicide: A Study in Sociology* (1897) that suicide is also a social phenomenon, shaped and influenced in powerful ways by forces outside the control of the individual. Durkheim demonstrated the need to study suicidality within its social and cultural contexts. We adopt this enlarged, sociological approach to analyze potential suicides in the Deuteronomistic History in chapter 1 and conclude that suicides, understood within the honor and shame culture of ancient Israel, may die in honor and even confer benefit to their family and those related to them. Chapter 2 examines Job as he considers whether life is worth living and traces how these musings imaginatively reexamine the relationship between life and death. We shall see in the book of Job adumbrations of the idea of vindication after death and the tactical use of a willing embrace of death as a means of affirming one's dignity.

Chapters 3 and 4 are studies of Samson. Taking advantage of the fact that Samson enjoys a rich and variegated history of interpretation already within biblical literature, we analyze the biblical Samson story (Judges 13–16)

Preface

through its later reception in John Milton's *Samson Agonistes*, Blind Willie Johnson's song "If I Had My Way I'd Tear This Building Down," and Augustine's "Sermon 364" to consider whether Samson represents a suicide terrorist or a redeeming hero.

Chapters 5, 6, and 7 are studies of three leaders in the biblical tradition who risk death for the sake of the group: Judah, Moses, and Esther. Each strategically embraces death in their negotiation with a more powerful other in order to save Israel: Judah to save Israel from devastating famine, Moses from divine wrath, and Esther from human hatred. These three characters demonstrate in their own ways that one's willingness to die can be employed as a tactic to redeem their people from death. They also discover in death a power to give life to others and, as a consequence, win the authority and charism necessary to lead.

Chapters 8, 9, and 10 turn to the topic of martyrdom. Chapter 8 offers a definition of martyrdom and reviews the figures studied up to this point through that lens. Chapters 9 and 10 are studies of the two martyrs in the Hebrew Bible: the Suffering Servant of Isaiah 53 and the authors of the book of Daniel who refer to themselves as the Wise. We will see in these chapters the emergence of the idea of vicarious suffering and the doctrine of the resurrection of the dead.

The book concludes with a summative review of the book and a brief consideration of whether God might die and be understood to express a willingness to die for the sake of Israel in the Hebrew Bible.

A Note to Method

Throughout, I have prioritized the interpretation of the biblical text and the illumination of the theme of the willingness to die over methodological consistency. Thus, while the biblical text almost always lies at the center, a variety of methods have been employed to open up and analyze the text and the relevant issues therein. In each case, I have tried to marry the best method for the task of studying the selected text and the chosen topic. For example, in chapters 3 and 4, which ask whether Samson is a suicide terrorist or a heroic redeemer (a question that is itself taken from the field of Milton studies), I employ a history-of-interpretation perspective to better appreciate the redactional tensions of the canonical text and their contribution to the ambiguity surrounding Samson in later reception history. In contrast, I take up the social theory of Michel de Certeau in chapter 7 to analyze Esther's gambit to access the power needed to save her people. In short, to be faithful to the text and to illuminate the topic of the willingness to die, I chose to be promiscuous as to method.

A downside of this methodological eclecticism is an increase in the complexity of the book and the potential impedance of the main argument. In a book that employs a single dominant method, once that methodology has been explicated and demonstrated, the argument can be laid out with fewer and fewer qualifications and explications (on the part of the author) and read with increasing ease and alacrity (on the part of the reader). In contrast, a methodologically diverse book, such as the present one, must slow down time and again to explain, clarify, and combat assumptive blinders. In writing a methodologically diverse book, I have perhaps risked oversaturating the colors and the contrast levels for the sake of achieving a more detailed and vibrant comprehension.

The result, practically speaking, is that this book can be read as a topically interconnected collection of individual essays. But to read this book only as an essay collection would miss out on the overarching and cumulative argument that I have tried to thread together. I have cut out vistas here and there, but I have not provided anything like an aerial view, because I do not think a clear and continuous history of development can be reconstructed. This is because the willingness-to-die tradition—which perhaps is as good a name as any for what this book tries to describe—is fed by multiple tributaries, including suicide, suicide attack, sacrificial death, and martyrdom. To introduce an explanatory image, these small and large tributaries pool together underground and, almost out of view, flow and, flowing gently, carve into the bedrock something new and revolutionary. The appearance of these new and revolutionary patterns of thinking at the fraught borderlands between life and death transforms the entire landscape of existence, for all the living and the dead.

Join me as we push off the bank.

ACKNOWLEDGMENTS

THIS STUDY WAS BEGUN IN THE SUMMER OF 2017, and much of the research for the book and the first draft of several of its chapters were completed in 2017–2018 during a research leave from Wesley Theological Seminary, to which I am grateful. I am likewise grateful to the Louisville Institute, whose First Book Grant for Scholars of Color provided additional financial support that made a yearlong leave possible, and to the Department of Classics and Ancient Mediterranean Studies at Penn State, in particular Aaron D. Rubin and Mark Munn, for hosting me as a visiting scholar during the leave.

I am much indebted to a number of friends, colleagues, and teachers, especially those who kindly read and offered erudite and incisive comments on all or a part of the manuscript: Jon D. Levenson, Janling Fu, Dong-Hyuk Kim, Jane E. Kim, Sathianathan Clarke, and Jean Dudek. I also profited from conversations with Sondra Wheeler, Cheryl Townsend Gilkes, and many others. Parts of chapter 5 have their origin in a paper I wrote for Professor Carolyn J. Sharp as an MDiv student in 2005 and benefited from her inspired teaching and detailed comments on that paper. Special thanks are due to the students of Wesley Theological Seminary who took the course "Willingness to Die in the Hebrew Bible" in the years 2016–2020. The book reflects their wisdom, learning, and insight. The errors that remain, needless to say, are strictly my responsibility.

A special note of thanks is due to the Faculty of Wesley Theological Seminary. During the first faculty meeting of 2015–2016, the Wesley Faculty discussed the murder of Reverend and State Senator Clementa C.

ACKNOWLEDGMENTS

Pinckney. He had been a student in our Doctor of Ministry program at the time Dylan Roof entered Mother Emmanuel African Methodist Episcopal Church, sat through the Bible study Pinckney led, and murdered him and eight other congregants. We were weighing the possibility of posthumously awarding Pinckney the DMin. Then came a comment that dispelled all hesitation. A colleague observed that Pastor Pinckney had died in the line of duty and that some among us must be willing to die to live out our Christian calling. The statement woke me as if from a slumber and watered the seed that has become this book.

I also owe much gratitude to my two editors. Andrew Knapp showed me kind and patient support since our first conversation about the project, and Laurel Draper and the team at Eerdmans have shepherded the volume through the publication process with expert efficiency. I must also thank my copyeditor, Blake Jurgens, whose expertise as an editor and biblical scholar improved my manuscript.

Urbana, Maryland
December 28, 2021

ABBREVIATIONS

AB	Anchor Bible
ABD	*Anchor Bible Dictionary.* Edited by David Noel Freedman. 6 vols. New York: Doubleday, 1992
b.	Babylonian Talmud
BDB	Francis Brown, S. R. Driver, and Charles A. Briggs. *A Hebrew and English Lexicon of the Old Testament*
BibInt	*Biblical Interpretation*
BZAW	Beihefte zur Zeitschrift fur die alttestamentliche Wissenschaft
CBQ	*Catholic Bible Quarterly*
COS	*The Context of Scripture.* Edited by William W. Hallo. 3 vols. Leiden: Brill, 1997–2002
ECC	Eerdmans Critical Commentary
FAT	Forschungen zum Alten Testament
FOTL	Forms of the Old Testament Literature
HBM	Hebrew Bible Monographs
HKAT	Handkommentar zum Alten Testament
HSM	Harvard Semitic Monographs
HTR	*Harvard Theological Review*
HTS	Harvard Theological Studies
IVBS	International Voices in Biblical Studies
JBL	*Journal of Biblical Literature*
JBQ	*Jewish Bible Quarterly*
JNES	*Journal of Near Eastern Studies*
JSOT	*Journal for the Study of the Old Testament*

ABBREVIATIONS

JSOTSup	Journal for the Study of the Old Testament Supplement Series
KTU	*The Cuneiform Alphabetic Texts from Ugarit, Ras Ibn Hani, and Other Places.* Edited by Manfried Dietrich, Oswald Loretz, and Joaquín Sanmartín. Münster: Ugarit-Verlag, 1995
LHBOTS	The Library of Hebrew Bible/Old Testament Studies
Louw-Nida	Johannes P. Louw and Eugene A. Nida, eds. *Greek-English Lexicon of the New Testament: Based on Semantic Domains.* 2nd ed. New York: United Bible Societies, 1989
LSJ	Henry George Liddell, Robert Scott, and Henry Stuart Jones. *A Greek-English Lexicon.* 9th ed. with revised supplement. Oxford: Clarendon, 1996
OBO	Orbis Biblicus et Orientalis
ORA	Orientalische Religionen in der Antike
OTL	Old Testament Library
SAOC	Studies in Ancient Oriental Civilization
SBLAIL	Society of Biblical Literature Ancient Israel and Its Literature
SBLStBL	Society of Biblical Literature Studies in Biblical Literature
SBLWAW	Society of Biblical Literature Writings from the Ancient World
SemeiaSt	Semeia Studies
SHBC	Smyth & Helwys Bible Commentary
TDOT	*Theological Dictionary of the Old Testament.* Edited by G. Johannes Botterweck and Helmer Ringgren. Translated by John T. Willis et al. 8 vols. Grand Rapids: Eerdmans, 1974–2006
VT	*Vetus Testamentum*
WBC	Word Biblical Commentary
ZAW	*Zeitschrift für die alttestamentliche Wissenschaft*

CHAPTER 1

Kings and Hero Men and Suicide in the Deuteronomistic History

Suicide: the voluntary destroying of a person's own life, by one's own means and procurement.

John Sym [1]

THE ENGLISH WORD "SUICIDE" WAS COINED in 1651 or 1652 by Walter Charleton, an English physician, and came into wide usage only in the eighteenth century;[2] but the phenomenon to which it points—the voluntary killing of oneself—has existed in all cultures from every time and place and elicits violent and often polar opposite responses. On the one hand, common is the belief that suicide violates a fundamental moral value, that it is a sin that must be strictly and often elaborately punished.[3] On the

---

1. Adapted from John Sym, cited in Michael MacDonald and Terence R. Murphy, *Sleepless Souls: Suicide in Early Modern England* (Oxford: Oxford University Press, 1990), 222.
2. David Daube, "Linguistics of Suicide," *Philosophy & Public Life* 1 (1972): 421–25.
3. In early modern England, for example, suicide was regarded as "bad death" and the ghosts of suicides were seen as "dangerous and intrusive," requiring elaborate burial practices to tame and keep at bay (MacDonald and Murphy, *Sleepless Souls*, 47). Thus, suicides were often buried under a highway or at crossroads with a stake driven through the body (*Sleepless Souls*, 44–49).

CHAPTER 1

other, some see suicide as an honorable act that can even expiate for past wrongs.[4] Either way, suicide is everywhere controversial: it is viewed as either a sin or an act of expiation, the spitting image of immorality or the highest expression of human liberty, the devil's work or a pathway heavenward. And these are just some of the extreme responses the topic of suicide has elicited. It is a topic about which one must choose sides.[5]

So what does the Bible say?[6]

Perhaps to the surprise of many, the Bible nowhere condemns suicide. In fact, some have argued that the Bible presents suicide as licit and even desirable.[7] As we will see in greater detail below, no one who voluntarily

---

4. The Stoic philosopher Seneca, for example, praises Cato's suicide as "a wide path to freedom" (cited in Arthur J. Droge and James D. Tabor, *A Noble Death: Suicide & Martyrdom among Christians and Jews in Antiquity* [New York: HarperCollins, 1992], 34). In a recent monograph on suicide in the ancient Near East, including in the Hebrew Bible, Jan Dietrich writes, "Der Selbstmord erweist sich in den meisten, wenn auch nicht allen biblischen und altorientalischen Fällen als ein Ehrphänomen: Hand an sich legt man um der eigenen Ehre und in den hellenistisch-jüdischen Texten auch um der Ehre Gottes willen." See *Der Tod von eigener Hand: Studien zum Suizid im Alten Testament, alten Ägypten und alten Orient*, ORA 19 (Tübingen: Mohr Siebeck, 2017), 19. As we shall see in greater detail, the biblical writers thought of self-killing as a means of preserving and, under certain cases, gaining honor.

5. The etymology of "suicide" mirrors the history of beliefs and attitudes concerning suicide. Daube ("Linguistics of Suicide," 422–24) argues that "sui-cide," which originally was hyphenated, may be a Latinization of John Donne's neologism, "self-homicide." Donne famously argued that "self-homicide" may or may not be a crime in *Biathanatos*, a book published posthumously against the author's wishes sometime between 1644 and 1647. Donne argued against the dominant legal and religious opinion that to kill oneself is to commit self-murder, a most serious crime and grave sin, and for that reason opposed publishing his apology for the right, under rare circumstances, for individuals to kill themselves. Charleton, in coining the neologism after Donne, agreed with Donne's measured defense of suicide. However, legal and religious attitudes have long remained hostile to defenses of suicide.

6. Biblical Hebrew has no word or phrase for suicide, and the expression מאבד את עצמו לדאת ("he that destroys his own self knowingly") first appears in Talmudic literature (Leon Nemoy, "A Tenth Century Disquisition on Suicide According to Old Testament Law," *JBL* 57 [1938]: 412; Daub, "Linguistics," 397). This means that the reader must discern whether an instance of death is to be considered suicide.

7. See Droge and Tabor, *Noble Death*; Dietrich, *Tod von eigener Hand*; James T. Clemons, *What Does the Bible Say about Suicide?* (Minneapolis: Fortress, 1989), 15–28.

kills himself in the Hebrew Bible is censured for the act, and some even receive honorable burials. For example, Samson, who kills himself in killing many Philistines, appears to win the narrator's praise for his final act, praise that reverberates in subsequent Jewish and Christian interpretative traditions: "So those he killed at his death were more than those he had killed during his life" (Judg. 16:30b).[8] In the New Testament, the Gospel of John presents Jesus not only as willing to die, but as dying voluntarily: "No one takes [my life] from me," Jesus says, "but I lay it down of my own accord" (John 10:18a). And Paul more than once expresses a preference for death as a pathway to heavenly bliss over the toils of life: "For to me, living is Christ and dying is gain. If I am to live in the flesh, that means fruitful labor for me; and I do not know which I prefer. I am hard pressed between the two: my desire is to depart and be with Christ, for that is far better; but to remain in the flesh is more necessary for you" (Phil. 1:21–24). "Dying," Paul says, "is gain" because to die is to "be with Christ." Paul is more than willing to die. He desires to die, "for that is far better."[9]

Despite these scriptural statements about voluntary death, both Jewish and Christian cultures have condemned suicide through the millennia. Late antique Jewish authorities generally prohibit suicide with exceptions made for extreme circumstances only.[10] And Christian theologians, es-

---

8. All English citations of the Bible are taken from the NRSV, unless otherwise indicated.

9. See Arthur J. Droge, "Suicide," *ABD* 4:225–31.

10. Yael Shemesh ("Suicide in the Bible," *JBQ* 37 [2009]: 157) reports that "Tractate Semahot (2:1) prescribes various sanctions against suicide victim and limits mourning rites for them. So does the *Shulhan Arukh* (Y. D. 345:1)" and notes that, in Jewish culture, "suicide is viewed sympathetically only in extreme cases, such as a threat to personal liberty as at Masada, or in attempts at forced conversion, as in Germany during the Crusades, in York in 1190, and other instances in medieval Europe." Nemoy ("Disquisition on Suicide," 412–13) writes, "In Rabbinic law suicide *per se* is forbidden, on both legal and moral grounds, except when it is the only way out of forced commission of one of the three capital sins—idolatry, murder, and adultery." For a fuller treatment, see Fred Rosner, "Suicide in Biblical, Talmudic and Rabbinic Writings," *Tradition: A Journal of Orthodox Jewish Thought* 11 (1970): 25–40. Rosner concludes, "Judaism regards suicide as a criminal act and strictly forbidden by Jewish law. The cases of suicide in the Bible as well as from the Apocrypha, Talmud and Midrash took place under unusual and extenuating conditions" (pp. 38–39).

pecially after Augustine, have condemned suicide as a crime and a sin.[11] Augustine influentially interpreted the sixth commandment, "You shall not murder" (Exod. 20:13), as precluding suicide, which he interpreted as self-murder.[12] With this, Augustine made it possible to equate suicide with the crime of murder and thus condemn suicides as murderers. In short, later Jewish and Christian opinions on suicide seem to disagree with explicit biblical statements about suicide. What the Bible permits, some have argued prescribes in certain circumstances, Jewish and Christian interpreters have consistently proscribed.

The reasons for the discrepancy between the explicit statements on suicide found in the Bible and subsequent Jewish and Christian customs regarding suicide are not difficult to surmise. Suicide as a lived reality, no less for the ancients than for later Jews and Christians, is a serious blow to the heart and fabric of human society in ways that seldom receive representation in biblical literature. Studies of suicide have failed to take sufficient stock, for example, of the fact that all examples of suicide in the Hebrew Bible come from one body of work scholars call the Deuteronomistic History (Deuteronomy–2 Kings, minus Ruth in the Christian canons), which likely stems from a more or less socially and ideologically homogenous group. As an epic retelling of Israel's history from its tribal origins in the late second millennium BCE to its demise in the sixth century, the Deuteronomistic History takes little interest in the experiences of everyday folk, much less in the obscure and relatively rare phenomenon of suicide committed by commoners. In short, the Deuteronomistic treatment of suicide should not be taken as representative of the entire Hebrew Bible or biblical Israel on the matter.

Fortunately, the Hebrew Bible contains profound thinking about death and life, specifically dealing with the question of when dying might become preferable to living, in the magnificent and enigmatic book of Job. Thus, in order to arrive at a fuller and necessarily more nuanced understanding of

---

11. See Droge and Tabor, *Noble Death*, 167–83; MacDonald and Murphy, *Sleepless Souls*; and George Minois, *History of Suicide: Voluntary Death in Western Culture*, trans. Lydia G. Cochrane (Baltimore: Johns Hopkins University Press, 1999).

12. See Augustine, *The City of God*, trans. Henry Bettenson (London: Penguin, 1984), 27, 31.

the Hebrew Bible's attitude toward the voluntary destroying of one's own life, in chapter 2 we shall examine Job on the question of whether life is worth living. At the end of our twin study of the Deuteronomistic History and Job, we will discover that the Hebrew Bible permits suicide under certain circumstances but also recommends, as is consonant with its generally high evaluation of human life, patient endurance through even horror and devastation. The Hebrew Bible provides neither simple condemnation nor simple approval of suicide. Its is a nuanced morality regarding suicide.[13]

Let us first turn to potential cases of suicide in the Deuteronomistic History: Abimelech son of Jerubbaal; Samson (briefly); Saul; Saul's squire, Ahithophel; and Zimri.

Abimelech Son of Jerubbaal (Judges 9)

Abimelech's death, if it is a suicide, is a case of assisted suicide. Mortally injured in battle, Abimelech commands his armor-bearer, "Draw your sword and kill me" (Judg. 9:54). Abimelech's motive for seeking death is clear: to avoid social shame.[14] "Kill me," he says, "so people will not say about me, 'A woman killed him'" (9:54). But is he a suicide?

Abimelech is a son of Gideon, who is called Jerubbaal in Judges 9. In his scheming to become king, Abimelech conspires with the people of Shechem to murder his seventy half-brothers, the sons of Jerubbaal who ruled over Israel. However, the relationship between Abimelech and the Shechemites sours, festers, then bursts into violence. At one point, Abimelech carries out a military campaign against the city of Thebez. He successfully lays siege to that city and even breaches its walls.[15] However,

---

13. Albert Bayet (*Le suicide et la morale* [Paris: Librarie Felix Alcan, 1922], 23) finds that attitudes toward suicide can be divided into a "morale *simple*" that condemns all suicides and a "morale *nuancée*" that condemns or pities, excuses or admires, instances of suicide case by case.

14. See Dietrich, *Tod von eigener Hand*, 77-82. About both Abimelech and Saul's respective deaths, Dietrich writes, "In beiden Fällen ist der Sinn der Selbsttötung die Verhinderung des 'sozialen Todes' und die Wahrung der eigenen Ehre" (p. 82).

15. The reason for Abimelech's campaign against Thebez is not clear. For an explanation based on the sociological model of the complex secondary chieftainship, see

during his attack on the strong fortress inside the city where the citizens have shut themselves in (9:51), "a certain woman threw an upper millstone on Abimelech's head, and crushed his skull" (9:53). It is then that Abimelech asks his armor-bearer to kill him lest he become a shameful byword, and his armor-bearer—unlike Saul's who under comparable circumstances refuses to obey his master (1 Sam. 31:4)—obliges his wounded king, thrusts him with a sword, and hastens Abimelech's death. The plan to preempt his becoming a byword for military incompetence, however, fails; for we have this story that details the circumstances of Abimelech's death, and the manner of Abimelech's death becomes the basis of a well-known military lesson by David's time: Do not fight immediately below fortified walls, lest you die shamefully like Abimelech (2 Sam. 11:21).

The Deuteronomistic scribe(s) who edited the account of Abimelech's rise and fall added a theological framework to a preexisting account of Abimelech's demise (Judg. 9:23–24, 56–57). This frame is a familiar prophecy-fulfillment formula. First, Judg. 9:23–24 announces the reason for God's involvement in history: God intervenes to punish Abimelech and the Shechemites for the part they played in slaying Abimelech's seventy brothers. Next, the story concludes with a summary fulfillment formula: "Thus God repaid Abimelech . . . and the people of Shechem" (9:56, 57). The Deuteronomistic History paints both the devastation that the Shechemites experience at Abimelech's hand and, more importantly for our purposes, Abimelech's death at the hand of a Shechemite woman as God's just punishment for past wrongs. The relevant question for us is whether and to what extent God's punishment took the form of suicide.

In order to answer this moral-theological question, we need first to ascertain whether Abimelech commits suicide. As noted above, Abimelech's death is not a straightforward case of suicide, and two factors recommend this qualification. First, Abimelech believes that he will soon die from the wound he suffered from the upper millstone a woman hurled at him. In fact, Abimelech is remembered in 2 Samuel 11 not as a suicide or even as a soldier who receives the *coup de grâce* but as someone who was killed by a woman (11:21), just as he feared he would be (Judg. 9:54). The comparison

---

Katie M. Heffelfinger, "'My Father Is King': Chiefly Politics and the Rise and Fall of Abimelech," *JSOT* 33 (2009): 289.

to Saul's death is instructive. Saul is badly wounded during a battle against the Philistines, but not so badly that he would inevitably or imminently die from the wounds (1 Sam. 31:3). Thus, he asks his armor-bearer, "Draw your sword and thrust me through with it, so that these uncircumcised may not come and thrust me through, and make sport of me" (31:4). Saul fears not that he will die from his current wounds but that the Philistines, finding him still alive, will kill him more painfully or, even worse, abuse him. Saul's relative vitality is likely the oft overlooked reason for the armor-bearer's refusal to obey Saul's command, for to thrust a wounded but lively man with the sword would be an act of murder.[16] The armor-bearer's refusal forces Saul's hand and he kills himself. In contrast, Abimelech, who asks for the *coup de grâce* to cover up his death-by-millstone, does not so much die by his own means and procurement, but mostly from a battle wound.

The second consideration that disqualifies Abimelech's death as a case of suicide is that he does not destroy his life with his own hands. He dies at the hand of the woman of Thebez and the hand of his armor-bearer. Interesting to consider in the latter case is the cultural understanding of so-called mercy killing in battle. Modern international law forbids the killing of both friendly and enemy wounded combatants (*The Geneva Convention of 12 August 1949*, chapter 2, article 12). In fact, the one who delivers the *coup de grâce* can be tried for homicide. In contrast, in the ancient world to die at the merciful hands of one's comrade appears to have been a relatively honorable way to die in battle, certainly more honorable than dying at the mocking hands of the enemy (so Saul) or at the hands of a woman with a household appliance (so Abimelech).[17] Thus, just as those who demand and receive a *coup de grâce* today are not considered suicides, neither

---

16. Diana V. Edelman (*King Saul in the Historiography of Judah*, JSOTSup 121 [Sheffield: JSOT Press, 1991], 284–85) offers a different opinion and suggests that Saul's anointed status explains his different treatment. See also the citation of Edelman in Pnina Galpaz-Feller, "Let My Soul Die with the Philistines (Judges 16.30)," *JSOT* 30 [2006]: 320n8. The question of whether someone wounded in battle might be able to survive given proper medical attention, even if he does not believe he will, continues to animate questions about the ethics of mercy killing.

17. Galpaz-Feller ("Let My Soul Die," 320) notes that the Abimelech story and the story of Deborah (Judges 4) testify to the "terrible shame of falling at the hand of a woman or having victory credited to a woman."

should Abimelech. Abimelech died due to an elementary tactical mistake, to his shame, or, to his honor, by mercy killing. In short, Abimelech is not a suicide.

To return to the theological question posed above, God's punishment of Abimelech does not take the form of suicide for the simple reason that Abimelech does not destroy his own life. Thus, suicide is neither here nor in the case of Saul, as we shall see below, a straightforward sign of divine disapprobation. The divine punishment of Abimelech occurs, according to the Deuteronomist, through the souring of Abimelech's relationship with the Shechemites, which leads to his shameful death at the hand of a woman and, just as important, the demise of his kingship.[18]

In sum, Abimelech was not a suicide but rather an opportunistic murderer of his half-brothers and a poor military strategist. The writers of the Deuteronomistic History portray his death as God's punishment for his fratricide. The manner of his death (by millstone), insofar as it brings Abimelech shame, may also be thought of as part of the divine punishment. However,

---

18. The downward spiral of Abimelech's career as king begins with highway robbery. Immediately following the announcement that God purposes to punish Abimelech (Judg. 9:23) is the statement that "out of hostility to him, the lords of Shechem set ambushes on the mountain tops. They robbed all who passed by them along that way; and it was reported to Abimelech" (9:25). The Shechemites who raid the passersby on the mountain top, likely merchants traveling through the region, are in effect robbing Abimelech, who as the king of the region would have collected taxes for protecting the trade routes. As the Gospel of Mark notes, "no one can enter a strong man's house and plunder his property without first tying up the strong man; then indeed the house can be plundered" (Mark 3:27). To rob merchants under the king's protection was to rob the king and to regard the king as weak. Abimelech rightly understands the affront to his kingship and engages in war against the Shechemites to reassert his authority and to punish the Shechemites. His first campaign is a success. He takes the city of Shechem, killing its residents and razing the city, and burns down the Tower of Shechem with all those inside who had fled there for protection (9:45–49). The narrator characterizes the fall of Shechem as divine punishment for the sin of the Shechemites. Abimelech's second campaign against Thebez ends in his own death. This is Abimelech's punishment. Important for the book of Judges, Abimelech's death also marks the end of the premature kingship of a man whose name means "My Father is King." On the importance of Abimelech to the structure of the book of Judges as an anti-Northern monarchic polemic, see Brian P. Irwin, "Not Just Any King: Abimelech, the Northern Monarchy, and the Final Form of Judges," *JBL* 131 (2012): 443–54.

that the immediate cause of death is the sword of his armor-bearer, which Abimelech requested, is not condemned. Rather, had it succeeded in its purpose to cover up Abimelech's death-by-millstone, it would have reduced Abimelech's dishonor rather than subtract from his moral standing.

Samson (Judges 13–16)

Samson appears to destroy his life by his own means and procurement. But his ultimate act is much more than a suicide, for it also crushes thousands under the monumental stones of a temple to Dagon like so many ripe grapes. In fact, the destruction of Philistine lives is Samson's primary goal, not the ending of his own life; Samson seeks vengeance, not suicide. Recall, in this light, Samson's final prayer, "Lord GOD, remember me and strengthen me only this once, O God, so that with this one act of revenge I may pay back the Philistines for my two eyes" (Judg. 16:28). He also prays, "Let me die with the Philistines" (16:30), but it is unclear whether he desired his own death in itself, even if he accepted it as a secondary inevitability. In short, Samson is willing to die because he wills to kill. For this reason, we will devote two later chapters to the discussion of Samson and ask whether Samson, as some have proposed, should be considered a suicide terrorist or, as others have claimed, a redeemer.

Saul (1 Samuel 31; 2 Samuel 1; 1 Chronicles 10)

Saul committed suicide or attempted to commit suicide, unless he did not. The Bible contains three accounts of Saul's death in 1 Samuel 31, 2 Samuel 1, and 1 Chronicles 10, and each account contains nontrivial differences that complicate our understanding of Saul as a suicide.

First Samuel 31:1–7 contains the oldest and the most approving account of Saul's death.[19] Saul's death takes place within the context of Israel's military

---

19. First Sam. 31:8–13 stems from a different tradition from the previous passage. Consider, for example, that while the Philistines are said to already have overtaken Saul

CHAPTER 1

campaign against the Philistines in which Saul is badly, but apparently not mortally, wounded by Philistine archers. Saul fears for good reason that, should the Philistines capture him alive, which seems inevitable, they will torment and humiliate him. Thus, Saul commands his armor-bearer, "Draw your sword and thrust me through with it, so that these uncircumcised may not come and thrust me through, and make sport of me" (1 Sam. 31:4a).[20] When the armor-bearer refuses his king—for unstated reasons, to which we will return shortly—Saul falls on his own sword and apparently dies (31:4b–5), and the narrator allows Saul's final words and action to stand without comment.

When the biblical writers leave uncommented such a fraught event like the suicide of a king, it invites interpretation. The difficulty for modern readers of the ancient text, however, is that the cultural codes that the biblical writers shared with their first audiences are alien to us. While we acknowledge that the meaning of texts is not trapped in the world of its author and can give rise to a range of interpretations, as literary theorists have taught us, we do well to begin with its first meanings.

The relevant symbolic matrix in which the biblical writers would have understood a suicide like that of Saul is that of an honor and shame culture.[21] Saul states that he wishes to die in order to avoid an ignoble death at the hand of the Philistines and further social shame. In contrast to Abimelech, whose death appears imminent and inevitable, that Saul will die from the wound he has already suffered is not clear. Thus, the potential shame that Saul would experience should he be captured by the Philistines is great. The primary ignominy would be death at the hands of those whom Saul derogatorily calls "these uncircumcised" (31:4). Adding insult to injury would be the treatment Saul expects at the hand of the Philistines, describing the abuse to which the Philistines will subject him and his body (31:8–10) with the verb *'ālal* that elsewhere refers to God's severe

---

in verse 2, in verse 8, the Philistines are said to do so only the next day. See Dietrich, *Tod von einiger Hand*, 63–64.

20. Dietrich (*Tod von eigener Hand*, 66) draws attention to Samson's treatment at the hand of the Philistines, who gouged out Samson's eyes and put his mutilated body on display as entertainment for the masses (Judg. 16:21, 25).

21. For a review of the honor and shame culture of ancient Israel, see Dietrich, *Tod von eigener Hand*, 19–58.

treatment of the Egyptians (Exod. 10:2) and the gang-rape of the Levite's concubine in Judges 19 (19:25).[22]

In addition to personal shame, because Saul is king, his death and abuse would entail shame for all Israel. The biblical writers spell out the group consequence clearly: "When the men of Israel who were on the other side of the valley and those beyond the Jordan saw that the men of Israel had fled and that Saul and his sons were dead, they forsook their towns and fled" (31:7). Saul's shame as king is tantamount to the shame of the people; his defeat is their defeat. Thus, within the honor-shame culture of ancient Israel, King Saul's suicide should be understood not as a cowardly and shameful act, but as an act taken to safeguard his honor and his nation's honor and to avoid shame for himself and his people.[23]

In contrast to 1 Samuel 31, 1 Chronicles 10 retells and recasts Saul's death as divine punishment. The postexilic Chronicles contains no story about Saul except a severely shortened account of his death.[24] The condensed story adheres closely to its source in 1 Samuel but adds a significant interpretative conclusion:

> [13] So Saul died for his unfaithfulness; he was unfaithful to the LORD in that he did not keep the command of the LORD; moreover, he had consulted a medium, seeking guidance, [14] and did not seek guidance from the LORD. Therefore the LORD put him to death and turned the kingdom over to David son of Jesse. (1 Chr. 10:13–14)

---

22. Dietrich, *Tod von eigener Hand*, 65–66.
23. Dietrich (*Tod von eigener Hand*, 67) agrees that Saul's suicide averts shame: "Sauls Selbsttötung selbst ist nicht schändlich; vielmehr soll Schande durch den Akt der Selbsttötung gerade abgewendet werden." Rosner ("Suicide in Biblical, Talmudic and Rabbinic Writings," 36) notes that Rabbi Jacob ben Asher did not consider King Saul "a wilful [*sic*] suicide," thus "entitled to all funeral rites." Stephen B. Chapman (*1 Samuel as Christian Scripture: A Theological Commentary* [Grand Rapids: Eerdmans, 2016], 17) writes, "The character of Saul may therefore be, and I argue must ultimately be, viewed christologically within Christian biblical theology. In his struggle to die, Saul adumbrates Christ ... Saul ... [is] a 'type' for Christ."
24. Saul Zalewski, "The Purpose of the Story of the Death of Saul in 1 Chronicles X," *VT* 39 (1989): 449–67.

Whereas 1 Samuel allows Saul the dignity of self-determination at the end of his life, as perhaps different from Abimelech, the Chronicler refuses him that honor. The Chronicler says that "the Lord put him to death."[25] Furthermore, the Chronicler transforms Saul's tragic, even heroic death in 1 Samuel into divine punishment: "Saul died for his unfaithfulness ... the Lord put him to death." In this way, Chronicles not only becomes an "anti-Saul document" but opens up the possibility of interpreting suicide as divine punishment, a possibility not present in 1 Samuel.

Second Samuel 1 contains a third account of Saul's death that diverges significantly from both 1 Samuel 31 and 1 Chronicles 10. Important to note is that 1 Samuel 31 leaves ambiguous the reason that Saul's armor-bearer refuses to offer the *coup de grâce* that Saul requests, stating only that the armor-bearer was scared (31:4). Also important to note is that 1 Samuel 31 does not explicitly state that Saul died immediately after falling on his sword, only that his armor-bearer thought that he had died (31:5). Significantly, the narrative in 2 Samuel 1, while not contradicting the account in 1 Samuel 31, plays on the narrative gaps and ambiguities of 1 Samuel 31 to demean Saul and glorify David.

In 2 Samuel 1, a young Amalekite gives his eyewitness account of Saul's death and the part he supposedly played in it. The young man claims that he found himself on Mount Gilboa and discovered there "Saul leaning on his spear" but still alive (1:6). Saul, after learning that the young man is an Amalekite, asks him to kill him, "Come, stand over me and kill me; for convulsions have seized me, and yet my life still lingers" (1:9). The young Amalekite reasons that Saul cannot survive his wound and, unlike Saul's armor-bearer, kills him.

David's response is important. David first mourns Saul and Jonathan "until evening" (1:12). This demonstrates the appropriateness of lament as a response to death, including potential suicide.[26] Only then does David address the young Amalekite, who must have expected a handsome reward

---

25. J. H. Price, "The Conceptual Transfer of Human Agency to the Divine in the Second Temple Period: The Case of Saul's Suicide," *Shofar* 34 (2015): 107–30.

26. Bruce C. Birch, "1 and 2 Samuel," *New Interpreter's Bible* (Nashville: Abingdon, 1998), 2:1209.

for having killed David's rival and for bringing to David the accoutrements of kingship: Saul's crown and armlet (1:10). Rather than award the Amalekite, however, David reprimands him for having stricken "the LORD's anointed" (1:14). What is here being underlined is David's reason for not having killed Saul himself when he previously had opportunities to do so (1 Samuel 24 and 26), which is juxtaposed to the Amalekite's unworthy action and the ambiguous action of Saul's armor-bearer. The armor-bearer, like David and unlike the Amalekite, had acted faithfully by not raising his hand against "the LORD's anointed."[27]

To summarize, the three biblical accounts of Saul's death show the range of possible responses to suicide. On the one hand, the earliest account in 1 Samuel 31 characterizes Saul's death as a tragic but honorable death. On the other, the account of his death in 1 Chronicles 10 recasts Saul's suicide as divine punishment for unfaithfulness. Already in the Hebrew Bible, then, we see suicide as a controversial topic. It cannot be said, as some have argued, that suicide is a noble death *tout court* or, in contrast, the height of human sinfulness. Rather, suicide is a complex issue about which contested narratives and interpretations are possible already within biblical literature.

Saul's Armor-Bearer (1 Samuel 31; 1 Chronicles 10)

Saul's armor-bearer's suicide receives minimal attention in both biblical and later Jewish and Christian writings. Both the Deuteronomistic History and Chronicles devote only two verses to him. He refuses to kill Saul, but after Saul kills himself the armor-bearer falls on his sword and dies. Second Samuel 1 provides a possible reason for the armor-bearer's refusal to kill Saul: He dared not lay a hand on God's anointed. Still, no reason for him killing himself is given.

The reason that Saul's armor-bearer kills himself may elude us, but the reason was likely quite obvious for an ancient audience: It was the duty

---

27. Note that David, in condemning the Amalekite who raised his hand against the anointed king, indirectly legitimizes his prior refusal to do so and thereby underlines the sanctity of the very office he now occupies.

of a servant to die with the master. The armor-bearer's suicide fits the definition of what the sociologist Émile Durkheim called obligatory altruistic suicide.[28] Altruistic suicide, according to Durkheim, results from an underdeveloped sense of self and the overattachment of one's identity to that of the group or another, such as one's master. In this light, the armor-bearer's identity was bound up in his relationship to Saul and lacked independence and individuation so that, when Saul died, he felt obliged to die with Saul.

Given the great cultural divide between ancient Israel and the modern West, many likely would consider the death of Saul's armor-bearer and other instances of altruistic suicide with a mixture of pity and disdain: Poor thing. How could he value himself so little that he would commit suicide just because his master died? However, it is far from clear that the armor-bearer's death would have been deplored in ancient Israel. It may indeed have been understood to be pitiable but nevertheless honorable not to survive one's master in such circumstances. If so, the example of Saul's armor-bearer teaches us that cultural frameworks play a powerful role in shaping the way we evaluate texts and their meaning, especially when they deal with such large and complex phenomena as life, death, and suicide. In fact, we must go further to note that cultural frameworks wield power over not only the assignment of meaning but also the decisions pertaining to life and death, as demonstrated by Saul's armor-bearer.

Ahithophel (2 Samuel 17)

Ahithophel's suicide takes place within a literarily accomplished telling of Absalom's rebellion, which plays out, on the one hand, the consequences of various past sins of David's household (2 Sam. 12:7–12; 16:20–23)[29] and, on the

---

28. Émile Durkheim, *Suicide: A Study in Sociology*, trans. John A. Spaulding and George Simpson, ed. with an introduction by George Simpson (London: Routledge, 2005), 175–86. See also Kalman J. Kaplan and Matthew Schwartz, "Suicide and Suicide Prevention in the Hebrew Bible," *Journal of Psychology and Judaism* 24 (2000): 99–109.

29. Absalom's rebellion may be read as the fulfillment of Nathan's oracle against David after David's adultery and murder and as Absalom's response to Amnon's rape of Tamar and David's inaction. See Michael Avioz, "Divine Intervention and Human Error

other, looks forward to the ascension of Solomon, the paradigmatically wise king, to the throne.[30] The account of the suicide event is simple enough:

> [23] When Ahithophel saw that his counsel was not followed, he saddled his donkey and went off home to his own city. He set his house in order, and hanged himself; he died and was buried in the tomb of his father. (2 Sam. 17:23)

However, beneath the orderly death of the wise man torrents of narrative and theological entanglements surge and rage. Ahithophel's suicide is more than the noble death of a revered statesman who sought, through self-violence, to avoid the public shame of professional defeat or the punishment a traitor to the throne might reasonably expect for himself and his family.[31] The narrative artfully plays out a theological lesson about the limits of human wisdom and the power of divine will.

Ahithophel begins his political career as a counselor to David, and the narrator likens Ahithophel's advice to "the oracle of God" (2 Sam. 16:23). For this reason, Ahithophel is also Absalom's first handpicked recruit to his rebellion against his father David. The narrator indicates the importance of Ahithophel's participation in Absalom's rebellion by framing and punctuating the story of Absalom's meteoric rise and swift fall from power with notices about Ahithophel joining Absalom (2 Sam. 15:12) and Ahithophel's death (17:23) as if to bind Absalom's fortunes to Ahithophel's.[32] As Ahithophel goes, so does Absalom.

---

in the Absalom Narrative," *JSOT* 37 (2013): 339–47. For a review of recent reconstructions of the redaction history of the passage, see Dietrich, *Tod von eigener Hand*, 148–50.

30. Song-Mi Suzie Park, "The Frustration of Wisdom: Wisdom, Counsel, and Divine Will in 2 Samuel 17:1–21," *JBL* 128 (2009): 453–67. Park notes that Absalom proves unfit for kingship by his failure to "discern what is wise from what is unwise" in contrast to Solomon (p. 466).

31. D. G. Schley ("Ahithophel," *ABD* 1:121) notes, "Ahithophel's role in Absalom's revolt earned him a permanent place in the later Syriac vocabulary, where his name became an adjective—*'aḥitōpēlājā*—meaning 'traitor.'"

32. Ahithophel, before joining Absalom's rebellion, is in his hometown of Giloh and not in Jerusalem, where you would expect to find the king's active counselors. Poor health is an unlikely reason for his retirement, as Ahithophel volunteers to lead an army of 12,000 against David (2 Sam. 17:1–3). It is possible that he resigned, voluntarily or

CHAPTER 1

When Ahithophel joins Absalom's rebellion, Ahithophel offers Absalom a twofold plan to usurp David's kingdom. Ahithophel first advises that Absalom take his father's concubines, thus symbolically taking David's royal authority, for himself: "Go in to your father's concubines, the ones he has left to look after the house; and all Israel will hear that you have made yourself odious to your father, and the hands of all who are with you will be strengthened" (2 Sam. 16:21).[33] By doing this, Absalom attains the prize of symbolic kingship.[34] It is at this point that the narrator notes that "the counsel that Ahithophel gave was as if one consulted the oracle of God" (2 Sam. 16:23). The notice indicates, on the one hand, that Ahithophel's counsel, while not itself an oracle of God, fulfills Nathan's oracle to David that God "will take your wives before your eyes, and give them to your neighbor, and he shall lie with your wives in the sight of this very sun" (2 Sam. 12:11).[35] Ahithophel's wisdom approaches divine will as much as is humanly possible. There is a darker side to the comparison, however. It casts the events about to unfold as a contest between Ahithophel's godlike human wisdom and God's will in human affairs.

The second part of Ahithophel's advice to Absalom is swift and decisive action. He advises that Absalom take immediate military action against David's disorganized and retreating forces as a means to solidify the kingship

---

otherwise, from the post. Scholars have speculated about the reason that Ahithophel chose to betray David, whatever his reasons for retirement. Particularly intriguing is the suggestion that Ahithophel is Bathsheba's paternal grandfather (2 Sam. 11:3; 23:34) who came to resent David's treatment not only of Bathsheba but also Tamar. See David Daube, "Absalom and the Ideal King," *VT* 48 (1998): 315–25, esp. 320–22. Less conjectural, if less interesting, is the suggestion that Ahithophel shared deep disappointment about David's rule with other Israelites.

33. "In the ancient Near East, the usurpation of the royal authority of one's father also meant the usurpation of his male virility, hence the great symbolic power of Absalom's act" (Schley, "Ahithophel," 121).

34. I do not call the public rape of women wise. Sexual assault is an unacceptable moral horror. What is wise, strictly within the narrative logic of story, is Absalom's heeding of Ahithophel's counsel as an effective means to achieving the end of becoming king. Absalom's sex act is not (only) about sex but about power, more precisely about claiming for himself the power his father had as king. See Hans J. L. Jensen, "Desire, Rivalry and Collective Violence in the 'Succession Narrative'," *JSOT* 55 (1992): 45–47.

35. Dietrich, *Tod von eigener Hand*, 150.

Absalom has symbolically claimed by taking David's concubines. "Let me choose twelve thousand men," Ahithophel says to Absalom,

> and I will set out and pursue David tonight. ² I will come upon him while he is weary and discouraged, and throw him into a panic; and all the people who are with him will flee. I will strike down only the king, ³ and I will bring all the people back to you as a bride comes home to her husband. You seek the life of only one man, and all the people will be at peace. (2 Sam. 17:1–3)

The proposed plan is a beautiful example of economy and unity in language, thought, and action. In following Ahithophel's first piece of advice, Absalom took the smaller part of the kingdom that David's concubines symbolized and must now take the greater part, the people symbolized as the bride, by following Ahithophel's second piece of advice. However, this plan requires swift action: the immediate striking down of Absalom's rival suitor, David. Across both counsels, Ahithophel restrains himself to a single image, a young groom (Absalom) in pursuit of his bride (the people), and mercifully limits the scope of violence to the rival suitor (David). Ahithophel expresses political wisdom distilled to its purest essence.[36]

David, who knew the power of Ahithophel's wisdom better than perhaps anyone, launches two campaigns to counter Ahithophel's counsel. The first is prayer: "David was told that Ahithophel was among the conspirators with Absalom. And David said, 'O LORD, I pray you, turn the counsel of Ahithophel into foolishness'" (2 Sam. 15:31). As we will discuss more fully below, the prayer finds fulfillment in the second half of the episode: "the LORD had ordained to defeat the good counsel of Ahithophel" (17:14bα).[37] David's initial prayer and its fulfillment form a neat theological

---

36. Ahithophel's advice, like Hushai's, is built on poetic insight but unlike Hushai's advice is far more economical. Park ("Frustration of Wisdom," 463) characterizes Ahithophel's terse style as "not formally wise." While I agree with Park that Ahithophel's advice evinces an austerity in contrast to Hushai's poetic flourish, I disagree that Ahithophel's advice is not wise in form. Because of the compact artistry of Ahithophel's advice, it requires wisdom to decipher, not unlike the sayings of Proverbs.

37. The verse continues, "so that the LORD might bring ruin on Absalom" (2 Sam. 17:14bβ). Absalom's ruin, which is the logical consequence of Ahithophel's fail-

CHAPTER 1

inclusio. The events that enfold within this theological frame, as is typical in the Deuteronomistic History, is a human drama of high political intrigue involving spies, secret liaisons, and a contest of wisdom.

David's second campaign against Ahithophel involves human actors. Hushai, another counselor to David and his friend, appears on the scene immediately after David's prayer and asks to join David as he flees Jerusalem (2 Sam. 15:32). However, David does not permit Hushai to accompany him into exile: "If you go on with me, you will be a burden to me" (2 Sam. 15:33). Instead, he sends Hushai to Absalom as a spy with plans to undermine Ahithophel's wisdom (2 Sam. 15:34–36). Whatever his internal protest and despite the risk to his own safety, Hushai enters Jerusalem, now the den of David's enemies, and begins the crucial contest of wisdom that will decide Absalom's, David's, and indeed Israel's future.

Hushai, because he is a well-known friend of David (2 Sam. 15:37; 16:16, 17), must first ward off Absalom's suspicions concerning his allegiance: "Is this your loyalty to your friend? Why did you not go with your friend?" (2 Sam. 16:17). Hushai does not disclose his clandestine plans, nor let on his hurt at David's apparent disregard for his safety in his statement, "You will be a burden to me . . . return to the city." With disarming flattery, Hushai wins Absalom's initial forbearance and, to maintain his cover, wisely remains silent as Absalom executes the first part of Ahithophel's twin strategy to take David's kingdom. Hushai knows that silence is a luxury he cannot long afford, but to speak would be to risk discovery and death, for Absalom and his men would not spare Hushai should they discover the hidden bodkin in Hushai's left hand.

Hushai bides his time while Absalom takes David's concubines. But, at Absalom's goading and also recognizing that Ahithophel has finally taken aim squarely at David, Hushai begins to execute David's command to "defeat for me the counsel of Ahithophel" (2 Sam. 15:34). Absalom has initially found Ahithophel's counsel for military action satisfactory. However, to

---

ure, is the tragic conclusion to Absalom's rebellion, tragic particularly for David who, at news of his son's death, wails: "O my son Absalom, my son, my son Absalom! Would I had died instead of you, O Absalom, my son, my son!" (2 Sam. 18:33; cf. 19:4). Divine response to human prayer, if we are right that God frustrates Ahithophel's counsel in response to David's prayer, can take unexpected and tragic form for the one who prays.

get a second opinion and test Hushai's loyalty, Absalom has Hushai also give his counsel. Hushai takes the opportunity to give a vivid and alluring counsel designed to undermine Ahithophel's pithy and austere advice and to use Absalom's psychological history against him.[38]

First, Hushai attacks Ahithophel head-on: "This time the counsel that Ahithophel has given is not good" (2 Sam. 17:7). Professional disagreements no doubt existed in ancient courts. However, for Hushai, whose loyalty was still under scrutiny, to disagree so publicly with Ahithophel's plan, especially when it was already approved as "right" by Absalom and the elders (2 Sam. 17:4), was to risk his own safety. Recall Micaiah son of Imlah's contestation of the court prophets (1 Kgs. 22:8–28) or Jeremiah, whose disagreement with the court landed him in prison and at the bottom of a cistern (Jeremiah 37–38). Hushai's naked disapproval of Ahithophel's advice may have been a desperate act more than a calculated risk. Indeed, Ahithophel's response to his defeat in this contest of wisdom, suicide by hanging, in part indicates the seriousness of Hushai's challenge. At risk was not only professional reputation but life itself. In this light, Hushai's challenge against Ahithophel is a manifestation of his incredible loyalty to David, his king and friend, and an indication of Hushai's willingness to die for him.

Next, Hushai deploys his finest rhetorical arsenal: evocative similes and vivid imagery to inspire in Absalom a childlike awe for his father as well as to feed his mimetic desire to be like his father.[39] Hushai instructs Absalom to remember that "your father and his men are warriors . . . enraged, like a bear robbed of her cubs" (17:8) and that Absalom, though a "valiant warrior, whose heart is like the heart of a lion," will melt with fear if he encounters them unprepared (17:10). Thus, Hushai advises Absalom to gather "all Israel . . . from Dan to Beersheba, like the sand by the sea for multitude" (17:11) and then descend on David's forces "as the dew falls on the ground" (17:12); for only utterly defeating David and his army to the point that "not even a pebble is to be found there" can ensure victory (17:13). In contrast to Ahithophel, Hushai argues that unwise half measures will not succeed against David.

---

38. See Park, "Frustration of Wisdom," 457–60.
39. Concerning mimetic desire, see Jensen, "Desire, Rivalry and Collective Violence," 45–47.

CHAPTER 1

Hushai's counsel, as some scholars have noted, is a "masterpiece of oriental eloquence," although I fail to see what is particularly oriental about the eloquence.[40] Rather, I would read it as a desperate deployment of his most powerful rhetorical arsenal. Hushai first reminds Absalom that David is "your father" three times (2 Sam. 17:8 [2×], 10), then inspires filial fear by evoking for Absalom an image of a youthful David as a capable and fearsome warrior, an image that would have resonated with Absalom's childhood memories of his father.[41] This is meant to delay Absalom from taking immediate military action. Second, Hushai baits Absalom's mimetic desire to be like his father—or better than his father—by calling Absalom "a valiant warrior, whose heart is like the heart of a lion" and by hypnotically dangling the Davidic promise of inheriting all of Israel and Judah, "from Dan to Beersheba" (see 2 Sam. 3:10; 24:2). In contrast to Ahithophel who depicts Absalom as a rival suitor to David, deploying a more politically fitting but psychologically distant analogy, Hushai exploits the psychologically potent familial paradigm of father and son. Ahithophel paints David exclusively as a figure of Absalom's mimetic desire: Absalom must displace David and take his harem and his bride. Hushai depicts David not only as the object of mimetic desire but also as a figure to be feared. Hushai reminds Absalom that the reason that he wants to be like David is precisely the reason that David must be feared: He is a mighty warrior. He is a bear robbed of her cubs. And Absalom is but his cub!

"Absalom and all the men of Israel" are hoodwinked and embrace Hushai's counsel as "better than the counsel of Ahithophel" (2 Sam. 17:14). They override the earlier decision by "Absalom and all the elders of Israel" who were initially convinced of Ahithophel's wisdom (2 Sam. 17:4). But Absalom's foolishness is understandable. Hushai's shiny and dizzying rhetoric obfuscates the austere beauty and wisdom of Ahithophel's counsel. Ahithophel's counsel is perhaps overly compact, requiring a clear and precise understanding of the political-military situation and an acute mind rare in such crisis moments, whereas Hushai lays bare the inner logic of

---

40. Hans Wilhelm Hertzberg, *I and II Samuel: A Commentary*. OTL (Philadelphia: Fortress, 1964), 351; also cited in Park, "Frustration of Wisdom," 454.
41. Park, "Frustrations of Wisdom," 458–59.

the argument with a series of evocative images. Hushai's baroque artistry defeats Ahithophel's more austere wisdom![42]

As noted above, though the events take place on the plane of human stratagems and executions, a theological frame brackets the entire episode. Thus, it can be said that Hushai succeeds not only thanks to his wisdom and artistry but ultimately because "the LORD had ordained to defeat the good counsel of Ahithophel, so that the LORD might bring ruin to Absalom" (2 Sam. 17:14). Absalom falls for Hushai's delaying tactics and seals his fate in part because God ordained it.

Absalom's decision to postpone military action buys Hushai time to inform David, giving David the opportunity to escape. And while Absalom readies an army for the inevitable confrontation with his father, Ahithophel, seeing that his counsel has been rejected and that David's victory is certain, acts both reactively and preemptively. He rides home, sets his house in order, and commits suicide. Ahithophel, perhaps the wisest man in all of Israel, whose wisdom rivaled God's, willingly and deliberately chooses death and leaves us asking, Why?

The stated reason for Ahithophel's suicide, that his counsel was not followed, reveals perhaps only half of his motivation.[43] As Dietrich underlines, the force of public shame in ancient Israel cannot be overstated. Ahithophel would have experienced the public rejection of his counsel as a kind of "social death," so joined was his identity with his public profession. Thus, Dietrich explains, Ahithophel retires from the public space of his humiliation to the privacy of his home to die in honor.[44]

Others have noted additional reasons for the suicide. For one, Ahithophel may have feared that, when Absalom's rebellion has inevitably failed and David has returned to power, he would die the shameful death of a traitor at David's hands. Relatedly, by preemptively killing himself, he may have wanted to spare his family the social and economic ruin of a traitor's household. For, as the story of Naboth's vineyard suggests, the property of an

---

42. Park, "Frustration of Wisdom."

43. Dietrich (*Tod von eigener Hand*, 152) disagrees, saying that the loss of honor due to his failure as a counselor is the only reason to be considered.

44. Dietrich, *Tod von eigener Hand*, 152.

executed criminal transfers to the king in ancient Israel (1 Kgs. 21:15–16).[45] Killing himself may have been a means to clear his family of guilt and to ensure their financial viability after his death.[46] Is this perhaps what is meant by the note that Ahithophel "set his house in order"?

If there is merit to these speculations, Ahithophel's measured decision to kill himself by hanging may be understood not only as an effort to preserve his own honor by avoiding a traitor's death but also as an act of self-sacrifice for the sake of his family. In dying by his own hand, Ahithophel ensures continued life for his household: his wife, children, and likely numerous servants. He dies not only to escape personal shame but also to preserve his family's honor. That is, he dies that he might give life. In this respect, it is important to note that Ahithophel is "buried in the tomb of his father" and receives no moral censure, neither from his family nor from the narrator (2 Sam. 17:23). Indeed, Ahithophel's manner of death may be understood as a testimony to his own faith in the wisdom of his counsel. In short, Ahithophel's suicide is presented as an honorable, even heroic, death.[47]

There remains for us to consider the theological aspect of the episode. Recall that Ahithophel fails to convince Absalom to follow his counsel because "the Lord had ordained" it. And since it is Absalom's rejection of Ahithophel's counsel that leads to his suicide, we might be tempted to ascribe ultimate responsibility for Ahithophel's death to God. Did God cause Ahithophel to commit suicide as a means to kill off a human rival in wisdom and to demonstrate divine superiority over human limitations?

The relationship between human volition and divine will is a complex issue throughout the Hebrew Bible, no less in the Deuteronomistic His-

---

45. Shemesh, "Suicide," 164.

46. The fate of those whom a suicide leaves behind was an important consideration. For example, in early modern England the suicide of a family member could leave the surviving family in financial ruin through forfeiture of their property as punishment for the crime of self-murder; see MacDonald and Murphy, *Sleepless Souls*, 119–21. Jennifer Michael Hecht (*Stay: A History of Suicide and the Philosophies Against It* [New Haven: Yale University Press, 2013], 116–48) turns the consideration of the community into a strong argument against suicide generally.

47. Dietrich, *Tod von eigener Hand*, 155.

tory. However, a careful consideration of the literary artistry of 2 Samuel 15–17 reveals important clues about the contours of the divine-human relationship within the passage.

A prominent feature of the narrative artistry of 2 Samuel 15–17 is its balanced symmetry.[48] Each point in the first half of the central story (2 Sam. 15:12–16:14) has a counterpoint in the second half (2 Sam. 16:15–17:23). Marking the outer frame of the narrative are Ahithophel's entrance and exit from the scene: Ahithophel leaves his hometown of Giloh to join Absalom's rebellion (15:12) and later abandons Absalom's rebellion and returns to Giloh, where he ends his life (17:23). Marking the narrative center, where the story transitions from a period of preparation to one of action, are the movement of David's weary forces from Jerusalem to the Jordan (16:14) and Absalom's movement into Jerusalem (16:15). Linking the opposed movement is Hushai's departure from David (15:37) to join Absalom (16:16).

Within these interwoven pairs, there is an important theological framework, as noted above. David's prayer marks the opening of the theological frame: "O LORD, I pray you, turn the counsel of Ahithophel into foolishness" (2 Sam. 15:31), and a narrator's note marks the closure: "for the LORD had ordained to defeat the good counsel of Ahithophel, so that the LORD might bring ruin to Absalom" (2 Sam. 17:14b). What the nested structure suggests is that the narrator attributes divine responsibility more heavily for the events that occur between David's prayer and its fulfillment; that is, for the events recounted within the theological frame (2 Sam. 15:31–17:14).

Now the complexities of both the Succession Narrative and the Deuteronomistic History as a whole advise against drawing hard conclusions about the boundary between human agency and divine will both in this episode and in the rest of the corpus. However, the clear framing of the sapiential contest between Ahithophel and Hushai allows us to say that, from the narrator's perspective, primary responsibility for defeating Ahithophel's wisdom and consequently for Absalom's ruin lies with God.[49]

---

48. For a slightly different construal of the chiastic structure, see Jan P. Fokkelman, *The Crossing Fates (I Sam. 13–31 & II Sam. 1)*, vol. 2 of *Narrative Art and Poetry in the Books of Samuel: A Full Interpretation Based on Stylistic and Structural Analysis* (Assen: Van Gorcum, 1986), 205; cited in Dietrich, *Tod von eigener Hand*, 151.

49. Indeed, the relationship between Ahithophel and divine involvement in historical reality is dense. It is almost as if Ahithophel is emptied of agency. His first coun-

All events outside that, including Ahithophel's premeditated suicide, are incidental consequences, driven more by human decision than by divine prescription. That is to say, Ahithophel's suicide was not the result of direct divine intervention in human affairs but the measured decision of a paradigmatically wise human individual. It was volitional death, not a form of divine punishment.[50] To deny that Ahithophel died of his own volition by his own means and procurement would be to deny him the dignity and honor the biblical text accords him by noting his godlike wisdom.

In summary, Ahithophel is presented as a wise man, whose wisdom is comparable to the oracles of God. And this man committed suicide and took decisive and premeditated action to end his life. His death, to be sure, is a tragedy, the lamentable consequence of a clash between human excellence and divine volition in the theater of political and military machinations. His death is also an expression of characteristic wisdom, especially given the cultural context. His death is honorable in that it anticipates foreseeable shame and admirable in that it provides a way for his family to survive. Ahithophel demonstrates that, in ancient Israel, one might kill himself for personal honor and to give life to his beloved family.

Zimri (1 Kings 16)

Zimri was king of Israel for seven days and commits suicide by burning down a royal palace over himself. While his death is evaluated as divine judgment for past sins, his self-destruction passes without comment.

Zimri participates in the story of turbulent political rivalries that plagued Northern Israel for much of its history. More specifically, he plays a pivotal role in the fall of the House of Baasha and anticipates the rise of the House of Omri. In the first part of Zimri's story (1 Kgs. 16:1–7), the prophet Jehu receives an oracle against Baasha that, because of his sins and

---

sel, heralded as comparable to an oracle of God, fulfills God's oracle. And his second counsel, whose wisdom remains unproven in fact, is defeated by God's intervention.

50. Shemesh ("Suicide in the Bible," 165) makes an interesting connection between Ahithophel's death and Absalom's: "Ahithophel's suicide, as well as the means [by hanging] . . . warns readers that Absalom's rebellion is doomed and even foreshadows Absalom's own death, which comes while he is hanging helplessly from a tree (18:10)."

the sins he caused Israel to commit, God will destroy the House of Baasha like the House of Jeroboam (1 Kgs. 16:1–3). Zimri fulfills that prophecy in the second part of the story (1 Kgs. 16:8–14). While Elah, Baasha's son and successor to the throne, is feasting in Tirzah, Zimri assassinates Elah and all his male kin and allies. The narrator then comments that Zimri fulfilled "the words of the LORD" (1 Kgs. 16:12). Zimri, it would appear, usurps Israel's throne with divine approval. However, God's approval does not last very long. Omri, the commander of Israel's army and Zimri's rival claimant to the throne, captures the city of Tirzah seven days after Zimri's ascension to the throne. Rather than surrender to Omri and face likely execution, Zimri retreats to the royal palace and burns down the house, killing himself and his companions in the process. Zimri's suicidal conflagration destroys the riches of the palace and leaves a dark mark in the archaeological record of Tirzah.[51] The narrator provides a concluding theological commentary: Zimri "burned down the king's house over himself with fire, and died—because of the sins that he committed, doing evil in the sight of the LORD, walking in the way of Jeroboam, and for the sin that he committed, causing Israel to sin" (1 Kgs. 16:18–19).

The immediate reasons that Zimri destroys his life and the royal palace are familiar to us from the above discussion. Zimri immolates himself to avoid the indignity and shame of being captured by his rival Omri and treated as a traitor to his king Elah. The motive to escape shame resonates with the reasons that Abimelech, Saul, and Ahithophel hastened their respective deaths. However, it is significant that Zimri's suicide does not benefit others, as might be argued about Saul's and Ahithophel's deaths. Rather, Zimri likely killed others trapped in the palace with him and destroyed royal property. That is, Zimri's motive for killing himself is self-centered and concerned not at all with benefiting others, even if the manner of his death does not attract particular censure or even comment from the narrator.

---

51. "In an archaeological dig at the site believed to be biblical Tirzah, a stratum dated to this period was found covered with ash and marks of charring. If the flames of the king's house spread to the town, these may be the scars of Zimri's history as King of Israel." Quote from Patricia Berlyn, "The Rise of the House of Omri," *JBQ* 33 (2005): 226; citing Roland de Vaux, "The Excavations of Tell el-Far'ah and the Site of Ancient Tirzah," *Palestine Exploration Quarterly* 88 (1956): 125–40.

CHAPTER 1

This is not to say that Zimri's death is neutral. As noted, the narrator twice condemns Zimri for the sin(s) he committed and for causing Israel to sin. There is, however, a small distinguishing feature in regard to Zimri's death. The narrator connects Zimri's untimely death to sin and raises the possibility that, similar to Saul's death in 1 Chronicles, untimely death and perhaps suicide itself might be understood as forms of divine retribution. Even if suicide was not categorically condemned as a moral wrong in ancient Israel, it seems to have been possible to view it as an act of divine displeasure and judgment.

Conclusion

Suicide, the voluntary destruction of a person's own life, by one's own means and procurement, is a fraught event. It is analyzable on psychological, political, cultural, social, historical, and theological levels. The complexities of suicide are compounded by the passions that the topic elicits, even more so when we talk about suicide as it is presented in the Bible.

I imagine, therefore, that the above discussion will elicit a range of strong responses. What I would underline are two themes that will be important to keep in mind for the rest of the book. The first is that the Hebrew Bible arises from an ancient and distant society whose culture is, for many of its modern readers, unfamiliar and strange. For example, that a wise and admirable person such as Ahithophel might kill himself to preserve his honor and to safeguard his surviving family from economic and political ruin may strike many modern readers as strange. However, such acts are not without modern parallels. In response to allegations of bribery, Roh Moo-Hyun, President of the Republic of Korea from 2002 to 2007 and a celebrated human rights lawyer, committed suicide by jumping off a cliff on May 23, 2009. The suicide helped turn the tide of rising criticism away from himself and back against his political rivals. In dying, then, Roh not only preserved his honor but may have increased his prestige as well—quite apart from whether he accepted bribes. He also shielded his family from public criticism and legal investigations; on account of his death, they could live on.

The second theme that bears remembering is the diversity of views that exist internal to the Hebrew Bible. We saw, for example, that there exist three traditions concerning Saul's death, one that seems to accept it as honorable (1 Samuel 31), another that characterizes it as divine punishment (1 Chronicles 10), and yet another that laments Saul's death as the result of a reprehensible disregard for the sanctity of the Lord's anointed (2 Samuel 1). Because the Hebrew Bible is a composite work, more a library than a single-authored book, we risk distorting its witness when we emphasize one passage or perspective over others in the name of simplicity, consistency, or any other external principle. The wide range of perspectives should be regarded as reflective of the complex realities of lived experience, then as now. With this in mind, we shall now turn to the book of Job, whose meditation on death arises from a set of concerns quite different from those of the Deuteronomistic History. In Job, we find a more existential meditation on death and its allure from the perspective of a righteous man in suffering.

CHAPTER 2

Job and the Problem of Suicide

There is but one truly serious philosophical problem, and that is suicide. Judging whether life is or is not worth living amounts to answering the fundamental question of philosophy. All the rest ... comes afterwards.

Camus, "The Myth of Sisyphus"[1]

THE DEUTERONOMISTIC SUICIDES we examined in the previous chapter, from Abimelech to Zimri, are kings and advisors to kings, hero men and chiefs. Though they were no doubt vulnerable to the ills that touch all human lives, the circumstances surrounding their deaths were extraordinary and altogether alien to the vast majority of people. Falling on one's own sword, for example, was a privilege and a dignity available only to the elite of society and burning down a palace would have been an unimaginable waste for all common folk.[2] Ordinary people who committed suicide died in relative obscurity, likely by hanging or jumping into water or off high places, though they were no doubt lamented by their friends and family.

---

1. Albert Camus, *The Myth of Sisyphus and Other Essays* (New York: Knopf, 1955), 3.
2. For example, Georges Minois (*History of Suicide: Voluntary Death in Western Culture*, trans. Lydia G. Cochrane [Baltimore: Johns Hopkins University Press, 1999], 16–18) notes that the manner of suicide differed between nobles and commoners in the Middle Ages; so too did the related laws and theoretical discussion of morality.

That is, there is a social dimension to suicide, and the suicide of the rich and the powerful and the ways in which they are represented, including the fact that their stories were preserved at all, differ significantly from the suicide of most common folk.

We find an unlikely representative of more common reflections on death and suicide in the Hebrew Bible in Job. It is important to remember that Job is a figure of legendary piety and wealth, which would seem to disqualify him as representative of the everyman, let alone the everywoman.[3] Yet, in the hands of a talented postexilic poet, Job articulates well the pain that many Israelites experienced in the aftermath of the greatest tragedy of Israel's history: the destruction of home and family, forced migration to alien lands, and the loss of one's livelihood and dignity.[4] In an important way, Job arguably becomes a kind of new Adam and a new kind of Adam. If Adam's journey was from paradise to the realities of historical existence, Job's journey is in the opposite direction. In the middle of the journey of our life, Job is thrust into a nightmarish world of pain and loss and must claw his way back toward paradise. Job never quite reaches his destination, but he does manage to end up about where Adam does: on earth in between heaven and hell. Thus, in treading the ancient path from loss toward recovery, Job becomes an archetype for the resilient sufferer. He muses on the allure of death and the relative worth(lessness) of life and probes the tragic depths of human existence that sometimes lead to voluntary death; he teaches us that human life can be full of agony, admitting that events occur that shatter assumptions about the meaningfulness and the goodness of the world and

---

3. A notable effort to read Job in light of the concerns of the poor comes from Gustavo Gutiérrez, *On Job: God-Talk and the Suffering of the Innocent*, trans. Matthew J. O'Connell (Maryknoll, NY: Orbis Books, 1987).

4. The date of the book of Job continues to be debated, and it remains uncertain when and where the various parts of the book were composed. I am convinced on multiple grounds (linguistic, theological, intertextual) that the book of Job is exilic at the earliest but more likely postexilic. See Marvin H. Pope, *Job*, AB 15 (Garden City, NY: Doubleday, 1965), xxx–xxxvii; or for a more recent review, Kathryn Schifferdecker, *Out of the Whirlwind: Creation Theology in the Book of Job*, HTS 61 (Cambridge; Harvard University Press, 2008), 13–21.

the worthiness of the self.⁵ In the end, however, he counsels endurance, though not necessarily patience, and even faithfulness.⁶

Along the way, Job discovers a new way to relate to death. Pain and loss drive Job toward death in the beginning of the book. He desires death as an escape from life's ills. By the end of the book, however, Job no longer desires death but is willing to die in defense of his integrity. That is, he embraces the possibility of death as a means of finding a reason to live. Job comes to see death as a portal to the fullness of life and not as necessarily an exit from the evils of life. The story of this transformation in the way Job relates to death follows.

Set Up

Job was first and foremost a pious man who earned, so it would seem, God's blessing (Job 1:1). His blessedness was paradigmatic. He had seven sons and three daughters, seven thousand sheep and three thousand camels, five thousand cattle and five thousand jennies, and many servants besides (1:2–3).⁷ And his piety was exemplary. After his children would fête together every day on choice meat and wine, served attentively by the servants, Job took care to offer sanctifying sacrifices for each of his children, anxious should they have gratuitously cursed God in their hearts (1:4–5). He was married, of course, and his wife enjoyed God's blessings with him. She would also suffer with Job the consequences of divine attention.

---

5. Ronnie Janoff-Bulman (*Shattered Assumptions: Towards a New Psychology of Trauma* [New York: Free Press, 1992], 6, 52), using the story of Job as an example, defines trauma as the shattering of three core assumptions about the world and ourselves: (1) The world is benevolent; (2) The world is meaningful; and (3) The self is worthy.

6. "The patience of Job" is legendary but largely fictional. The patience of Job comes from the KJV translation of the Greek ὑπομονή, which is better translated as "endurance." It has been suggested that the allusion is to the Testament of Job, not the Hebrew Bible book of Job. See Christopher R. Seitz, "The Patience of Job in the Epistle of James," in *Konsequente Traditionsgeschichte: Festschrift für Klaus Baltzer zum 65. Geburtstag*, ed. Rüdiger Bartelmus, Thomas Krüger, and Helmut Utzschneider, OBO 126 (Göttingen: Vandenhoeck & Ruprecht, 1993), 373–82.

7. On the significance of the numbers, see Pope, *Job*, 7.

In two divine counsels in heaven (1:6–12; 2:1–6), Job's piety becomes a topic of debate. God asks the Satan, one of the divine beings,[8] "Have you considered my servant Job? There is no one like him on the earth, a blameless and upright man who fears God and turns away from evil" (1:8; 2:3a). Each time he is asked, the Satan questions the purity of Job's piety: "Does Job fear God for nothing?" (1:9). He then suggests that Job fears God because of blessings:

> [10] Have you not put a fence around him and his house and all that he has, on every side? You have blessed the work of his hands, and his possessions have increased in the land. [11] But stretch out your hand now, and touch all that he has, and he will curse you to your face. (1:10–11)

The Satan's suggestion is to unlink piety and blessings and see whether, even when piety appears to lead to suffering, Job will choose to fear God. God permits the Satan to carry out the proposed trials.

The first trial strips Job of all his blessed possessions in the opposite order listed by the narrator earlier: the cattle and jennies first, then the sheep and camels, and finally, and inevitably, Job's children and many servants (1:14–19).[9] To great dramatic effect, the lone survivor from each scene of disaster runs to Job and recounts the devastation in a repetitive style: "While he was still speaking another one came and said, '. . . I alone have escaped to tell you'" (see 1:13–19). In this way, the author makes the reader of his tale stand next to Job, to hear the bad news directly from the servants and to react to the news alongside Job. The author effectively collapses together the world of the story and the world of the reader in order to juxtapose and so accentuate the difference between the reader's likely response to the disasters and Job's.[10] The reader perhaps raises her fist in anger and utters a not-so-gratuitous curse in her heart; but Job in contrast:

---

8. "The Satan" is not the diabolic figure of Christian mythology. See Ryan Stokes, "Satan, Yhwh's Executioner," *JBL* 133 (2014): 251–70, and the works cited therein.

9. This is the first example of chiasm that characterizes the artistry of the earliest layer of the Joban tradition. See Paul K.-K. Cho, "The Integrity of Job 1 and 42:11–17," *CBQ* 76 (2014): 230–51, esp. 232–34.

10. On the hermeneutical importance of distinguishing between the world of the reader and the world of Job, see Michael V. Fox, "Job the Pious," *ZAW* 117 (2005): 351–66.

> ²⁰ fell on the ground and worshiped. ²¹ He said,
> "Naked I came from my mother's womb,
> and naked shall I return there;
> the LORD gave, and the LORD has taken away;
> blessed be the name of the LORD." (1:20–21)

Job demonstrates impossible composure and unbelievable piety, while the reader ponders incredulously: Blessed be the name of the LORD for the death of your children?

When the story continues, Job's extraordinarily pious words bring about further pain, not its cessation. At the second divine meeting, God again boasts of Job's faithfulness, while admitting to the Satan, "you incited me against him, to destroy him for no reason" (2:3b). The Satan does not apologize or admit defeat but rather proposes more extreme vetting: "Skin for skin! All that people have they will give to save their lives. But stretch out your hand now and touch his bone and his flesh, and he will curse you to your face" (2:4–5). God sanctions the further testing, and the Satan "went out from the presence of the LORD and inflicted loathsome sores on Job from the sole of his foot to the crown of his head" (2:7). The sores incidentally make Job appear a serious sinner for, according to Deuteronomy, those who break the covenant with God are so punished (Deut. 28:27, 35). From this point on, already denuded economically, Job is made to suffer in his body and, more importantly, socially.[11] His wife, who knows best the depth of Job's piety and suffers with him the loss of property, children, and status, advises that Job abandon God who would punish a righteous man and end the needless suffering: "Curse God, and die" (Job 2:9).[12] Job's three friends, Eliphaz, Bildad, and Zophar, come to console and comfort Job but, in presuming that Job has sinned against God—that is, in reading the outer sign of Job's skin disease through the lens of the Deuteronomic code—become instead Job's true tormentors. Though this was not their initial intent, they come to deny him honor and

---

11. Paul K.-K. Cho, "Job 2 and 42:7–10 as Narrative Bridge and Theological Pivot," *JBL* 136 (2017): 870–75.

12. On the ambiguity of Job's wife's advice, see Cho, "Job 2 and 42:7–10," 871–73.

Job and the Problem of Suicide

rob him even of basic respect. To use Deuteronomic language, they treat Job as "an object of horror, a proverb, and a byword" (Deut. 28:37).

The table is thus set.

"He Cursed the Day of His Birth"

Job responds to his wife's provocative advice, "Curse God, and die" (2:9b), initially with an ambiguous but far-from-impious statement: "You speak as any foolish woman would speak. Shall we receive the good at the hand of God, and not receive the bad?" (2:10a). He attributes both the good and the bad to God but does not accuse God of wrongdoing. He suggests that doing so would be foolishness (2:10b). Then the friends who arrive belatedly and sit with him in silence for seven days and seven nights elicit Job's first unguarded words (Job 3). And in the long conversation that ensues, Job agonizes over the very questions his wife had posed: whether it is acceptable, under circumstances such as his, to blame God or even to curse God for the unwarranted suffering, and whether it might be better to die rather than to continue his tortured existence. Job provides no straight response to these questions, for none is possible, but takes us on a deeply human journey from initially desiring death to being willing to die for a chance at renewed life. Along the way, he crosses imaginatively into the land of the dead and beyond on several occasions.[13]

It is true, as scholars have rightly noted, that Job never expresses a desire or a plan to kill himself anywhere in his speeches.[14] Nonetheless, it is clear that Job at points engages in suicide ideation, for death is not a mere rhetorical device for Job but an alluring existential option. And Job's first words in the poetic core unambiguously and quite artfully declare his death wish, which reverberates throughout his speeches.

Job's first soliloquy (Job 3) after sitting in silence for seven days and seven nights is the heart-wrenching lament of someone wishing that he

---

13. For an in depth examination of the death theme in Job, see Dan Mathewson, *Death and Survival in the Book of Job: Desymbolization and Traumatic Experience* (LHBOTS 450; New York: T & T Clark, 2006).

14. Dietrich, *Tod von eigener Hand*, 12–17.

had never been born or, short of that, had died soon after birth before experiencing the recent tragedies. Job declares,

> ³ Let the day perish in which I was born,
> and the night that said,
> "A man-child is conceived."
> ⁴ Let that day be darkness!
> May God above not seek it,
> or light shine on it.
> ⁵ Let gloom and deep darkness claim it.
> Let clouds settle upon it;
> let the blackness of the day terrify it.
> ⁶ That night—let thick darkness seize it!
> let it not rejoice among the days of the year;
> let it not come into the number of the months.
> ⁷ Yes, let that night be barren;
> let no joyful cry be heard in it. (Job 3:3–7)

Job, as the narrator correctly notes, "cursed the day of his birth (*yômô*, lit. 'his day')" with these words (3:1). In so doing, Job does more than that. He reaches back to creation language, found in the first chapters of Genesis, and redeploys it for a purpose directly opposed to creation.

First, Job declares his wish to destroy, one might even say "uncreate," the day on which he was born, and with it the very possibility of his life, in language stolen from Genesis 1. Recall that, on the first day that God began creating the heavens and the earth, God commands, "Let there be light (*yəhî 'ôr*)" (Gen. 1:3a). Job echoes this divine utterance and reverses it. He dares command, to translate the Hebrew woodenly to better bring out the similarity of Job's words to God's, "That day, let there be darkness (*yəhî ḥōšek*)" (Job 3:4aα).[15] Job directly counters divine speech and directs

---

15. For a fuller discussion of creation language in Job 3, see Michael Fishbane, "Jeremiah IV 23–26 and Job III 3–13: A Recovered Use of the Creation Pattern," *VT* 21 (1971): 151–67; Valerie Fortsman Petty, "Let There Be Darkness: Continuity and Discontinuity in the 'Curse' of Job 3," *JSOT* 98 (2002): 89–104; and Schifferdecker, *Creation Theology in the Book of Job*.

his malcontent over "his day," the day of his birth, to the day of cosmic becoming, the world's birthday. Within this dramatic setting, Job damns his life with destruction; but the negative allusion to Genesis indicates that Job in fact condemns all creation. He wishes both that he did not exist and that creation did not exist.

Second, Job reaches beyond the day of his birth and curses the very night of his conception. Job wishes to outrun the harbinger of glad tidings, "A man-child is conceived!" (3:3b), and to anticipate him with his prophylactic curse, "let that night be barren" (3:7a). Job knows, of course, that life is not a matter of words only, so he curses also the pleasure of coitus that makes conception possible: "Let no joyful cry be heard in it" (3:7b).[16] In some sense, Job wishes to negate Adam's ecstasy at awakening to the newly created Eve that made him break out into poetic song: "This at last is bone of my bones and flesh of my flesh," and the passion that makes men leave their parents to form new families with women (Gen. 2:23-24). Job's despair that curses the night of his conception takes aim at the fundamental social glue and creative force, which is the sexual attraction between a man and a woman and the joy of conjugal consummation.

Job's imprecatory lament, then, is double-edged. It concerns his particular circumstance and, what more, the cosmic and social reality as such. He wishes that light, the very foundation of the cosmos, were darkness (note that "darkness" is the dominant theme in 3:3-10); and he wishes that sexual pleasure, the fundamental generative social force, were null and rather dull: "let no joyful cry be heard" in the night. In sum, the Joban poet transforms Job's personal tragedy into a platform from which to examine the basic question of human existence and cosmic ordering.

It is not possible to say with certainty what historical event motivated the Joban poet to compose the tortured poetry of Job. At one level, the story of Job alone, the utter destruction of a seemingly perfect life, provides ample motivation. And the book supplies the self-generative dra-

---

16. David J. A. Clines (*Job 1-20*, WBC 17 [Nashville: Thomas Nelson, 1989], 85-86) writes, "The 'cry of joy' (רננה, not 'triumphing' as in 20:5) he wishes had never been uttered is the sound of his parents' lovemaking that resulted in his conception (so also Terrien), or perhaps the joyful singing of the epithalamium or wedding ode, if it is to be assumed that the wedding night is the night of conception (Fohrer)."

matic situation (a disputation in dialogue form) that explains and makes space for maximal flexibility to explore, to abandon, and to develop numerous and diverse themes. Thus, we need to assume nothing other than the personal tragedy of an individual to understand Job. At the same time, many scholars suspect that a large-scale traumatic event lies behind the Joban tradition, such as the experience of the Babylonian exile and its aftermath. Though caution is advisable because of the paucity of historical reference in the book, it is not difficult to imagine behind Job's pained words the destruction of homeland, the forced migration of a significant portion of the surviving population, and the widespread disruption to social, religious, and economic life. Similarly, one could imagine behind the friends' speeches a struggle to find some solid ground in the midst of the widespread disruption. That is to say, Job and his friends do not speak just as individual personalities but also as representatives of larger groups. Job never becomes everyman or everywoman—and the specificity of his persona is important for the dramatic power of the book—but the rhetorical ambition of the Joban poet, which reaches to the ends of the earth and to heaven and hell, resonates with authenticity because the suffering of innumerable lives lies behind Job's personal story. Furthermore, when read against the disorder brought about by the historical tragedies of exile, the traditionalism of the friends becomes understandable as authentic voices within the community that long for a return to traditional normalcy—an idealized dream against the challenges of reality.

In sum, Job does not stand alone, neither when he utters a desperate desire for death nor when, at the end, he stands up to God for his honor and his dignity. Job stands for the exilic and postexilic communities, the community of the traumatized, and perhaps also for all humanity. His journey is representative of suffering human beings everywhere.

"I Choose Death Rather Than This Body"

The theme of voluntary death, which Job's wife first clearly articulates (2:9b) and Job embraces in his opening soliloquy (Job 3), courses throughout Job's poetic speeches. The theme develops in two somewhat contradictory trajectories until the denouement in Job's final speech (Job 29–31).

Job and the Problem of Suicide

First, there are the passages in which Job explores the allure of death. Second, there is Job's imaginative search for hope through death. These antithetical developments culminate when Job stands before God and wagers his life in defense of the integrity of his life. We turn first to Job's suicidality.

After Job 3, Job next expresses his desire for death in response to Eliphaz's first speech (Job 4–5). Job complains that his suffering, if such a thing can be weighed, is heavier than "the sand of the sea" (6:2–3). He then names God as the author of that suffering:

> ⁴ For the arrows of the Almighty are in me;
> my spirit drinks their poison;
> the terrors of God are arrayed against me. (6:4)

Then comes the death wish:

> ⁸ O that I might have my request,
> and that God would grant my desire;
> ⁹ that it would please God to crush me,
> that he would let loose his hand and cut me off! (6:8–9)

Job does not here threaten to kill himself. He only says that he wishes that God would kill him.[17] However, we misunderstand Job if we, with some scholars, interpret these and other similar statements as a prayer for deliverance only: "Thus, the death wish in the book of Job does not aim for death but rather for the preservation of life."[18] It would be more correct to say that Job's death wish here and in other passages to be discussed below asks for the cessation of unbearable and unrelenting suffering—*even if that should mean death*. It is literally true that "no suicide is in view, only a desire that God would allow him to die."[19] Furthermore, as we will discuss, Job

---

17. Dietrich, *Tod von eigener Hand*, 16.
18. Kathrin Liess, "Todessehnsucht," in *Wörterbuch alttestamentlicher Motive*, ed. Michael Fieger, Jutta Krispenz, and Jörg Lanckau (Darmstadt: WBG, 2013), 405; cited in Dietrich, *Tod von eigener Hand*, 17; my translation.
19. Dietrich, *Tod von eigener Hand*, 16; my translation.

moves toward affirming the value of life over death by the conclusion of the dialogue. Nevertheless, Job displays clear signs of suicidality, according to a consensus list of warning signs for suicide, including "talking ... about death, dying, or suicide" and "acting," or in Job's case, speaking "reckless or engaging in risky activities, seemingly without thinking."[20] Job knows that his words are reckless and rash and may exacerbate his troubles (6:3; cf. Prov. 20:25). Yet he speaks and speaks, and ultimately makes a vow of innocence at the risk of his life (Job 31).

Job again expresses a desire to die in Job 7 in his impassioned first response to Eliphaz. He begins this section by characterizing human life as a daily torment, full of ceaseless labor and punctuated by restless sleep (7:1–4). If there is a silver lining to human existence, it is that life is mercifully brief: "My days are swifter than a weaver's shuttle ... my life is a breath ... As the cloud fades and vanishes" (7:6a, 7a, 9a). After describing human life in general, Job then complains of his particularly vexing lot in life. If all human beings have a "hard service on earth" (7:1), Job says that his lot is harder, for his overseer is none other than the divine warrior:

> [12] Am I Sea, or Dragon,
> that you set a guard over me? (7:12, adapted from the NRSV)

Job feels that the oppression he experiences is categorically more severe than that experienced by other human beings. His is cosmic, proportional to the animosity God the creator has toward primordial forces of chaos, Sea and Dragon.

We see glimpses of the cosmic monsters Sea and Dragon throughout the Hebrew Scriptures under various names, including Leviathan and Rahab. We find an illustrative passage in Psalm 74:

---

20. See Table 2 in M. David Rudd et al., "Warning Signs for Suicide: Theory, Research, and Clinical Applications," *Suicide & Life-Threatening Behavior* 36 (2006): 259. Rudd et al. divide the list of warning signs for suicide into two tiers, the first requiring immediate and professional intervention and the second directing that the individual get help but not necessarily immediate assistance. Job displays behavior consistent with signs from both the first and second tiers. Job's obsession with death, especially his own death, is obvious. He also speaks "reckless" (see Job 6:3; 7:11).

Job and the Problem of Suicide

¹² Yet God my King is from of old,
working salvation in the earth.
¹³ You divided Sea[21] by your might;
you broke the heads of Dragon[22] in the waters.
¹⁴ You crushed the heads of Leviathan;
you gave him as food for the creatures of the wilderness.
(Ps. 74:12–14, adapted from the NRSV)

The historical devastation that forms the background to Psalm 74 is the destruction of the Jerusalem Temple in 587 BCE and the subsequent Babylonian exile. These experiences were, from the perspective of the psalmist, not only a disaster of world-historical significance but indeed of cosmic consequence. The destruction of the Temple especially was understood as equivalent to the destruction of the center of the world.[23] The result was the unleashing once again of the mythic forces of chaos, which the monstrous Sea and the many-headed Leviathan embody. This is the reason that the psalmist calls on the God of old, whose victory over these primordial monsters led to the creation of order and vitality, to take up arms against Sea and Dragon and to slay and defeat them, that life and goodness might return.

To return to Job, by comparing himself to Sea and Dragon, Job suggests that the cosmic might of God that crushed primordial monsters is arrayed and deployed against him. The glory of God in creation and the world-historical puissance of God who acts in history, Job says, are responsible for his personal tragedy. We might be tempted, in light of the bathic resonance of "against chaos, against Babylon, and against my skin," to dismiss Job's self-comparison to mythological monsters as so much exaggeration

---

21. The translation differs from NRSV and follows the Hebrew, since "sea" (ים) appears without a definite article. It is likely the proper name of a Canaanite deity of the sea, also found in the Ugaritic Baal Cycle.

22. Reading תנין ("dragon") for Hebrew תנינים ("dragons") to parallel the singular Leviathan.

23. See the excellent discussion in Jon D. Levenson, *Sinai and Zion: An Entry into the Jewish Bible*, New Voices in Biblical Studies (New York: HarperCollins, 1985), 111–37; see also, Paul K.-K. Cho, *Myth, History, and Metaphor in the Hebrew Bible* (Cambridge: Cambridge University Press, 2019), 71–73.

born out of debilitating anguish. What we must not dismiss, however, is the seriousness of suffering that can inspire such a comparison. Job, and the people whom he represents, suffers pain and loss beyond words, a pain that undoes the world.

After comparing himself to Leviathan, Job turns to the theme of sleep, the moments of respite that, like the moments at the bottom of the hill for Camus's Sisyphus, make the daily labor bearable and possibly even enjoyable.[24] Unfortunately, Job says that even the small grace of sleep is denied him and instead turned into torture:

> [13] When I say, 'My bed will comfort me,
> my couch will ease my complaint,'
> [14] then you scare me with dreams
> and terrify me with visions . . . (7:13–14)

Hard labor by day and ominous visions by night drive Job to choose death over tormented life:

> [15] . . . so that I would choose strangling
> and death rather than this body. (7:15)

According to the logic of the complaint, Job would choose a life of hard labor free from nightly torment over voluntary death. However, Job does not harbor hope that either sleep or daily life will give him redeeming pleasure. In Job's imagination, God is a fierce champion with his bow drawn against humanity and most pointedly against Job.[25] Job believes that God hunts him as if he were a monstrous beast and finds himself helpless against the Almighty. Defeated and trapped like prey, Job's thoughts gravitate toward death, not so much as an end to life but as a release from restless horror

---

24. Camus, *Myth de Sisyphe*, 168: "Je laisse Sisyphe au bas de la montagne! On retrouve toujours son fardeau. Mais Sisyphe enseigne la fidélité supérieure qui nie les dieux et soulève les rochers. Lui aussi juge que tout est bien. . . . La lute elle-même vers les sommets suffit à remplir un coeur d'homme. Il faut imaginer Sisyphe heureux."

25. Job imagines God as a warrior who fights against him throughout the dialogues. See, for example, Job 6:4; 7:20; 10:16; 16:7–17.

that is synonymous with living.²⁶ At this point in the dialogue, death for Job is an alluring existential option as the sole available escape route out of a desperate and aversive situation.

Job again takes up the theme of God as the enemy and his fantasy for stillbirth in his response to Bildad's first speech (Job 8). Job begins the second half of his response with a forthright declaration: "I loathe my life" (10:1aα). Job, immediately after confessing his desire for suicidal hanging, had said, "I reject my life" (7:16).²⁷ In comparison, that he now loathes his life instead of categorically rejecting it may be understood as "a somewhat less nihilistic attitude."²⁸ Indeed, Job's mood is not all gloom and doom. He recalls with apparent gratitude past divine kindnesses: "Your hands fashioned and made me . . . You clothed me with skin and flesh . . . You have granted me life and steadfast love" (Job 10:8a, 11a, 12a). However, his words quickly become caustic as he turns from remembrances of things past to present realities, which appear all the more dire against the backdrop of the happy days of yore:

> ¹⁶ Bold as a lion you hunt me;
> you repeat your exploits against me.
> ¹⁷ You renew your witnesses against me,
> and increase your vexation toward me;
> you bring fresh troops against me. (10:16–17)

Before, Job felt as if God was hunting him, but now God has transmogrified in Job's traumatized imagination from a mighty warrior (6:4) into a leonine deity (10:16). The terror of divine pursuit cows Job into despair, and he returns to the fantasy of his own stillbirth:

---

26. For further discussion on Job's experience of defeat and entrapment, see Paul K.-K. Cho, "'I Have Become a Brother of Jackals': Evolutionary Psychology and Suicide in the Book of Job," *BibInt* 27 (2019): 208–34.

27. NRSV translates both מאס ("reject, despise, spurn, disdain"; 7:16) and קוט ("feel anger, loathing"; 10:1) as "loathe." The difference may be subtle but important. Clines (*Job 1–20*, 244) notes, "The injection of this feeling of disgust [in 10:1] . . . may even be a positive sign, a token of a somewhat less nihilistic attitude." The object "life" is not expressed in 7:16 but is implied.

28. Clines, *Job 1–20*, 244.

CHAPTER 2

> ¹⁸ Why did you bring me forth from the womb?
> Would that I had died before any eye had seen me,
> ¹⁹ and were as though I had not been,
> carried from the womb to the grave. (10:18–19)

Job, in his opening soliloquy, had decried that he did not die upon birth:

> ¹¹ Why did I not die at birth,
> come forth from the womb and expire? (3:11)

Job's complaint in the earlier soliloquy is impersonal, a formal desire for early expiration. If Job blames anyone, he blames his mother for nurturing him upon birth (3:12). In his response to Bildad, Job directs his plaint against God who "fashioned and made" him, brought him "forth from the womb," "clothed [him] with skin and flesh," and even "granted [him] life and steadfast love." But to what end? In Job's reconstruction of his life story, God has orchestrated his creation, birth, maturation, and his blessed flourishing precisely for the sardonic pleasure, at the end, to hunt him as a lion hunts its prey and to look on as Job cowers at the onslaught of divine troops.[29] That is why God brought him forth from the womb, in his mind: to torture him. In Job's mind, God is a puppet master who laughs maniacally at the dark comedy of reasonless destruction.

We know that Job's reconstruction of his life story as the story of a pet in the hands of a sadistic deity is incorrect. We know because we have the narrative prologue in which God makes his love for Job clear (Job 1–2). What is important is that Job does not know that he is wrong. He is not privy to the divine conversations that led to his recent tragedies. From Job's limited perspective, his nightmarish autobiography is not only an intellectual possibility but a lived reality. Thus, if we take Job's reconstruction of his story as earnest—and we ought to, though his friends do not—then Job's desire to die, either at God's hand (6:8–9) or at his own (7:15),

---

29. Clines (*Job 1–20*, 251) writes, "his unwished-for existence has become but the outworking of the perverse divine plan (vv. 13–14)." For an extended metaphor in which Job pictures God as an attacking warrior and predator, with numerous troops and ravenous horde in tow, see Job 16:6–17.

becomes understandable. We can pity him for imperfect knowledge. We cannot doubt that he would die and why.

"There Is Hope for a Tree"

Job's relationship to death does not remain constant. At the same time that Job runs toward death, he also attempts to jump over death. In fact, Job comes imaginatively to think of death as a gateway to a yet unknown world where hope and joy remain possibilities.

Job's imaginative and surprisingly hope-filled exploration of the land beyond death begins already in his opening soliloquy (Job 3). We saw above that Job desires that he were already dead. The concrete reason for his death wish is that suffering has become synonymous with life. Job concludes his opening lament with these plaintive words:

> [25] Truly the thing that I fear comes upon me,
> and what I dread befalls me.
> [26] I am not at ease, nor am I quiet;
> I have no rest; but trouble comes. (Job 3:25–26)

Life has become a living nightmare with no possibility of rest or the Sisyphean moment at the foot of the hill whence to appreciate the day's toil (and accomplishment). For Job, life is the relentlessness of trouble that comes without cessation.

Already in the first speech, the reality of pain and loss are not the only forces that push Job toward death. Pulling from the other side of death is the possibility of rest and the allure of an existence free from fear. In the middle of his opening speech, Job imagines life beyond death. If he were already dead, Job says,

> [13] Now I would be lying down and quiet;
> I would be asleep; then I would be at rest
> [14] with kings and counselors of the earth
> who rebuild ruins for themselves,
> [15] or with princes who have gold,

> who fill their houses with silver. . . .
> ¹⁷ There the wicked cease from troubling,
> and there the weary are at rest.
> ¹⁸ There the prisoners are at ease together;
> they do not hear the voice of the taskmaster.
> ¹⁹ The small and the great are there,
> and the slaves are free from their masters. (3:13–15, 17–19)

Job imagines that what awaits him in the land of the dead are quiet, sleep, and rest—the very things whose absence makes life so unbearable. Job strikes a note of sadness in this passage when he speaks of kings and advisors to kings, hero men and chiefs, who will lose their gold and houses of silver upon dying (3:13–15). This is understandable, for, as he later admits, he counts himself among wise counselors and mighty kings (29:21–25). However, in a significant expression of solidarity with common folk, Job characterizes the ambitions of the elite in life as rebuilding "ruins for themselves" (3:14) and celebrates the liberation of prisoners and slaves from their taskmasters and masters (3:18–19). Job, in a sense, repents of his past life. He recognizes that his material possessions count little in the face of physical and social torment, and he finally empathizes with his many servants who died tending his sheep and serving his children: "There the prisoners are at ease together . . . and the slaves are free from their masters" (3:18–19). There is salvation in death for slaves and prisoners, and also for someone like Job, from the senseless selfishness of rebuilding ruins, the torment of restless work, and the dread of ever coming disaster.

Job again peers beyond death in chapter 14 in an extended comparison of human and plant life and achieves a remarkable insight. Job initially compares the effervescence of flowers to the brevity of human life:

> ¹ A mortal, born of woman, few of days and full of trouble
> ² comes up like a flower and withers,
> flees like a shadow and does not last. (14:1–2)

This is a fitting metaphor, for flowers were thought to be paradigmatically short-lived. For example, the psalmist writes,

> ¹⁵ As for mortals, their days are like grass;
> they flourish like a flower of the field;
> ¹⁶ for the wind passes over it, and it is gone,
> and its place knows it no more. (Ps. 103:15–16;
> > see also Isa. 28:1, 4; 40:6–8)

The comparison to flowers, meant first to highlight the fleeting nature of human life, however, continues to work metaphorically to change Job's conceptualization of human life, first in a subtle, then in a dramatic way.

Flowers, in addition to withering quickly, signify flourishing and beauty in biblical thought. Thus, the psalmist writes that "they flourish like a flower," and the poet of the Song of Songs uses floral metaphors to describe the beauty lovers see in each other:

> ¹⁴ My beloved is to me a cluster of henna blossoms
> in the vineyards of En-gedi. (Song 1:14)
>
> ¹ I am a rose of Sharon,
> a lily of the valleys.
> ² As a lily among brambles,
> so is my love among maidens. (2:1–2)
>
> ¹³ His cheeks are like beds of spices,
> yielding fragrance.
> His lips are lilies
> distilling liquid myrrh. (5:13)

The loveliest things in life call to mind flowers, and vice versa. No surprise, then, that when Job compares human life to flowers, though he does so initially to underline life's brevity, what comes to mind next is the goodness of human life. Thus, Job, who once complained of the hardship laborers experience (7:1–2), pleads:

> ⁶ look away from them, and desist,
> that they may enjoy, like laborers, their days. (Job 14:6)

Laborers can enjoy daily life, Job admits. That is, human life is not all trouble but can be pleasant, if only God would leave human beings alone. Flowers subtly but surely infuse Job's gloom with pleasant aromas, the scent of living water.

Job's thinking about life changes in a more dramatic way when he exchanges floral imagery for an arboreal one:

> ⁷ For there is hope for a tree,
> if it is cut down, that it will sprout again,
> and that its shoots will not cease.
> ⁸ Though its root grows old in the earth,
> and its stump dies in the ground,
> ⁹ yet at the scent of water it will bud
> and put forth branches like a young plant. (14:7–9)

Job in this passage moves from thinking of the all-too-brief life cycle of flowers to that of trees and discovers that not all plants are alike. While flowers wither never to bloom again, the same is not true for trees. A tree that has apparently died, Job observes, can come back to life even after being cut down. What is needed is the mere "scent of water" and the dead trunk pushes forth saplings. The dead can give life. The dead can come back to life, Job discovers.

However, when he turns from the aroboreal frame of reference to the human, Job quickly realizes that no analogical movement from death to life is possible in human life:

> ¹⁰ But mortals die, and are laid low;
> humans expire, and where are they?
> ¹¹ As waters fail from a lake,
> and a river wastes away and dries up,
> ¹² so mortals lie down and do not rise again;
> until the heavens are no more, they will not awake
> or be roused out of their sleep. (14:10–12)

Momently Job hopes, a precious and rare virtue in Job, but appears immediately to abandon even imagined resurrection. Yet hope lingers, and the reviving tree sows a seed of doubt whether Job really knows that "mortals die . . . and do not rise again." Job gives articulation to his budding and speculative hope in a remarkable passage:

> [13] O that you would hide me in Sheol,
> that you would conceal me until your wrath is past,
> that you would appoint me a set time, and remember me!
> [14] If mortals die, will they live again? (14:13–14a)

Job imagines Sheol, the land of the dead, as potentially a hiding place where God(!) will shield him from God's own wrath and, remembering him, bring him back to life. Life after death is possible, Job thinks, if only God would make it so. This hopeful thought, the result of imaginative wandering inspired by a metaphor, leads to perhaps the most daring question in all of Job: "If mortals die, will they live again?" Can the dead come back to life?

Job abandons this line of inquiry and concludes that God, far from being the agent who will make resurrection a reality, "destroys the hope of mortals" (14:19b). However, though the metaphorical exploration produces no hardy hope, it nevertheless changes Job's mental landscape in a profound way. Job had previously reconstructed his life story as a divinely orchestrated nightmare that concluded with God hunting him like a lion until his death in "the land of gloom and chaos" (10:1–22). Such gloomy narrative reconstructions were the basis of Job's death wish. Death as soon as possible was the best ending to his tortured existence. But the floral and arboreal metaphors enable Job to reimagine death as potentially a gateway to a new hope and to a God(!) who redeems. Death graced by flowers, to borrow from Dante and Frost, changes from a devastating end into a fork in the middle of our life's journey onto a way that may lead on to way.

The hope that blooms with flowers and then with trees gives way to clearances in Job's mental field of vision that ramify into new narrative possibilities for hope beyond death. And perhaps the most powerful, if also the most perplexing, vision of hope beyond death comes in Job 19:25–27:

> [25] For I know that my Redeemer lives,
> and that at the last he will stand upon the earth;

CHAPTER 2

> ²⁶ and after my skin has been thus destroyed,
> then in my flesh I shall see God,
> ²⁷ whom I shall see on my side,
> and my eyes shall behold, and not another.
> My heart faints within me! (19:25–27)

The Hebrew of these crucial verses is difficult, and we cannot discuss, let alone resolve, the many semantic and interpretative issues here.[30] What is important for our purposes is to explore the various ways in which Job in this passage begins to reimagine the landscape of death and its relation to life.

In the imagined future of the famous passage, Job has died. Job says that his "skin" (*'ôr*) has been destroyed, and the phrase translated above "in my flesh" (*mibbəśārî*) (19:26b) can be and likely should be translated "without my flesh."[31] In this light, recall that, in the second divine conversation between God and the Satan, both "skin" (*'ôr*) and "flesh" (*bāśār*) are related to human life (2:4–5). God protects Job's life in permitting the Satan to strike only his "bone and flesh" (2:5), whereas the Satan implies that one's "skin" is equivalent to one's life: "Skin for skin! All that people have they will give to save their lives" (2:4). For one's skin to be destroyed and for one to be separated from her flesh, it is safe to presume, implies her death. Moreover, Job appears to assume his own death in the preceding passage, where he expresses his desire for a written and permanent record of his words (19:23–24). In sum, Job's vision of the redeemer, thus also of his redemption, assumes his death.[32]

The identity of the redeemer remains a matter of debate. Scholarly opinions gravitate toward two major options: the redeemer is God himself or a third, neutral party.[33] A proposed third theory is that the redeemer is

---

30. See Clines, *Job 1–20*, 457–68; C. L. Seow, *Job 1–21: Interpretation and Commentary* (Grand Rapids: Eerdmans, 2013), 802–8, 823–27.

31. Seow, *Job 1–21*, 826.

32. Clines (*Job 1–20*, 465) distinguishes between what Job knows ("his death before vindication, but vindication thereafter") and what he desires ("a face to face encounter with God this side of death").

33. See Norman C. Habel, *The Book of Job*, OTL (Philadelphia: Westminster, 1985), 305–7, for arguments for and against identifying the redeemer as God and arguments for identifying the redeemer as a third party.

none other than Job himself. No interpretation has won consensus status, no surprise given the freighted and ambiguous nature of the issue. However, arguments from the various sides of the debate helpfully illumine different dimensions of the book.

To turn first to God as the redeemer, the core of the argument that the redeemer is God has to do with the terms Job uses to describe the redeeming figure: Job uses terms closely associated with God in other biblical corpora. For example, God is referred to as "redeemer" (*gō'ēl*) in the Psalms (Pss. 19:15[14]; 119:154)[34] and in Deutero-Isaiah (Isa. 41:14; 44:6, 24; 47:4; 48:17; 49:7, 26; 54:5, 8);[35] Deutero-Isaiah calls God "the Last (*'aḥărôn*)," as in "I am the First and I am the Last" (Isa. 44:6; 48:12) (the same term, *'aḥărôn*, is often translated adjectivally in Job 19:25 as "at the last," but some scholars argue that it is actually a divine epithet);[36] and God is elsewhere often designated as "living" (*ḥāy*).[37] Job does not name God directly but refers to God using divine epithets.

Against viewing God as the redeemer, it has been noted that "since the lawsuit here stands in the context of a dispute with God, it seems unlikely that God himself would appear as vindicator and legal attorney against himself."[38] It is true that Job at points rejects that God will be the source of his deliverance. However, it is claiming too much to say that to identify God as a redeemer is "a complete reversal in the pattern of Job's thought to date" and that this pattern "persists after this famous cry of hope" until the end of his speeches.[39] As we noted above, Job entertains, if only momently, the possibility of God hiding him in Sheol and reviving him after God's wrath has passed (14:13). Job is capable of inconsistency, calling on God to save him against God. In addition, as I will argue below, Job's final speech, which is an oath of innocence, is predicated on his faith that God as the ultimate judge will clear Job's name and restore him to honor. C. L.

---

34. Habel, *Job*, 305.
35. JiSeong James Kwon, *Scribal Culture and Intertextuality: Literary and Historical Relationships between Job and Deutero-Isaiah*, FAT 2.85 (Tübingen: Mohr Siebeck, 2016), 17.
36. Seow, *Job 1–21*, 806–7.
37. For a summary of arguments, see Habel, *Job*, 305.
38. H. Ringgren, *TDOT* 2:350–55; cited approvingly in Clines, *Job 1–20*, 459.
39. Habel, *Job*, 306.

Seow may be correct that Job calls God "the redeemer" ironically, but it is nevertheless an interpretation that the ambiguous text invites and, to an extent, fulfills.[40] For example, recall that God vindicates Job at the end, saying to Eliphaz:

> [7] My wrath is kindled against you and against your two friends; for you have not spoken of me what is right, as my servant Job has. [8] Now therefore take seven bulls and seven rams, and go to my servant Job, and offer up for yourselves a burnt offering; and my servant Job shall pray for you, for I will accept his prayer not to deal with you according to your folly; for you have not spoken of me what is right, as my servant Job has done. (Job 42:7–8)

God calls Job "my servant" twice, states that Job has spoken "what is right," and elevates him to the honored position of priestly intercessor for his friends.[41] God as the referent in Job 19:25 cannot be ruled out.

Scholars who argue that the redeemer in Job 19:25 is not God but rather a third party usually emphasize the connection of the verse to other passages in which Job imaginatively hopes for either a neutral umpire who might arbitrate the judicial encounter between God and Job (9:33), or a "witness in heaven ... that vouches for me ... [and] maintain[s] the right of a mortal with God" (16:19, 21).[42] The redeemer, according to this line of reasoning, is not a *de novo* figure but the development of a prior motif. The mysterious redemptive figure represents Job's resilience in the face of overwhelming disaster. A Job who can imagine a redemptive figure demonstrates that Job is in the process of rebuilding a world that is meaningful, a world in which justice is possible, and an understanding of himself as one worthy of redemption.

In addition to these two dominant interpretations of Job's redeemer, David J. A. Clines has argued that the redeemer is none other than Job himself

---

40. Seow (*Job 1–21*, 805) writes, "So, while Job may not have had a sudden reversal of his view of God, he certainly must have had God in mind ... , if only ironically."

41. The writer of Job 42:7–10 is the Joban poet responsible for much of the poetic core; see Cho, "Job 2 and 42:7–10."

42. Habel, *Job*, 306; Seow, *Job 1–21*, 805.

or, more precisely, Job's own outcry for justice.[43] This interpretation picks up the important theme of self-agency in the book. Throughout most of the poetic dialogues, Job experiences himself as helpless, either to escape the aversive situation or to stand and face his adversaries. We often find Job declaring that he feels like a trapped animal or a city under siege (see 16:7–17).[44] But, in the middle of the dialogues, he begins to discover that he has a voice:

> [18] O earth, do not cover my blood;
> let my outcry find no resting place. (16:18)

After Cain has murdered his brother Abel, God says to Cain, "What have you done? Listen; your brother's blood is crying out to me from the ground!" (Gen. 4:10). Job's plea is a clear allusion to this Genesis passage, marked by three thematic words: "earth" (referring to "ground" in Genesis), "blood," and "outcry" ("crying out" in Genesis). Through the allusion, the Joban poet indicates Job's realization his innocent blood and outcry can advocate for him, even if that should happen after his death. Job discovers that he has a voice and that his voice has agency.

Clines equates Job's outcry to the "witness in heaven" mentioned in the following verse:

> [19] Even now, in fact, my witness is in heaven,
> and he that vouches for me is on high . . .
> [21] that he would maintain the right of a mortal with God,
> as one does for a neighbor. (16:19, 21)

Clines finds it difficult to believe that this "witness in heaven" is God or anyone else. He writes, "What is in heaven 'now' and had not been before the dialogue began is Job's own protestation of innocence and his formal disposition that requires God to give an account of himself."[45] Next, Clines identifies, a bit too woodenly in my opinion, the redeemer in Job 19:25 as the heavenly witness, thus to Job's own outcry. The "redeemer," according

---

43. Clines, *Job 1–20*, 459.
44. See Cho, "Evolutionary Psychology and Suicide in the Book of Job."
45. Clines, *Job 1–20*, 390.

CHAPTER 2

to this interpretation, is Job himself. Clines does not entertain the possibility that a heavenly being, either God or someone else, who hears and takes up Job's defense of his innocence is the heavenly witness in 16:19—the better option, in my opinion. Nevertheless, Clines is right to note that Job begins to rediscover his own voice and its value. Job has not lost all hope nor is so utterly defeated that he cannot advocate for himself.

Who is the redeemer Job claims to know? The text, we must be honest, is ambiguous. And that ambiguity reflects the uncertainty of Job's claimed knowledge. Job knows *that* there is a redeemer but not necessarily the identity of the redeemer. And it is important that Job does not know for dramatic reasons. He does not know why he suffers nor at whose hand. Thus, he does not know the reason that he should continue to live and remain pious toward God. Nothing is certain. His entire world is at sea where the wind, the rain, and the waves shatter past certainties. But Job in 19:25, in claiming that there is a redeemer, begins to build a raft. It is not possible to say that Job believes this redeemer to be God, or someone else, or himself. What we can say is that Job claims to know of the existence of a redeemer, and this claim signals a tremendous transformation.

What has been transformed? Job previously imagined his life as a cruel farce, orchestrated by a sadistic deity. In contrast, Job begins now to imagine and to hope that his life could become a heroic epic with a blessed and flourishing beginning, unfathomable trials, then triumph. Job does not yet know how or who will bring about the triumph. However, the crucial fact is that he has begun to believe that the world and his life are redeemable and, just as important, worthy of redemption. His life and the world are not things Job wishes categorically to destroy as he once did (Job 3) but rather things he hopes might be redeemed. The anguish of "Let the day perish . . ." has transformed into a new hope: "I know that my Redeemer lives."

"I Hold Fast My Righteousness"

With his declaration in Job 27:2–7, Job turns decisively from desiring death toward affirming life. Moreover, he trades his two previous narrative structures—the first in which death meant escape from the ill that is life, and the second in which redemption was imaginable only after death—for a third in which a willingness to die purchases him the possibility of restoration in his present life. Job says,

> ² As God lives, who has taken away my right,
> and the Almighty, who has made my soul bitter,
> ³ as long as my breath is in me,
> and the spirit of God is in my nostrils,
> ⁴ my lips will not speak falsehood,
> and my tongue will not utter deceit.
> ⁵ Far be it from me to say that you are right;
> until I die I will not put away my integrity from me.
> ⁶ I hold fast my righteousness, and I will not let it go;
> my heart does not reproach me for any of my days. (27:2–6)

The first thing to note is that Job, with these words, swears on his life. This signifies that he now sees his life as something valuable; it can form the basis of a promise. Also note that, even in a complaint against God "who has taken away my right / and ... who has made my soul bitter," Job acknowledges that the breath that gives him life is "the spirit of God." With this, Job effectively rejects his wife's advice, "Curse God and die!" (2:9). He does not curse God, but rather identifies God as the source of his vitality. Neither does he choose death, but rather holds on to God and to his life.

Second, Job swears on his life that he is righteous: "I hold fast my righteousness" (27:6). In so doing, he refuses the advice of his friends. They had consistently counseled that Job "agree with [God], and be at peace" (22:21). That is, they had advised Job to admit that he had sinned and deserved punishment, then to repent and pray for healing, assuring him that God would respond graciously and restore him to blessedness.[46] Many readers of Job have condemned Job's friends as lousy comforters—essentially agreeing with Job (13:4; 16:2)—and found it curious that so much space is given for them to speak their nasty and judgmental words

---

46. Carol A. Newsom (*The Book of Job: A Contest of Moral Imaginations* [New York: Oxford University Press, 2003], 90–129) helpfully interprets the friends as sympathetically trying to return Job to narrativity by placing Job's experience of suffering within a traditional plot that moves from sin, punishment, repentance, to restoration.

(see especially Job 22). Yet, their tenacious commitment to a Deuteronomistic interpretation of Job's punishment, especially his skin disease, as the result of sin is important (Job 2:7; Deut. 28:27, 35). On the one hand, it highlights by way of contrast the conviction necessary for Job to hold on to his righteousness. Neither tradition nor the prevailing opinion among his peers can shake Job's integrity. On the other, the friends' traditionalism reflects the difficulty that a traumatized person or society experiences abandoning the older assumptive systems of meaning that once provided them with stability, even if those systems lead to self-condemnation. In the aftermath of traumatic events, it is not only third-person observers who blame the victim for the perpetrator's crime but also the victim herself who finds it difficult to find "a balance between unrealistic guilt and denial of all moral responsibility."[47] What we have in the dialogue is Job's heroic insistence on his worth and innocence against the countertestimony of his friends and social circle, who speak with the weight of traditional authority and the violence of mobs.[48]

What I am arguing is that the Joban dialogue pits against each other two competing discourses that can arise after large-scale disruptive experiences. On the one hand, Job represents the individual victim who must find a new language with which to describe his unspeakable experience and the shattered world born through the wound of trauma. The new language is halting and tortuous, more pidgin than a full language, precisely because he is in the process of creating language that did not exist before. On the other hand, the friends speak the language of the larger group for whom it would be preferable to explain (away) the disturbing event as unremarkable by using the available resources of the traditional theological framework.[49] The language of tradition is fluent—except when it comes to the issue of the unspeakable trauma. Thus, in order to hold on to its

---

47. Judith Lewis Herman, *Trauma and Recovery: The Aftermath of Violence from Domestic Abuse to Political Terror*, rev. ed. (New York: Basic Books, 1997), 68. For the tendency to blame the victim, see pp. 114–17.

48. For a provocative interpretation of the social dimension of Job's suffering, see René Girard, "'The Ancient Trail Trodden by the Wicked': Job as Scapegoat," *Semeia* 33 (1985): 12–41.

49. For a helpful contrasting view of Job's friends, see Newsom, *Contest of Moral Imagination*, 90–129.

fluency and legitimacy—that is, the illusion of mastery—the language of tradition must exorcise the traumatic, of which it cannot speak. The drama of language plays out in the dialogue between Job and his friends. Job struggles to give an account of his anomalous experience; but the friends claim that the anomaly is accounted for by the ordinary rules of tradition. The inevitability of the contest lies in the fact that Job has no choice but to acknowledge the shattering of the world, for the shattering is enacted in his person. In contrast, the friends feel compelled to hold on to order and stability, even if it means they must abandon the victim. And the contest is one that cannot end in a draw.[50]

When Job takes a stand against the friends' claim that no human being can be righteous before God and wagers his life on his integrity, Job is doing more than standing up for himself. He is standing up against the assumptions of tradition and its social rules and theologies. He is a man raising a defiant fist against a particular vision of the world and its God.

The bold ambition of Job's wager comes into clear view in his final speech in Job 29–31. Job's final speech is comprised of three parts. In the first section (Job 29), Job reviews his past life as an honored elder who attained the highest ethical and moral standard and exercised his considerable influence and authority with equity and compassion. Job presents a longing portrayal of a lost golden age: "O that I were as in months past" (29:2), Job bemoans, remembering his experiences of God's presence (29:2–6) and the honor and reverence of lads, elders (29:8), and even princes (29:9). Indeed, Job portrays himself as the defender of the poor, the orphan, and the widow and the bane of criminals (29:11–17); he was a king (29:25).

The second section is an anguished plaint of his lamentable present after the tragedies (Job 30). Far from an honored member of society, Job complains that he is treated worse than even the "senseless, disreputable brood" (30:8). In fact, the very disreputable brood whom Job derides as more animal than human, who were once forced to live in the wilderness (30:3–8), now look down on him: "And now they mock me in song / I am a byword to them" (30:9). No longer at the center, Job finds himself as far as is imaginable from human society among animals. Thus, he declares, weeping:

---

50. See Jon D. Levenson's review of Newsom's *Contest of Moral Imagination* in *JR* 84 (2004): 271–72.

> ²⁹ I am a brother of jackals,
> and a companion of ostriches. (30:29)

Job signals with this admission the total loss of honor and utter shame. He experiences a kind of social death in a society in which some commit suicide in order to "escape the desecration of one's own name and reputation."⁵¹ He is no longer human. He is no longer a descendent of Adam who rejected the animals as a companion fit for him (Gen. 2:18–20); he is the animal rejected by Adam.

In chapter 31, the last section of Job's final speech, Job does not commit suicide but expresses his willingness to accept extreme punishment, including death, should he be shown not to have been righteous in a series of self-imprecatory oaths. This is his ultimate attempt to escape shame and recover his honor. The "implied ethical system" to which Job holds himself accountable, as one scholar notes, involves "not merely external actions but also inner attitudes and principles of ethical thinking."⁵² Another scholar declares that "[i]t cannot be disputed that Job who utters the oath of purity in chapter 31 stands almost alone upon an ethical summit."⁵³ For Job

> wishes disaster on himself not only for overt actions like withholding food from the starving slave (vv. 16–17) but also for inward attitudes: despising the justice due to the slave (v. 13), depending on wealth and power (vv. 24–25), being pleased ('stirred,' *'rr*, 'emotionally moved') at an enemy's misfortune (v. 29), and concealing himself because of fear of someone else's displeasure (vv. 33–34).⁵⁴

According to the logic of self-imprecation, Job places himself under a binding curse should his claim to the highest standard of ethical and moral action and thought prove false. He also binds God to respond, either to

---

51. Dietrich, *Tod von eigener Hand*, 40; my translation.

52. Edwin M. Good, *In Turns of Tempest: A Reading of Job* (Stanford: Stanford University Press, 1990), 309.

53. Georg Fohrer, "The Righteous Man in Job 31," in *Essays in Old Testament Ethics (J. Philip Hyatt, In Memoriam)*, ed. James L. Crenshaw and John T. Willis (New York: Ktav, 1974), 19.

54. Good, *In Turns of Tempest*, 313.

carry out the curse or to declare Job's innocence. Job expresses a willingness to die for the integrity of his person and in so doing obligates God to respond.[55] He has once again changed his relationship to death and so also the role death plays in his life story. His willing embrace of death, should he prove to be guilty of even a peccadillo of deed or thought, opens up the possibility that God will declare his innocence, restore him to honor before his fellow, and pave the way for a full and dignified life. Job's willingness to die makes redemption in life imaginable.

In his powerful self-imprecatory vow of righteousness, Job makes an important self-comparison to Adam, which unfortunately many translations obscure. Here is a translation that makes the reference to Adam explicit:

> [33] If I have concealed my transgressions like Adam,
> by hiding my iniquity in my bosom,
> [34] because I stood in great fear of the multitude,
> and the contempt of families terrified me,
> so that I kept silence, and did not go out of doors. (31:33-34, adapted from the NRSV)

The Hebrew translated "like Adam" in verse 33 is $kə'ādām$. The phrase can be translated, as it is in many versions, as "like a human being," but can likewise be translated as "like Adam." If the latter translation is correct, Job may be understood as referring to the story in Genesis 2-3 of the first human being, who, with his wife, hides from God after disobeying the command not to eat of the tree of knowledge of good and evil (Gen. 3:8).[56] Job claims that, unlike the first Adam, he does not hide because of sin, but rather that he has no sin to hide. The claim is that "Job surpasses Adam; he is truly blameless in thought, word, and deed."[57]

The narrative and theological implication of Job's self-comparison to Adam is great. Job, in chapter 3, attempted to undo creation, both the

---

55. Good, *In Turns of Tempest*, 314.
56. David J. A. Clines, *Job 21-37*, WBC 18A (Nashville: Thomas Nelson, 2006), 1030; Habel, *Job*, 438.
57. Habel, *Job*, 438.

cosmos as well as human society, with language stolen from Genesis: "That day, let there be darkness . . . that night . . . let no joyful cry be heard in it" (3:4, 7). In 31:33–34, Job appears to propose a new beginning, a new Genesis, which begins not with the failed first Adam, but with Job as the new Adam. There is hubris here. What God created Job declares faulty and proposes that the world should begin anew with him. But there is also admirable confidence in how Job stands up for himself and walks bravely after unimaginable tragedy. Job has come a very long way since his opening soliloquy. He has come from desiring to destroy the world so there would be no possibility of his life story to providing a full account of his own life story. He summarizes the past (Job 29), gives an evaluation of the present (Job 30), and takes matters into his own hands to ensure the possibility of a future (Job 31). He has come from denying the possibility of narrative to wagering his life for the possibility of narrative continuation.

Job cannot say at the conclusion of his final speech what his future will hold. What is important for our argument is that he boldly steps into that future, whether it be weal or woe, whether God strikes Job for his false claim to impossible righteousness or affirms Job's righteousness, clearing him of social shame and restoring him to honor. The miracle at the heart of the book of Job is this internal transformation: that Job, without social support or divine prodding, of his own volition and strength turns from contemplating suicide to wagering his life on his integrity for the possibility of proving his worth and of life after loss. By renegotiating his relationship to death, Job has given new shape to life, his and everyone else's.

Conclusion

I stated above that Job represents the contemplations of common folk on suicide. If Job had committed suicide by hanging, as he said he wants to (7:15), he would have died because of the loss of his children, his financial ruin, the pain in his bone and flesh, the torment of social shame, and the senselessness of the world—that is, for a set of reasons rather different from what drove Abimelech and Zimri to choose death, but ones not unlike those that have driven common folk throughout the ages to suicide.

But Job does not commit suicide and, in this sense, Job as a representative of common folk carries a strong message against suicide, even despite unimaginable horror and devastation. Job embodies, perhaps better than any other character in the Bible, hell in which some live, an endless and existential hell. And Job in the poetic dialogue gives full expression to this pain—with laments, complaints, and curses—and, after all that, receives divine approval for having spoken what is right (42:7, 8). Job does not deny the reality of senseless horror and, in the longest poetic lament in the Bible, gives full expression to its experience in speeches that reflect the deepest sorrow and even delusional flights of fancy. Yet, at the end, Job does not commit suicide and ceases even to ask that God end his life.

Rather than die, Job stands up before God and before his fellow and takes hold of life in the strongest terms possible. He is willing to die for the right to continue living as a person of integrity. And he does this as a representative of all human beings—as a new Adam. Unlike Adam, Job's story begins in a world shot through with tragic incoherence and, from within that very real place, he rejects the counsel of despair and chooses to rise and live day after day, one hundred and forty years' worth of days (42:17). He chooses, with his wife, to make love, to give birth, to dare call their children beautiful—Jemimah, Keziah, and Keren-happuch—all the while teaching them of both loss and gain, of blessings and curses. The heroism of Job is the heroism of the everyday, the boring choice to rise early in the morning, saddle the donkey, and go to work—and laugh.

What has permitted Job's high resilience, I suggest, is not a dogmatic demonization of suicide as self-murder nor its glorification as the highest expression of human self-determination. It is the courage and the freedom to think and speak honestly and earnestly through the irresolvable issues that attend the greatest question that any person can face: "whether life is or is not worth living." The book of Job does not, to my mind, provide definite answers to the many profound questions it raises. But if there is one lesson I am certain the book teaches, it is the high value of life—for the enjoyment of which much pain might be endured, though not necessarily patiently. The final word in Job, in short, is that beauty that deeply delights the soul is possible, even given great sorrow and suffering.

CHAPTER 3

Was Samson a Suicide Terrorist?

... those two massy Pillars
With horrible convulsion to and fro
He tugg'd, he shook, till down they came, and drew
The whole roof after them with burst of thunder
Upon the heads of all who sat beneath.

John Milton, Samson Agonistes, 1648–52[1]

THE STORY OF SAMSON, AS IT IS preserved in Judges 13–16, is a narrative gem, be it a rough and uncut one, that reflects and refracts the light of inquiry with dizzying, often illusive, brilliance. For, depending on the angle of approach, Samson's face shines or darkens into a thousand and

---

I presented earlier versions of the present chapter to the faculty of Wesley Theological Seminary on October 22, 2018 and at the History of Interpretation program unit at the Annual Meeting of the Society of Biblical Literature in Denver on November 17, 2018, and thank those who were present for their critique and engagement. I also thank Jane E. Kim for her thoughtful, challenging, and expert comments on an earlier version of the chapter. A part of the chapter is adapted from Paul K.-K. Cho, "Biblical Samson, Milton's *Samson Agonistes*, and Modern Terrorism," in *Studies in the History of Exegesis*, ed. Mark Elliott, Raleigh C. Heth, and Angela Zautcke (Tübingen: Mohr Siebeck, 2022), 141–55.

1. Unless otherwise noted, citations from Milton come from John Milton, *Complete Poems and Major Prose*, ed. Merritt Y. Hughes (Upper Saddle River, NJ: Prentice Hall, 1957).

one hues: Does the angelic annunciation in Judg. 13:5 indicate that Samson will become a heroic judge who will at last "begin to *redeem* Israel from the hand of the Philistines" or a dud who can manage only to "*begin* to redeem Israel"?[2] In his adventures, does he prove himself a saint, a Nazirite set apart for God, or a lecherous sinner, undone by his bloody lust? And in dying by his own hands—by his own hands!—does he prefigure Christ or commit mass murder? Each episode in the story invites multiple readings and even contradictory interpretations so that no part of Samson's story permits easy summation or evaluation: not the birth narrative, not the sexually charged violence that punctuates his life, and not least the narrative of his voluntary death.

In this and the following chapter, we shall focus on Samson's death and consider whether it constitutes an act of terrorism or redemption, arguing in this chapter that Samson is no terrorist and, in the next, that he can be considered a redemptive figure under certain circumstances. Before we turn our attention to the end of the Samson story, however, it bears reviewing the entire story to highlight details important to the following discussion.

The Samson Story

The story of Samson begins with the familiar but deeply enigmatic account of his birth in Judges 13 involving a Danite man named Manoah, his unnamed wife, and an angel of Yhwh, who refuses to disclose his name. The angel of Yhwh first appears to Manoah's wife and announces to her, among other things, that she who has been barren will bear a son who is to be set apart as a Nazirite from birth and will begin to deliver Israel from the Philistines (Judg. 13:3–5).[3] Manoah, after his wife tells him of the angel's visit, entreats that the angel appear to him as well. The angel does return

---

2. Emphasis added.
3. On Nazirite vow, with attention to its social, historical, and literary contexts, see Susan Niditch, *The Responsive Self: Personal Religion in Biblical Literature of the Neo-Babylonian and Persian Periods* (New Haven: Yale University Press, 2015), 72–89, esp. 78–89.

CHAPTER 3

but again to the woman, who calls Manoah to the field where the angel has come to her for the second time. Throughout the encounter, Manoah appears confused—about the angel's identity and intent (13:15–23)—and dimwitted, especially compared to his perceptive wife. Indeed, the angel's insistence on appearing only to the woman paints Manoah as inessential to Samson's birth and later maturation. The promised child is the woman's child, not Manoah's, and a child of God, a Nazirite from birth. The conclusion of the birth account nicely summarizes Manoah's unimportance: "The woman bore a son, and named him Samson. The boy grew, and the LORD blessed him" (13:24). Manoah, if he is indeed the father, is an absent father.

Given the narrative paralepsis of Manoah's fatherhood, it is not surprising that speculations arose that the angel, not Manoah, fathered Samson, an interpretation the nuances of the Hebrew support.[4] According to the NRSV, the unnamed woman, after the first angelic visitation, informs Manoah, "A man of God came to me" (13:6), but the underlying Hebrew often has a sexual connotation implying coitus and can be translated, "A man of God came in to me." For example, the same phrase occurs in 16:1 and clearly implies sexual intercourse: "Once Samson went to Gaza, where he saw a prostitute and went in to her." That the angel comes (in) to the woman in the field, while she is alone without her husband, during the second visit further heightens the sexual nuance (13:9).[5] There is another detail that suggests angelic fatherhood. At the conclusion of the first (sexual) encounter, the angel informs the woman, "You shall conceive and bear

---

4. Josephus, *Jewish Antiquities, Books V–VIII*, trans. H. St. J. Thackeray, Loeb Classical Library (Cambridge: Harvard University Press, 1968), 5.124–27; Pseudo-Philo, *Liber Antiquitatum Biblicarum*, 42; cf. Gen. 6:1–5. See Marc Zvi Brettler, *The Book of Judges* (London: Routledge, 2002), 44–49.

5. According to Deut. 22:25–27, a woman raped in the field is assumed to be innocent. See also §12 of "The Middle Assyrian Law," trans. Martha Roth (*COS* 2:126:353–60): "If a wife of a man should walk along the main thoroughfare and should a man seize her and say to her, 'I want to have sex with you!' — she shall not consent but she shall protect herself; should he seize her by force and fornicate with her . . . they shall kill the man; there is no punishment for the woman" (cf. §§14–16 and 56). See also Philippe Guillaume, *Waiting for Josiah: The Judges*, LHBOTS 385 (New York: Bloomsbury, 2004), 168.

a son" (13:5; cf. v. 7). The Hebrew, again, can be translated otherwise as, "Look, you are with child and shall bear a son." A comparable construction occurs in the famous Immanuel passage in Isaiah: "Look, the young woman is with child and shall bear a son" (Isa. 7:14). Since Manoah's wife was barren before the angelic encounter (Judg. 13:3) but is "with child" by the end—and it nowhere says that Manoah "went in to" or "knew" his wife—what may be insinuated is that Samson is of a mixed divine and human parentage. Samson, it is implied, is a human-divine child of the unnamed woman and the angel who refuses to disclose his name.

Traditio-historically, Judges 14–15 contains the oldest stories about Samson, likely dating from Israel's tribal period, and centers on Samson's comic-tragic marriage to an unnamed Philistine woman: the riddle of "out of the eater . . . something sweet" (14:5–18), the hapless thirty of Ashkelon (14:19), the inferno of paired foxes (15:4–6), and the heap (ḥămôr) of bodies slaughtered with the jawbone (ləḥî) of a donkey (ḥămôr) at Lehi (leḥî) (15:9–17). These narratives, along with the Gaza episode (16:1–3), showcase Samson's superhuman strength and thus raise the question of its source.

Judges 14–15 interestingly does not speculate about the source of Samson's strength, but the surrounding narratives do provide two distinct sets of answers. The Delilah episode (Judges 16) explicitly raises the question and provides two somewhat ambiguous answers. Delilah, at the bidding of the Philistine lords, repeatedly asks Samson, "Please tell me what makes your strength so great, and how you could be bound, so that one could subdue you" (16:6; cf. 16:10, 13, 15). And Samson, after rebuffing her three times, reveals the secret on the fourth occasion: "A razor has never come upon my head; for I have been a nazirite to God from my mother's womb. If my head were shaved, then my strength would leave me; I would become weak, and be like anyone else" (16:17). The answer, however, not unlike the answer to Samson's riddle about "out of the eater . . . something sweet," is ambiguous. Samson binds his strength symbolically to his Nazirite status but also talismatically to his unshorn hair (16:17) and leaves open whether his strength is a matter of religious belonging—the fact that he, as a Nazirite, belongs to God—or a purely physical phenomenon, something bound up in his hair.

The secret of Samson's strength is, in fact, more complicated even than that, for the birth narrative in Judges 13 provides two additional explanations. The first alternative explanation is "the spirit of Yhwh," which begins to stir Samson in Mahaneh-dan (13:25) and returns at critical moments in Samson's life to endow him with immense physical strength (14:6, 19; 15:14; cf. 16:20, 28). The motif of Yhwh's spirit suggests that Samson's strength is a situational, divine dispensation. The second alternative explanation suggests the very opposite, that Samson's strength is a permanent attribute of his birth. As noted above, Samson's birth narrative suggests a mixed divine-human parentage. If this is correct, Samson is the last of the Nephilim, the legendary giants born of the union between the sons of God and the daughters of human beings, "the heroes that were of old, warriors of renown" (Gen. 6:4).[6] According to this explanation, Samson possesses his strength by virtue of his human-divine constitution.

To summarize, the Samson story attributes Samson's strength to four different sources: his unshorn hair; the periodic onrush of Yhwh's spirit; his status as a Nazirite; and his divine-human parentage. Important for the discussion below is that the proliferation of the explanations for Samson's strength, precisely because of the overdetermination, obscures the cause of Samson's renewed strength before his suicide attack.

Judges 16 opens with a brief story of Samson's entrance into (presumably through the city gate to visit a prostitute) and exit from (in the middle of the night, with the city gates slung across his ginormous shoulders) Gaza (16:1–3). The fantastical story nods to Samson's gigantic form and sets the scene for the next two episodes by introducing the relevant themes: Samson's love of women, the antagonism between Samson and the Philistines, and the enigma of Samson's prodigious strength.

The Delilah episode expertly interweaves the various themes from the previous episodes, from Samson's love of women to the theme of riddling, and precipitates, after the shocking revelation of Samson's Nazirite secret, toward death (16:4–22). Once Samson's hair has been cut and Samson is rendered merely human, the Philistines bind and blind him;[7] and,

---

6. Brian R. Doak, *The Last of the Rephaim: Conquest and Cataclysm in the Heroic Ages of Ancient Israel* (Cambridge: Harvard University Press, 2012).

7. There is a debate concerning who exactly shaves Samson's hair, whether it is Delilah or the Philistine men. See Cornelis Houtman, "Who Cut Samson's Hair? The Interpretation of Judges 16:19a Reconsidered," in *Samson: Hero or Fool? The Many Faces of Samson*, ed. Erik Eynikel and Tobias Nicklas, TBN 17 (Leiden: Brill, 2014), 67–86.

Was Samson a Suicide Terrorist?

while Samson's shorn hair begins to grow back in the dark, dank dungeon (16:22), the Philistines celebrate his capture and apparent defeat with a great sacrifice to Dagon at the temple, singing:

> ²³ Our god has given Samson our enemy into our hand.
> ²⁴ Our god has given our enemy into our hand,
> the ravager of our country, who has killed many of us.
>   (16:23b, 24b)

Hubris and animus animate the final scene at the temple of Dagon, which will be a focus of our inquiry below. Blinded by recent triumph, the Philistines bring the blind Samson into the temple to provide entertainment to the thousands in attendance at the festive sacrifice. Thus, Samson gains entrance into the sacred temple and, after doing the Philistines' bidding, prays that God return to him his strength. His strength renewed—it is not clear how, whether with the growing hair, by divine gift, or by some other means—Samson tears down the two supporting pillars of the temple and brings death on those gathered at the temple and on himself. Samson forfeits his life to avenge, as he puts it, "one of my two eyes" (16:28).[8] In so doing, does he also begin to deliver Israel from Philistine hands? Or does he commit an act of terrorism?

Two Faces of Samson's Death

Samson's voluntary death, at first glance, falls squarely within the Deuteronomistic pattern of death chosen for reasons of honor we examined in chapter 1. His dramatic capture, the blinding of his eyes, and his enslavement to grind grain and provide on-demand entertainment for the Philistine throng bring personal and national shame. They form the basis for the Philistine taunt song: "Our god has given Samson our enemy into our hand." This is the kind of shameful outcome Saul obviates by bravely falling on his sword before the Philistines can capture him alive (1 Sam. 31:1–7) and which Abimelech tries but fails to prevent despite his

---

8. Against the NRSV, following the Hebrew, which reads אחת משתי עיני.

choosing to die "so that people will not say about me, 'A woman killed him'" (Judg. 9:54; see 2 Sam. 11:21). Samson dies by his own means and procurement to curtail the proliferation of personal humiliation and, from the perspective of the Deuteronomistic Historian, national and religious shame as well. His death puts a gag on the Philistine boast at Samson's, Israel's, and YHWH's expense. To boot, Samson's suicide attack, true to the annunciatory prophecy, "begins to deliver Israel from the hand of the Philistines" in handing the Philistines an unexpected blow (13:5). Samson's chosen death, within the honor and shame cultural matrix of ancient Israel, is an honorable act.[9]

Yet, Samson's death, no less than the stories of his birth and life, defies summarization—or rather, radiates outward speculatively and invites diverse interpretations. For our present purpose, we will focus on two extremes of the interpretative tradition concerning Samson's death, touching on relevant aspects of his birth and life as necessary. In the next chapter, we will consider positive, traditional interpretations of Samson's death as a redemptive act. In the present chapter, we turn to the negative interpretation, made more urgent by the events of September 11, 2001, that Samson's death is an act of suicide murder comparable to those carried out by modern terrorists. Throughout both chapters, we will mine the complex relationship between death and life that obtains in the Samson tradition, particularly the central issue of giving (up) life, to argue that Samson's suicide attack, while clearly terrible, has facets that, when seen from a particular angle and under certain lighting conditions, shine hope and life into a dark situation.

Let us first turn to the interpretation that Samson is a terrorist.

Is Samson a Terrorist?

After September 11, 2001, Samson has not infrequently been yoked with the title "terrorist." Norman Mailer, for example, calls the suicide terrorists of 9/11 "Muslim Samsons,"[10] and Joseph Jeter writes, "Samson was

9. Dietrich, *Tod von eigener Hand*, 222–31.
10. Norman Mailer, *Why We Are at War?* (New York: Random House, 2003), cited

a terrorist. At least he was if you were a Philistine."[11] More significantly, J. Cheryl Exum, a prominent biblical scholar of Samson, provides a considered argument that the biblical Samson leads a life of terrorism that culminates in what she calls the "ultimate terrorist act," his suicide attack on the Philistines at the feast to Dagon.[12]

Exum identifies four "wanton terrorist act[s]" in the Samson story. Samson's first terrorist act, according to Exum, occurs during his own wedding feast. Samson engages his Philistine guests on a wager for "thirty linen garments and thirty festal garments" (Judg. 14:12). The guests must provide the solution by the end of the seven-day feast to Samson's riddle: "Out of the eater came something to eat / Out of the strong came something sweet" (Judg. 14:14), or pay up. When the guests succeed—by extracting the answer from Samson's bride or, as Samson puts it, by plowing with his heifer (14:18)—Samson rushes to Ashkelon, kills thirty men, and despoils them of their garments, which he gives to his guests as fulfillment of his debt. Exum objects that "Samson's response . . . is out of proportion to his guest's chicanery" and that Samson kills the Ashkelonite men "who have done nothing to him."[13] According to Exum, the disproportionality of Samson's response and the innocence of his victims make Samson's murderous theft a terrorist act.

Samson's second terrorist act, according to Exum, is his burning the Philistine grain fields and olive orchards in retaliation to his father-in-law giving his wife to a friend in marriage (Judg. 15:1–5). Recall that Samson sets the grain fields and the olive orchard aflame by tying a torch between pairs of foxes during the harvest. The disproportionality of the destruction and the innocence of the victims—not the offending father-in-law or the friend but Philistine "children as well as men and women"—

---

in Feisel G. Mohamed, "Confronting Religious Violence: Milton's *Samson Agonistes*," *Publications of the Modern Language Association* 120 (2005): 327.

11. Joseph R. Jeter Jr., *Preaching Judges* (St. Louis: Chalice, 2003), 116, cited in J. Cheryl Exum, "The Many Faces of Samson," in *Samson: Hero or Fool? The Many Faces of Samson*, ed. Erik Eynikel and Tobias Nicklas, TBN 17 (Leiden: Brill, 2014), 17.

12. Exum, "Many Faces of Samson," 17.

13. Exum, "Many Faces of Samson," 19. For further discussion of the concept of proportionality and innocence in the Samson story, see Helen Paynter, "'Revenge for My Two Eyes': Talion and Mimesis in the Samson Narrative," *BibInt* 26 (2018): 133–57.

qualify the agricultural conflagration, for Exum, as a "large-scale wanton terrorist act."[14]

Third, Samson slaughters a thousand Philistines with a fresh jawbone of a donkey. When the Philistines learn that Samson ravaged the harvest out of anger that his father-in-law had married away his wife, they burn the wife and her father to death. They also pressure the Judahites to hand Samson over to them. Three thousand Judahite men bind a willing Samson and hand him over to the Philistines, their overlords. When the Philistines approach to take him away, Samson easily frees himself from the ropes and handily kills a thousand Philistines (15:9–17). Exum again objects to the disproportionality: "The Philistines' rather feeble attempts to rid their country of a fierce destroyer pale in comparison to Samson's vendettas against the Philistines."[15]

Samson's final act of terrorism, according to Exum, is his pulling of the temple of Dagon down on himself and the three thousand Philistine men and women gathered, ironically, to celebrate Samson's capture (16:23–30). Samson reveals the secret of his strength, the unshorn hair of a lifelong Nazirite, to Delilah, who sells the secret to the Philistine lords. Armed with knowledge and scissors, the Philistines finally capture Samson, gouge his eyes, shackle him in bronze fetters, and imprison him. But then they make a strategic mistake. They bring Samson into the temple to provide entertainment at the festive sacrifice to Dagon. Samson seizes the opportunity to revenge, as he puts it, "one of my two eyes" by pulling the temple down on himself and the Philistine congregation (16:28). Again, Exum bases her judgment that this is Samson's "ultimate terrorist act" on the principles of disproportionality and innocence: "This is killing on a huge scale and surely would include many innocent people. . . . On what scale of justice can destruction of this extent qualify as 'vindication for one of my two eyes'? It is vastly out of proportion."[16]

In addition to the principles of proportionality and innocence, Exum identifies motivation as a criterion for evaluating whether something is a terrorist act. She notes, for instance, that Samson's motivation for his var-

---

14. Exum, "Many Faces of Samson," 18.
15. Exum, "Many Faces of Samson," 19.
16. Exum, "Many Faces of Samson," 17, 18.

ious violent acts is vengeance, "not any higher ideal."[17] Then, she finds that God provides the "higher ideal," which is "not religious, but nationalistic."[18] She further insinuates that, since God is the source of Samson's occasional and permanent power, God may be seen as the terrorist mastermind to Samson the suicide bomber: "Samson is an instrument in the plan of a god who is 'seeking an occasion against the Philistines.'"[19] In this way, Exum provides, if not a definition of terrorism, the criteria by which one might evaluate an act as terrorist or not: proportionality, innocence, and motivation. She also raises the crucial question about the relationship between Samson's actions and God's plan. Not Samson's various acts of violence alone but they coupled with God's masterplan, according to Exum, meet the definitional requirements of terrorism.

Is Milton's *Samson Agonistes* a Terrorist?

It was John Milton's *Samson Agonistes*, not the biblical Samson, whose connection to terrorism first became a topic of serious discussion after 9/11. And while studied explorations of the biblical Samson's relation to terrorism have been sparse—as of this book's writing there is only Exum's—the debate about *Samson Agonistes* and terrorism has become a sizable cottage industry for students of Milton. We can take advantage of this development and use the discussion in Milton studies as a helpful framework and lens to supplement the more meager discussion within biblical scholarship. So we enlist Miltonic scholarship, *Samson Agonistes*, and Milton himself as co-readers of the biblical story. We shall find in Milton a most sensitive reader of Scripture, whose supple rewriting of Samson as a heroic slayer of tyrants reveals the artful ambiguities of the biblical story and challenges any easy conclusion that labels Samson a terrorist.

John Milton (b. 1608–d. 1674) was an early modern English poet who went blind "Ere half [his] days" circa 1657—a disability that connects him

---

17. Exum, "Many Faces of Samson," 18.
18. Exum, "Many Faces of Samson," 18.
19. Exum, "Many Faces of Samson," 18.

to Samson.[20] He is best known for the Christian epics *Paradise Lost* (1667; abbreviated *PL*) and *Paradise Regained* (1671; abbreviated *PR*). Admirers of these works have found it curious, even embarrassing, that Milton wrote a dramatic rendition of the Samson story, *Samson Agonistes* (1671; abbreviated *SA*) toward the end of this life. What has especially intrigued and puzzled readers is that *Samson Agonistes*, a work published as a companion piece to the decidedly pacifist *Paradise Regained*, seems to celebrate Samson's violent suicide attack.

In his autobiographical Sonnet XIX (1652) Milton asks what service he, whose "light is spent" and who is gradually becoming blind, might render God: "Doth God exact day-labor, light denied"? (l. 7). In response, Milton introduces a motif that will grow in importance in his later poetic creations: "They also serve who only stand and wait" (l. 14). Milton claims that patient forbearance—to stand and wait—despite life's cruel reality is a service, perhaps even the best service, that human beings can render God (ll. 10–11).

Nearly two decades after writing Sonnet XIX, Milton elevates the posture of standing (one's ground) and faithfully waiting (on God) to epic and theological heights in his account of Christ's victorious confrontation against Satan in *Paradise Regained*, a rewriting of Jesus's wilderness temptations after forty days of fasting found in the Synoptic Gospels (Matthew 4; Mark 1; Luke 4). Toward the climactic end of the poem, Satan presents Jesus with the third and final temptation atop the highest tower of the Jerusalem temple. Satan says to Jesus, "Cast thyself down; safely if Son of God," and quotes Scripture, that God the Father "will give command / Concerning thee to his Angels, in thir hands / They shall up lift thee, lest at any time / Thou chance to dash thy foot against a stone" (*PR* 4.555–59).[21]

Satan, with these words, attempts to shake Jesus's faith that he is the Son of God and to tempt him, with a scripturally inspired test, so as to attain evidence for his (unstable) faith: If you jump from this tower, you will perish, unless, of course, you are the Son of God, in which case, as it says in Scripture, the Father will command the angels to protect you. For Jesus to fall from the temple tower to demonstrate to Satan, and thus to

---

20. John Milton, Sonnet XIX, l. 2.
21. Note that the order of temptations in Milton is different from the biblical order.

himself, that he is the Son of God would provide visual proof for his faith. It would also falsify his faith—for "faith is the assurance of things hoped for, the conviction of things not seen" (Heb. 11:1)—and consequently destroy Jesus as the Christian redeemer.[22] In short, what is at stake atop the temple tower is no less than the entire redemptive history of Christian faith. For Jesus to fall—to temptation and from the tower—within the Miltonic universe would constitute the second fall, greater by far.

The poem continues with Jesus's all-important response and Satan's dramatic reaction:

> To whom thus Jesus. Also it is written,
> Tempt not the Lord thy God; he said and stood.
> But Satan smitten with amazement fell. (*PR* 4.560–62).

This is the precise moment when, within Milton's Christian mythology, Jesus claims his divine sonship—Jesus by faith takes Satan's hypothetical "if you are the Son of God" as true and rejects the need for evidence—and begins to regain the paradise lost by "Man's First Disobedience" (*PL* 1.1). And how is paradise won, according to Milton? Christ speaks and stands; Satan is silenced and falls. In his earlier Sonnet XIX Milton had asked, "Doth God exact day-labor, light denied?" The full answer, which he discovers only in 1671, is not "They also serve who only stand and wait," but "He redeems the world who stands his ground and waits in faith."

The scene of Christ's triumphal speech and standing, "he said and stood," has been rightly celebrated for its pacifism.[23] It is an awesome testimony to the primacy of interior faith in Milton. It has also been contrasted to the bloody violence that concludes *Samson Agonistes*, which, as noted above, was first published with *Paradise Regained* as the second work in a single volume: *Paradise Regain'd. A Poem in IV Books. To which is added Samson Agonistes*. Why did Milton bind *Samson Agonistes* to *Paradise Regained*?

---

22. The internal faith that is not founded on outward evidence is an important theme in Milton; see the introduction to Stanley Fish, *How Milton Works* (Cambridge: Harvard University Press, 2001).

23. See, for example, Angela Balla, "Wars of Evidence and Religious Toleration in Milton's *Samson Agonistes*," *Milton Quarterly* 46 (2012): 65–85, esp. 66, 77, 79.

CHAPTER 3

Toward the end of *Samson Agonistes*, Samson, blinded and in chains, is called to the temple to entertain at the feast to the Philistine deity Dagon. After performing the commanded acts of strength and might, Samson requests to be stood "Between the pillars . . . That to the arched roof gave main support" (*SA* 1630, 1634). This is where Samson performs his final act, standing between the two towering pillars. A messenger, who witnessed the event firsthand, recounts the deed:

> As with the force of winds and waters pent
> When Mountains tremble, those two massy Pillars
> With horrible convulsion to and fro
> He tugg'd, he shook till down they came, and drew
> The whole roof after them with burst of thunder
> Upon the heads of all who sat beneath,
> Lords, Ladies, Captains, Counsellors, or Priests,
> Thir choice nobility and flower. (*SA* 1647–54)

In stark contrast to Jesus who "said and stood," Samson "tugg'd, he shook." Violent, murderous action replaces faithful and patient testimony.

The conjoined publication of *Paradise Regained* and *Samson Agonistes* has rightly led to their comparison, for the juxtaposition highlights Samson's violence against Jesus's pacifism: What does Samson's violent and outward deed have to do with Jesus's internal faith? Does Samson's suicide attack complement Christ's redemptive patience as yin yang, as some say it does?[24] Or does Christ's pacifism condemn Samson's militancy, as others argue?[25] Is Milton's Samson a terrorist? The roots of this debate date back to at least the 1960s.[26] And, in the wake of 9/11, John Carey has added fuel to the smoldering fire with a provocatively titled article, "A Work in Praise of Terrorism?: September 11 and *Samson Agonistes*."[27]

---

24. Elizabeth Oldman, "Milton, Grotius, and the Law of War: A Reading of Paradise Regained and Samson Agonistes," *Studies in Philology* 104 (2007): 540–75, esp. 550–75.

25. Not all scholars are convinced that we should read *Samson Agonistes* with *Paradise Regained*. See, for example, Dennis Brown, "Moral Dilemma and Tragic Affect in Samson Agonistes," *Literature and Theology* 20 (2006): 91–106.

26. Alan Rudrum, "Milton Scholarship and the *Agon* over *Samson Agonistes*," *Huntington Library Quarterly* 65 (2002): 465.

27. John Carey, "A Work in Praise of Terrorism? September 11 and *Samson Ago-*

Was Samson a Suicide Terrorist?

"A Work in Praise of Terrorism?"

Carey's suggestion that Milton's *Samson Agonistes* can be read as a work in praise of terrorism begins with Carey's reading of Stanley Fish's reading of *Samson Agonistes*, which is a rewriting of the biblical Samson story, the result of Milton's reading of the Bible. We need concern ourselves with neither the full history of reading nor the details of the history of scholarship, but a wide brush stroke summary will help identify key issues in Milton studies that will help illumine the issue in the biblical Samson story.

Samson Agonistes is a one-act (closet) play. The play begins toward the end of the Samson story proper, with Samson already bound and blinded and sitting in a Philistine prison. Earlier events in Samson's life are recounted through dialogues between Samson and his three main interlocutors—Manoah his father, Dalila his wife (biblical Delilah), and Harapha the Philistine giant and father of Goliath (*SA* 1247–49; see 2 Sam. 21:22)—in addition to the Chorus. The end of the play recounts the scene at the Philistine feast to Dagon, where Samson commits his suicide attack. The relevant history of scholarship begins with Samuel Johnson's observation about the narrative structure of the play, that it "has a beginning and end which Aristotle himself could not have disapproved" but that "it must be allowed to want a middle, since nothing passes between the first act and the last, that either hastens or delays the death of Samson."[28] Johnson's point is that *Samson Agonistes* tells the story of Samson's beginning (through Samson's dialogues with his interlocutors) and end (as it happens) but not the middle, which should explain how Samson goes from the beginning to the end.

Stanley Fish takes up the Johnsonian observation about the missing middle and, in his 2001 book *How Milton Works*, argues that "mystery . . .

---

nistes," *Times Literary Supplement* (6 September 2002): 15–16. For insightful critiques of Carey's article, see Mohamed, "Confronting Religious Violence," esp. 327–29; Ryan Netzley, "Reading Events: The Value of Reading and the Possibilities of Political Action and Criticism in *Samson Agonistes*," *Criticism* 48 (2006): 509–33; Rudrum, "Milton Scholarship."

28. Samuel Johnson, "The Rambler. Numb. 139. Tuesday, 16 July 1751," in *The Works of Samuel Johnson, LL.D.*, ed. Arthur Murphy, 12 vols. (London, 1806), 5.436; cited in Warren Chernaik, "Tragic Freedom in *Samson Agonistes*," *The European Legacy* 17 (2012): 204.

lies at the heart of Samson's action" in *Samson Agonistes*.[29] That is, Fish argues that no cause-and-effect relationship can be discerned in *Samson Agonistes*, not from divine inspiration to Samson's marriages or to his final suicide attack. The poem provides no clear reason for Samson's actions, whose motivation remains a mystery. There is no middle to the plot that explains how Samson moves from the beginning to the end, from his miraculous birth to his murderous death. More importantly, Fish argues that Samson himself remains ignorant of any reason that he should act one way or another. Samson's actions, to misuse a Kierkegaardian term but only slightly, are leaps of faith.

What this means is that the conflict at the center of *Samson Agonistes* is not social, military, or even theological, but hermeneutical—and ultimately existential: How do we know how to conduct our lives if we desire to conform to God's will? According to this reading, Samson's heroism does not lie in his final, climactic act but rather in his relinquishing of the need to understand God's will as a prerequisite for taking action. That is to say, Samson's heroic accomplishment is not the suicide attack on the Philistines but decidedly more internal. It is that he "leaves off assuming that he can decipher God's will"[30] but decides nevertheless to act in the belief, by faith, that his action "is an expression, however provisional, of his reading of the divine will."[31] Fish goes on to say—and this is the controversial part—"insofar as [Samson's action] represents his desire to conform to that will . . . [it] is a virtuous action."[32] For Fish, Milton portrays Samson's suicide attack as virtuous insofar as it is an act of faith, and as heroic insofar as that faith is not based on certain knowledge or understanding—for faith is "the substance of things hoped for, the evidence of things not seen." That Samson believes that he acts in conformity with the divine will is necessary and sufficient. "*No other standard of evaluating it exists.*"[33]

---

29. Fish, *How Milton Works*, 396–97.
30. Fish, *How Milton Works*, 473.
31. Fish, *How Milton Works*, 426.
32. Fish, *How Milton Works*, 426.
33. Fish, *How Milton Works*, 426.

Was Samson a Suicide Terrorist?

John Carey finds Fish's reading of *Samson Agonistes* objectionable. If Fish understands *Samson Agonistes* as a work in praise of faith, Carey argues that that makes *Samson Agonistes* a work in praise of terrorism:

> The events of [9/11] are like a devilish implementation of [Fish's] arguments. The similarity between the biblical Samson and the hijackers of [9/11] are obvious. Like them Samson sacrifices himself to achieve his ends. Like them he destroys many innocent victims, whose lives, hopes and loves are all quite unknown to him personally. He is, in effect, a suicide bomber, and like the suicide bombers he believes that his massacre is an expression of God's will. Applying Fish's opinion about Samson to the events of September 11 we find that the action of the murderers was, in so far as they desired to conform to the divine will, 'virtuous' and 'praiseworthy,' and *'no other standard of evaluating it exists.'*[34]

Carey is careless here and misrepresents Fish.[35] He also slips uncritically between talking about Fish's interpretation of Milton's *Samson Agonistes* and the biblical Samson. One moment he says that the events of September 11 "seem like a devilish implementation of [Fish's] arguments"; the next, he writes that the "similarities between the *biblical* Samson and the hijackers are obvious."[36] Carey's slippage, however, is significant, for it is symptomatic of a wider cultural unease not only with Milton's work or Fish's reading of it, but ultimately with the biblical source material, revealing that Carey's critique is not only about *Samson Agonistes* but also about the Samson of Judges, not only about Fish's praise of Milton's Samson but also about Jewish and Christian glorification of Samson as a mighty judge of Israel, a hero of faith, or a forerunner of Christ. He also correctly places the pulse on the central issue, which is not the outward violence of Samson's deeds—which, in any case, is undeniable—but the missing middle, the mystery at the heart of the drama, the reason that Samson does what he does. Carey correctly underlines that what differentiates an act of terrorism from other

---

34. Carey, "A Work in Praise of Terrorism?" 15.
35. Mohamed, "Confronting Religious Violence," 329.
36. Emphasis added.

acts of terrifying violence is the purpose for which it is carried out. The impulse behind the act.

Defining Ancient Terrorism

The term "terrorism" came into usage only in the late eighteenth century in France, and hundreds of definitions are currently in use in a variety of fields of study.[37] Thus using the term and concept to analyze *Samson Agonistes*, let alone the biblical Samson, would not only constitute anachronism but also risk definitional confusion. In this regard, Timothy Howe and Lee L. Brice deserve our gratitude for editing *Brill's Companion to Insurgency and Terrorism in the Ancient Mediterranean*, which demonstrates the analytical value of examining ancient texts through the modern lens of terrorism, with Brice in particular providing a definition of terrorism.

Brice wades through the definitional and conceptual jungle that attends the study of terrorism, helpfully summarizes the literature, and provides definitions of two types of terrorism. Brice first notes that there are two components to terrorism: the violent act that terrorizes and the ideology that motivates the action. In this regard, he correctly notes that all forms of terrorism involve acts of terror: the "practice of calculated, demonstrative, direct violent action without legal or moral restraints, targeting mainly civilians and non-combatants, performed for its propagandistic and psychological effects on various audiences and conflict parties."[38] The ideology for which acts of terror are undertaken differentiates the two types of terrorism. First, Brice defines "state terrorism" as "the intentional use or threat of violence by state agents or their proxies against individuals or groups who are victimized for the purpose of intimidating or frightening a broader audience."[39] Second, he defines "revolutionary terrorism" as "the

---

37. Lee L. Brice, "Insurgency and Terrorism in the Ancient World," in *Brill's Companion to Insurgency and Terrorism in the Ancient Mediterranean*, ed. Timothy Howe and Lee L. Brice (Leiden: Brill, 2016), 12.

38. Brice, "Insurgency and Terrorism," 13.

39. Brice, "Insurgency and Terrorism," 15.

use of terror as an insurgent strategy with the goal of overthrowing the state, and so is sometimes called anti-state terrorism."[40]

Brice's definitional discussion nicely clarifies the categorical distinctions already described by Exum and Carey that can help structure the discussion to follow. On the one hand, Exum worries about the innocence of Samson's victims and the disproportionality of his violence. We can take this to refer to the act of terror that makes up the practical side of *terror*ism. On the other, Carey and Exum worry about the motive behind Samson's acts of terror*ism*, about the goal that stands behind Samson's decision to act. Important to keep in mind for the discussion to follow is that the two together, an act of terror and the terrorist ideology, but neither alone, make up terrorism.

Let us turn first to Samson's act of terror and its victims, then to Samson's motivation, which will bring us also to the question of Samson's connection to God.

The Act of Terror in Judges and in *Samson Agonistes*

There can be little doubt that Samson's dying act in both the biblical narrative and Milton's play terrifies. The Philistines in Judges, even before the event at the temple, feared Samson as "our enemy ... the ravager of our country, who has killed many of us" (Judg. 16:24), and the immensity of their fear underlies the ecstasy of their celebration of Samson's capture. And Milton registers the terror of Samson's act in describing it in the language of theophany: "As with the force of winds and waters pent / When Mountains tremble ... / ... burst of thunder" (cf. Exodus 19). However, while the biblical narrative and *Samson Agonistes* agree about the terrible terror of Samson's dying attack, their difference concerning Samson's victims disqualify *Samson Agonistes*, but not necessarily Judges, as a text in praise of terrorism. Samson's dying attack in Judges can be characterized, according to Brice's definition, as an act of terror but not that of *Samson Agonistes*.

40. Brice, "Insurgency and Terrorism," 14.

CHAPTER 3

Let us begin with Judges. The biblical story states that before Samson collapses the load-bearing pillars of the Dagan temple, "the house was full of men and women; all the lords of the Philistines were there, and on the roof there were three thousand men and women" (16:27). That is, the biblical writers distinguish between "the lords" who are inside the temple and the commoners who are on the roof. We find a similar distinction in the summary description of Samson's suicide attack: "the house fell on the lords and all the people who were in it" (16:30). What is curious is that while a distinction is made between the lords of the Philistines and common folk, they are killed together without discrimination.

It is tempting to attribute the biblical animosity toward both the noble and common folk to a general hatred for all Philistines: The Philistines are Israel's archetypical enemies; thus, every Philistine by his or her membership in the group deserves retaliatory death. To so generalize, however, would be to miss significant details of the story, details that provide reasons for the animosity internal to the Samson story and, as we shall see further below, offer a countertestimony to a general hatred of all Philistines.

Let us begin by acknowledging that the biblical narrative provides reasons for Samson's hatred of the Philistines, thus justifying his dying attack even if we conclude that these reasons do not seem to fully justify the attack in our opinion. When we do so, we might notice that there is a disjunction between the stories we find in Judges 14–15 and Judges 16. Note, in this regard, that the events of Judges 14–15 are all interrelated; a matrix of motifs, themes, and plot interweave through the disparate episodes and bind them together into a narrative whole: the riddle of "out of the eater . . . something sweet" builds on an earlier encounter with a lion on the way to Timnah and leads to the slaughter of thirty Ashkelonites; Samson's enraged departure from Timnah and belated return only to find his wife was married off to another continue the earlier theme of Samson's marriage to a Philistine woman and lead to the conflagration of Philistine fields and vineyards and ultimately to the slaughter of one thousand at Lehi. Further marking the unity of these stories is the formulaic concluding notice that Samson "judged Israel in the days of the Philistines twenty years" (15:20).

The result is that when the Samson story continues in Judges 16, it is as if a new story begins with no connection with what has happened. There is a repetition of themes and motifs between Judges 14–15 and Judges 16 but no sense of narrative continuity.[41] The effect is to restore Samson to a prior state of naivety, if not innocence. There is an effort to erase Samson of his past by thematically and structurally portraying him as (once again) a young man who falls in love with a woman and wants nothing better than to live out his days peacefully in her embrace before he is rudely interrupted by the Philistines, first in the middle of the night at Gaza, then repeatedly in the valley of Sorek. The Philistines, the narrative reset seems to say, are the provocateurs who throw the proverbial first stone, not Samson. Samson is the unprovoked victim who, having been denied satisfaction and love and having been violently captured and humiliated, justifiably seeks revenge.

The nobles of the Philistines debut as a distinct group in the Delilah episode. They are the ones who recruit, to use a term taken from the world of espionage, Delilah as an asset against Samson (16:5, 8, 18). They pay her, supply her, and maintain a line of communication with her. While the Philistine lords are a distinct group and play the role of financier and mastermind, their crime is thematically attributed to the entire Philistine population in at least two ways. First, both the narrator and Delilah repeatedly refer to the midnight ambush in Delilah's bedroom as "the Philistines": "The Philistines are upon you, Samson," says Delilah repeatedly (16:9, 12, 14, 20); and the narrator writes, "So the Philistines seized him and gouged out his eyes" (16:21). The ambush, which was likely arranged by the Philistine nobles, metonymically embodies the will of all the Philistines, not just the nobles. The part stands for the whole.

The transference of the nobles' guilt to all the Philistines takes on concrete form at the temple scene. The Philistine lords and the people first echo each other in their praise of Dagon for Samson's capture. We first learn that "the lords of the Philistines gathered to offer a great sacrifice to their god Dagon and to rejoice their victory; for they said, 'Our god has given Samson our enemy into our hand'" (16:23). Then, the people join the lords, saying, "Our god has given our enemy into our hand, the ravager of our country, who has

---

41. On the structural and thematic parallels between Judges 14–15 and Judges 16, see J. Cheryl Exum, "Aspects of Symmetry and Balance in the Samson Saga," *JSOT* 19 (1981): 3–29.

killed many of us" (16:24). The lords and the people, while forming distinct groups, are united in their enmity toward Samson and, from the perspective of the biblical writers, their idolatrous praise of Dagon. Their socioeconomic differences explain the distinct roles they play in the narrative and their separate seating at the temple, some inside and some on the roof; but their shared enmity and idolatry justify their shared judgment. From the perspective of the biblical writers, all the Philistines participate in the capture of Samson by espionage, the violent mutilation of his body, and the idolatrous worship of Dagon. Though not equally, all the Philistines are guilty.

Exum challenges the biblical portrayal of Samson as a naïve youth by raising the issue of proportionality and innocence. The blind and weakened Samson, when he prays to God to strengthen him one last time, makes clear his motive for the attack: "so that by this one act of revenge I may avenge the Philistines for one of my two eyes" (16:28). Exum argues that Samson's retaliatory attack, which she describes as his "ultimate terrorist act," is "vastly out of proportion" with the wrong done to him: "[Samson's dying attack] is killing on a huge scale. . . . On what scale of justice can destruction of this extent qualify as 'vindication for one of my two eyes'?"[42]

It is interesting that Exum brings up the notion of proportionality precisely at this juncture, for the mention of recompense for the loss of an eye brings to mind Leviticus 24: "Anyone who maims another shall suffer the same injury in return: fracture for fracture, eye for eye, tooth for tooth; the injury inflicted is the injury to be suffered" (24:19–20; see also Exod. 21:24; Deut. 19:21). Read through the lens of pentateuchal law, Samson's dying attack, which kills "more than those he killed in his life" (16:30), is precisely not "eye for an eye" and lacks Levitical proportionality. From Samson's perspective, his dying attack is revenge for only one of his eyes. From the perspective of the Philistines and Mosaic law, his attack exceeds what might be reasonably considered proportional revenge. To kill thousands in retaliation for the loss of his eyes, let alone one of his eyes, does not adhere to the principle of "eye for an eye." Or, in the language of Brice's definition of a terrorist act, Samson's attack is "violent action without legal or moral restraint."

In addition to the issue of proportional justice, Samson's attack would qualify as an act of terror only if the Philistines are "civilians and non-

---

42. Exum, "Many Faces of Samson," 17, 18.

combatants" rather than belligerent militants. In this regard, Exum challenges the biblical portrayal of all Philistines as participants in Samson's capture, imprisonment, and blinding and states that those killed "surely would include many innocent people."[43] She questions whether all the Philistines are guilty, combatants in actuality or potential, and, in so doing, forces us to consider whether the depiction of an entire population as guilty and therefore deserving a violent death is not reflective of a terrorist ideology.[44]

In this light, note that the Philistines gathered at the temple, recalling earlier episodes in the Samson story, characterize Samson as "our enemy ... the ravager of our country, who has multiplied our slain" (16:24). It turns out that the Samson story does not in fact begin anew in Judges 16. Samson may have once again fallen in love with a woman as if for the first time, but he cannot undo what he has already done (in Timnah, Ashkelon, and Lehi). The result is that the depiction of the Philistines as the initial provokers of Samson proves false. The Philistines may not be innocent when they capture Samson—his head shaven and asleep in Delilah's knees (almost like an innocent babe)—but they were not unprovoked. They do not capture and blind a naïve lover but someone they can reasonably call "the ravager of our country, who has multiplied our slain."

In conclusion, Samson's dying attack, already within the context of biblical law and narrative, cannot be cleared of the charge of an act of terror on ethical and moral grounds. Furthermore, it can arguably be characterized as "violent action without legal or moral restraint, targeting mainly civilians and non-combatants," based on pentateuchal law. It is, according to Brice's definition, an act of terror and satisfies half of the definition of terrorism. (We will discuss whether we can ascribe a terrorist ideology to Samson below.)

If the biblical writers distinguish between Philistine lords and commoners for narrative reasons (the lords have the financial means to recruit Delilah), Milton transforms the distinction to spare the common folk for religious and political reasons. Here is again the pivotal moment in *Samson Agonistes*:

---

43. Exum, "Many Faces of Samson," 17.
44. I thank Sondra Wheeler for our conversations about the ethics of terrorism and other aspects of this chapter.

CHAPTER 3

> As with the force of winds and waters pent
> When Mountains tremble, those two massy Pillars
> With horrible convulsion to and fro
> He tugg'd, he shook till down they came, and drew
> The whole roof after them with burst of thunder
> Upon the heads of all who sat beneath,
> Lords, Ladies, Captains, Counsellors, or Priests,
> Thir choice nobility and flower [. . .]
> Samson, with these immixed, inevitably
> Pulled down the same destruction on himself;
> The vulgar only scap'd, who stood without. (1647–54, 1657–59)

Milton's distinction between "thir choice nobility and flower" and "the vulgar" echoes the biblical distinction between the Philistine lords and the common folk. Novel in Milton is the idea that the vulgar escaped death because they "stood without," that is, outside the temple walls.

Saving the Philistine folk from death required on the part of Milton an architectural innovation. Milton pictures the temple as a theater, "half round, on two main pillars vaulted high. / With seats where all the lords . . . might sit . . . / The other side was open, where the throng / On banks and scaffolds under sky might stand" (1606–10). Milton's reconstruction differs from the biblical narrative, which places the common folk on the roof of the temple. However, Milton trades one spatial consistency for another. Placing the vulgar outdoors under the open sky allows Milton to save the common folk and honor the fact that Scripture says that only the people *in* the temple died: "the house fell on the lords and all the people who were in it" (Judg. 16:30), but not those on the roof, so technically outside the temple. That is, through an act of willful misreading, Milton valorizes the biblical distinction between the lords and the common folk and kills the former and spares the latter, who were denied access to the literal seats of power and prestige inside the temple.

Milton's prose writings help clarify the reason that Milton distinguishes between the nobility and the vulgar in *Samson Agonistes*. In his "Defense of the People of England," Milton references Ehud and Samson in defending the regicide of Charles I.

Was Samson a Suicide Terrorist?

> None but a country's foe thinks a tyrant is her king. It matters not whether Eglon was a foreigner and our man a native, since they were both enemies and tyrants. If it was right for Ehud to slay the one, it was right for us to punish the other. Even the heroic Samson, though his countrymen reproached him saying, Judges 15, "Knowest thou not that the Philistines are rulers over us?," still made war single-handed on his masters, and, whether prompted by God or by his own valor, slew at one stroke not one but a host of his country's tyrants, having first made prayer to God for his aid. Samson therefore thought it not impious but pious to kill those masters who were tyrants over his country, even though most of her citizens did not balk at slavery.[45]

The circumspect comment, "whether prompted by God or by his own valor," is important, as we will see below. What bears noting at this junction is that, insofar as the Israelites saw the Philistines as their masters, Milton considers the Philistines to have been tyrants over Israel. What *Samson Agonistes* clarifies for us is that Milton considered only the Philistine elites to be guilty of tyranny but not the common folk. It is because the Philistine elites are tyrants, according to Milton, that their death can be justified.

How about Philistine commoners? According to Milton, they deserve toleration, not violence. As some scholars note, Milton praises toleration in his prose works.[46] For example, in *Of Reformation*, Milton states that individuals should be allowed to use "the ability of searching, trying, examining all things, and by the Spirit discerning that which is good."[47] Indeed, far from praising religious violence, Milton laments its use: "How many persecutions then, imprisonments, banishments, penalties and stripes; how much bloodshed have the forcers of conscience to answer for, and protestants rather than papists!"[48] Milton decries the use of violence to coerce

---

45. John Milton, "A Defense of the People of England," in *Complete Prose Works of John Milton*, ed. Don M. Wolfe, 8 vols. (New Haven: Yale University Press, 1953–1982), 4:302, cited in Tobias Gregory, "The Political Messages of *Samson Agonistes*," *Studies in English Literature, 1500–1900* 50 (2010): 175–203, see 186.
46. Balla, "Wars of Evidence," 77–80.
47. *Complete Prose Works* 1:566, cited in Balla, "Wars of Evidence," 78.
48. *Complete Prose Works* 7:253, cited in Balla, "Wars of Evidence," 79.

CHAPTER 3

inward conversion. In addition to the above and other prose writings that promote toleration, there is also *Paradise Regained*, in which "the Son's toleration of Satan exemplifies how readers ought to behave toward those who contest their faith and practice."[49] Recall that Jesus, after Satan's temptations, speaks against Satan but takes no action against him: "To whom thus Jesus. Also it is written, / Tempt not the Lord thy God; he said and stood / But Satan smitten with amazement fell" (*PR* 560–62). According to Milton, common folk, even when they hold bad views, even if they are Philistines, even if they should be the devil, deserve not violence but toleration, a chance to discern that which is good, free from the coercion of tyrants.

Milton's Samson, then, commits tyrannicide, not a "violent action without legal or moral restraints, targeting mainly civilians and non-combatants." Samson punishes the Philistine lords who are tyrants, enemies to the freedom of conscience, and liberates not only Israel but also Philistine commoners from tyranny. In short, *Samson Agonistes* is a work in praise of tyrannicide, not of terrorism. Milton's Samson, in his prose and in his poetical works, is a hero whose suicidal attack, it might be argued, begins to deliver Israel and Philistine commoners from the tyranny of the Philistine nobility.

To summarize, we can commute the charge against Milton's Samson from terrorism to tyrannicide on account of Milton's conscientious exclusion of common folk from death precisely because they are excluded from the halls of power. However, we cannot make a similar argument for the biblical Samson. The biblical Samson's final act remains troubling and in need of further examination before we can conclude that he too is no terrorist. Thus, we turn to the issue of Samson's motivation and the concomitant issue of divine responsibility.

Samson's Motive and the Divine in *Samson Agonistes* and Judges

In *Samson Agonistes*, when a Philistine officer informs the blind Samson of the Philistine lords' wish that he come to the temple of Dagon and give public display of "thy strength . . . surpassing human rate . . . To honor this

---

49. Balla, "Wars of Evidence," 77. Throughout this article Balla makes the argument that *Samson Agonistes* is itself a work in praise of tolerance.

great Feast" to Dagon (*SA* 1313, 1315), Samson initially refuses. He cites, first of all, Hebrew law: "Our Law forbids at thir Religious Rites / My presence" (1320–21). He also proffers his sense of self as a second reason for his refusal: "Myself? my conscience and internal peace. / Can they think me so broken, so debas'd / With corporal servitude, that my mind ever / Will condescend to such absurd commands?" (1334–37). In short, Samson refuses to play the "fool or jester" for the Philistines for religious and personal reasons (1338). His duty to God forbids it, and his pride disallows it.

But he changes his mind, and Samson ultimately decides to go. The reason for the change, which lies at the center of the debate about *Samson Agonistes* and terrorism, is not immediately clear. Milton registers the mystery in the Chorus, who upon hearing of Samson's decision to go to the temple of Dagon say: "How thou wilt here come off surmounts my reach" (1380). Samson's explanation further enshrouds his motive in mystery: "I begin to feel / Some rousing motions in me which dispose / To something extraordinary my thoughts" (1381–83). What are these "rousing motions," and where do they come from? What impels Samson to make this mysterious decision to enter Dagon's temple against religious law and his sense of dignity?

One thing is clear: Samson's decision to enter the temple in obedience to the Philistine command is voluntary. Before announcing his decision to go, Samson reasons: "The Philistian lords command: / Commands are no constraints. If I obey them, / I do it freely" (1371–73). Having first refused to obey—thus having demonstrated his willingness to offend the Philistine lords and bear the consequences, that is, having shown that no "outward force constrains" his internal decision (1369)—Samson can now claim that his obedience is also a free act of his will: "But who constrains me to the temple of Dagon, / Not dragging?" (1370–71). He reasons that, if someone is willing to disobey a command, then, even when he obeys, he does so freely.

Samson reiterates the same point after having demonstrated his "strength . . . surpassing human rate" in an address to the Philistine audience:

> Hitherto, Lords, what your commands impos'd
> I have perform'd, as reason was, obeying,
> Not without wonder or delight beheld.
> Now of my own accord such other trial

> I mean to show you of my strength, yet greater;
> As with amaze shall strike all who behold. (1640–44)

The point here is that Samson obeyed the Philistine command to provide entertainment as a means to pursue his own volitional end. Samson then proceeds to carry out his attack, which was the final cause for changing his mind about the Philistines' "absurd commands":

> those two massy Pillars...
> He tugg'd, he shook, till down they came...
> Upon the heads of all who sat beneath. (1648, 1650, 1652)

In sum, Samson changes his mind and obeys the Philistines of his "own accord" in order to execute his plan to kill the Philistine lords in a final display of "my strength, yet greater."

Clarity concerning the final cause does not, however, resolve the enigma of "some rousing motions" that set the entire sequence of events in motion. We do not know the source of the "rousing motions," and, more pointedly, we must consider whether they have their source in God. In this regard, scholars have heard in Samson's "rousing motions" an echo of the earlier "intimate impulse" that, Samson said, had moved him to marry a Philistine woman. Samson explains:

> They [Samson's parents] knew not
> That what I motion'd was of God; I knew
> From intimate impulse, and therefore urg'd
> The marriage on, that, by occasion hence,
> I might begin *Israel's* deliverance—
> The work to which I was divinely call'd. (221–26)

Samson, at the time of his marriage to the Philistine woman of Timnah, enjoys an uncomplicated hermeneutic. He interprets the "intimate impulse" as having its source in the divine and so says that he "knows" that what he desires to do, marry the Philistine woman, is "of God." Furthermore, he interprets the marriage itself as a divinely sanctioned occasion to begin the work of delivering Israel. At this early stage in Samson's story, there is no mystery between divine cause and human action. God inspires, and Samson acts.

What, then, is the relationship between this earlier "intimate impulse" and the later "rousing motions"?

There are at least two ways of reading the echo between the "intimate impulse" and the "rousing motions," which one scholar describes as the "traditional view" and the "revisionist view."[50] Samson already at the beginning of *Samson Agonistes* fears that, through his own fault, he has lost the ability to read the workings of the divine in his life, this inability symbolized in his physical blindness. He remains physically strong but spiritually blind, and so laments:

> O impotence of mind in body strong!
> But what is strength without a double share
> Of wisdom? Vast, unwieldy, burdensome,
> Proudly secure, yet liable to fall
> By weakest subtleties. (52–56)

In *Samson Agonistes*, Samson retains, or has already regained, his physical strength as he sits in the Philistine jail before entering Dagon's temple. What he has lost is the ability to see, both physically and spiritually. He is a rudderless and wayward ship filled to the brim with trinitrotoluene, a weapon of mass destruction.

The traditional interpretation of *Samson Agonistes* says that Samson, through his conversations with Manoah, Dalila, and Harapha—which structurally mirror Christ's three temptations in *Paradise Regained*—regains his spiritual sensitivity to the prodding of the Holy Spirit so that, at the end of the play, he can again sense and obey the "rousing motions" as divine command to "*Israel* from *Philistian* yoke deliver" (*SA* 39).[51] *Samson Agonistes*, according to this reading, is a comedy with the expected U-shape of glory, fall, and redemption, in which Samson is a genuine hero.

The revisionist interpretation contends the opposite, that "Samson is a

---

50. Rudrum, "*Agon* over *Samson Agonistes*," 465.
51. Rudrum, "*Agon* over *Samson Agonistes*," 465.

false hero, contrasted to the true heroism of the Son in *Paradise Regained*."[52] The "rousing motions," according to this interpretation, are Samson's own delusion and are not of divine origin. This would mean that his dying attack is the result of a murderous impulse fueled by personal vengefulness and not divine motivation. He remains "[impotent] of mind in body strong" and acts without the necessary double share of wisdom. Samson is a fool, and his dying attack is a foolish act.

Stanley Fish carves out an option somewhere between the traditional and revisionist views. Fish questions whether we can know that God is or is not behind Samson's "intimate impulse" and "rousing motions." What we know is that while Samson attributes the "intimate impulse" to God, he does not explicitly do so with the "rousing motions." In the former case, Samson thought he knew that his "intimate impulse" was of God and so acts with innocent confidence; in the latter, he acts though he is unsure that the "rousing motions" are indeed from God. That is, Samson acts on faith that the "rousing motions" are from God, not from knowledge. As we saw, Milton's Samson, even before he enters Dagon's temple, is physically capable of mass destruction. What he lacks is the internal conviction that must propel outward action. And, according to Fish, if Samson becomes a hero at the end of *Samson Agonistes*, he becomes a hero of faith, a hero who overcomes the hermeneutical need for certain knowledge in order to live, or try to live, in accordance with God's will.

So what is Samson's motive for acting in *Samson Agonistes* and what is the relation of his motive to the divine? If we can trust Fish's brilliant, if somewhat unorthodox, reading of *Samson Agonistes*, we cannot know (and Milton does not want us to know) whether God impels or arouses Samson to do anything, only that Samson acts first out of naïve certainty, then out of genuine faith—that is, blind faith—and that his action "is an expression, however provisional, of his reading of the divine will." Milton does not resolve the mystery at the heart of Samson, which Milton sees as a matter of internal, not external, capacity. To return to Milton's perspicacious words from "Defense of the People of England," he leaves open the issue of whether Samson's action was "prompted by God or by his own valor."

We can transpose the debate concerning Samson's "rousing motions" to

---

52. Rudrum, "*Agon* over *Samson Agonistes*," 465.

another scene, which has a direct parallel in Judges, as a means of returning to the biblical account. Prior to addressing the Philistines before tearing the temple down, Samson, we are told, holds his

> ... head a while inclin'd,
> And eyes fast fixt he stood, as one who pray'd,
> Or some great matter in his mind revolv'd. (1636–38)

The biblical parallel to this scene is Judg. 16:28: "Then Samson called to the LORD and said, 'Lord GOD, remember me and strengthen me only this once, O God, so that with this one act of revenge I may pay back the Philistines for one of my two eyes.'" In the Bible, Samson prays to God, but no indication is given whether God answers him. That is, there is a mystery about how Samson comes to regain his strength. Milton transforms the biblical mystery about the source of Samson's renewed strength into an internal matter: Does Samson reach out to God in prayer or ponder within himself? In so doing, Milton forces us to question, against what is habitually assumed, whether we know that God answered Samson's prayer and strengthened him one last time.

In Judges, Samson clearly states his motive for his suicide attack in Judg. 16:28: revenge for one of his eyes. As scholars have noted, Samson's destruction of Dagon's temple for the loss of his eyes fits the pattern of citing personal grievances as justification for acts of violence established throughout the Samson story. Recall that a private bet with his wedding guests leads to the killing of thirty men in Ashkelon, that his wife's marriage to another man leads to the burning of fields of grain and fruit, and his capture by a group of Philistines leads to the slaughter of a thousand people. The question that arises and which we will take up is how to interpret the disproportionality between cause and effect, between the personal offense that Samson suffers and the death visited on thousands of Philistines.

One option is to follow Exum, who argues that Samson is a terrorist, because he is not, "as Samson says on one occasion, 'blameless in regard to the Philistines when I do evil to them' (15:3)."[53] His violent acts of revenge

---

53. Exum, "Many Faces of Samson," 20.

unjustifiably exceed in scope and scale the offending event. The biblical tradition itself nods at the notion of proportionality by alluding to the pentateuchal principle of "eye for an eye" (Lev. 24:19–20). We are made to wonder whether Samson killing three thousand Philistines is a justifiable recompense for "one of [his] eyes." A second option, to which we turn below, is to see if the biblical story supplies additional reasons to supplement Samson's insufficient justification for his outsized acts of violent revenge. When we do, what we find is God in the background as planner and enabler.

We should begin the discussion of God's role in the Samson story with the acknowledgment that God's relation to Samson's motivations and actions is complex. The complexity, in part, can be attributed to the compositional history of the Samson story, which we will discuss in greater detail in the next chapter. For the purposes of the present discussion, it suffices to distinguish between the core of the Samson story, Judges 14–15, and the frame, Judges 13 and 16. The core is the oldest layer of the Samson tradition and stems from Israel's tribal period, whereas the frame stems from or after the monarchical period.[54] In the older core narrative, God unambiguously enables Samson's violent attacks on the Philistines but has the modest goal of retaliatory revenge. In the later frame narrative, God's goal is Israel's liberation and the overthrow of the Philistines, but God has an ambiguous and somewhat tenuous relation to Samson's physical power. Let us first turn to the core of the Samson story.

In Judges 14–15, the most explicit statement concerning the goal God desires to achieve through Samson comes on the occasion of Samson's marriage to a Philistine woman: "[Samson's] father and mother did not know that this was from the LORD; for he was seeking a pretext to act against the Philistines" (Judg. 14:4). The statement makes clear that the reason for Samson's parents' disapproval of Samson's proposed marriage to a Philistine woman, in part, arises from their ignorance of God's plans. What remains unclear is whether Samson was aware of the divine plan and what the divine plan consisted of.

Concerning whether Samson thought there was a divine purpose for his marriage, we noted above that Milton interpreted Judg. 14:4 to mean that Samson knew that the marriage "was of God"—a case of confusing personal

---

54. See Brettler, *Judges*, 41–44.

libido for divine destiny, if there ever was one. However, this interpretation is far from certain. In fact, more fitting to the biblical account would be the interpretation that Samson was ignorant of God's plan to use the marriage as an occasion against the Philistines. If we assume that Samson had planned to marry, to riddle, and to have his wife married off to his friend, all to the end of harming the Philistines, that is, if we think of Samson as a strategist with the end goal of doing violence against the Philistines, then the story loses all dramatic feeling. If Samson's goal was to find "a pretext to act against the Philistines," he could have done so with far less self-harm. No, in the core of the Samson story, Samson consistently acts for personal and largely private reasons against the Philistines. If the story espouses a larger group goal against the Philistines, that goal resides with God alone.

This brings us to what God wants: What does God intend to accomplish by acting against the Philistines? The Hebrew word (*tō'ănāh*), translated "pretext" in the phrase "a pretext to act against the Philistines," appears only once in the Hebrew Bible. This rare word derives from a root (*'nh*) meaning "to be opportune" and means something like "opportunity."[55] In other words, God takes advantage of an opportunity that arises unexpectedly thanks to Samson. To put it negatively, Samson's marriage is not a part of a grand divine strategy. The modesty of the tactical opportunity that God seizes upon reflects Israel's historical situation as the weaker party in relation to the more culturally, economically, and militarily advanced Philistines. God, like the Israelites, has to resort to tactical opportunism to carry out smaller and larger acts of rebellion against the Philistines.

That one must resort to tactical opportunities, as we shall see in our discussion of Esther, does not preclude the possibility of a grand anti-state strategy. So, it is possible that, in seizing on the opportunity of Samson's marriage, God is thought to have in mind the deliverance of Israel from the Philistines "by overthrowing the [Philistine] state." However, while deliverance for Israel is indeed God's goal in the canonical form of the Samson story, it is not yet the goal in the tribal core of the Samson story. We know this because the text does not state that this is the goal, and because of the conclusion of this layer of the tradition in Judges 15. The concluding episode recounts the devastating and, from the perspective

---

55. BDB, s.v. "תֹּאֲנָה," and "III אָנָה."

of an Israelite, satisfying death of a thousand Philistine men at the hand of Samson (15:14–17). But, as if to acknowledge that deliverance has not been accomplished, Samson asks that God provide water to quench his terrible thirst, lest he "fall into the hands of the uncircumcised" (15:18). The Philistines remain a threat to Samson and, by extension, to Israel. Then comes the concluding notice: "[Samson] judged Israel in the days of the Philistines twenty years" (15:20). The remark acknowledges that, while Samson achieved a momentary victory over the Philistines, Israel continues to live under Philistine domination.

To summarize, what God purposes through Samson falls far short of an overthrow of Philistine rule and aims at something like an opportunistic retaliation against an oppressive force. It is true that, in the older core of the Samson story (Judges 14–15), God directly and unambiguously enables Samson's violence against the Philistines (14:6, 19; 15:14). God enables Samson's acts of terror. However, the purpose of these acts is more revenge and retaliation than revolution and the overthrow of Philistine rule. Judges 14–15, in conclusion, is not a text in praise of terrorism, because the act of terror is not conjoined to an ideology of terrorism.

If, in Judges 14–15, God is portrayed as the source of Samson's strength but as having modest ambitions against the Philistines, the opposite is true in Judges 13 and 16. In the frame narratives, God's goal is the more expansive one of deliverance for Israel, what Brice might call an "insurgent ideology." However, whether and how God empowers Samson to perform terrorist acts is unclear. First, in regard to God's plan, the angel of the LORD clearly declares to Samson's mother that God plans to "begin to deliver Israel from the hand of the Philistines" through Samson (13:5). This annunciatory declaration would seem to closely align divine purpose and Samson's destiny: God means to save Israel and to do so through Samson. This would be true except for the word "begin." The word "begin" creates a considerable gap between Samson and divine purpose; to begin to deliver may mean anything from "to have barely begun" to "to have almost finished." The gap nods to the fact that the Philistines remain a threat long after Samson and may indicate, on the part of the writers of Judges 13, a wariness about yoking God and Samson too closely together.

The unease in placing God's goal of Israelite deliverance squarely on Samson's shoulders is also reflected in the conclusion of the Samson story.

Was Samson a Suicide Terrorist?

In his prayer to God, Samson characterizes his dying attack on the Philistines as "this one act of revenge... for one of my two eyes" (16:28). That is to say, even as an act of personal revenge, Samson's mass murder of thousands of Philistines only begins to avenge the animus Samson feels toward the Philistines. It is an incomplete revenge, as his deliverance will be incomplete. That is, the motif of one-of-two eyes connects with the opening angelic annunciation that Samson will only manage to begin to deliver Israel. The motif also resonates with the summary remark about Samson's career: "[Samson] had judged Israel twenty years" (16:31; cf. 15:20). The length of Samson's rule at twenty years is significant. The usual length of a judge's rule is forty years (see Judg. 3:11; 8:28). Thus, to say that Samson ruled for only twenty years comments not only on the relative brevity of Samson's life, but also on his failure to complete the work of delivering Israel from Philistine rule. God purposed to deliver Israel, but Samson can only manage to begin the work.

We also see the nonalignment between divine purpose and Samson in the obfuscation that surrounds the connection between Samson's strength and God. As noted above, the older Samson tradition in Judges 14–15 clearly states that God enabled Samson to carry out his acts of violence on the Philistines (14:6, 19; 15:14). The later narratives of Samson's birth and death, however, proliferate explanations of Samson's strength and, as a result, confuse the precise role God plays in Samson's suicide attack. We noted above that the frame narrative proposes that Samson's strength derives from his divine-human parentage (Judges 13), or his Nazirite status (16:17), or his unshorn hair (16:17, 22), or directly from God (13:25; 16:28). In fact, the latter two sources of strength are mentioned but are not confirmed as the actual source of Samson's renewed strength in the temple scene. Bound and blinded in the Philistine prison, Samson's hair, the narrator informs us, "began to grow again after it had been shaved" (16:22). This note raises the possibility that Samson's strength had begun to return with the growing hair. In contrast, however, Samson's dying prayer to God ("remember me and strengthen me only this once" [16:28]) suggests that Samson's strength has not returned and will return only at the pleasure of God. But the narrator does not confirm that God listened to Samson's prayers and strengthened him again. In sum, the narrator leaves the question of how Samson regains his strength unanswered. More than that, the narrator frustrates our desire for certainty by purposely providing at least two possibilities: Samson's strength returns talismanically with his hair or as a situational divine dispensation.

Where does that leave us?

We argued, in regard to Milton's *Samson Agonistes*, that Samson is not a terrorist because Samson's act of terror is not "without legal or moral restraints, targeting mainly civilians and non-combatants." Milton's Samson commits tyrannicide and scrupulously, on the part of Milton, spares the commoners. Regarding the biblical Samson, we found that Samson committed an act of terror "without legal or moral restraints, targeting mainly civilians and non-combatants." However, we cannot label him a terrorist because he holds no terrorist ideology that can be characterized as either state or revolutionary terrorism; Samson acts consistently for personal reasons.

God, however, can be said to harbor what Brice might call a revolutionary ideology—the plan to deliver Israel from the hand of the Philistines. This makes it possible, by joining Samson's act with God's ideology, to argue that Judges 13–16, as Carey said of *Samson Agonistes*, is a text in praise of terrorism. However, I demur to the conclusion because of the composite nature of Judges 13–16. For, if the biblical Samson story is a text in praise of terrorism, it is only myopically so when we read the text without attention to the important tensions and countervailing voices at work in the biblical text between the older core narratives and the later frame narratives. The frame narratives, in which God desires to deliver Israel from Philistine domination, obfuscate whether God is the source of Samson's strength; and the core narratives, in which God clearly empowers Samson's violent acts, limit God's goal to enacting opportune acts of retaliation, not to overthrowing the Philistines. The Samson story as we have it in the Hebrew Bible is multilayered, and each layer of composition contains not only its own stories about Samson, but also its own ideology, and we must attend to these complexities before concluding whether Samson should be considered a terrorist or a redemptive figure. We shall tackle that task in the next chapter.

Dalila, Delilah, and Jael

I would like to conclude with a final textual indication of the unease the authors of the frame narratives felt about the link that the core narratives assume between God and Samson. We can recover this textual indication by reading the biblical story alongside Milton.

We noted that the biblical writers of Judges 16 obfuscate the source of Samson's renewed strength precisely at the moment of his suicide attack. In so doing, they hide the nature of the divine involvement in his mass murder. This brings us back to Milton's *Samson Agonistes*. Recall that Milton hedged whether Samson prayed to God or enjoyed a moment of internal reflection before taking decisive action to demolish the temple of Dagon: "[his] head a while inclin'd, / And eyes fast fixt he stood, as one who pray'd, / Or some great matter in his mind revolv'd" (*SA* 1686–88). That is to say, Milton shows himself a most acute reader of Scripture in finding "mystery ... at the heart of Samson's action."[56] Milton heard in the silence over whether or not God answered Samson's prayer to renew his strength a reluctance on the part of the biblical writers to confirm divine involvement in Samson's dying attack; then, with his characteristic subtlety and genius, Milton translated the moment of outward prayer in Judges into a moment of profound internal mystery in *Samson Agonistes*. Did Samson incline his head in prayer or in contemplation?

There is another moment in Milton's rewriting of the Samson story that sheds brilliant light on a moment of considerable interest to our question about whether Judges 13–16 should be considered a text in praise of terrorism. It has to do with Delilah, whom Milton, following the Greek translation and for metrical reasons, calls Dalila.

Milton portrays Dalila as Samson's wife. (Judges is silent on the matter and notes only that Samson loved her [Judg. 16:4].) Samson's conversation with Dalila in *Samson Agonistes* focuses on Dalila's betrayal, on what motivated Dalila to break her conjugal duty to Samson and to betray his secret to the Philistines. Many reasons are proffered but toward the end of their conversation, Dalila explains:

> My name perhaps among the Circumcis'd
> In *Dan*, in *Judah*, and the bordering Tribes,
> To all posterity may stand defam'd,
> With malediction mention'd, and the blot

56. Fish, *How Milton Works*, 396–97.

> Of falsehood most unconjugal traduc'd.
> But in my country where I most desire,
> In *Ekron, Gaza, Asdod,* and in *Gath*
> I shall be nam'd among the famousest
> Of Women, sung at solemn festivals,
> Living and dead recorded, who to save
> Her country from a fierce destroyer, chose
> Above the faith of wedlock bands, my tomb
> With odors visited and annual flowers. (*SA* 975–87).

Dalila argues that her betrayal of Samson against "wedlock bands" will win her everlasting honor among the Philistines and that her self-sacrificial deed will be "sung at solemn festivals." Dalila is no hero in Milton's work, but she provides a convincing and reasonable Philistine perspective on the Samson situation: Samson has terrified the Philistines, killing the innocent as well as the guilty. Thus, to help bind him is to help stop an enemy of the state, to betray him is to save many lives. Dalila is a hero. At least she is if you are a Philistine!

What Dalila says next is remarkable. Just as Milton advanced the biblical examples of Ehud and Samson to defend the regicide of Charles I, Milton's Dalila advances the biblical example of Jael to defend her betrayal of Samson:

> Not less renown'd than in Mount *Ephraim,*
> Jael, who with inhospitable guile
> Smote *Sisera* sleeping through the Temples nail'd. (988–90)

Dalila argues that her betrayal of Samson is analogous to Jael's betrayal of her husband Heber, whose people, the Kenites, were allied to Sisera (Judg. 4:17). Jael becomes an Israelite heroine by betraying her husband. She kills Israel's enemy (4:9) and is memorialized for her heroic deed in the ancient Song of Deborah: "Most blessed among women be Jael" (5:24). To return to *Samson Agonistes,* just as Jael and her deed are "sung at solemn festivals" in Israel, so Dalila imagines that she and her deed too will be in Philistia. In short, Dalila conceives herself as a Philistine Jael and trades "faith of wedlock bands" for a "tomb / With odors visited and annual flowers," fidelity to husband for patriotism to country, carnal happiness for eternal fame.[57] These are heroic virtues that, as one scholar has argued, Samson himself will take up. Samson dismisses Dalila—as a false embodiment of Jael—but Jael whom Dalila invokes and imitates endures as a model for Samson himself.[58] One might say that Dalila delivers the Miltonic Samson from self-pity and self-doubt by resurrecting from Hebrew lore the ghost of Jael and sitting her before him for imitation. Samson arguably outdoes Dalila in imitating Jael, but he imitates Dalila in imitating Jael. Dalila, in short, saves Samson so that he might save Israel.[59]

But what prompted Milton to liken Dalila to Jael? Milton's remarkable defense of Dalila and his sympathy for the Philistine perspective with reference to Jael likely stem ultimately from the biblical text, which Milton could read in Hebrew. The Hebrew of Judg. 16:14, which recounts Delilah's third attempt to discover Samson's Nazirite secret, begins:

> *wattītqaʿ bayyātēd . . .*
> And she thrust with the peg . . .

The Hebrew does not make sense in context: "And she thrust with the peg. Then she said to him, 'The Philistines are upon you, Samson!'" The awkwardness of the Hebrew has led many English translators to conclude that the Hebrew text must be the result of scribal error. Thus, many English

---

57. See Paula Loscocco, "'Not Less Renown'd than Jael': Heroic Chastity in *Samson Agonistes*," *Milton Studies* 40 (2001): 181–200. Loscocco reads Dalila as introducing Jael as a heroic type that Samson takes up to move toward his resolution to act at the end.

58. Loscocco, "Heroic Chastity in *Samson Agonistes*," 187. She writes, "Dalila may be gone, but through her going Jael and Judith remain, spectral and (at least partially or temporarily) masculine figures that increasingly haunt and hover over Milton's hero, guiding him back to godly intimacy." Later she states, "Indeed, a distinctly heroic tone enters Milton's poem with Dalila's invocation of Jael, a tone that transfers to Samson, as a kind of recovered masculinity, almost as soon as Dalila speaks and leaves" (p. 188).

59. Susan Ackerman ("What If Judges Had Been Written by a Philistine?" *BibInt* 8 [2000]: 33–41) examines these Miltonic verses in considering the Philistine perspective on Samson but does not discuss the possible biblical source of Milton's inspiration, on which below.

translations follow the Greek[60] and/or fill in the gaps with details from the previous verse. For example, the NRSV expands, "And she thrust with the peg," into, "So while he slept, Delilah took the seven locks of his head and wove them into the web, and made them tight with the pin...." But is the Hebrew text really the result of an error?

Here, Milton's decision to portray Dalila as imitating Jael is instructive, for the enigmatic Hebrew phrase: "And she thrust with the peg" repeats precisely the account of how Jael kills Sisera:

> *wattītqaʿ ʾet-hayyātēd bəraqqātô* . . .
> And she drove the peg into his temple . . . (Judg. 4:21)

Far from a scribal error, the Hebrew of Judg. 16:14 may be a deliberate allusion to Judg. 4:21, an intertextual link between the Hebrew hero Jael and the Philistine hero Delilah. This, it seems to me, is precisely the textual detail that Milton, the supreme reader of the Bible that he was, worked out in having Dalila compare herself to Jael. Note that Dalila mentions the exact scene in which "Jael . . . Smote *Sisera* sleeping through the Temples nail'd." In turn, Milton helps us to see that what we have in the Hebrew of Judg. 16:14 is a hidden record of a biblical writer considering, however tentatively through his allusive arts, the Philistine perspective on Delilah and so also on Samson. If Delilah's deed is comparable to Jael's, then Samson is the Philistine's Sisera, the hated enemy God has ordained destroyed. Indeed, looking forward to after Samson's capture, this is exactly what the biblical writers have the Philistines say for themselves: "Our god has given Samson our enemy into our hand . . . the ravager of our country, who has killed many of us" (16:23, 24). It has become commonplace for commentators on the Samson story to say that "Samson was a terrorist. At least he was if you were a Philistine," as if they are saying something new and shocking. As it turns out, it was a perspective as old as Milton and arguably original to the biblical authors themselves.

---

60. Judg. 16:14 LXX: καὶ ἐκοίμισεν αὐτὸν Δαλιλα καὶ ἐδιάσατο τοὺς ἑπτὰ βοστρύχους τῆς κεφαλῆς αὐτοῦ μετὰ τῆς ἐκτάσεως καὶ κατέκρουσεν ἐν τοῖς πασσάλοις εἰς τὸν τοῖχον.

Was Samson a Suicide Terrorist?

Conclusion

The presence of an intertextual and allusive possibility that the biblical writers were sympathetic to the Philistine perspective does not change our judgment concerning Samson. But it does teach us that the biblical writers were not deaf to contrarian voices, even if they contradict the dominant opinion regarding the archetypal enemy of the Israelites, the uncircumcised Philistines. Reading Judges with Milton, in short, encourages us to consider anew those enigmatic details and the fraught silences of the biblical text to see if they lead to a "way [that] leads on to way," that opens on to "counter, original, spare, [and] strange" narrative landscapes, hidden just out of view beyond roads "less traveled by."[61]

---

61. Robert Frost, "The Road Not Taken," in *The Poetry of Robert Frost: The Collected Poems*, ed. Edward Connery Lathem (New York: St. Martin's Griffin, 1969), 105.

CHAPTER 4

The Other Samsons

Well, if I had my way
If I had a, a wicked mind
If I had a, ah Lord, tear this building down.
...
Lord, if I had my way
Well, if I had a, a wicked world
If I had a, ah Lord, tear this building down.

Blind Willie Johnson,
"If I Had My Way I'd Tear the Building Down"[1]

A RESPONSE TO THE CHARGE THAT Samson is a terrorist must contend with the long tradition that sees Samson as a redeemer and, within Christian tradition in particular, a prefiguration of Christ. This is what we shall do in this chapter by examining the biblical rewritings of the Samson story, as well as its postbiblical reception. We shall find that both inner and extrabiblical interpretations of Samson wrestle with the negative aspects of Samson—his inordinate love of women and his suicide attack, among others—but at the end celebrate him as a redeeming hero: Samson is a

---

1. I thank Cheryl Townsend Gilkes for directing my attention to these lyrics, which can be found at https://genius.com/Blind-willie-johnson-if-i-had-my-way-id-tear-this-building-down-lyrics.

troubling figure but also a figure who in no small measure gives hope and encouragement to various reading communities. In fact, our thesis needs to be bolder for, already within the Hebrew Bible, Samson participates in the formation of a hope in a Davidic redeemer yet to come. Samson, through a long tradition of rewriting and rereading, becomes himself a redeemer and a prefiguration of a still greater and future savior.

The Many Faces of Samson and the Compositional History of Samson

The many faces of Samson—which darken and illumine with each encounter—stem in part from the complex compositional history of the biblical narrative. Scholars have noted that the Samson story is a composite comprised of at least three major blocks of tradition, each belonging to a different stage of literary growth: Judges 13, Judges 14–15, and Judges 16.[2] The oldest tradition likely hails from Israel's tribal period, when Israelite tribes indeed lived under the shadow of the more technologically and culturally advanced Philistines, and makes up the core of the biblical account found in Judges 14–15.[3] At a later stage, during Israel's monarchic period, the annunciation of Samson's birth (Judges 13) was prepended to the core narrative, and this expanded version of the Samson story was integrated into the book of Judges and so also into the Deuteronomistic History, which stretches from Deuteronomy to 2 Kings. Judges 16 was likely appended at a still later period during Israel's exile in Babylon when the Deuteronomistic History was updated to reflect the new historical reality. Each stage in the literary history of Samson, as we shall see below, coincides with a reassessment of Samson. A straightforward culture hero in the earliest layer of the tradition, Samson becomes an increasingly complex figure of light and shadows, participating fully in the development of the multilayered Deuteronomistic tradition and in the formation of expectations

---

2. See Jichan Kim, *The Structure of the Samson Cycle* (Kampen: Kok Pharos, 1993) for a review of scholarship. See also Brettler, *Judges*, 41–44, for arguments that the Samson story is composite.

3. See, for example, 1 Sam. 13:19–20. Philistines were expert metalsmiths during a time when Israelites lacked the technology.

for a future redeemer. Later interpretations of Samson, both Jewish and Christian, will reflect and refract the complex richness of this innerbiblical development.

Samson in the Time of Tribal Israel (Judges 14–15)

Judges 14–15 stem from Israel's tribal period and contain stories first told orally—perhaps around the stereotypical campfire—among Israelites dominated by their Philistine neighbors.[4] These stories of a preternaturally, indeed, divinely strong Israelite who pummels so many Philistines are revenge fantasies not unlike those whispered among dominated groups everywhere throughout history. Samson, during this early stage of the tradition, embodies Israel's hidden hope one day to have their way with the Philistines. This would have been most poignantly so for the tribe of Dan, whence Samson hails, who will lose their homeland on the south Mediterranean coast to the Philistines (see Josh. 19:41–46; Judg. 13–16) and be forced to migrate to a new location inland in the northern part of Israel (see Josh. 15–19; Judg. 1:27–34).[5] For the tribe of Dan, and also for other Israelite tribes during the period of Philistine domination, Samson was an uncomplicated hero, a redeemer of the weak.[6]

But what did the Israelites think about his violence and sexual transgressiveness? The short answer is that the Israelites, the weaker, dominated group in relation to the Philistines, would have found in what may look

---

4. For a detailed argument for the oral origins during the tribal period of much of the Samson story, see Serge Frolov, *Judges*, FOTL (Grand Rapids: Eerdmans, 2013), 256–63. On orality in Judges, see Susan Niditch, *Judges: A Commentary*, OTL (Louisville: Westminster John Knox, 2008), 14–18, 142, and see 154, for a discussion on the early origin of the Samson story.

5. On forced migration, see John Ahn, *Exile as Forced Migrations: A Sociological, Literary, and Theological Approach on the Displacement and Resettlement of the Southern Kingdom of Judah*, BZAW 417 (Berlin: De Gruyter, 2011). For a reassessment of the history of Dan's migration and its dating to the time of Josiah, see Guillaume, *Waiting for Josiah*, 133–41.

6. On the Philistines, see Peter Machinist, "Biblical Traditions: The Philistines and Israelite History," in *The Sea Peoples and Their World: A Reassessment*, ed. Eliezer D. Oren (Philadelphia: University of Pennsylvania Press, 2000), 53–69.

like faults from one perspective the admirable qualities of a culture hero.[7] Allow me to explain.

The weak, in order to fight the strong, must take advantage of whatever opportunity presents itself. That is, as a noted philosopher and sociologist correctly notes, the tactics of the weak against the strong "depends on time—it is always on the watch for opportunities that must be seized 'on the wing'" as opposed to the dominant strategy to control space at all times.[8] For example, we see evidence of Philistine domination over the Israelites in that the Philistines drive out the Danites to occupy for themselves the coveted coastal region, which they stud with five cities: Ashdod, Gaza, Ashkelon, Gath, and Ekron, whence to project power far beyond the region (Josh. 13:3; 1 Sam. 6:17).[9] In short, the Philistines as the dominant power seek to and succeed in controlling the spatial dimension of a shared reality. In contrast, the weaker Israelites lose control of the region and must be tactical, taking advantage of whatever opportunities arise, in their efforts to infiltrate Philistine society and to retaliate against the Philistines. Within this context, Samson's lack of sexual and martial discipline, attributes that make Samson a liminal and transgressive figure, affords him an important tactical advantage against the hegemonic structures of the Philistines.[10] They give him the necessary flexibility to take advantage of opportunities for revenge as they arise.

Consider, first of all, Samson's initial entrance into Philistine society. His desire to marry a Philistine woman and the events that follow give Samson (and God) opportunities to harm numerous Philistines. Without

---

7. Susan Niditch, "Samson as Culture Hero, Trickster, and Bandit: The Empowerment of the Weak," *CBQ* 52 (1990): 608–24.

8. Michel de Certeau, *The Practice of Everyday Life*, trans. Steven Rendall (Berkeley: University of California Press, 1984), xix.

9. On the importance of coastal cities, see Lawrence E. Stager, "Port Power in Early and the Middle Bronze Age: The Organization of Maritime Trade and Hinterland Production," in *Studies in the Archaeology of Israel and Neighboring Lands: In Memory of Douglas L. Esse*, ed. S. R. Wolff, SAOC 59 (Chicago: Oriental Institute, 2001), 625–38.

10. For Samson as a liminal hero, see Gregory Mobley, "The Wild Man in the Bible and the Ancient Near East," *JBL* 116 (1997): 217–33; Mobley, *Samson and the Liminal Hero in the Ancient Near East*, LHBOTS 453 (New York: T&T Clark, 2006). David might be compared profitably to Samson, whose comparable unconventionality gave him access into the Philistine army.

CHAPTER 4

the outburst of illicit and frankly crude passion ("Get her for me, because she pleases me") to which his parents dutifully object (Judg. 14:3),[11] Samson would not have had the opportunities, whatever his personal reasons, to enact Israel's vengeance against the Philistines. Consider also Samson's entrance into Gaza and ultimately into the Philistine temple. Samson's infiltration is made possible by his sexual desires, first for a prostitute in Gaza, then for Delilah in the valley of Sorek. In this light, consider also the episode of Samson's death, which was written during the exilic period when Israel was again the weaker in an asymmetric relationship, and the opportunistic manner in which he gains access to the monumental temple and destroys it and its Philistine occupants (16:23–30). Samson does not will his way in, as might a general in command of a powerful army, but enters only at the invitation of the Philistines (16:25), and he is able to locate the two massy pillars thanks only to the attendant's unsuspecting help (16:26). Not unlike the tribes of Israel, Samson must create and take advantage of every opportunity to act against the Philistines. Thus, tribal Israel, seeing themselves in Samson, would have accepted, if not celebrated, his uncontrolled sexual desires as a tactical advantage and rejoiced in his violence as enactments of their (hidden) desire for revenge against Philistine oppressors.

To summarize, as a hero of the weak, Samson in Judges 14–15 reflects Israel's dominated status and employs opportunistic tactics against the Philistines. As one scholar put it, even Samson's riddle (14:12–14) "is an attempt to have power over his inlaws" and, more generally, the Philistine guests, and his agricultural (15:1–5) and martial violence (15:14–17) are acts of social banditry that involve "the resistance to rich foreign conquerors or oppressors, a response to some significant alteration of a perceived 'traditional order' of things."[12] This characterization of Samson as tactical in the early tradition applies also to God, who is said to seek "a pretext to act against the Philistines" with no reference to any grand strategy for

---

11. Samson's parents represent the majority opinion of the Israelites who favor nonaggression and nonengagement. Compare, for example, that the Judahites willingly hand over Samson to the Philistines (Judg. 15:9–13). However, it is the "hidden transcript" of vengeance and retaliation that God endorses (14:4).

12. Niditch, "Samson as Culture Hero," 620–21, 622.

delivering the Israelites from the Philistines (14:4). In short, Samson is Israel's Robin Hood and achieves his heroism by trickery and banditry. And the beleaguered Israelites would have celebrated their hero with uncomplicated delight in the safety of each other's company, safe from the surveillance of the hated Philistines, saying: He killed how many of them and with what? A thousand with the jawbone of an ass![13]

Samson in the Time of the Monarchy (Judges 13–15)

In the seventh century BCE during the reign of Josiah king of Judah (640–609 BCE), a gifted historian (or group of historians), whom scholars call the Deuteronomistic Historian, integrated the Samson story into an expansive account of Israel's history, the so-called Deuteronomistic History. And this integration of a tribal tradition into a work of national historiography transformed Samson from a hero into an antihero.

How did this transformation occur?

The Deuteronomistic History is a monumental work of ancient historiography, stretching from Deuteronomy to Kings, and it traces the story of the landless Israelites from the time of Moses, still outside the promised land, through times of conquest, loss, and resurgence up to the reign of Josiah king of Judah. It is a history in praise of Judah, the lone surviving tribe after the Assyrian conquest of the Northern Kingdom in 722 BCE, and especially of King Josiah, who likely commissioned the work. The Deuteronomistic Historian depicts Josiah as the ideal king (cf. Deut. 6:4–5; 2 Kgs. 23:25) who has the ambition to restore Israel to the height of its territorial expanse achieved under David and to reform Israelite religion in conformity to the Mosaic laws of Deuteronomy (2 Kgs. 22–23). Josiah, in the Deuteronomistic History, is David and Moses both. And Samson, in this new literary and ideological context that lauds the kingdom of Judah and Josiah, territorial domination, and religious conformity, loses much

---

13. Frolov (*Judges*, 267) writes, "Problematic as they are, all these traits are rendered tolerable, if not admirable, by the punisher framework as long as they contribute to unbridled aggression against the audience's boogeyman; indeed, it is none other than YHWH herself that puts them to use in such a way (14:4)."

of his folksy luster and becomes encrusted with rust. New compositional additions to the Samson story as well as the new literary context contribute to Samson's eclipse. What tribal Israel found advantageous—his martial might and his sexual transgressiveness—become suspicious and even deplorable when seen through the lens of monarchy; and Samson, no longer himself the sun, changes into a dimly glowing signpost pointing to a hero yet to come.

The Deuteronomistic Historian, in integrating the Samson story into his larger work, added the annunciation of Samson (Judges 13) to the earlier tradition (Judges 14–15) and, among other editorial changes, added a summative framework to the cluster of stories. At the beginning, the Historian added the refrain, "The Israelites again did what was evil in the sight of the LORD, and the LORD gave them into the hand of the Philistines forty years" (Judg. 13:1) and, at the end, the summary statement, "And he [Samson] judged Israel in the days of the Philistines twenty years" (Judg. 15:20). By means of these and other compositional and editorial contributions, the Deuteronomistic Historian effectively recasts Samson the hero to play two less flattering roles within a new expanded drama. First, within the book of Judges, Samson participates in the progressive devolution of the office of judge as its final occupant and anticipates the chaos and civil strife that will erupt after his death (Judges 17–21).[14] Second, in the Deuteronomistic History, Samson plays the role of foil to David—who in contrast to Samson unifies the tribes of Israel under one monarchy and completes Israel's deliverance from the Philistines.[15] Samson, once the little sun, darkens, and his inner light flickers only to point to a future redeemer, to David.[16]

The Deuteronomistic additions to the Samson tradition, the annunciation and the framework, tell a part of the story of Samson's transformation. First, the Deuteronomistic Historian modeled Samson's annunciation on

---

14. Samson is not the last judge in the Deuteronomistic History, since Samuel acts very much like a judge. However, within the book of Judges, Samson is the last.

15. Machinist ("Philistines," 55) writes, "David, in sum, achieves the permanent solution over the Philistines that eluded his predecessors . . . the Philistines never regaining the power they had enjoyed to threaten Israel."

16. The name Samson (שִׁמְשׁוֹן) is related to the Hebrew שֶׁמֶשׁ ("sun"), and the ending may be the Hebrew diminutive, giving us the meaning "little sun." See Robert G. Boling, *Judges*, AB 6A (Garden City, NY: Doubleday, 1975), 225.

the Gideon story. More specifically, the Historian modeled the scene of Manoah's sacrifice (Judg. 13:15–25) on that of Gideon's (6:11–24): Both Manoah and Gideon present offerings of a kid and meal on a rock to an angel, and both fear for their lives when they belatedly realize that the divine being is the angel of YHWH. The purpose of the parallel, in addition to creating a literary bond between Gideon and Samson, may be to critique the doubt that motivates Gideon by associating him with the buffoon Manoah and to denigrate the dimwitted Manoah by connecting him with Gideon. The parallel also works to contrast Manoah with his perceptive wife.[17] The unstated point is that Samson is from ambiguous stock.

More revealing of the Deuteronomistic Historian's design for Samson are the refrains that bracket the narrative. The Samson story, as does every story of a major judge, begins with the notice that the Israelites "did evil in the eyes of the LORD" (Judg. 2:11; 3:7, 12; 4:1; 6:1; 10:6; 13:1). What follows after the declaration of Israel's evil is the repeated motif of Israel's subjugation to a foreign power for a period of time, in Samson's case to the Philistines for forty years (13:1). The introductory refrain thus raises the expectation that Samson will repeat the comedic structure of the careers of the other major judges: sin, subjugation, repentance, deliverance, and a period of peace (see Judg. 3:7–11). Indeed, Samson arrives on the scene with much promise: he is a Nazirite from birth and possibly of partial divine parentage.

Samson, however, ultimately proves a disappointment. At the conclusion of the Samson story, the Deuteronomistic Historian writes, "And he judged Israel in the days of the Philistines twenty years" (15:20). The implication of the Deuteronomistic frame—which states that the Philistines rule over Israel for forty years but that Samson judges for only twenty years—is that twenty years of Philistine oppression remain after Samson's death. Samson does not complete the full cycle typical of a judge and usher in a period of peace after redemption. His career, so also Israel's redemption, is abortive. The abortive nature of Samson's career in retrospect clarifies the meaning of the angel's somewhat enigmatic statement to Samson's mother: "you shall conceive and bear a son . . . who shall *begin* to deliver Israel from the hand of the Philistines" (13:5, emphasis added). Begin to deliver.

---

17. See Guillaume, *Waiting for Josiah*, 166–68.

CHAPTER 4

That is, fail to deliver. To put it boldly, the Deuteronomistic Historian, by adding the scene of Samson's annunciation (13:2–25) and supplying the summative framework (13:1; 15:20), transforms Samson the tribal hero into a national disappointment. In the earlier layer of the tradition, Samson is a culture hero who carries out longed-for revenge against the Philistines; in the national history of the Deuteronomistic Historian, he is a failure—a great potentiality ultimately unrealized.

This judgment, that Samson is a failure, taints even the details of the Samson story that the Deuteronomistic Historian did not himself compose or edit. We noted above that Samson's violence and sexual transgressiveness, within the historical context of tribal Israel, are assets that contribute to Samson's tactical advantage against the hegemony of the Philistines. If not celebrated, the violence and transgressiveness were accepted as necessary to the end of taking opportunistic revenge against a more powerful enemy. Within the national historiography that is the Deuteronomistic History, however, Samson's tribal assets become national liabilities and morally suspect. It is not that the Deuteronomistic Historian changes the details of the story, but the change in the stories that frame the older stories warps the lens through which Samson is perceived and judged. To provide two crosscultural examples, Hong Gildong and Robin Hood are heroes from the perspective of the weak; but from the perspective of the state, they are thieves and social agitators. So too is Samson.

First, the Deuteronomistic Historian, for whom the book of Deuteronomy is a kind of theological and political foundation, would have found Samson's love of foreign women to be contrary to the health and flourishing of Israel as Yhwh's people. Samson's parents state a mild form of this official position in response to Samson's desire to marry a Philistine woman from Timnah: "Is there not a woman among your kin, or among all our people, that we must go to take a wife from the uncircumcised Philistines?" (14:3). And while no Deuteronomic law forbids intermarriage with Philistines—perhaps the enmity needed no articulation due to the visceral hatred of Philistines among the people—it is not difficult to imagine Deuteronomy saying about the Philistines what it says explicitly about the Hittites, the Girgashites, the Amorites, the Canaanites, the Perizzites, the Hivites, and the Jebusites: "Do not intermarry with them . . . for that would turn away your children from following me, to serve other gods" (Deut. 7:3–4). That is, Samson's sexual outburst, tolerated within tribal Israel as a tactical necessity, would have received censure from the Deuteronomistic Historian, who wrote from the perspective of an established state.

Second, the Deuteronomistic Historian, as an official historian of the state, is likely to have found Samson's unconventional, guerilla-like tactics inadequate to the task of liberating Israel and, beyond that, downright troubling. This is the reason that Samson is depicted as able only to begin to deliver Israel and, as we noted in the previous chapter, the reason that the Deuteronomistic Historian likens Delilah to the Israelite hero Jael and so Samson to Sisera, Israel's enemy. Samson's violent outbursts may have satisfied the need for tribal Israel to vent its pent-up aggression against the Philistines but could not serve as the basis of a successful campaign to liberate Israel. In fact, itself a state with territorial ambitions, Israel would have found Samson's use of nonconventional martial tactics contrary to its strategies for spatial domination.

The Deuteronomistic Historian's disapproval of Samson comes into clearer view when we consider the overall thrust of the book of Judges. The structure of Judges is complex and evinces no clear overall plan. There is a repeated cycle of "apostasy, oppression, repentance, and deliverance" that structures the major narratives of the book but nothing like a well-sorted chiasmus.[18] This is in part because, as we shall see below, the narrative that begins in Judges continues into 1 and 2 Samuel: the deliverance Samson begins David completes. Nevertheless, scholars have noticed an overall pattern of decline in which Samson is a significant punctum.

The stories of the major judges participate in two interrelated patterns. The first is geographical: the stories begin in the south, in Judah, and move north, to Dan.[19] The second is evaluative: the judges become progressively less reliable and less honorable, starting with Othniel and Ehud and concluding with Jephthah and Samson. The result is that only the southern judges are unambiguously good while the northern judges are ambiguously bad. As for Samson, "[w]ithin the broader context of Judges, Samson is a negative role model."[20] No surprise, then, that Samson's death

---

18. See Frolov, *Judges*, 25–27; Brettler, *Judges*, 9–12.
19. Brettler, *Judges*, 111.
20. Brettler, *Judges*, 112.

precipitates a kingless chaos and a civil conflict throughout all Israel that threatens the survival of one of its tribes, Benjamin (Judges 17–21). The period of judges devolves as the leadership moves from south to north and ultimately brings Israel into a state of crisis in which "all the people did what was right in their own eyes" because "in those days there was no king in Israel" (Judg. 17:6 and 21:25; cf. 18:1, 19:1). Furthermore, not only does Samson mark the end of the ill-fated period of judges, he anticipates the waywardness of the kingless people, who do "what was right in their eyes." Note, in this regard, how Samson explains his transgressive desire for the Philistine woman of Timnah. "Get her for me," Samson says to his parents, "because [to translate the Hebrew literally] she is right in my eyes" (14:3). Samson, the last judge, leads the Israelites by example, not to repentance and redemption, but to decay and destruction: he, as they, does what is right in his eyes.

While Samson plays an almost thoroughly negative role within the book of Judges, he gains a positive dimension within the larger context of the Deuteronomistic History as a whole. Himself a failed redeemer, he anticipates David who will complete the redemptive work that Samson began. To revisit the Deuteronomistic annunciation of Samson's birth in this light, to say that Samson will "begin to deliver Israel" is to acknowledge that Samson contributes positively to the total redemptive pattern even if he himself does not complete it. It is to anticipate the one who will finally finish delivering Israel from the hand of the Philistines. And that, within the Deuteronomistic History, is none other than King David.

In order to appreciate how David completes the redemptive arc Samson only begins, we must look beyond Judges into the books of Samuel and the intervening figures of Samuel and Saul. First, Samuel reflects and complements Samson. Like Samson, Samuel is born to a barren woman (1 Samuel 1), is a Nazirite (1 Sam. 1:22), fights the Philistines (1 Samuel 4–7), and receives a judge's summation: "Samuel judged Israel all the days of his life" (1 Sam. 7:15).[21] Furthermore, Samuel is said to defeat the Philistines and so appears, at first glance, to complete the work that Samson began:

---

21. See Fred Blumenthal, "Samson and Samuel, Two Styles of Leadership," *JBQ* 33 (2005): 108–12; Lara van der Zee, "Samson and Samuel: Two Examples of Leadership,"

> ¹³ So the Philistines were subdued and did not again enter the territory of Israel; the hand of the LORD was against the Philistines all the days of Samuel. ¹⁴ The towns that the Philistines had taken from Israel were restored to Israel, from Ekron to Gath; and Israel recovered their territory from the hand of the Philistines. There was also peace between Israel and the Amorites. (1 Sam. 7:13-14)

Samson and Samuel together, it would appear, complete the typical cycle of a judge's career: sin, subjugation, repentance, deliverance, and peace.

But Samuel does not actually complete the work Samson began. The problem with seeing Samuel as the ideal complement to Samson is that the Philistines continue to wreak havoc for the Israelites after Samuel's death and that Samuel, whatever else he is, is still a judge-like leader and characterized as such: "Samuel judged Israel all the days of life."[22] In other words, Samuel, while clearly effective and honored as a leader, is too much like Samson truly to offer a lasting solution to the problem of leadership that judges as a group and Samson in particular represent in Israel. According to the Deuteronomistic History, only a king and only a king from the south—specifically from Judah and not from the tribe of Benjamin—can lead Israel. That is, it has to be David.

If the book of Judges is about the heroism of Israel's judges and, toward the end, about their failures, epitomized in Samson, then it is also about kings. The story of Abimelech, whose name literally means "my father is king" and is himself made king (Judg. 9:6), problematizes the institution of king (Judges 9). The parable of Jotham (9:7-15) and the fratricide that clears the path to Abimelech's kingship—which God punishes with death— offer biting criticism of the potential evils of kingship. Whatever the reservations about kingship, however, the final chapters of Judges (Judges 17-21) offer explicit endorsement for kingship. In the absence of a king, these

---

in *Samson: Hero or Fool? The Many Faces of Samson*, ed. Erik Eynikel and Tobias Nicklas, TBN 17 (Leiden: Brill, 2014), 53-65.

22. Samuel is a complex figure who occupies multiple roles; he embodies the offices of judge (1 Sam. 7:15), priest (1 Sam. 3), prophet/seer (1 Sam. 3 and 9), and kingmaker (1 Sam. 10, 12, 15-16). In addition, he may be seen as king-like in that he tries to establish a hereditary form of leadership: "When Samuel was old, he made his sons judges over Israel" (1 Sam. 8:1).

chapters argue, everyone did what is right in their eyes, leading to idolatry, civil strife, and widespread immorality. As the programmatic verse Judg. 2:17 makes clear ("Yet they did not listen even to their judges"), judges are inadequate to the task of leading Israel. And as the repeated refrain at the end of the book makes clear ("In those days there was no king in Israel..."; see 17:6; 18:1; 19:1, 21:25), the problem is the lack of a king. The solution, by implication, is kingship.

The book of Judges as a whole also argues that the best king, like the best judges, will come from the south, specifically from Judah. As noted above, the early and the only unambiguously good judges come from the south. As leadership moves northward, the quality "goes south." Now both Judah and Benjamin are southern tribes, and the first two good judges are from these tribes. Othniel, the first judge, is from Judah. This is not stated explicitly, but Othniel is the son of Kenaz, the brother of Caleb (Judg. 3:9), and we know that Caleb inherits Judah (Josh. 14:6–14). Ehud, the second judge, is a left-handed Benjamite. (Note the irony of a left-handed "Benjamite," which literally means "son of the right hand.")[23] That the first two good judges hail from Judah and Benjamin reflects the fact that the first two kings of Israel, Saul and David, are from these tribes, Saul from Benjamin and David from Judah. However, the book of Judges is not neutral regarding Judah and Benjamin but objects strongly to any Benjamite claim to the throne, and thus to Saul's kingship.

Key to the rejection of Benjamin (and Saul) are the final chapters of Judges, especially Judges 19. Recall that it is the people of Gibeah, a town in Benjamin (19:14), who rape and murder the Levite's concubine, an event that precipitates the civil war that nearly destroys the tribe of Benjamin. The Levite sends a message to all Israel concerning the murderous rape, "Has such a thing ever happened since the day that the Israelites came up from the land of Egypt until this day? Consider it, take counsel, and speak out" (Judg. 19:30). The message is a call to arms against Benjamin, and the civil war that ensues nearly destroys the tribe of Benjamin (21:3). The post-Samson era marks the darkest period in Israelite history, when "there was no king in Israel" and "all the people did what was right in their

---

23. On Ehud's left-handedness, see Suzie Park, "Left-Handed Benjamites and the Shadow of Saul," *JBL* 134 (2015): 701–20.

own eyes." And the event that epitomizes that darkness happens in Gibeah of Benjamin.

That a narrative against Gibeah preemptively disqualifies Saul's kingship becomes clear in Samuel, when it is revealed, and emphasized, that Saul is not only a Benjamite but also from Gibeah (1 Sam. 10:26). Judges 19 also not so subtly endorses David. Before choosing to lodge in Gibeah, where he will allow his concubine to be raped and murdered, the Levite explicitly rejects Jerusalem, at that time still occupied by the Jebusites: "We will not turn aside into a city of foreigners, who do not belong to the people of Israel; but will continue on to Gibeah" (Judg. 19:12). The Levite's rejection of Jerusalem and subsequent choice of Gibeah will prove fatal for his concubine and for the Benjamites. The narrative seems to say, "If only he had chosen Jerusalem." This barely disguised narrative regret anticipates David who chooses, conquers, and makes the place that the Levite rejects the capital of a united Israel, transforming Jerusalem into Zion, the enduring center and symbol of Israelite religion and political power (2 Sam. 5:6–9). The city the Levite rejects becomes the foundation to the United Kingdom.

The books of Samuel make further claim to the primacy of David as the contrapuntal to Samson over Saul. Saul, far from delivering the Israelites from the Philistines, commits suicide in anticipation of an imminent defeat and humiliation in Philistine hands (1 Samuel 31). David, in contrast to Saul and in fulfillment of the promise inherent in Samson's birth, as one biblical scholar puts it, "achieves the permanent solution over the Philistines that eluded his predecessors": Samson, Samuel, and Saul.[24] David defeats the Philistine champion Goliath (1 Samuel 17) and, after having infiltrated the Philistine camp in duplicitous service (1 Sam. 27:1–28:2), deals a permanently crippling blow to the Philistines at the Valley of Rephaim (2 Sam. 5:17–25). Not only that, David unifies the tribes of Israel under one king and establishes a new capital in the neutral—neutral because it belongs historically neither to the north nor to the south—territory of Jerusalem.

To summarize, the Deuteronomistic Historian transforms Samson, on the one hand, from a culture hero into a national disappointment, into an antihero who fails to deliver Israel. On the other, Samson becomes the

---

24. Machinist, "Philistines," 55.

antitype that anticipates David. The Deuteronomistic Historian, through a variety of means, disqualifies the alternatives to David, Samuel and Saul. Samuel rises as a towering leader in the book of Samuel. He combines the offices of priest, prophet, judge, and even king. However, even as he offers a compelling vision of effective leadership, Samuel is too similar to Samson: born to a barren woman, a Nazirite, and a judge. Saul, the first king of Israel, stands a head taller than any other Israelite, quite literally (1 Sam. 9:2). Nevertheless, he is marred from the moment he is born, being a Benjamite and from Gibeah, all the way to the moment of his death: he commits suicide, not unlike Samson, but unlike Samson does no damage to Israel's enemies the Philistines. At the end, David stands alone to complete the work that Samson, Samuel, and Saul failed to accomplish, "Israel from Philistian hands deliver," and replaces the inadequate office of judge with kingship. The judge is dead, long live the king! Samson, as a figure of promise and in failing that promise, participates intimately in the formation of a pro-Davidic tradition.

Samson in the Time of the Babylonian Exile (Judges 13–16)

The Deuteronomistic History, which was written in the seventh century, celebrated the tribe of Judah and Josiah. But time rolled on, and the monumental document that was the preexilic edition of the Deuteronomistic History soon became outdated by historical events: Josiah dies in battle in 609 BCE, and Babylon conquers Judah in 597 BCE and destroys Jerusalem and the temple in 587 BCE, and exiles a significant portion of the Judahite population, thus inaugurating the period of the Babylonian exile.[25] An update to the Deuteronomistic History was required, and so an exilic edition of the Deuteronomistic History was produced. This exilic document recounts the fate of Judah after Josiah, including the heart-wrenching death of Zedekiah, the last king of Judah, and in so doing interweaves the story

---

25. For a history of the exile, see Rainer Albertz, *Israel in Exile: The History and Literature of the Sixth Century B.C.E.*, trans. David Green, SBLStBL 3 (Atlanta: Society of Biblical Literature, 2003), 45–131.

The Other Samsons

of Samson to proclaim a message of hope and fury that resonates with ancestral voices stretching as far back as Genesis.[26]

Nebuchadnezzar, the king of Babylon, first conquers Judah in 597 BCE. At that time, he takes King Jehoiachin along with other Judahite nobles into exile and crowns Zedekiah vassal king over Judah. A decade later, Zedekiah rebels against Babylon. Nebuchadnezzar's response is decisive. He captures and destroys much of Judah, including Jerusalem and the temple. While the Babylonians lay siege on Jerusalem, Zedekiah attempts to flee the capital city by night. But he is captured, and he and his family are brought before Nebuchadnezzar at Riblah. There, Nebuchadnezzar executes Zedekiah's children before his eyes, then has Zedekiah blinded—searing the image of his children's brutal murder as his final visual memory. Furthermore, Nebuchadnezzar has Zedekiah bound in bronze fetters. The exilic Deuteronomistic Historian writes, "They slaughtered the sons of Zedekiah before his eyes, then put out the eyes of Zedekiah; they bound him in bronze fetters (*nəḥuštayim*) and took him to Babylon" (2 Kgs. 25:7, adapted from the NRSV).[27]

The exilic Deuteronomistic Historian, who updated the Deuteronomistic History to include the story of Zedekiah, also appended the story of Samson's death (Judges 16) to the intermediate version of the Samson story (Judges 13–15). Read together, the similarities between the two scenes of the demise of the two failed leaders, one the last judge of Israel and the other the last king, stand out. Both are captured by the enemy; both are blinded; both are bound in bronze fetters; and both are brought into enemy territory. In fact, the scenes of the binding of Zedekiah and Samson are told in the same terms, down to the rare word translated "bronze fetters": "they... bound him in bronze fetters (*nəḥuštayim*)[28]" (Judg. 16:21; cf. 2 Kgs. 25:7).[29] These parallels suggest that the Deuteronomistic Historian means for Zedekiah to be seen in light of Samson, and vice versa.

---

26. Frank M. Cross, *Canaanite Myth, Hebrew Epic: Essays in the History of the Religion of Israel* (Cambridge: Harvard University Press, 1973), 274–89.

27. Following the NRSV but with "bronze fetters" for the Hebrew נחשתים.

28. נחשתים appears seven times in the Hebrew Bible, three times in connection to Zedekiah (2 Kgs. 25:7; Jer. 39:7; 52:11), once to Samson (Judg. 16:21), once to Abner (2 Sam. 3:34), once to Manasseh (2 Chr. 33:11), and once to Jehoiakim (2 Chr. 36:6).

29. My translation, to show the parallel to 2 Kgs. 25:7.

CHAPTER 4

To appreciate fully how Samson functions as a revelatory window onto the presentation of Zedekiah, we need to note the one significant difference between the account of Samson and that of Zedekiah: Samson performs an act of suicide attack (some have considered an act of suicide terrorism) against the enemy; but Zedekiah lives on. Or, more accurately, the Deuteronomistic Historian provides no conclusion to Zedekiah's story, the only instance in which an account of a king's life is left open-ended in all of the Deuteronomistic History. (The death of every other king is narrated with the significant exception of Jehoiachin, whom the Deuteronomistic Historian leaves elevated and seated at the table of the Babylonian king [2 Kgs. 25:27-30], on which below.)[30] The unusual silence concerning the end of Zedekiah's life invites speculation, and the words: "they bound him in bronze fetters" triggers the analepsis back to the Samson story that helps fill in the silence.

When Zedekiah's story breaks off, the parallels between Samson and Zedekiah suggest that we transpose what happens in Samson's story to Zedekiah's. That is, the interrupted repetition of the plot of Samson's story in Zedekiah's suggests that what follows Zedekiah's blinding and binding will deliver a significant blow to the Babylonians, just like Samson's, and begin to deliver Israel. As one scholar put it, the account of Samson's suicide attack "is meant as consolation, suggesting that the blinding and killing of Zedekiah (=Samson) will soon bring death to the Babylonians and ultimate restoration to Israel."[31] Samson, as a proleptic fulfillment of Zedekiah's revenge on Babylon, becomes once again a hero of vengeance who comforts his contemporaries and gives hope to future Israelites in exile. Samson reverberates with the fury of those who were made to witness their children's murder—and resonates with their longing for revenge.

The binding of Zedekiah and Samson is more than consolation for the exilic community, who find themselves, again like tribal Israel, subjugated under a foreign power. The binding of Samson and Zedekiah signals a subtle but, for those sensitive to the inner logic of the Deuteronomistic

---

30. On the final passage in 2 Kings, see Jon D. Levenson, "The Last Four Verses in Kings," *JBL* 103 (1984): 353-61; Michael J. Chan, "Joseph and Jehoiachin: On the Edge of Exodus," *ZAW* 125 (2013): 566-77.

31. Brettler, *Judges*, 58.

History, bold claim for the future redemption of Israel through a Davidic redeemer to come. Zedekiah, like Samson, can only begin to deliver Israel from the hand of the Babylonians. But Samson, so also Zedekiah, anticipates a Davidic king to come who will complete the redemptive work already begun. If we can extend the similitude between Samson and Zedekiah in this way, the concluding passage of the Deuteronomistic History concerning Jehoiachin takes on added significance:

> [27] In the thirty-seventh year of the exile of King Jehoiachin of Judah, in the twelfth month, on the twenty-seventh day of the month, King Evil-merodach of Babylon, in the year that he began to reign, released King Jehoiachin of Judah from prison; [28] he spoke kindly to him, and gave him a seat above the other seats of the kings who were with him in Babylon. [29] So Jehoiachin put aside his prison clothes. Every day of his life he dined regularly in the king's presence. [30] For allowance, a regular allowance was given him by the king, a portion every day, as long as he lived. (2 Kgs. 25:27–30)

Recall that Jehoiachin was taken into exile in 597 BCE. And he, the sole surviving Davidic king after Zedekiah's (unreported) death, the conclusion of the Deuteronomistic History seems to state, rises from prison as if from the grave and ascends to a seat of honor and privilege. His story, with echoes of Joseph's rise from an Egyptian prison, resonates with that earlier story of yet another Israelite who was wrongfully imprisoned, rises to great prominence, and uses his powers "to preserve a great people" (Gen. 50:20). The comparison is highly suggestive: Joseph saves Jacob his father, his eleven brothers, and their children. That is, Joseph saves the eponymous ancestors of Israel and its tribes. Jehoiachin, in so far as he is Joseph *redivivus* as a Davidic king, will restore the people of Israel and its tribes.

The binding of Samson to Zedekiah, thus, brings us back to Joseph—then forward to exodus. If Samson looks forward to the first, historical David, then Zedekiah looks forward to a second David, a type of David, in Jehoiachin, who in turn looks backward to Joseph who saved Jacob. And we find that Jacob, whom God renames Israel, was forced to migrate to a foreign land, just as the current generation of Israelites were forced to migrate to Babylon. However, the descendants of Israel did not remain in Egypt. The story of Joseph precedes the story of Israel's exodus from Egypt, the return to Canaan through the wilderness, and God's enthronement in Zion. That is, Jehoiachin who looks back to Joseph also looks forward to the (second) exodus (out of Babylon). The dizzying reverberations of themes and motifs from Genesis to 2 Kings crescendos to announce, in cryptic but in no less certain terms, a second exodus, this time from Babylon back to Zion.

To summarize, during the exilic period Samson and specifically his suicide attack acquire yet another layer of signification. There is a recrudescence of the Samson of the tribal period, whose opportunistic heroism shines once again through the encrusted rust of the monarchic period. Samson's opportunistic infiltration into the heart of enemy territory, the temple of their deity, epitomizes the tactics of the weak and his suicide attack the weapon of the weak.[32] Once again the weaker party in relation to the Babylonian empire, Judah rediscovers a hero in Samson. Furthermore, bound to Zedekiah, Samson's role as foil to and anticipation of the future David becomes amplified into a prophetic hope for a Davidic king to come in a yet uncertain future, who will deliver Israel from its Babylonian yoke and lead it back to Zion—in a second exodus.

Postbiblical Samson

The canonical story of Samson, as we began to explain above, participates in a complex web of significations that oscillates between light and dark. It reaches back to Genesis and forward to 2 Kings, intimates the divine and anticipates a Davidic redeemer to come, recalls the primeval Rephaim and prophesies a second exodus, the return from the Babylonian exile. That is, Samson contributes to a multivocal and multilayered act of communication as it echoes and resonates with texts far and near and blasts a symphonic message as clear as it is intricate. The Samson story is full of nostalgic longing for a home already lost, seizes present opportunities and underlines its failures, and dares to hope for a future redemption lit

---

32. Ian Hacking, "The Suicide Weapon," *Critical Inquiry* 35 (2008): 1–32.

dimly by the afterglow of distant memories. It would thus not be a great exaggeration to say that Samson holds in his two meaty hands ropes that connect Genesis to 2 Kings, as well as things in between and beyond. It is no surprise, then, that Samson enjoys a varied and rich body of interpretations in the postbiblical era.[33] That richness prohibits anything like a thorough consideration of the history of interpretation, and we will have to be content with a brief overview of interpretations that represent Samson as a hero of the weak and as a prefiguration of Christ.

Samson the Hero of the Weak

As one scholar aptly puts it, "Samson's reception among early Jewish commentators is mixed."[34] (The same can be said of Samson's reception in all traditions.) For the rabbis of early Judaism, as for the biblical writers, Samson's assets were equally his liabilities, depending on the context of the interpretation. For example, Samson's enormous strength is often compared to that of Goliath. On the one hand, in Ecclesiasticus Rabbah Samson and Goliath are named as those who increase strength to their demise, whereas David and Judah do so to their benefit (Eccl. Rab. 1.18).[35] On the other, Samson's strength, again compared to Goliath's, is a source of ethnic pride in Leviticus Rabbah. When non-Israelites boast, "Who is wise like Balaam? And who is wealthy like Haman? And who is strong like Goliath?" Israelites are instructed to respond, "Ahithophel, was he not wise? Korah, was he not wealthy? Samson, was he not strong?" (Lev. Rab. 5.3).[36] Samson's strength, a fault when considered within the context of an inner-Jewish discussion, is presented as an asset in the context of an intraethnic contest.

The same is true even for Samson's transgressive sexual desire. It comes as no surprise that rabbinic authorities criticize Samson's desire for Philistine women. Rabbi Isaac, who likens Samson's desire for Philistine women to a desire for "something unclean," is typical (Num. Rab. 9:24). But even

---

33. See David M. Gunn, *Judges Through the Centuries* (Oxford: Blackwell, 2005), 170-230. Also, see Michael Krouse, *Milton's Samson and the Christian Tradition* (Princeton: Princeton University Press, 1949).
34. Gunn, *Judges*, 172.
35. See Gunn, *Judges*, 173.
36. Translation mine. See Gunn, *Judges*, 173.

CHAPTER 4

Samson's transgressive and defiling sexuality can become a source of ethnic pride given the right context. According to one Jewish legend, the Philistine Goliath's strength stemmed from his father, and his father was none other than Samson—through one of his several Philistine sexual partners![37] Again, in a multiethnic context in which Jews would have been a minority, a potential fault becomes an asset, a source of pride, for claiming that the mightiest of Israel's enemies inherited their strength from an Israelite source.[38]

A similar ambivalence about Samson but ultimate celebration of him as a hero of the weak characterize Blind Willie Johnson's celebrated song, "If I Had My Way I'd Tear This Building Down." Here is the refrain:

> Well, if I had my way
> Well, if I had a, a wicked world
> If I had a, ah Lord, tear this building down.

The body of the song conflates the Timnite woman and Delilah, offers the biblical reservation against marrying the Philistine woman, "Can't you find a woman of your kind and kin?" but withholds ultimate judgment. One suspects that the song dismisses the objection against marrying a Philistine woman, for it is Samson's falling to the woman's wiles that gives him the opportunistic access to the building to be torn down. If the song is uncertain about the merits or demerits of Samson's relation to Philistine women, it is less so about Samson's use of martial strength. The refrain, repeated five times, makes clear that the destruction of "this building," equated by parallelism to "a wicked world," is a longed-for fantasy for the singer. "If I had my way" is the artist's plaintive refrain. The singer is weak and cannot have his way, but were he strong enough and could have his way, his act

---

37. Gunn, *Judges*, 173. See Louis Ginzberg, *The Legends of the Jews*, 6 vols. (Philadelphia: Jewish Publication Society, 1909–1928), 4:250n29.

38. "Even this severe punishment produced no change of heart. He continued to lead his old life of profligacy in prison, and he was encouraged thereto by the Philistines, who set aside all considerations of family purity in the hope of descendants who should be the equals of Samson in giant strength and stature" (Ginzberg, *Legends of Jews*, 4:121).

of just vengeance against the wicked world would look like what Samson actually did: "If I had a, ah Lord, tear this building down."

As euphoric as the revenge fantasy is, true to the biblical source, Johnson's song artfully acknowledges the dark side of even imagined violence. In this regard, consider the first stanza, which essentially repeats the refrain but features one key difference:

> Well, if I had my way
> If I had a, a wicked mind
> If I had a, ah Lord, tear this building down.

"If I had," not a "wicked world," but a "wicked mind," reads the opening lines. The song acknowledges with brilliant simplicity that even imagined, just revenge stems from at least a hint of inner wickedness. The overwhelming wickedness of the world drowns out the initial self-reflection in the rest of the song, but the existence of the introspective self-doubt in the song owes not a little to the complexity of the biblical Samson. The song acknowledges that Samson's vengeance, which it ultimately celebrates, stems from a timely opportunity made possible by an initial act of questionable values ("Can't you find a woman of your kind and kin?") and that the destruction of the wicked world cannot erase all traces of the inner wickedness of longing for violence.

Blind Willie Johnson, then, no less than the biblical writers, refrains from giving himself and his "kind and kin" a moral carte blanche in celebrating Samson as a hero of the weak, the downtrodden, and the wronged in society. He sings longingly, "Lord, if I had my way . . . If I had a, ah Lord, tear this building down." At the same time, he acknowledges that desiring to tear down even a wicked world has the potential to taint the mind with wickedness. It is possible to seek justice and to do good for the wrong motive, as it is possible to do evil for just and even admirable reasons. Complex is the moral landscape of human existence in which Samson lives.[39]

39. For further discussion of Blind Willie Johnson's song, see Nyasha Junior and Jeremy Schipper, *Black Samson: The Untold Story of an American Icon* (New York: Oxford University Press, 2020), 58–60 and notes. This important book was published after the completion of the present chapter, precluding the opportunity for detailed engagement. In any case, I found the nuanced discussion of the Black Samson tradi-

CHAPTER 4

Samson the Redeemer

The strongest interpretation of Samson as a redemptive figure comes in Christian tradition, starting already in the New Testament (Heb. 11:32–34) and continuing well into the present. The christological interpretation of Samson burgeoned during the patristic period among allegorists.[40] Ambrose seems to have been the first to offer an allegorical interpretation of Samson as a figure of Christ, claiming almost comically that "all true believers cling to Christ, the head of the Church, just as Samson's locks clung to his head."[41] Ambrose's younger contemporary Augustine offers a more sustained and sophisticated christological interpretation of Samson in his monumental *The City of God* and in a sermon on Samson.[42] Augustine, as do other serious interpreters of Samson, wrestles with the dark side of Samson, but nevertheless finds in him a redeeming figure who, as Augustine influentially argues, anticipates Christ.

Augustine solidifies the (Western) Christian opinion against suicide in *The City of God*. He equates suicide to murder in writing that "anyone who kills himself is a murderer" (*City of God*, 1.17). He bases his opinion on his reading of the Ten Commandments: "In fact we must understand [suicide] to be forbidden by the law 'You shall not kill,' particularly as there is no addition of 'your neighbour' as in the prohibition of false witness, 'You shall not bear false witness *against your neighbour*'" (*City of God*, 1.20). The sixth commandment, "Do not murder," the argument goes, does not discriminate as concerns the victim, and thus also forbids mortal harm against the

---

tion in America to be in agreement with the findings of the present work, namely that Samson continues to be a complex figure capable of diverse and sometimes opposed interpretations.

40. For a helpful review of this period, see Krouse, *Milton's Samson*, 31–45.

41. Krouse, *Milton's Samson*, 40. The Latin text of Ambrose, *Expositio in septem visiones libri Apocalypsis*, Patrologia Latina 17, cited in Krouse (40n26), reads: "Samson Christum significat: per capillos vero omnes electi disignantur. Et sicut capilli adhaerent capiti, ita et omnes justi adhaerent Christo, qui caput est omnium electorum suorum."

42. Translations of these works taken from Augustine, *The City of God*, trans. Henry Bettenson (London: Penguin, 1984); Augustine, "Sermon 364," in *Sermons 341–400*, trans. and notes by Edmund Hill, ed. John E. Rotelle, vol. III/10 of *The Works of Saint Augustine: A Translation for the 21st Century* (Brooklyn: New City, 2017), 276–81.

self. (A nontrivial consequence of Augustine's argument against suicide is the diminution of a person's freedom to self-determination regarding how and when one dies, including euthanasia for reasons of chronic illness.)

Augustine's firm stance concerning the sinfulness of self-murder is such that it enables him to make a significant contribution to sexual ethics and to our thinking about disabilities. In instances of rape, Augustine argues—controversially for his time—the guilt resides in the perpetrator only and the victim remains pure. He writes,

> There will be no pollution, if the lust is another's. . . . Now purity is a virtue of the mind. . . . What sane man will suppose that he has lost his purity if his body is seized and forced and used for the satisfaction of a lust that is not his own? . . . if [purity] is a quality of the mind, it is not lost when the body is violated. (*City of God*, 1.18)

In so arguing, Augustine speaks against women killing themselves to avoid being raped or after having been sexually violated, a practice that was lauded among Christians and pagans alike. In fact, by going against contemporary opinion, Augustine famously condemns Lucretia, a Roman noblewoman usually praised for committing suicide after being raped by a king's son. Augustine objects that the rapist suffers a lesser punishment than the victim:

> But how was it that she who did not commit adultery received the heavier punishment? For the adulterer was driven from his country, with his father; his victim suffered the supreme penalty. If there is no unchastity when a woman is ravished against her will, then there is no justice in the punishment of the chaste. (*City of God*, 1.19)

A woman's suicide comforts the male audience, perhaps especially the husband for whom the wife's death proves to him her innocence and faithfulness. But Augustine looks through the woman's eyes, who suffers first the trauma of rape by one man and (self-)murder because of social pressures to prove her innocence. There is no reason for victims of sexual assault, Augustine writes, to be ashamed, and it is no justice for victims to suffer death, actual or symbolic, at the very real hands of social opinion.

CHAPTER 4

In cases of sexual assault, the guilt and the shame lodge themselves in the perpetrator only; the victim remains pure, her virtue untouched by vulgar hands.

Augustine's argument against suicide also leads to a revolutionary insight concerning physical disabilities, though this is less fully explored: "The body is not holy just because its parts are intact, or because they have not undergone any handling. Those parts may suffer violent injury by accidents of various kinds" but remain holy (*City of God*, 1.19). This insight has profound implications for thinking about disabilities, about the dignity and worth of those living with disabilities of one sort or another—about the shame experienced by and imposed on the disabled in contrast to, as Augustine sees it, their enduring worth before God and fellow human beings. No physical attribute can serve as a heuristic index for virtue, which in its interiority enjoys a vitality distinct from material existence.

As can be seen, the interpretation of suicide as self-murder, a sin and a crime of the highest order, is productive for Augustine. The complexities of Scripture and of life, however, meant that Augustine had to contend with exceptions to his general condemnation of murder and suicide as self-murder. To account for the many exceptions, Augustine reasons that those who commit homicide at the commandment of a just authority, for example God or the State, do not commit murder. Thus, he justifies wars waged "on the authority of God" and criminal executions on the "authority of the State" (*City of God*, 1.21). Augustine names specific examples that conform to the above principle from Scripture. They include Abraham, Jephthah, and Samson. Of Abraham's willingness to kill his son, Augustine writes: "far from being blamed for cruelty he was praised for his devotion; it was not an act of crime, but of obedience." Abraham's willingness to kill his son is indicative of a sacrificial posture of obedience, not of murderous sinfulness.[43] Augustine is less certain about Jephthah: "One is justified in asking," writes Augustine, "whether Jephthah is to be regarded as obeying a command of God in killing his daughter" (*City of God*, 1.21). Samson, who commits suicide and commits mass homicide in killing himself, proves

---

43. *City of God*, 1.21. See also Jon D. Levenson, *The Death and Resurrection of the Beloved Son: The Transformation of Child Sacrifice in Judaism and Christianity* (New Haven: Yale University Press, 1993), 111–24.

most troubling for Augustine, and he returns to the issue again and again. Augustine's instinct is to justify Samson, but a nagging feeling persists.

Augustine initially offers the pat justification that Samson's suicide attack "can only be excused on the ground that the Spirit... secretly ordered him to do so" (*City of God*, 1.21). Samson, like Abraham, was obeying a just and higher authority. In revisiting this answer, however, Augustine acknowledges the mystery at the heart of the enigma that is Samson and anticipates Milton in discovering Samson's hidden consciousness. Augustine turns again to the question of women who kill themselves to escape "those who threaten their chastity by throwing themselves into rivers for the stream to whirl them away to death" and whom the church venerates as martyrs (*City of God*, 1.26). Augustine, no political revolutionary, refuses to contradict the church and advises caution: "I do not presume to make a hasty judgement on their case. I do not know whether divine authority convinced the church by cogent evidence that [the women's] memory should be honoured in this way; it may well be so." Augustine pleads ignorance concerning the possibility of divine inspiration on the part of the woman and the church. He then likens the case of women suicides venerated as martyrs to Samson: "we are bound to believe in Samson's case," as in the case of the women, "that they acted on divine instruction and not through a human mistake—not in error, but in obedience" (*City of God*, 1.26).

Augustine writes that he is "bound" to consider Samson as ordered secretly by God to suicide. Augustine is so bound because he is unwilling to challenge the authority of Scripture, for Hebrews 11 states that Samson is a saint. He is also bound "to believe" because he does not know if divine authority indeed prompted Samson to commit his suicide attack. For Scripture—and Augustine is a supreme reader of Scripture—nowhere states explicitly that the Spirit commanded Samson's suicide attack. Scriptural praise of Samson as a saint, on the one hand, and its silence about the role of the Spirit, on the other, clearly irritated Augustine's discerning mind.

Augustine ultimately takes refuge, anticipating Milton, in the hiddenness of human consciousness: "We have only a hearsay acquaintance with any man's conscience; we do not claim to judge the secrets of the heart. 'No one knows what goes on inside a man except the man's spirit which is in him' (1 Cor. 2:11)" (*City of God*, 1.26). Augustine—the genius who discovered, and some would say helped invent, human consciousness—finds in Samson a seed of the mystery of human consciousness.[44] In this sense, Samson is immune to our probing and remains free from our readerly desire to impose clear and immutable meaning to his actions. To this most glorious and surprising aspect of Samson, his deep and mysterious interiority, Milton gives most apt articulation a millennium after Augustine: "I begin to feel / Some rousing motions in me which dispose / To something extraordinary my thoughts." More than "something extraordinary," it is the "thoughts," that is, Samson's mind, that remains wonderful in its unfathomableness.

Augustine deals more explicitly and with more theological ingenuity with what he considers to be Samson's faults in a sermon on Samson.[45] The sermon offers an allegorical reading of Samson that explicates, and so creates, parallels between details of the Samson story and Christ's person, life, and work. Like Ambrose, Samson's hair is of interpretive interest to Augustine: The hair, in which resides Samson's strength, covers the head like a veil, so "Christ had his strength in a veil, when the shadows of the old law were covering him"; the shaving of Samson's head indicates that the "law was ignored, and Christ suffered"; and that the hair grew again signifies persistence of unbelief, even after Christ's resurrection (*Sermon 364*, 6).

The central point of Augustine's figural reading of Samson is that Samson's death anticipates Christ's redemptive death. He concludes: "This mystery was very clearly fulfilled by our Lord Jesus Christ; because our redemption was accomplished by him in his death in a way that it had certainly not been celebrated by the life of him who lives and reigns forever and ever. Amen" (*Sermon 364*, 6). It is well that Augustine characterizes the prefiguration as a "mystery," for how Samson's death in fact prefigures Christ's redemptive work is a riddle which takes the entire sermon to unravel. Samson's suicide, as noted above, escapes condemnation within Augustinian thought only with reference to the opacity of human interiority. That it should work salvation is far from clear, a puzzle with many interlocking pieces.

---

44. Harold Bloom, *Genius: A Mosaic of One Hundred Exemplary Creative Minds* (New York: Warner Books, 2002), 82–89.

45. The sermon, known as "Sermon 364," appears to be of dubious or mixed authorship, with some scholars attributing the sermon to Caesarius of Arles. See *Sermons 341–400*, 281n1.

The Other Samsons

The key to Augustine's reading of Samson is the invention of two Samsons: the historical Samson and the "mystical Samson." Splitting Samson into two allows Augustine to pursue two levels of allegorical reading and, as needed, to distinguish Samson's wickedness from Christ's perfection. Augustine begins by signaling his ambivalence about Samson: "Whether [Samson] is a just man is wholly uncertain; the justice of this man is profoundly obscure" (*Sermon 364*, 2). Samson is a riddle, not unlike the riddle he put to his Philistine guests, in need of decipherment. And Augustine turns Samson's obscure ambiguity into a theological asset and finds a way to argue that Samson's ambiguous goodness, the fact that his goodness is intermixed with wickedness, renders him a more fitting allegory of Christ. Augustine notes that "the whole Christ . . . is both head and body; just as Christ is the head of the Church, so the Church is the body of Christ" (*Sermon 364*, 3). Within the framework of an ecclesial Christology, Augustine asserts that the mystical Samson signifies Christ the head of the Church, who is perfect in every way, and that the historical Samson signifies the Church the body of Christ, which contains both "strong members" as well as "weak ones." The mystical Samson, who signifies Christ, can do no wrong; but the historical Samson, who signifies the Church, can do both wrong and right. If Samson is "profoundly obscure," it is because he represents the whole Christ, the head and the body, and the weak and the strong parts of the body.

How does Augustine transform Samson's death into a mystery that Christ's death fulfills? To begin at the end, Augustine elaborates that Christ, like Samson, "while being destroyed himself . . . overwhelmed his adversaries, and his own death meant the slaughter of his persecutors" (*Sermon 364*, 6). In the case of Samson, the identity of Samson's persecutors, and so his victims, is clear: the Philistines. In the case of Christ, the matter is more complex. Augustine, in naming Christ's enemies, repeats the ugly anti-Semitic trope that the Jews killed Christ: "Christ was both arrested and killed by the Jews." But it would be a mistake to understand the Jews as Christ's true enemies and thus those whom Christ's death destroys. For Christ does not kill the Jews. Rather, Christ's enemy, so the object of his destruction, is blindness—which Augustine says inflicted the Jews in the time of Christ and continues to inflict all people.

Augustine writes, "So the blindness which they inflicted on him, signified the blindness of the Jews; Christ was both arrested and killed by the Jews; but he, rather, slew those who killed him. *So his enemies brought him in to make fun of him* (Judg. 16:25)" (*Sermon 364*, 6). The allegorical relationship between Samson and Christ is far from clear, and it is important to keep in mind the distinction between the historical and the mysterious levels of signification. On the one hand, Samson's enemies are historical. On the other, Christ's enemy is mysterious and is the blindness that leads Jews, in Augustine's reconstruction of the passion narrative, to arrest and kill Christ. Augustine's decision to read Samson's death as a prefiguration of Christ's death forces this reading and saves Augustine, at least in this instance, from fulsome and foul anti-Semitism. Christ's enemies are blindness and unbelief, which affect the Jews and the body of Christ—which is the basis for Augustine's claim that Christ's death accomplishes "our redemption." Christ, in himself being destroyed, slaughters that which destroys him, namely blindness: unbelief that keeps the affected from knowing "Christ either performing miracles or ascending into the heavenly sphere" (*Sermon 364*, 6). And the blindness of unbelief is a reality then in Christ's time and now in Augustine's. That is the figural meaning of Samson's hair growing back. Blindness endures.

Two other episodes from the Samson story fill out Augustine's reading of Samson as prefiguring Christ's redemptive work: the riddle and the visit to Gaza. Augustine writes that the riddle, "*From the eater there issued food, and from the strong there came forth sweetness* (Judg. 14:14)," signifies "Christ rising from the dead" (*Sermon 364*, 3). Augustine nicely ties the eater to the common biblical and ancient Near Eastern depiction of death as an indiscriminate and ravenous devourer: "death which devours and consumes all things."[46] The food that proceeds from death is none other than Christ, for Christ is "the living bread, who [came] down from heaven (John 6:41)" (*Sermon 364*, 3). Rising with Christ from the dead, in Augustine's reading of the riddle, are Christians. For this reading, the lion (not the eater) signifies the dead Christ from whose body comes a swarm of bees, the source of the sweet honey.

---

46. *Sermon 364*, 3. See also Paul K.-K. Cho and Janling Fu, "Death and Feasting in the Isaiah Apocalypse (Isaiah 25:6–8)," in *Intertextuality and Formation of Isaiah 24–27*, ed. Todd Hibbard and Hyun Chul Paul Kim, SBLAIL 17 (Atlanta: Society of Biblical Literature, 2013), 117–42, esp. 120–25.

Augustine's interpretation of Samson's visitation of a prostitute in Gaza takes full advantage of his ecclesial Christology again to argue that the episode prefigures the resurrection. Augustine writes that Samson's visit to a harlot is "impure." "But," he continues, "if he did it as a prophet, it's a sacred sign . . . by reason of some mystery" (*Sermon 364*, 5). That is, Samson's visitation to a prostitute can be both impure and sacred, a figuration of the body of Christ and Christ the head of the Church. Samson's visit to Gaza, interpreted as a deed of the mystical Samson, opens up the possibility of interpreting the entire scene as looking forward to resurrection. "[T]he harlot's house was a representation of hell," Augustine begins. This makes Samson's descent foreshadow Christ's descent into hell and Samson taking away the gates of the city signify Christ's taking away the gates of hell, thus "depriving death of its dominion" (*Sermon 364*, 5). That is, after Samson's/Christ's visitation to hell, resurrection becomes possible—not only for Christ but also for the faithful.

Samson as a figure of Christ, especially of Samson's violent suicide as prefiguring Christ's redemptive death, offers significant interpretative challenges. Augustine strongly condemns suicide, and Christ does not slaughter anyone in dying. But Augustine's ecclesial Christology offers a sophisticated, multilayered, and, I might add, sinuous allegorical reading of Samson's death and other episodes from the story to paint a fulsome understanding of Christ's death as destroying the blindness of unbelief and his resurrection as destroying the dominion of death, so as to make general resurrection possible. Samson is not an easy figure for Augustine, whose suicide and sexual transgressions receive his disapproval, but, for all that, Samson proves a sophisticated figuration of the whole Christ, not only the head, but also the body.

Conclusion

How the dead come to inspire hope and to give life to the living, if we take the story of Samson as an example, is multifaceted and mysterious and, for all that, no less powerful and miraculous. We began with a consideration of the very real possibility that the dead, far from giving life, can kill in examining the more recent claim that Samson is a suicide terrorist—or at least he is if you are a Philistine. We argued that the danger of taking inspiration for terrorism from Samson is real. We also argued that to claim that Samson is a suicide terrorist, without qualification, misses the self-criticism contained in the biblical text in the reference to Jael and Sisera and the structure of the book of Judges, and turns a blind eye to the quite elaborate ways in which Samson contributes to the redemptive message of the Hebrew Bible and biblical tradition.

Samson is not a hero in a simple way. He disallows the possibility of any wholesale praise or condemnation. And his death especially shimmers, as if by moonlight, like the dark, deep sea that hides a tremendous mystery. Readers over the millennia have seen both monstrous beasts and one like a Son of Man in the waters. And we do well to acknowledge the monster even as we take stock of the redeemer. Samson reminds us that, while death may give life, it is without question death.

CHAPTER 5

Judah's Scepter

I am the good shepherd. The good shepherd lays down his life for the sheep.

John 10:11

LEADERSHIP IS A CENTRAL CONCERN throughout the Hebrew Bible. Judges and kings, priests and prophets, mothers and sons, God, and many besides lead and fail to lead throughout biblical history. Much has been written about the qualities of a biblical leader, but one quality I would like to focus on that has escaped attention is the leader's willingness to die for the group. I shall argue that one's willingness to die comes to be understood as the unleashing of the full life force of both the individual and the divine for the benefit of the group. The transaction is not unidirectional, however, for a leader who is willing to die for the group receives, in return, a charisma that exceeds the usual value of an individual life. The willing leader comes to embody the life force of the group and of its deity. In this way, leaders who demonstrate a willingness to die for the group earn the right to lead and, what is more, usurp the mysterious and transcendental power of death, for the good of the group and themselves.

Samson the Pivot

The connection between willingness to die and leadership appeared already in our discussion of Samson. The history of Samson's career within the development of the biblical tradition is ultimately tragicomical. He is, at the beginning of the tradition during Israel's tribal period, a bawdy simpleton of preternatural strength whose unsavory qualities allow him, quite despite his own intentions, to enact Israel's revenge fantasies against their cultural and military betters, the Philistines. If we were to look for an analogy in popular culture, Samson is more Inspector Gadget than Superman. This is the Samson we find in Judges 14–15. However, when he enters the world of the preexilic Deuteronomistic History and its epic account of Israel's history from the career of Moses to Josiah's religious reform, Samson gains a birth narrative (Judges 13) and changes into an uncouth failure who marks the end of the heroic age of judges (Judges 3–16) and the beginning of civil strife and chaos within Israel (Judges 17–21). Israel's true enemies, who were up to this point imagined as external (the Ammonites, the Midianites, the Philistines), it turns out, come from within—and they look rather like Samson, who does whatever is right in his own eyes (cf. Judg. 14:3, 17:6).

Samson's fall from grace during the monarchic period sets him up for an eventual rise in the exilic edition of the Deuteronomistic History in which he, having gained an end-of-life narrative (Judges 16), proleptically deals a mortal blow to the enemy and gives hope to the exilic community living under Babylonian rule. It is in dying that Samson regains his honor—lost through repeated failures, first at the hand of a Timnite woman, then again at the hand of Delilah—and accomplishes what the exilic Historian presents as an act of heroism: "So those he killed at his death were more than those he had killed during his life" (Judg. 16:30b).

The ethical issues surrounding Samson's attack and death are complex, and we gave space to them in the previous two chapters. What is of importance for the present argument is that the Deuteronomistic framing renders Samson's death—which Samson willingly embraces, saying, "Let me die with the Philistines" (Judg. 16:30)—a sacrifice for the sake of Israelite deliverance. That is, Samson's voluntary death becomes the decisive means by which he fulfills the angelic announcement to his mother that he "shall begin to deliver Israel from the hand of the Philistines" (13:5). He does not complete the task, but he gets halfway there. Furthermore, Samson's end, bound to Zedekiah's by the common motifs of blinding and bronze fetters (Judg. 16:21; 2 Kgs. 25:7), signals to an exilic audience that there is a leader who, though terrorized and humiliated by the Babylonians, will die like Samson and deal a blow to the enemy. He, no more than Samson, completes the task of delivering the Israelites. But he, no less than Samson, looks forward to a Davidic king, Jehoiachin, who will like Joseph keep many alive for the eventual return home in a second exodus. It is this canonical, redemptive Samson who, while far from erasing the philistine brute of past traditions, will resonate time and again with the longing for revenge and liberation among the weak and oppressed Jewish, Christian, and other reading communities.

In sum, the Samson tradition, with the logic of a palimpsest, adumbrates an emerging economy of death willingly embraced for the sake of a group: Willing death recasts the willing dead in heroic form, giving him retrospective honor and splendor he may not have earned in life. An issue of narrative ethics arises. Since the dead cannot tell their own stories, anyone who claims to speak for the dead first commits theft, then potentially bears false testimony.[1] (We shall discuss this issue at greater depth when we turn to the topic of martyrdom.) The economy of willing death, in any case, bleeds into the economy of the penultimate step before voluntary death: the willingness to die. Not only those who indeed die for the sake of the group but also those who demonstrate a willingness to die for the group may receive in return a hero's honor and splendor. The crucial difference, of course, is that those who are willing to die do not necessarily die, so that they can spend their earned heroism in life—to lead honorably and thus to cement their leadership or spend it nefariously for their own benefit. The moral hazard—that no actual death purchases the honor and splendor of leadership—potentially reduces expressions of a willingness to die for the group to mere rhetoric. Yet, even as rhetoric, such expressions exercise power over life and death. And the writers of the Hebrew Bible, with boldness as well as sophistication, explore and develop the fraught relationship between leadership and a willingness to die for the group. We shall examine in this chapter how Judah demonstrates his fitness to lead

---

1. Consider the structural analysis of myth by Roland Barthes in "Myth Today," in *Mythologies*, trans. Annette Lavers (New York: Hill and Wang, 1972), 107–64, in particular the analysis of the black soldier saluting the French flag (pp. 115–26).

CHAPTER 5

through a demonstration of a willingness to die for the group and turn to Moses and Esther in the following chapters.

Joseph's Descent

The Joseph story (Genesis 37–50), in which Judah plays a decisive leadership role, is a work of literary genius. It weaves a rich, colorful tapestry of family intrigue and individual maturation into a history about a people on the move, traveling in caravans through the vast landscape of an ancient world, from Canaan down to Egypt and, eventually, back again, and together and apart through a tumultuous history of famine and survival, oppression and liberation, and forced migration and return home. Of the many themes that animate the story, one is leadership, and central to the development of that theme is the idea that a leader should be willing to suffer a great deal, even death, for the sake of the group.

Joseph is not the leader in the Joseph story. He is, of course, the central protagonist, but is ostracized from the group from the beginning and something of an outsider to his family to the end. Joseph's journey is more personal than communal and his role more functional than dynamic. His childhood dreams, with their far from childish consequences, already mark him as singular and set apart. And, from the time his brothers throw him into the pit until his brothers bow to him in supplication for his forgiveness after their father's death, Joseph travels through space and time very much alone.

First, Joseph travels alone deeper and deeper into the nadir regions of life—from the pit in Canaan down to Egypt and from Egypt down to the cavernous prison, forgotten and presumed dead by all, except God. Then, Joseph's rise from the depths (I dare add, of death, so his resurrection) is meteoric. Overnight, Joseph the prisoner becomes Joseph the viceregent in Egypt. However, though he orchestrates the survival of many lives through the famine of famines, he remains alone and lonely on the throne to the end. Recall that, after Jacob's burial, Joseph's brothers come *tous ensemble* to beg for forgiveness in the name of their deceased father: "Your father gave this instruction before he died, 'Say to Joseph: I beg you, forgive the crime of your brothers and the wrong they did in harming you.' Now therefore please forgive the crime of the servants of the God of your father" (Gen. 50:16–17). In response, it says, "Joseph wept" (Gen. 50:17). Joseph's tears remind us that Joseph is, toward the end of the story as he has been throughout, a man of sorrows and full of tears (42:24; 43:30; 45:3; 50:17).[2] There has been consolation along the way: the birth of Manasseh and Ephraim and the reunion with his family, most importantly with his younger brother Benjamin and his father Jacob. But until the end, Joseph remains misunderstood, feared, and unloved by his family. In a word, he is alone, and that is the simple and sufficient reason that Joseph cannot be a leader. For leaders, though they often experience loneliness, cannot be alone.

Joseph was not, however, utterly alone throughout his eventful life. As we are repeatedly told, "the LORD was with him" (39:2, 3, 21, 23). The short statement reveals the theological core of the Joseph story and the vital theological function Joseph plays within the story of Israel. That God was with Joseph—in the pit, in Egypt, and in the prison—presumes that God journeyed with Joseph as he descended into regions dark and deep, then up out of his prison clothes and into the royal garb of an Egyptian governor. God, in other words, goes into exile with Joseph, suffers with him in his descent into deathliness, "in order to," as Joseph comes to realize, "give life to many people" (Gen. 50:20, my translation).[3] Joseph suffers deathlike pain—and with him God also—in order to give life to others. That is, if Joseph functions within the Joseph story as the preserver of life so that Israel not only survives the widespread famine but in fact increases in number "very greatly, so that the land was filled with them" (Exod. 1:7; see Gen. 46:3), it is because, in a profound and mysterious way, God is with Joseph in his experience of deathliness and in his rise from the pit to abundant life. Joseph dies and with him is God who also resurrects him.

In this way, Joseph plays an important role in the development of the biblical idea that deathliness may be a portal into more abundant life. Nevertheless, Joseph is not a leader in Israel, and cannot be. The full reason is

---

2. Joseph cries when the seams between what I call different levels of representational realities begin to tear.

3. God, who goes to Egypt with Joseph, may be fruitfully compared with Ezekiel's conception of God as departing the desecrated Jerusalem temple and going into exile with the Jews to be "a sanctuary to them for a little while in the countries where they have gone" (Ezek. 11:16).

that he neither leads the family of Israel into Egypt nor leads the people of Israel out of Egypt in fulfillment of the Abrahamic promise (Gen. 15:13–16). Joseph prepares the right conditions for Israel's sojourn in Egypt; but it is Judah who leads the family down to Egypt, not Joseph. Likewise, Joseph takes the family back to Canaan to bury Jacob—with the Pharaoh's permission but without their children or flocks[4]—but he brings them back again to Egypt, his adopted home (Gen. 50:6–14). We will need to wait for Moses to lead the people out of Egypt. Joseph, in short, is a conduit figure for God's sacrificial love for Israel that preserves and multiplies the people, but he does not enact God's historical volition for Israel, that they journey down to Egypt and ultimately back to Canaan, the land of promise (Gen. 15:13–16). No, Joseph can only participate in that historical movement in and out of Egypt as something carried, first as a slave to be sold for economic gain, then as bones carried out of Egypt and across the wilderness into the land flowing with milk and honey (Gen. 50:25; Exod. 13:19; Josh. 24:32).

Judah's Compromise

The theme of leadership in the Joseph story plays out in the sibling rivalry between Judah and Reuben, with Judah, not the eldest son Reuben, rising from the fray blessed and charged with leadership (49:8–12).[5] And Judah earns the right to lead—for himself and, by metonymy, for the tribe of Judah and ultimately his descendant David—by demonstrating that he is willing to suffer a great deal, even death, for the sake of the group. Judah is the first figure in the Hebrew Bible who, by demonstrating a willingness to die, gives life to the group and wins for himself the charism necessary to lead.

The story of Judah's rise to leadership is a story of maturation. The beginning of the Joseph story highlights Judah's shortcomings but also

---

4. That Joseph goes up to Canaan without the flocks and the children is significant because these are precisely the items that, in Exodus, Moses refuses to leave Egypt without (see Exod. 10:7–11, 21–29).
5. Reuben's demotion in the story of Joseph may reflect the historical disappearance of the tribe of Reuben from among the tribes of Israel.

Judah's Scepter

his promise. Jacob, who favors Joseph above his other sons, sends Joseph to check up on his brothers who are out pasturing the flock in Shechem (Gen. 37:12–13). When Joseph's brothers see the "master dreamer" from a distance and begin to conspire to kill Joseph (Gen. 37:18–19), Reuben seeks to save him and has the brothers throw Joseph into a pit (37:22). Reuben, according to the narrator, planned to "rescue him out of their hand and restore him to his father" (37:22). However, before carrying out his plan, Reuben inexplicably exits the scene, leaving behind a trail of good intentions and the others eating and brooding over Joseph's fate. Reuben says later that he had asked the brothers "not to wrong the boy" but in the same breath confesses his failure to persuade them: "But you would not listen" (42:22). We also learn that Joseph pleaded for mercy with his brothers but that they ignored him: "We saw his anguish," the brothers confess later about the event, "when he pleaded with us, but we would not listen" (42:21). Refusal to listen either to their eldest or younger brother characterizes the brothers. They are a stiff-necked lot.

In this confused scene of tearful pleading and unheeded advice incarnadined with fraternal jealousy and hatred, Judah finds a way forward. During the repast conversation among the brothers about what to do with Joseph, Judah notices a caravan of Ishmaelites passing by on their way down to Egypt and proposes that the brothers not kill Joseph but sell him to the Ishmaelites for financial gain and, he adds, "for he is our brother, our own flesh" (37:27). The other brothers follow Judah's lead and have Joseph sold down to Egypt.[6]

Reuben's plan to save Joseph and to return him to Jacob is more morally commendable than Judah's proposal. The key difference, however, is that Reuben, in planning to act alone, fails to lead the group and loses the opportunity even to attempt rescue. What more, he ignores the very real hatred animating his brothers' bloodthirst with the result that they ignore him. In contrast, Judah's plan to save Joseph from death represents a pragmatic compromise between Reuben's idealism and the other brothers' murderous hatred. Judah appears, from a certain angle, to be a greedy opportunist. He reasons, "What profit is it if we kill our brother?" (37:26)

---

6. Note the source critical entanglement in Gen. 37:28. Who is responsible for taking Joseph to Egypt, the Midianites or the Ishmaelites?

and proposes to sell his brother for twenty pieces of silver in Judas-like fashion (cf. 37:28 and Matt. 26:15). At the same time, Judah takes the opportunity to remind the group that Joseph, hate him as they might, is still "our brother, our own flesh," and subtly but significantly leads the group toward right action and also right thinking. Reuben occupies the higher moral ground, but he fails to lead. Judah fails to cast the highest moral vision for the group but pragmatically guides the group away from fratricide.

To summarize, Judah is an imperfect leader at the beginning of the Joseph story, but his leadership avoids repeating Cain's archetypal crime, delivers Joseph from death, and contributes to the narratively necessary transportation of Joseph from Canaan to Egypt. To read this early scene through the lens of the ending, recall that Joseph says of his sale to Egypt toward the conclusion of the story, "Even though you [my brothers] intended to do harm to me, God intended it for good, in order to give life to a numerous people, as he is doing today" (Gen 50:20, my translation). Among the brothers who took part in sending Joseph down to Egypt, Judah alone participates on the divine side of the equation, for he too, like God, "intended it for good, in order to preserve," if not a numerous people, Joseph, his brother, his own flesh, who in turn with God's help will save a numerous people. At the beginning of the story, Judah leads, if imperfectly, and participates in the divine economy of salvation.

Tamar's Veil

The next episode in the Joseph story, Genesis 38, appears misplaced if we think that the Joseph story is only about Joseph, so much so that scholars once confidently wrote that Genesis 38 "has no connection with the drama of Joseph, which it interrupts" and proposed its excision.[7] However, the chapter seems rather well-placed when we realize that the Joseph story is as much about Judah as it is about Joseph.[8] Genesis 38 recounts the story

---

7. E. A. Speiser, *Genesis*, AB 1 (Garden City, NY: Doubleday, 1964), 299. See also Claus Westermann, *Genesis 37–50*, trans. John J. Scullion (Minneapolis: Fortress, 1982).

8. Gary A. Rendsburg, "David and His Circle in Genesis XXXVIII," *VT* 36 (1986):

of Judah's growth and maturation into a figure able to lead his father and his brothers, that is, Israel and its tribes.

Genesis 38 begins with Judah's voluntary departure from his brothers—structurally and verbally mirroring Joseph's forced departure[9]—and recounts a generational family drama of marriage, birth, and death. Once settled near an Adullamite named Hirah, Judah marries a Canaanite woman named Shua. The daughter of Shua or, to transliterate the Hebrew, Bath-shua (38:12; 1 Chr. 2:3) gives birth to three sons: Er, Onan, and Shelah (38:2-5). The thick middle of the drama begins after Er, the firstborn, marries Tamar, a woman of uncertain, possibly Canaanite, ethnicity.

No sooner does Er marry Tamar than God kills Er because, as the text tersely explains, Er was wicked in God's eyes (38:7). So Judah gives Tamar to Onan to fulfill his levirate duty and sire a son to carry on his brother Er's name (Deut. 25:5-10). But Onan practices *coitus interruptus* and shirks his brotherly duty. This displeases God, who kills Onan (38:10).[10] Judah,

---

438-46. For connections to the rest of the Joseph story, see Levenson, *Death and Resurrection of the Beloved Son*, 157-64.

9. Levenson, *Death and Resurrection of the Beloved Son*, 158.

10. At this point in the narrative, Tamar becomes a misfit, neither an unmarried virgin nor a child-bearing wife. She finds herself without the necessary connection to the patriarchy, a problem the levirate law is supposed to remedy by requiring the brother of the deceased husband to marry his widowed sister-in-law and raise up an offspring for his brother (Deut. 25:5-10). The offspring would preserve the name of the deceased and inherit his property. The offspring would also provide the otherwise disenfranchised, childless widow with a binding and protective connection to her husband's household. Susan Niditch comments: "In terms of long-range security in the social structure, it is more important for a woman to become her children's mother than her husband's wife" ("The Wronged Woman Righted: An Analysis of Genesis 38," *HTR* 72 [1979]: 145). The levirate law extends "patriarchal protection" to the childless widow. P. Cruveilhier ("Le lévirat chez les Hébreux et chez les Assyriens," *Revue Biblique* 34 [1925]: 524-46) emphasizes this humane aspect of the Israelite levirate law in a comparative study of the law in Israelite and Assyrian societies. The Assyrian levirate law, he argues, is primarily mercantile in its interest: "le lévirat assyrien avait uniquement pour fin de permettre à la famille du beau-père de conserver les droits acquis par des donations antérieures" (p. 534). The Assyrian levirate law does not take into account whether the widow is childless or not, and the fundamental motive for the family of her deceased husband to provide a husband from within the family has to do with the marriage payment: "En négligeant au contraire la question de l'existence d'enfants, le

having lost two sons in quick succession, withholds his youngest, Shelah, from Tamar. Instead Judah postpones the marriage, understandably citing Shelah's youth, and unforgivably sends the widowed Tamar back to her father's house. "Remain a widow in your father's house," Judah says to Tamar, "until my son Shelah grows up" (38:11). Judah, we are told, feared for Shelah's life (38:11). His fear, however, could not have been purely paternal. It was likely also selfish, for Shelah's death would end Er's, Onan's, Shelah's, and very likely also Judah's line. Fear for himself in part motivated Judah's refusal to surrender Shelah to Tamar and to the dictates of biblical law.

In order to appreciate the genius of the Judah-Tamar drama that unfolds, it is helpful to understand the patriarchal society in which it takes place. Patriarchy, to be somewhat reductive, is a social order founded on phallocentric authority and value and is, as such, self-defining and self-referential; patriarchy defines itself and defines others in reference to itself by assigning value to other members of society according to their relation to members of the patriarchy. Within this androcentrism, a female person's status is derivative of her relationship to a male figure, first to her father, then to her husband, and finally to her son.[11] Susan Niditch identifies two broad categories for womanhood in the patriarchal society of ancient Israel: "She is either an unmarried virgin in her father's house or she is a faithful, child-bearing wife in her husband's or husband's family's home."[12]

To return to our story, Tamar, after Er's and Onan's death and before she is married to Shelah, occupies a liminal space within a patriarchal so-

---

Recueil de lois assyriennes nous manifeste qu'un tel but n'a nullement préoccupé l'auteur de son droit de lévirat. La fin ... n'est autre que la récupération d'un droit acquis par le paiement de biens matrimoniaux" (p. 542). If the rationale behind the Assyrian levirate law is financial, Israelite levirate law as articulated and depicted in Gen. 38, Deut. 25:5–10, and Ruth, is motivated by "une profonde charité fraternelle" (p. 546). Cruveilhier, no doubt, overemphasizes the difference, but he is correct to point out that the levirate law as we find it in the Hebrew Bible is not essentially a mercantile law. It is genuinely concerned with the well-being of the deceased husband and the surviving wife. This charitable aspect of the biblical levirate law has Hermann Gunkel (*Genesis*, trans. Mark E. Biddle [Macon, GA: Mercer University Press, 1997], 398) assign the cause of the Lord's displeasure with Onan, who refuses to fulfill his levirate duty, to his "lack of love for his deceased brother."

11. Niditch, "Wronged Woman," 145.
12. Niditch, "Wronged Woman," 145.

ciety with only the most tenuous claim to Judah's household and protection. Tamar's situation becomes doubly tenuous when Judah forces her to return to her father: She becomes not only a childless widow in her husband's family's house but also a non-virgin in her father's house. At this tense, dramatic juncture in the story, Tamar is without home or foothold in society. She stands before a perilous precipice on the edge of patriarchy into which Judah, it would appear, hopes she would fall and disappear. However, Tamar refuses and takes matters into her own hands and leads the story toward its shocking conclusion. In the process, she places patriarchal values under question, teaches Judah lessons vital to his future leadership role, and bears, quite despite the wishes of the patriarch Judah, the ancestor of David and the future kings of Israel and Judah. That is, Judah has Tamar to thank for his maturation into a worthy leader, and the tribe of Judah and its kings owe their very existence to Tamar, a (mere) woman and an outsider to Israel.

Many days, likely years, pass after Judah sends Tamar to be a widow in her father's house. In the meanwhile, Judah himself becomes a widower, and Tamar observes that "Shelah was grown up, yet she had not been given to him in marriage" (38:14). Judah's continued refusal to marry Tamar to Shelah now seriously jeopardizes the continuation of Judah's line, not only those of Er and Onan, since Judah has no son other than Shelah who can perpetuate his name. It also jeopardizes Tamar's survival. Should her father die, should another woman be given to Shelah in marriage, should Judah forget and ignore her, Tamar's place within society would disappear like footprints on desert sand dunes. Judah does not recognize the peril that lies before him. Nor does he concern himself with Tamar's plight. So Tamar takes her fate and that of Judah into her own hands.

We noted above that Tamar is a liminal figure within patriarchy. Judah, in sending the widow Tamar back to her father's house in violation of his duty to her, effectively places her outside the norms and protection of patriarchal society. Put negatively, Judah makes Tamar an outsider to patriarchy and its protections. Positively, she is set free from the regulations of patriarchy that has disenfranchised her to define and enact her own identity and agency within patriarchy whose rules no longer apply to her. Tamar takes hold of that freedom and takes off her widow's garment, the public sign of her social status, and, as an act of self-definition and defiance, "put[s] on a veil, wrap[s] herself up, and [sits] down at the entrance to Enaim, which is on the road to Timnah," to intercept Judah on his way to shear his sheep (Gen. 38:14).

Now, what's in a veil?

Scholars have observed that brides likely wore veils in ancient Israel.[13] Thus, it is possible that Tamar, by donning the veil and appearing before Judah, hoped to remind him that she is a bride to Shelah and to shame him into fulfilling his duty as patriarch and marry her to the now fully grown Shelah as promised. Possible also is that Tamar used her free agency to invent for herself a more dramatic role, namely that of a harlot, for prostitutes too wore veils and stood on roadsides. If the former possibility is correct, then when Judah fails to recognize his daughter-in-law and mistakes her for a prostitute and propositions her for sex, Tamar lives into his male fantasy (which reveals itself as having to do with both sex and patriarchy, on which below) and uses her invited access to manipulate him and the norms of patriarchy for her own ends. If the latter, Tamar in effect invents an alternate, representational reality in which she is a prostitute and uses her creative power as author and actor within that "fictional" play to control Judah, who behaves exactly as Tamar expects he would, and to create for herself a future reality in which she can survive and even flourish.

Why might Tamar choose to put on the mask of a harlot?

The harlot is a peculiar woman in a patriarchal society. On the one hand, the prostitute is the ultimate misfit. As proposed above, patriarchy assigns social values to its members in relation to itself. According to this self-referential logic, the prostitute is precisely that woman who perfectly opposes its definition of the ideal woman, for her sexuality is beyond the control of patriarchy. On the other hand, we see Judah readily, though not without a certain desire for secrecy, embrace the harlot. The patriarch desires the harlot. In short, the harlot is both the ultimate outsider and the ultimate insider within patriarchy. Phyllis Bird well articulates this essentially ambiguous status of the harlot: "A fundamental and universal

---

13. Jan William Tarlin, "Tamar's Veil: Ideology at the Entrance to Enaim," in *Culture, Entertainment and the Bible*, ed. George Aichele, JSOTSup 309 (Sheffield: Sheffield Academic, 2000), 178. See also Phyllis Bird, *Missing Persons and Mistaken Identities: Women and Gender in Ancient Israel* (Minneapolis: Fortress, 1997), 200.

feature of the institution of prostitution wherever it is found is an attitude of ambivalence. The harlot is both desired and despised, sought after and shunned."[14] Furthermore, Bird strikes upon the fundamental difference between the harlot and all other women in a patriarchal society when she comments, "What a man desires for himself may be quite different from what he desires for his daughter [including, I would add, his daughter-in-law] or wife."[15] In other words, the harlot is not defined in relation to the patriarchy; she does not fall under the logic of its self-referentiality. Rather, she falls under the logic of patriarchal self-definition; she reflects the patriarchy itself and does not stand in relationship to it. The harlot is "what a man desires for himself" (self-definition), not "what he desires for his daughter or wife" (self-referentiality).

It is precisely because patriarchy sees itself, or at least its desire, in the harlot, that it sanctions prostitution. At the same time, it is because patriarchy cannot control the harlot that it casts harlots into the liminal shadows of its society. To speak in symbolic and structural terms, a harlot symbolizes the ultimate outsider who penetrates into and lies at the very heart of patriarchy as the hidden center of its self-definitional and self-referential logic. Prostitution is the mirrored image of patriarchy, its structural opposite, and as such the epitome of an alternate reality to patriarchy in which a woman can define herself and exercise control over herself and others not only within the limited arena of her sexuality but also more expansively over her own body and over her economic and social situation. Prostitutes, it should be noted, are the rare women in the Hebrew Bible who rule over their own household.[16] I do not mean by this to glorify either the institution or the practice of prostitution as an antidote to patriarchy. I do mean, however, to note that prostitution, whatever one thinks of it morally or ethically, is a structural corollary and logical complement to patriarchy.

14. Bird, *Missing Persons*, 201.
15. Bird, *Missing Persons*, 201.
16. Recall that Rahab has a house of her own: "So they went, and entered the house of a prostitute whose name was Rahab, and spent the night there" (Josh. 2:1). Other women who are said to have a house(hold) of their own are Shiphrah and Puah (Exod. 1:21) and Job's three daughters, Jemimah, Keziah, and Keren-happuch (Job 42:14). Note that the Hebrew Bible records the names of these women, a relatively rare phenomenon.

CHAPTER 5

Thus, if Tamar chooses to play the part of a prostitute it is because she, as a widow in her father's house, stands outside the norms and strictures of patriarchy just like the prostitute and, therefore, can freely choose one or the other role. And if Tamar plays the part of a prostitute, it is because a prostitute is desired (according to the logic of self-definition), in critical contrast to the undesired widow sent away from her in-laws (according to the logic of self-referentiality). The result is that, in donning the veil of a harlot, Tamar takes hold of power and agency that come with desirability and gains access, from the margins of society the widow shares with the harlot, to the seat of patriarchal power as only a harlot can. Even if Tamar puts on a bride's veil, the result is the same. When Judah mistakes Tamar for a prostitute and she chooses to live into his fantasy, she chooses in that instant not only to claim the powers of the harlot but also that of author, the architect of reality. For, in either case, Tamar invites Judah to enter and live in an alternate, representational reality in which Tamar chooses to be a prostitute and allows him to be a credit customer, who gives up his seal and cord and his staff—symbolic representations of his honor and identity—to guarantee payment and secure her services, sleeps with her, and impregnates her (38:15–18). Tamar, a woman, creates, maintains, and exercises control over a not-so-fictional reality as its playwright and actor. She is there at the beginning and the middle of the one-act play and directs and guides the story toward the desired end. And, as if to show that social identity and status are as thick as gossamer and tulle, Tamar enters and exits from the representational reality of the play by the simple act of doffing a widow's garment and putting on the shimmering veil of a harlot. In constructing an alternate reality, she simultaneously reveals the constructed nature of social customs and identities, and so their fragility. She also discovers her considerable agency as an architect of reality.

Some three months after Judah's encounter with the harlot by the roadside, Tamar is brought before Judah, "pregnant as a result of whoredom" (Gen. 38:24), and cast mercilessly before the patriarch for judgment. Judah reflexively pronounces, "Bring her out, and let her be burned" (Gen. 38:24). In condemning without reflection the very person he embraced without hesitation, Judah puts on display his own hypocrisy as well as that of patriarchy.[17] "What a man desires for himself" (the self-definitional aspect

---

17. Bird, *Missing Persons*, 205.

Judah's Scepter

of patriarchy) and "what he desires for his daughter[-in-law]" (the self-referential aspect of patriarchy) collide head-on and reveal what deconstructionists might call the unthought thought at the structural center of patriarchy. The result: "Things fall apart; the centre cannot hold."[18]

Tamar is not caught unawares by Judah's harsh judgment. She anticipated that this would happen, for she knows the rules of the game. So as to lay bare the internal contradiction of patriarchy and Judah's actions, as she is being dragged out to be burned, Tamar produces Judah's identifying objects and declares that she is pregnant by their owner. "Recognize," she pleads, "whose these are, the signet and the cord and the staff" (38:25 my translation).[19] Tamar returns to Judah his authority and honor she had stolen from him and simultaneously reveals that, up to this point, Judah has acted without either. Judah, in recognizing them as his, recognizes the coexistence of the harlot he enthusiastically embraced some three months ago as custom permits and the widowed daughter-in-law he means now to kill under the cover of law. With the authority he had sold to the harlot, Judah condemns his daughter-in-law; and with the authority he receives back from his daughter-in-law, he exonerates her.[20] Tamar stages Judah's recognition of his hypocrisy and wrongdoing and enables him to declare, "She is more in the right than I, since I did not give her my son Shelah" (38:26).

That Tamar needs a man, the very man who most wronged her, to justify her may disappoint modern feminists, who may wish that she deconstruct patriarchy *tout court* and erect in its place a more just and equitable society. Yet we must recognize that Tamar's choice to return and to return to patriarchy its authority—which she has unveiled to be largely

---

18. W. B. Yeats, "The Second Coming," first published in 1919 in *The Dial*.

19. Cf. Gen. 37:32 and 38:25 where the only two occurrences of הכר־נא ("recognize") in the Hebrew Bible occur. See Levenson, *Death and Resurrection of the Beloved Son*, 158.

20. Here the pattern of patriarchy reaffirming its authority is repeated as in the case of the levirate law. But Tamar's vindication is predicated upon Judah's reputation being inextricably tied to Tamar, thus introducing an ironic complication. If Judah condemns Tamar, he must at the same time condemn himself—for Tamar as harlot reflects Judah's own self-defined identity as a patriarch who requires access to the sexual excesses of the harlot. Condemning Tamar would be tantamount—both ideologically and narratologically—to condemning himself. In short, Tamar has usurped the self-defining authority of the patriarchy for herself and has forced the patriarch to be defined in relation to herself. She sits on the throne of patriarchy's self-definition, if only for a passing moment.

symbolic—is a pragmatic and necessary compromise for Tamar's survival and flourishing in her time and space. She could not dismantle an entire cultural norm in one fell swoop and reasonably expect to live in it. Nevertheless, the achievement of her theft and restoration of Judah's authority is considerable. In orchestrating the situation so that the patriarch publicly condemns her, "Let her be burned," one moment and the next justifies her, "She is more in the right than I," Tamar demonstrates courage and exposes the contingency of patriarchal power: courage because she risks death "to expose the foolishness and fragility of Israelite patriarchy even while appearing to perpetuate it";[21] and contingency because she reveals that patriarchal authority is no natural attribute, an inalienable possession of male members of society. Rather, patriarchal authority, like authority generally, is contingent and ambiguous and can be used for justice as well as for injustice. Tamar also discovers and exercises her power as author and actor, which she uses to save herself and ensure the survival of Judah's line, the tribe of Judah, and the house of David. Judah feared that Tamar was an agent of death who, having killed Er and Onan, would kill Shelah; Tamar, in risking death and being willing to die, demonstrates that she is an agent of life who, despite Judah's machinations, saves herself, Judah, and his line. She gives life by embracing the possibility of death.

The fruits of Tamar's brave ingenuity are twofold. Biologically and historically, Tamar gives birth to twins, one of whom, Perez, is ancestor to the history-making David and the kings of Israel and Judah (Ruth 4:18–22; 1 Chr. 2:1–16).[22] The sapiential consequences are more important to the Joseph story: Judah learns the vital importance of letting go of beloved sons, even after great loss (of two sons) and the possibility of greater loss (of his beloved son), and experiences firsthand what it means to be a substitute (for Shelah to Tamar).[23] These two lessons prepare Judah to play a vital leadership role in the story of Israel within the Joseph story, the family's migration down to Egypt, their survival, and flourishing.

21. Tarlin, "Tamar's Veil," 176–77.
22. It is indeed interesting that David, in numerous narratives, is said to be of a mixed lineage that includes, at minimum, the nameless Canaanite wife of Judah, Tamar the Canaanite, and Ruth the Moabite. See Nadav Na'aman, "Ḫabiru and Hebrews: The Transfer of a Social Term to the Literary Sphere," *JNES* 45 (1986): 271–88.
23. Levenson, *Death and Resurrection of the Beloved Son*, 163–64.

Judah's Scepter

Judah's Willingness to Die

The story of Judah's rise to leadership after the Tamar incident culminates in Judah's demonstration of his willingness to suffer a great deal, even death, to ensure the survival of the group. Seen as a continuation of the events of Genesis 38, Judah wins the role of leader among his brothers by putting into practice the lessons painfully learned from the Tamar episode.

A severe famine threatens the survival of Jacob's household. When Jacob learns that there is surplus grain for sale in Egypt, he sends his remaining sons, minus Benjamin, to Egypt to buy grain. The sons return from Egypt with grain but without Simeon. To Jacob's dismay, they also return with the money (42:35).[24] Is it possibly the sale- or blood-price for Simeon? Have Jacob's sons again profited from a brother's demise? His sons explain,

> [30] The man, the lord of the land, spoke harshly to us, and charged us with spying the land. [31] But we said to him, "We are honest men, we are not spies. [32] We are twelve brothers, sons of our father; one is no more, and the youngest is now with our father in the land of Canaan." [33] Then the man, the lord of the land, said to us, "By this I shall know that you are honest men: leave one of your brothers with me, take grain for the famine of your households, and go your way. [34] Bring your youngest brother to me, and I shall know that you are not spies but honest men. Then I will release your brother to you, and you may trade in the land." (42:30–34)

Despite the fulsome explanation, Jacob assumes that Simeon, like Joseph, is dead and dismisses the possibility of sending Benjamin with his sons (42:36). Like Judah, he has lost two sons and refuses to release a third.

Reuben steps in and attempts to convince Jacob to entrust Benjamin to him so that they can return to Egypt to save Simeon. He says to Jacob, "You may kill my two sons if I do not bring [Benjamin] back to you. Put him in my hands, and I will bring him back to you" (42:37). Reuben's offer of his two sons as surety reveals for Jacob Reuben's fundamental misapprehension of the situation. As Jacob's response indicates, to lose two

---

24. Levenson, *Death and Resurrection of the Beloved Son*, 161–62.

sons is tantamount to himself dying: "[Benjamin's] brother is dead, and he alone is left. If harm should come to him ... you would bring down my gray hairs with sorrow to Sheol" (42:38). Reuben does not understand that for a father to lose two sons is also for himself to die. A proportional guarantee, if that is what Reuben wishes to offer, would have to include the offer of his own life. And how would the loss of two grandchildren console a father bereaved of two sons? Jacob's suspicion that his sons have sold or killed yet another brother for financial gain stands and so too his grip on Benjamin.

The family eventually exhausts the purchased grain supply. Joseph would have known that, before the seven years of famine concluded, his brothers would need to come back or face starvation. He would wait and see what his brothers will do with the responsibility to save Simeon from a hostile Egyptian lord and with Benjamin in their care. Did Joseph imagine that it would not be a deficit in fraternal love (for either Simeon or Benjamin) but an excess of paternal love (for Benjamin) that would prevent the brothers from returning (not unlike how Jacob's excessive and exclusive love for Joseph contributed to his demise)? For it is Jacob's continued refusal to entrust Benjamin to his brothers' care that prevents the brothers' journey back to Egypt.

At this point in the narrative, Judah intervenes to loosen Jacob's deathly grip on Benjamin. He says to Jacob,

> [8] Send the boy with me, and let us be on our way, so that we may live and not die—you and we and also our little ones. [9] I myself will be surety for him; you can hold me accountable for him. If I do not bring him back to you and set him before you, then let me bear the blame forever. [10] If we had not delayed, we would now have returned twice (Gen. 43:8–10).

Reuben, who bargained to take Benjamin to Egypt immediately after their return, appears to have wanted to deliver Simeon with little thought for the wellbeing of their father or the family. In contrast, Judah confronts his obstinate father and identifies the group's survival as the necessary reason: "that we may live and not die—you and we and also our little ones." Also in contrast to Reuben, Judah does not barter with the "little ones," and instead makes them the explicit object in need of deliverance. He instead offers himself as surety for Benjamin. He expresses a willingness to be a substitute for Benjamin even in death for the sake of the group's survival. Judah says in effect, "I am willing to die so that we may live." His willingness to die will prove to be a means of giving life to the group.

Judah's words move Jacob to let Benjamin go in a beautiful instance of narrative and paternal analogy: The father who knows the pain of losing two sons and the importance nevertheless of releasing the third convinces a father who believes he has lost two sons to risk losing a third for the sake of the group. The money his sons brought back the last time still bothers Jacob: "Perhaps it was an oversight," not payment for some nefarious activity, he dares to hope and sends double the money with which to pay back a debt and to purchase more grain (43:12). Only then does he say the dreaded words: "Take your brother also, and be on your way again to the man. . . . As for me, if I am bereaved of my children, I am bereaved" (43:13–14).[25]

Before the journey down to Egypt and back is over, Judah faces a situation in which he must make good on his promise to stand surety for Benjamin and demonstrate his full maturation since the beginning of the Joseph story. In Egypt, Joseph has Benjamin framed for theft (44:1–12). When Judah proposes that all the brothers become slaves as punishment, Joseph insists that Benjamin alone shall be punished (43:16–17). At this, Judah demonstrates his willingness to die the symbolic death of slavery in the place of Benjamin before Joseph and his brothers.

Judah recounts in full the brothers' experience of the past events with emphasis on Jacob's particular love for Benjamin. He reasons that, because Jacob's "life is bound up in the boy's life" (44:30), Jacob will die from sorrow should Benjamin not return (44:31). Judah concludes the most pathetic speech:

> [32] For your servant became surety for the boy to my father, saying, "If I do not bring him back to you, then I will bear the blame in the sight of

---

25. The Hebrew here is beautifully terse: ואני כאשר שכלתי שכלתי. As has been noted, Jacob's resolve echoes that of Esther: וכאשר אבדתי אבדתי (Esth. 4:16).

my father all my life." ³³ Now therefore, please let your servant remain as a slave to my lord in place of the boy; and let the boy go back with his brothers. ³⁴ For how can I go back to my father if the boy is not with me? I fear to see the suffering that would come upon my father. (44:32–34)

Judah admits that Jacob will not literally die, only suffer great sorrow. But Judah knows the depth of that sorrow, for he himself has experienced such loss. Judah also acknowledges Jacob's favoritism, that his own death will bring their father less sorrow than Benjamin's. But Judah chooses to love the son the father favors and to protect him out of love for their father, for he knows personally that a father's favor is profound and beyond reason. Joseph, who earlier was the object of fraternal hatred because of paternal favor, must most keenly perceive the dramatic transformation in Judah: Judah, who willingly sold him to Egypt precisely because he was favored, is now willing to voluntarily put on the yoke of Egyptian slavery instead of the favored Benjamin for the sake of their father. The curtain falls; the play ends. Moved by Judah's self-sacrifice and no longer able to control himself, Joseph weeps and reveals himself to his brothers, "I am Joseph" (45:1–3). The stage is set for Israel's deliverance from famine and migration to Egypt.

One may reasonably argue that Joseph has orchestrated Judah's transformation into an empathic son and sacrificial brother, just as Tamar orchestrated Judah's repentance in Genesis 38. It was after all Joseph who created the alternate reality in which he is a non-Hebrew-speaking Egyptian governor and his brothers are Canaanite spies. It was likewise Joseph who authored the requisite scenario: hold Simeon hostage, demand that Benjamin be brought, and place Benjamin in mortal jeopardy. The analogy with Tamar, however, is misleading, for whereas Tamar maintains control throughout the ordeal (with the possible exception of the very beginning), Joseph sets the stage and provides stage directions in Egypt but exerts no control over the crucial events that happen in Canaan. For example, Joseph has nothing to do with Judah's vitally important experience with Tamar or his offering himself as surety for Benjamin to Jacob. We see Joseph's relative lack of control in his genuine surprise when Judah offers to take Benjamin's place: "Then Joseph could no longer control himself. . . . And he wept" (45:1, 2). Joseph establishes the right conditions, but the credit for the critical transformation belongs to Judah.

Judah's Scepter

Before we discuss Jacob's testamental blessing on Judah, let us analyze the historical significance of Judah's self-sacrificial attitude. Judah's willingness to suffer a great deal, even slavery and death, in order to save Jacob is symbolic of the willingness of the tribe of Judah and Judah's most famous sons, the Davidic kings, to suffer for the sake of the people of Israel. That is, Judah does not merely deliver his father Jacob from going down to Sheol in sorrow but delivers Israel from starvation and so literal death. And how does Judah achieve this? By demonstrating his willingness to protect the most vulnerable brother, that is, the little tribe of Benjamin whose life is bound up with Israel's. We could say that Judah saves the whole by protecting the weakest member of the group. The theme of Judah saving Benjamin reflects the historical fact that Benjamin alone remains part of the Southern Kingdom of Judah after the schism of Israel after Solomon's death in 928 BCE. Literarily and canonically, Judah saving Benjamin reprises and corrects the dark narrative in which the Israelite tribes, led by Judah, nearly destroy Benjamin in the civil strife that breaks in the wake of Samson's death (Judges 20–21). Judah, in the Joseph story, reflects wisdom learned through history that the survival of the group is contingent on the survival of the least among them.

"Your Father's Sons Shall Bow Down before You"

Judah's future leadership among the tribes of Israel receives explicit treatment in Jacob's deathbed blessings in Genesis 49. Jacob says to his sons, "Gather around, that I may tell you what will happen to you in days to come" (49:1). What follows is Jacob's testament that in part adumbrates the future history of the tribes of Israel beginning with Reuben, the eldest, to Benjamin, the youngest. Fourth in line is Judah who nevertheless receives the prophetic blessing of preeminence and leadership.

Jacob disqualifies his eldest son Reuben for leadership, because he "went up onto my couch" (49:4). The reference is to an earlier incident recounted in Gen. 35:22 in which Reuben "went and lay with Bilhah his father's concubine" and reflects the disappearance of the tribe of Reuben in history. Jacob likewise disqualifies Simeon and Levi, again referencing an earlier incident found in Genesis 34 but also the role they will play in

Exodus 32, because of their propensity for violence and anger (49:5–7). This brings us to Judah:

> ⁸ Judah, your brothers shall praise you;
> your hand shall be on the neck of your enemies;
> your father's sons shall bow down before you.
> ⁹ Judah is a lion's whelp;
> from the prey, my son, you have gone up.
> He crouches down, he stretches out like a lion,
> like a lioness – who dares rouse him up?
> ¹⁰ The scepter shall not depart from Judah,
> nor the ruler's staff from between his feet,
> until tribute comes to him;
> and the obedience of the people is his.
> ¹¹ Binding his foal to the vine
> and his donkey's colt to the choice vine,
> he washes his garments in wine
> and his robe in the blood of grapes;
> ¹² his eyes are darker than wine,
> and his teeth whiter than milk. (Gen. 49:8–12)

The passage is not without its difficulties, including the crucial phrase translated "until tribute comes to him" (49:10bα) and the vine-wine metaphor of verses 11–12.[26] The difficulties, ambiguities, and ironies notwithstanding, the general significance of Jacob's blessing is clear: "Judah will continuously enjoy royal power to which even non-Israelite populations will eventually submit."[27] Verse 8 seems to transfer Joseph's elevated status among the brothers, revealed to him in his teenage dreams (Genesis 37), to Judah: The brothers will bow to Judah, not Joseph. The lion imagery, associated with royalty in ancient Israel and more broadly in the ancient Near East, is

---

26. See Richard C. Steiner, "Poetic Forms in the Masoretic Vocalization and Three Difficult Phrases in Jacob's Blessings: יֶתֶר שְׂאֵת (Gen 49:3), יְצוּעִי עָלָה (49:4), and יָבֹא שִׁילֹה (49:10)," *JBL* 129 (2010): 209–35; Serge Frolov, "Judah Comes to Shiloh. Genesis 49.10bα, One More Time," *JBL* 131 (2012): 417–22. On Gen. 49:11–12, see Edwin M. Good, "The 'Blessing' on Judah, Gen 49.8–12," *JBL* 82 (1963): 427–32.

27. Frolov, "Judah Comes to Shiloh," 422.

unambiguously positive (49:9).²⁸ Verse 10, whatever the significance of the much-debated phrase *yābō' šîlōh*, clearly states that Judah will wield royal power symbolized in the scepter and the staff. And verses 11–12 paint a picture of paradisiac abundance. Judah will reign forever and in abundance.

Joseph also receives unambiguous blessings from Jacob: "blessings of heaven above, blessings of the deep that lies beneath, blessings of the breasts and of the womb" (49:25). But Judah has stolen Joseph's blessing of preeminence. Judah, not Joseph, emerges from the Joseph story endowed with enduring leadership. This reflects the role Judah plays during the united monarchy and the survival of the Southern Kingdom of Judah after the demise of the Northern Kingdom (that is, the tribes of Joseph) in 722 BCE. And the basis of Judah's right and privilege to rule, it must be underlined, lies in his demonstration of a willingness to suffer a great deal, even death, for the sake of the group. Judah volunteers to suffer the symbolic death of slavery instead of Benjamin, the weakest member of the group, in order to save their father, the eponymous ancestor of Israel, from death. That is, the "scepter shall not depart from Judah, nor the ruler's staff from between his feet" precisely because Judah was willing to die for the sake of Israel. In demonstrating that he is willing to die for the group, Judah gives life to others and wins for himself the charism necessary to lead.

Conclusion

That a willingness to suffer for the sake of the group constitutes a qualification for legitimate rule is no mystery; and, as mere rhetoric, it has little power. But when words are married to conviction and conviction to deeds, there is perhaps no greater source of moral authority for leadership. The connection between legitimate leadership and a willingness to suffer for the group finds perfect biblical expression when the Johannine Jesus, building on the oracle of Ezekiel in which leaders are cast as shepherds (chapter 34), declares, "I am the good shepherd. The good shepherd lays down his life for the sheep" to save them from the wolf (John 10:11). Long

---

28. Brent A. Strawn, *What Is Stronger Than a Lion? Leonine Image and Metaphor in the Hebrew Bible and the Ancient Near East*, OBO 212 (Göttingen: Vandenhoeck & Ruprecht, 2005).

before Jesus, however, we find this thematic already in the Hebrew Bible, in an inchoate form in the Samson tradition and in a more mature form in the Joseph story. On the one hand, God suffers with Joseph the deathly descent into the pit, down into Egypt, and into prison on the way toward resurrection and the deliverance of many lives from death. God embraces death as a means to give life or, in Joseph's words, "Even though you intended to do harm to me, God intended it for good, in order to preserve a numerous people" (Gen. 50:20). On the other, Judah willingly offers himself to save Benjamin from slavery and his father from sorrowful death and, as a result, wins the right to rule over his brothers. Judah's embrace of death is the foundation of the Davidic kingship. Put together, willingness to die for the sake of the group releases the divine power for life and procures for the willing the mysterious blessing to stand as first among equals as leader: "Judah, your brothers shall praise you . . . your father's sons shall bow down before you."

The difficult link between the willingness to die and the burden of leadership receives continued consideration in the biblical tradition in connection to Moses and Esther, to whom we turn in the next chapters.

CHAPTER 6

Moses from the Breach to the Cleft

"The Lord brought us forth from Egypt"—not by an angel, not by a seraph, nor by an agent, but the Holy One, blessed be He, Himself.

Haggadah[1]

THE BOOK OF EXODUS TELLS THE STORY of Israel's birth as a nation, of its deliverance from "the house of slavery" and entrance into a covenantal relationship with YHWH (Exod. 20:2). The first of the two events, the exodus proper, understandably receives more attention and acclaim for its message of liberation from despotic oppression and genocidal hatred. But the second event, the binding of Israel to God, is equally important to biblical tradition and proves more difficult to achieve than the first. Deuteronomy memorably describes Egypt as the "iron-smelter" (Deut. 4:20). And if Israel comes out of the fire of Egypt as smelted iron, then forging Israel into God's covenantal partner might be compared to turning formless metal into a goodly tool, the arduous and patient process of casting and hammering to polishing and buffing. That is, Israel becomes God's

---

1. The Haggadah is the liturgy for the celebration of the Passover Seder and as such commemorates Israel's deliverance from Egypt. The quoted portion of the Haggadah comments on Deut. 26:8 and is taken from David Henshke, "'The Lord Brought Us Forth from Egypt': On the Absence of Moses in the Passover Haggadah," *AJS Review* 31 (2007): 61.

CHAPTER 6

people through an ongoing process initially of radical transformations, then of granular refinements. And Moses demonstrates admirable leadership through this process in crisis after crisis to bind Israel to God and God to Israel.

Of the many crises that punctuate Israel's journey through the Red Sea and across the Jordan River, down Mount Sinai and up Zion (Ps. 114:3, 5)[2] none of them threatens the divine-human relationship and, as such, defines that relationship more fundamentally than the events surrounding the golden calf as recounted in Exodus 32–34. During this most precarious and delicate situation, Moses again fulfills his duty as intermediary between God and Israel with uncommon sensitivity and decisiveness. He saves Israel from utter destruction at God's wrath, tames the flames that threaten to evaporate the people, and, more critically than that, pushes God from behind the veil of mystery into a shocking self-revelation and self-definition. With boldness and vulnerability founded on a willingness to die, Moses compels God, who first appeared in mystery and in fire as "I AM WHO I AM" (Exod. 3:14), to declare, "I will be gracious to whom I will be gracious, and I will show mercy to whom I will show mercy" (33:19, adapted from the NRSV).[3] The indeterminate *idem per idem*, thanks to Moses's audacious request to see God's glory (33:18), becomes infused with grace and mercy that, while not incapable of exclusion, free God to embrace even sinners (34:6–7).

In sum, Israel's journey out of Egypt toward the land of promise reaches its apex at Mount Sinai when God begins to dwell among Israel. But before that most difficult and beautiful union can become a reality, a harrowing crisis comes that threatens to undo the very possibility of that relationship: the crisis of the golden calf. However, Moses steps into the breach and brings the two parties together to forge a union at once impossibly fragile, because of the incompatibility of sinfulness and holiness, and inestimably strong, because the guarantor of the relationship is none other than the gracious God of mercy. At the heart of Moses's success, as we shall see, is a

---

2. On the equation of the Red Sea and the Jordan River, see Ps. 114:3, 5. On the close relationship between Sinai and Zion, see Jon D. Levenson, *Sinai and Zion: An Entry into the Jewish Bible* (New York: HarperCollins, 1985).

3. G. S. Ogden, "Idem per Idem: Its Use and Meaning," *JSOT* 53 (1992): 107–20.

willingness to die, first to stand with the people in punishment, and second to risk death to draw the gracious and merciful God from behind the veil.

The Goal of Covenantal Union and the Problem of Sin

The goal of the encounter at Sinai, after Israel's miraculous deliverance from the Egyptian house of slavery, is to make manifest the theological claim that Yhwh is Israel's God and that Israel is God's people (Exod. 6:7; 20:2). To this end, God and Israel enter into a covenantal relationship defined by Israel's grateful obedience to divine law (Exod. 19–24), grateful because, as God reminds the people, "I am the Lord your God, who brought you out of the land of Egypt, out of the house of slavery" (20:2). That the story of prior divine deliverance grounds Israel's covenantal obligation to God is an oft forgotten but vitally important datum.[4] Grace, not law, is the foundation for Israel's covenant with Yhwh. Next, God instructs the construction of a sanctuary in which God is to dwell among Israel: "And have them make me a sanctuary, so that I may dwell among them" (25:8). However, when God "finished speaking with Moses," having relayed to him the architectural, material, esthetic, and personnel details for the tabernacle (31:18), the events surrounding the golden calf interrupt the expected transition from command (Exodus 25–31) to fulfillment (Exodus 35–40) and significantly retard narrative progress. In this way, the golden calf incident dramatizes the formidable obstacle that stands in the way of realizing the divine-human union, namely, the violent incompatibility of human sin and divine holiness.

In Exodus 32, the people have been waiting for Moses to return from atop Mount Sinai for forty days and, afraid that Moses has died or, worse, abandoned them, demand that Aaron "make gods (*'ĕlōhîm*) for us, who shall go before us," because, they reason, "this Moses, the man who brought us up out of the land of Egypt, we do not know what has become of him" (32:1). The perceived crisis, from the perspective of the people, is that of absence and abandonment, Moses's absence interpreted as divine abandonment. That is, in asking that Aaron produce a replacement for the

---

4. See Levenson, *Sinai and Zion*, 36–42.

man Moses, the people demonstrate that there has been a prior substitution of Moses for God. There is a sin more primal than Israel's so-called original sin.[5] The people already see Moses as God, and the golden calf is but the latest outward expression of a prior inner corruption.

The unfortunate irony of Israel's panic and hasty attempt to remedy the perceived crisis of divine abandonment is that God was all the while making provisions to dwell among the people. God, for the past forty days, had given Moses detailed instruction on how to "make me a sanctuary, so that I may dwell among them" (25:8). Moreover, as one biblical scholar has pointed out, the telling of the golden calf incident echoes God's very first words to Moses on Mount Sinai. The similarities highlight the transgressive deviance of Israel's impatience.[6] Just as God instructs Moses to ask the Israelites for offerings of various material goods for the construction of the tabernacle (25:2–7), so too Aaron asks for and receives gold jewelry from the people for the golden calf (32:2–3). And just as the tabernacle is to facilitate divine presence (25:8), so too the golden calf is understood to embody the divine (32:4). The similarities reveal a basic agreement in what the people desire for themselves and what God desires for them: to be led and guided through the wilderness into the promised land by the God of the exodus. At the same time, the overall similarity underlines that the sinfulness that threatens Israel's existence is not some radical love of evil but the fearful groping and grasping for good with anxiety borne out of a lack of trust and loyalty. Sin, in other words, may have more to do with means than with ends, more with perversions of good than radical commitment to evil.

Another aspect of the perversion is the evil of mediated divine presence or, more accurately, the assumption on the part of the people and Aaron that they can make God present in a mediating figure. Aaron and the people revel—celebrate with song and dance and feast on drink and food—at their own power to conjure God. "They" (the people alone or Aaron and the people together, it is not clear) say of the calf, "These are your gods (*'ĕlōhîm*), O Israel, who brought you up out of the land of Egypt!" (32:4;

---

5. Thomas B. Dozeman, *Exodus*, ECC (Grand Rapids: Eerdmans, 2009), 685.
6. R. W. L. Moberly, *At the Mountain of God: Story and Theology in Exodus 32–34*, JSOTSup 22 (Sheffield: JSOT Press, 1983), 48.

cf. 1 Kgs. 12:28). Then Aaron builds an altar and declares *ex post facto* a "festival to the LORD" (32:5). Aaron and the people believe that they have made YHWH present again in a cultic object and so feast in revelry at the supposed return of God. It will be only after much bloodshed that the people realize that they cannot domesticate the divine presence and that the mediation of the divine presence—be it by an angel, a Moses, or especially a golden calf—is an evil thing (33:4).

The ferocity of God's response to the manufacture and celebration of the golden calf clarifies the seriousness of the people's transgression. God announced to Moses, "I have seen this people, how stiff-necked they are. Now let me alone, so that my wrath may burn hot against them and I may consume them" (32:9-10). The presence the people had sought and thought they could control, it turns out, is a consuming fire that renders even a moment's cohabitation potentially devastating. The task that lies before Moses, in the face of what appears to be an imminent dissolution of the union, is to find a way to bridge the gap so that God—as the Haggadah has it, "not . . . an angel, not . . . a seraph, nor . . . an agent, but the Holy One, blessed be He, Himself"—can be said to have delivered the people. Moses does so in two movements, each marked by a willingness to die.

"Blot Me Out of the Book"

Exodus 32–34 shows evidence of a complex history of composition and redaction with perplexing and intriguing doublets and editorial seams, not least of which is the similitude between the golden calf and Moses.[7] For the purposes of the present argument, we need not attend to these issues. However, it is important to keep in mind that the following argument is a distillation of the relevant issues from the complex matrix of textual issues and other entanglements.

God's initial response to the golden calf, as we noted above, is decisive. It is also a test of sorts for Moses. Here is the full text:

---

7. On source-critical issues, see Dozeman, *Exodus*, 575-81; on the homology between Moses and the golden calf, see Dmitri Slivniak, "The Golden Calf Story: Constructively and Deconstructively," *JSOT* 33 (2008): 19-38.

> ⁷ The LORD said to Moses, "Go down at once! Your people, whom you brought up out of the land of Egypt, have acted perversely; they have been quick to turn aside from the way that I commanded them; ⁸ they have cast for themselves an image of a calf, and have worshipped it and sacrificed to it, and said, 'These are your gods, O Israel, who brought you up out of the land of Egypt!'" ⁹ The LORD said to Moses, "I have seen this people, how stiff-necked they are. ¹⁰ Now let me alone, so that my wrath may burn hot against them and I may consume them; and of you I will make a great nation." (Exod. 32:7–10)

God commands Moses to go down to see the people's sin for himself. However, God also delays Moses. Not only does God invite intervention on the part of Moses to act against the threatened destruction, God also lays before Moses a test. Before God will permit Moses to descend the mountain, God appears to ascertain whether Moses might want to be rid of the people and become a second Abraham to a new Israel.

First, God clarifies the nature of the people's sin by referring to the Israelites as "your," that is, Moses's people. In echoing the people, God indicates that the heart of the issue is not that the people have displaced God for the golden calf but that they have displaced God for Moses. Before the people refer to the calf as "your gods . . . who brought you up out of the land of Egypt," they first refer to Moses as "the man who brought us up out of the land of Egypt." Moses will need to demonstrate that he understands the part he plays in the people's idolatry as a more potent temptation for idolatry than the golden calf.

Second, God presents a test for Moses, to see whether Moses desires to displace the people and become a second Abraham. God couples getting rid of the people, whom God characterizes as "stiff-necked" and therefore troublesome, with a temptation for Moses: the honor of becoming the progenitor of a great nation. There is a faint but distinct echo of the Noah story in the overall scenario: God desires to destroy a sinful population and start anew with a single righteous person. The resonance with the Abrahamic tradition is even clearer. Note, in this regard, that God repeats to Moses almost the exact same promise made to Abram:

wəʾeʿeśkāləgôy gādôl
I will make of you a great nation. (Gen. 12:2)

wə'ē'ēśeh 'ôtkā ləgôy gādôl
Of you I will make a great nation. (Exod. 32:10)

The only change is that the objective pronominal suffix of Gen. 12:2 indicating Abram, *-kā* ("you"), has been separated from the verb to emphasize that Moses shall be made into a great nation: "*of you* (*'ôtkā*) I will make a great nation." As the slight change indicates, the temptation for Moses is to rid himself of the troublesome people and to claim for himself the honor of being the new Abraham.

Along with the test, God also provides a way out for Moses. God's request, "Now let me alone," underlines the possibility precisely of not leaving God alone to intervene against "the disaster" God has planned against the people (32:14). Moses does exactly that and responds:

> ¹¹ O LORD, why does your wrath burn hot against your people, whom you brought out of the land of Egypt with great power and with a mighty hand? ¹² Why should the Egyptians say, "It was with evil intent that he brought them out to kill them in the mountains, and to consume them from the face of the earth"? Turn from your fierce wrath; change your mind and do not bring disaster on your people. ¹³ Remember Abraham, Isaac, and Israel, your servants, how you swore to them by your own self, saying to them, "I will multiply your descendants like the stars of heaven, and all this land that I have promised I will give to your descendants, and they shall inherit it forever." (Exod. 32:11–13)

Moses first addresses the mischaracterization of the Israelites as his people, not God's, and redescribes Israel as "your," that is, God's "people, whom you brought out of the land of Egypt with great power and with a mighty hand." Moses understands that the golden calf is epiphenomenal and points to a deeper, prior perversion that implicates him.[8] Then, pointing out the public relations implications of destroying God's people, Moses begins his attempt to stay God's hand from striking the people. Think of what the Egyptians will say, Moses argues. Also demonstrating that he recognizes the test intended for him, Moses explicitly names Abraham, along

---

8. On the similarities between Moses and the golden calf, see Slivniak, "Golden Calf Story."

CHAPTER 6

with Isaac and Israel, as the true receiver of God's promise of innumerable progeny and land, not him. Moses refuses to permit the destruction of the people, however troublesome they may be, and to become a second Abraham. He thereby successfully convinces God to relent from "the disaster that he planned to bring on his people" (32:14).

The dialogue between God and Moses continues after Moses goes down the mountain, sees the gravity of the situation for himself, and returns in the hope of making atonement for the people's sin (32:30). It is Moses who speaks first: "Alas, this people has sinned a great sin; they have made for themselves gods of gold. But now, if you will only forgive their sin—but if not, blot me out of the book that you have written" (32:31–32). How do we understand Moses's request for forgiveness? And what is the relationship between his offer of himself with the words "blot me out of the book" and the request for forgiveness?

Before returning to the mountain top, Moses told the people that he will go to YHWH to "make atonement" (*kāpar*) for the people's sin (32:30). We learn what it might mean for Moses to make atonement earlier in Exodus 29–30. In Exodus 29, God instructs Moses concerning the ordination rites of Aaron and his sons for the priesthood, including the requirement of offering a sin offering for atonement and making atonement for the altar (29:36–37). Atonement, in this instance, involves repeated animal sacrifice. A related but more elaborate atonement ritual is detailed in Leviticus 16 for the Day of Atonement involving, among other rituals, animal sacrifice and blood manipulation (see also Exod. 30:10). In Exod. 30:12, God describes a different atonement requirement when a census is taken of the population: "When you take a census of the Israelites to register them, at registration all of them shall give a ransom (*kōper*) for their lives to the LORD, so that no plague may come upon them for being registered." The registration is of males at least twenty years old, likely for military service. And the ransom (*kōper*, the nominal form of the verb "to make atonement") may be understood as a prospective atonement for bloodshed committed during battle.[9]

---

9. William Johnstone, *Exodus 20–40*, SHBC 2B (Macon, GA: Smyth & Helwys, 2018), 324–26.

Moses from the Breach to the Cleft

Given the discussion of atonement requirements in Exodus 29–30, Moses would have known that making atonement for the people's sin involved considerable cost, either in the form of animal sacrifice or monetary ransom. What is noteworthy, then, is that Moses goes up Mount Sinai ostensibly to make atonement for the people's great sin with neither gold nor goat, with neither a ransom nor an animal sacrifice. Moses goes up alone. One must wonder, therefore, on what basis Moses asks God to forgive the great sin that the people have committed.

Given that Moses approaches God empty-handed, it would be accurate to say that Moses offers nothing in requesting that God forgive the people. Moses is not attempting to negotiate forgiveness. He is requesting that God do so. This means that, if God does forgive the people, it will have to be a free act of God who chooses to do so, quite contrary to the laws God has prescribed in Exodus 29–30, without having received either sacrifice or ransom. Some may wish to disagree that Moses offers God nothing and argue that Moses offers himself as a sin offering. This would be a mistake. Moses does not offer to be punished in place of the people but to stand with the people in punishment. Radical identification, not substitution, underlies Moses's tactics: If God will not forgive the people, then Moses demands that God "blot me out of the book that you have written," presumably along with the people.

The identity of "the book that [God has] written" is uncertain. In the immediate context, the only thing God has written are the tablets of covenant, which Moses has already shattered (32:19). What might be in view, then, is something like either "the register of the house of Israel" (Ezek. 13:9) or the "book of remembrance" (Mal. 3:16). If the former is in view, in reaffirming his identity as one with the people, Moses forecloses the possibility of God's proposed plan: first destroy the people, then make Moses into a great nation (Exod. 32:10). If God rejects the Israelites as God's people, then Moses will also be left out of "the register of the house of Israel," thus leaving God with no name to populate "the register." Therefore, if God is to have a people, it will have to include the Israelites, who have sinned a great sin.

If the "book of remembrance" is in view, then Moses willingly embraces something more terrible than death in asking that he be blotted out from the book. According to Malachi, the "book of remembrance" records

CHAPTER 6

"those who revered the LORD and thought on his name" (Mal. 3:16). These, God says, are God's "special possession" and will be spared on the day of judgment (3:17). The others, described as "all the arrogant and all evildoers," are to be burned up, leaving them "neither root nor branch" (4:1). Thus, if the book of remembrance is in view, Moses willingly embraces perhaps not immediate death, but a punishment worse than death: not only exclusion from God's fold but also unimaginable horror under eschatological judgment.

To summarize, in asking to be blotted out from the book God has written, Moses rejects the possibility of glory, of becoming a second Noah or Abraham, and instead chooses the possibility of postmortem punishment with the people. In boldness founded on a willing embrace of death, Moses offers God two choices: Forgive the people in an act of pure grace; or, if not, punish the people, himself included.

God rejects Moses's offer: "Whoever has sinned against me I will blot out of my book" (32:33), and promises to punish the people for their sin "when the day comes for punishment" (32:34). The day comes soon, it would appear: "Then the LORD sent a plague on the people, because they made a calf—the one that Aaron made" (32:35). God's response of word and deed, despite its apparent clarity, however, resists a simplistic reading about either the nature of the punishment or the possibility of forgiveness. In regard to punishment, God appears to reject corporate responsibility in refusing to punish Moses. At the same time, God punishes all the people without regard to their individual involvement in what the text awkwardly ascribes to both the people and Aaron: "because they made a calf—the one that Aaron made."[10] The ambiguity calls for a more nuanced understanding of responsibility. There is such a thing as corporate responsibility: the people and Aaron together bear the sin, whatever the specific role they played in the manufacture of the calf; but there are also limits to corporate responsibility. Moses cannot be punished for sin committed without his knowledge and away from his sphere of influence. A corollary conse-

---

10. The JPS avoids the problem of agency by offering a different possible translation: "Then the LORD sent a plague upon the people, for what they did with the calf that Aaron made."

quence is the rejection of vicarious suffering: Moses cannot take on the punishment instead of the people.

God's response to Moses also does not fully resolve the question of forgiveness and, in fact, nuances it. In between promising (32:33) and enacting punishment (32:35), God says to Moses, "But now go, lead the people to the place about which I have spoken to you; see, my angel shall go in front of you" (32:34a). That is to say, punishment precludes neither the possibility nor the necessity of forgiveness. In fact, God's plan to continue his covenantal relationship with the people, be it in a reduced form with Moses and an angel as God's proxy, requires that God, at some level, forgives the people. Moses, through his daring proposal to be blotted out of God's books with the people, has advanced the conversation beyond the binary of sin and punishment toward forgiveness and accommodation. The extent of God's forgiveness and accommodation, not whether God will destroy the people and start anew, is the new starting point of the discussion moving forward. How tightly will God embrace the sinful people—and at what cost to whom?

"Show Me Your Glory, I Pray"

The crisis set in motion by the golden calf continues in Exodus 33, where the search for a lasting solution to the problem of sin moves decisively toward a conclusion. Exodus 33, it must be admitted, is riddled with compositional and redactional complexities that make easy comprehension impossible.[11] However, the overall thrust of the dialogue between God and Moses is not too difficult to follow. The conversation moves from the earlier threat of divine withdrawal and wrath (32:10) through an intermediate stage of mediated presence (33:1-3) toward full divine presence and grace (33:18-23). Moses, after having saved the people from divine wrath, pushes for God's full presence and a deeper revelation of God, even as the danger of God's holy presence for the stiff-necked people becomes clearer.

Exodus 33 again underlines the danger God's presence poses to the people and clarifies the extent of accommodation needed to make the divine-

---

11. Dozeman, *Exodus*, 688-700

CHAPTER 6

human cohabitation possible. After God reiterates that an angel will lead the people to the promised land, God states the reason for refusing to accompany the people: "I will not go up among you, or I would consume you on the way, for you are a stiff-necked people" (33:3). The same message is repeated in Exod. 33:5, and it is important to note that God and Moses characterize the people as "stiff-necked" throughout the passage. In fact, before the covenant renewal in Exodus 34, Moses again describes the Israelites as "a stiff-necked people" (34:9). The people have not changed and may be incapable of changing. What this means is that for God to "dwell among [the people]" changes will have to take place almost exclusively with God. God must change because the people will not.

When the people learn that God will "send an angel," and will not personally go among the people (33:2), the immediate assessment is that, to translate the Hebrew woodenly, it is an "evil word" (33:4). We might balk at the characterization of God's mediated or ambassadorial presence in an angel as evil, but that would be to fail to understand the controversy at the heart of the golden calf episode. As detailed above, the sin at the heart of the golden calf episode is the desire to make God present in a mediating figure, which explicitly takes the form of a golden calf but implicates the more primal temptation to see Moses as the mediating presence. The Haggadah, the liturgical celebration of the Passover Seder, correctly identifies the core theological problem of the golden calf episode when it states, "'The Lord brought us forth from Egypt'—not by an angel, not by a seraph, nor by an agent, but the Holy One, blessed be He, Himself." The redeeming figure cannot be, obviously, the golden calf, but neither can it be either an angel or even "an agent," that is, Moses.[12] It must be God, and anything else would be inadequate and as such an evil. In this light, the people's ritual response to God's decision not to accompany them but to send an angel instead symbolically demonstrates that they understand the seriousness of the situation. The people mourn and remove their ornaments as if at a funeral (33:4). What more, God commands the people to remove their ornaments as if to enact a divorce (33:5).[13] The people and

---

12. Henshke, "Lord Brought Us Forth."

13. Dozeman, *Exodus*, 722. Levenson (*Sinai and Zion*, 75–80) interprets the covenant language used to describe Israel's relationship with God and the implied image

God understand the sending of a substitutionary angel as either a kind of death or, more aptly, as a precursor to divorce.

Important at this stage of the conversation between God and Moses is Moses's tactical use of his favored status before God. The description of the "tent of meeting" is somewhat odd and appears out of place within the literary context (33:7–11). Whatever else its function, however, it establishes Moses's intimate relationship with God. We learn, for example, that God "speak[s] to Moses face to face, as one speaks to a friend" in the tent of meeting (33:11). Moses is a friend to God, that is, a companion of intense intimacy and trust.[14] And Moses evokes precisely this relationship as he begins negotiations with God: "You have said, 'I know you by name, and you have also found favor in my sight'" (33:12; cf. 33:17). What does Moses do with his favored status? He risks it, and not only it but also his life to demand that God, not an angel or an agent, lead the people.

Moses continues:

> [12] See, you have said to me, "Bring up this people"; but you have not let me know whom you will send with me. Yet you have said, "I know you by name, and you have also found favor in my sight." [13] Now if I have found favor in your sight, show me your ways, so that I may know you and find favor in your sight. Consider too that this nation is your people. (33:12–13)

To Moses's request to see God's ways, that is, to see how exactly God will lead the people, God responds, "My presence will go with you, and I will give you rest" (33:14). Moses pushes for firmer commitment, saying, "If your presence will not go, do not carry us up from here" (33:15), to which God capitulates, citing Moses's favored status: "I will do the very thing that you have asked; for you have found favor in my sight, and I know you

---

of marriage in the verse positively to argue, "At the heart of Israel's relationship with YHWH lay a dialogue of love" (75). For a fuller treatment of this theme, see Levenson, *The Love of God: Divine Gift, Human Gratitude, and Mutual Faithfulness in Judaism* (Princeton: Princeton University Press, 2016).

14. Saul M. Olyan, *Friendship in the Hebrew Bible* (New Haven: Yale University Press, 2017), 5, 7.

by name" (33:17). Then, Moses risks his life and dares ask, "Show me your glory, I pray" (33:18).

To ask to see God's glory, that is, something of God's essence, and not only to know God's ways, we soon learn, is a matter of life and death. God informs Moses, "But you cannot see my face; for no one shall see me and live" (33:20). The request to see God's glory, therefore, indicates a willingness to die on the part of Moses. Furthermore, hidden in it is a plea for accommodation. Moses knows the mortal danger that God's holy presence poses for the people and for himself, but he has demanded and received assurance that God indeed will accompany the people. What is yet unknown is how this may be possible. And in asking to see God's glory, Moses at the same time asks God to demonstrate how the divine-human union between God and Israel might be achieved. And that is precisely what God provides. God says:

> [21] See, there is a place by me where you shall stand on the rock; [22] and while my glory passes by I will put you in a cleft of the rock, and I will cover you with my hand until I have passed by; [23] then I will take away my hand, and you shall see my back; but my face shall not be seen. (33:21–23)

In this brief and delicate interaction between the transcendent God and fragile humanity, we find demonstrated the solution to the problem sin poses to the desired union. It will be God who provides the accommodation by shielding and protecting the human during an encounter with the divine: "I will cover you with my hand."

The principle of divine accommodation receives fuller expression in God's remarkable self-definition that accompanies the self-revelation: "I will make all my goodness pass before you, and will proclaim before you the name, 'the LORD'; and I will be gracious to whom I will be gracious, and [I] will show mercy on whom I will show mercy" (33:19). The proclaimed name, YHWH, refers back to Exod. 3:13–16 when God first revealed the divine name to Moses. At that time, the revealed name was accompanied by a mysterious, to say the least, definition: "I AM WHO I AM" (3:14). It is a name and a definition that declares radical freedom and eschews any commitment to an ethic or morality. In contrast, in response to Moses's request to see God's ways and God's glory, God fills out the mystery with divine "goodness" and defines God's radical freedom as a freedom to be gracious and show mercy. The mysterious and enigmatic *idem per idem*, "I AM WHO I AM," is inflected with grace and mercy to become, "I will be gracious to whom I will be gracious, and I will show mercy on whom I will show mercy."

The LORD, the LORD, a God Merciful and Gracious

The first recipient of divine grace and mercy, doled out as a free act of God, is Moses. But the benefactors of the new mode of divine cohabitation with humanity will come to include all of Israel when God, in renewing the covenant with the people (Exodus 34), declares once again the name, YHWH, then provides a more expansive definition:

> ⁶ The LORD passed before him, and proclaimed,
> "The LORD, the LORD, a God merciful and gracious,
> slow to anger, and abounding in steadfast love and
>   faithfulness,
> ⁷ keeping steadfast love for the thousandth generation,
> forgiving iniquity and transgression and sin,
> yet by no means clearing the guilty,
> but visiting the iniquity of the parents upon the children
> and the children's children, to the third and fourth
>   generation." (34:6–7)

Within the confines of this chapter, we cannot fully analyze these verses, which some have called the theological heart of the Hebrew Bible and whose importance is attested by its repetition throughout the Hebrew Bible.[15] What we will focus on is the implication of the declaration for our understanding of God, sin, and suffering.

Perhaps the first thing to note is that God's self-definition includes the attribute of justice.[16] While just punishment for sin does not fully express

---

15. Num. 14:18; Neh. 9:17; Pss. 86:15; 103:8; 145:8; Jer. 32:18; Joel 2:13; Jonah 4:2; Nah. 1:3; cf. also 2 Chr. 30:9; Neh. 9:31; Pss. 111:4; 112:4; 116:5.

16. Nahum M. Sarna, *Exodus* (Philadelphia: Jewish Publication Society, 1991), 216.

who God is, justice remains a reality in the human-divine relationship. The emphasis, however, clearly falls on divine compassion and graciousness. Steadfast love, faithfulness, loyalty, and forgiveness define God's moral character and thus God's relationship with Israel, and it is God's compassion and graciousness that form the basis for the renewal of the covenant. The common misapprehension that the God of the Hebrew Bible is a God of law and justice, thus of punishment and wrath, is undone at God's full self-disclosure in these verses. Not only is Israel's obedience to covenant law predicated on a prior history of God's liberatory action on behalf of Israel, but the renewal and continuation of that relationship also rest on the character of God, which in these verses is revealed as fundamentally and predominantly defined by compassion and graciousness, steadfast love and faithfulness, loyalty and forgiveness.

That YHWH is compassionate and gracious does not transform the character of the people. They remain, as Moses acknowledges, "a stiff-necked people" (34:9). In order for YHWH to renew the covenant and "take [Israel] for [God's] inheritance," therefore, God must choose to "pardon [their] iniquity and [their] sin" quite apart from Israel's transformation (34:9). That is to say, as Moberly puts it, Israel's sinfulness "is the reason for Yahweh's mercy" and "brings about his mercy."[17] God chooses to be gracious to Israel, and God chooses to show mercy on Israel as an expression of divine freedom (33:19). And God's free choice to forgive "the stiff-necked people" is the one necessary and sufficient ground for the covenantal relationship.

The remaining question concerns the economy of divine forgiveness. The paradox of divine graciousness is that its cause, sin, is the very thing that also causes God's wrath and judgment.[18] And the golden calf episode has made it abundantly clear that the result of God's righteous anger is death and destruction. The theological problem that rises is what to do with the death and the destruction that sin produces when God forgives sin and exercises his self-declared freedom to be gracious to whom God will be gracious and to show mercy on whom God will show mercy (33:19). This is an issue that the Exodus text neither raises nor addresses. However, when we read this passage with the full Christian canon in view, then we

---

17. Moberly, *Mountain of God*, 89.
18. Moberly, *Mountain of God*, 89.

might wonder whether God absorbs the deathly fruit of sin when he graciously forgives sin without exacting punishment. In other words, God's self-definition as "a God merciful and gracious" may imply God's commitment to suffering the consequence of sin, which is in part death and destruction. This does not mean that God dies, but it is as close as perhaps is imaginable. For God to be gracious, forgiving iniquity and transgression and sin, God must suffer a great deal. And it is on the basis of this divine self-sacrificial grace that the covenantal relationship between God and Israel can be established and renewed.

Conclusion

Moses arguably risks death twice in Exodus 32–34. He first binds his fate with the sinful people, even should it mean punishment worse than death, in a bid to convince God to forgive the people's great sin. He again risks death in asking to be shown God's glory. God's self-revelation and self-definition that follow demonstrate *in nuce* the grace and mercy God must exhibit for it to be possible for the holy God to dwell among a stiff-necked people. God's self-definition as a "God merciful and gracious," in other words, forms the one necessary foundation for the renewed covenantal relationship between God and Israel. God's graciousness and compassion do not do away with the human responsibility to obey in grateful response to God (34:7), but they free the covenantal relationship from dependence on human righteousness. The people may continue to be stiff-necked, but God's freedom to forgive sin in gracious compassion becomes the sufficient foundation for the establishment and survival of the relationship. This also means that God decides to take on himself the deadly consequences of sin, whatever that might mean in fact for God.

CHAPTER 7

Queen Esther's Gambit

Give us grace, O God, to dare to do the deed which we know cries to be done. Let us not hesitate because of ease, or the words of men's mouths, or our own lives. Mighty causes are calling us—the freeing of women, the training of children, the putting down of hate and murder and poverty—all these and more. But they call with voices that mean work and sacrifices and death. Mercifully grant us, O God, the spirit of Esther, that we say: I will go unto the King and if I perish, I perish—Amen.

W. E. B. Du Bois[1]

ONE MORE FIGURE ARISES IN THE HEBREW BIBLE who, at the risk of her own life, saves the people of God: Esther. These three—Judah, Moses, and Esther—form the triumvirate of savior figures in the Hebrew Bible who save the entire people of God from different forms of utter destruction: Judah from devastating famine, Moses from divine wrath, and Esther from human hatred. There is no other who can join their rank; the three

---

I gratefully acknowledge the permission of the editors of the *Journal of Biblical Literature* to publish chapter 7, "Queen Esther's Gambit," which appeared in a slightly different form as "A House of Her Own: The Tactical Deployment of Strategy in Esther," *JBL* 140 (2021): 663–82.

1. W. E. B. Du Bois, *W. E. B. Du Bois and the Sociology of the Black Church and Religion, 1897–1914*, ed. Robert A. Wortham (New York: Lexington Books, 2018), 128. I thank Veronice Miles for bringing this prayer to my attention.

stand alone together: father of kings, prophet-priest-judge-legislator, and queen of a world empire.

Esther demonstrates her willingness to die for the sake of the people in entering King Ahasuerus's presence unbidden. On learning from Mordecai, her cousin and childhood guardian, of the mortal danger facing all Jews throughout the vast Persian empire, Esther asks Mordecai for neither encouragement nor advice, but commands him:

> Go, gather all the Jews to be found in Susa, and fast for me, and neither eat nor drink for three days, night and day. I also, with my maids, will likewise fast. Then I will go to the king, though it is against the law. And if I perish, I perish. (Esth. 4:16)

Her announced entrance into the king's inner court will be her gambit, an opening move with considerable risk. Should her tactic fail, that is, should she be put to death as law dictates (4:11), her elaborate strategy for deliverance would come to a premature and utter end. She does not fail, of course, and we can best appreciate Esther's brilliant heroism when we analyze her plan within the multilayered reality in which she lived. Esther fully recognizes her intersectional identity as a woman, a queen, and a Jew and devises a most appropriate combination of tactics and strategies to undo the murderous design of Haman and the foolishness of Ahasuerus to save her people.

Michel de Certeau's Strategies and Tactics

Before we analyze the social, political, and legal world of the book of Esther, which should be differentiated from the historical realities of the Persian empire,[2] and in preparation for the analysis of Esther's ingenious

---

2. Adele Berlin (*Esther* [Philadelphia: Jewish Publication Society, 2001], xxx) writes that "Esther's image of Persia is stereotypical" of the ways in which Greeks depicted the Persians. This observation allows us to date the book of Esther to between the late Persian and the early Greek periods, so between 400–200 BCE (p. xli). On the creative deployment of stereotypical depictions of the Persians in Esther, see Peter Machinist,

CHAPTER 7

maneuverings therein, it will be helpful to review Michel de Certeau's twin concepts of strategy and tactic.[3]

According to de Certeau, strategy requires the presence of three elements: a subject with power and will, a place over which the subject exercises power and will, and subjective others. Given these elements, a person can be said to be strategic if she manages her relation to others in and through the place over which she has power. Strategy thus has to do with establishing and maintaining control over space—in part as a means of managing irregularities that fluxes in time introduce. To give examples from Esther that I will examine in detail below, the physical barriers as well as the legal customs that bar those dressed in sackcloth from entering the palace (Esth. 4:2) and anyone from approaching the king uninvited (4:11) manage the people's access to the king, especially in times of crisis, by controlling movement in the spaces that surround the king. As we shall see, imperial power in Esther is in part made palpable as control over space and conforms to de Certeau's insight that strategy is "a triumph of place over time."[4]

In contrast to strategy, for which the vagaries of time are nuisances and threats, fluxes in time are essential to tactics because tactics has no place proper to itself. "The space of the tactic," de Certeau writes, "is the space of the other."[5] This means that those who resort to tactics are the dispossessed, the weak, and the dominated who have no place over which they exercise control and who therefore must take advantage of opportunities that irregularities in time open up in spaces not their own. For example, the employee in the company building, the colonized in their own homeland, and the female in a phallocentric society must take advantage of opportune changes that occur in spaces controlled by others to seize momentarily a desired good otherwise denied them, such as a nap, an opportunity to assemble, or a chance to lead. This means that to be tactical is to be opportunistic. As de Certeau puts it:

"Achaemenid Persia as Spectacle. Reactions from Two Peripheral Voices: Aeschylus, *The Persians* and the Biblical Book of Esther," in *Eretz-Israel* 30 (2018): 109–23.

3. See especially Michel de Certeau, *The Practice of Everyday Life*, trans. Steven Rendall (Berkeley: University of California Press, 1984).

4. De Certeau, *Everyday Life*, 36.

5. De Certeau, *Everyday Life*, 37.

because it does not have a place, a tactic depends on time—it is always on the watch for opportunities that must be seized 'on the wing' . . . it must constantly manipulate events in order to turn them into 'opportunities.' The weak must continually turn to their own ends forces alien to them.[6]

De Certeau's use of the word "manipulate" is important and points to a concept analyzed by James C. Scott under the phrase "weapons of the weak."[7] The charge that the relatively powerless are conniving, disingenuous, or tricksy reflects the ideology of the powerful, who would rather do without the nuisance. However, to manipulate, to be tactical, and to take advantage of fleeting opportunities are for the weak to exercise the limited power at their disposal.

To return to Esther, we shall see that Esther makes ingenious use of a combination of tactics and strategies that befit her intersectional and multilayered identity, first to win a momentary strategic advantage and then to transform her weaknesses into weapons to undo the enemy and save many lives.

The World of Esther and Esther in the World

Esther's subjective position, as it is represented in the book of Esther, is characterized by intersectionality, and Esther moves and has her being within three overlapping structures of power.[8] The first is the arena of gen-

---

6. De Certeau, *Everyday Life*, xix.
7. James Scott, *Weapons of the Weak: Everyday Forms of Peasant Resistance* (New Haven: Yale University Press, 1985).
8. On Esther's intersectional identity, see, e.g., Randall Bailey, "'That's Why They Didn't Call the Book Hadassah!': The Interse(ct)/(x)ionality of Race/Ethnicity, Gender, and Sexuality in the Book of Esther," in *They Were All Together in One Place: Toward Minority Biblical Criticism*, ed. Randall C. Bailey, Tat-siong Benny Liew, and Fernando F. Segovia, SemeiaSt 57 (Atlanta: Society of Biblical Literature, 2009), 227–50; Greg Goering, "Intersecting Identities and Persuasive Speech: The Cases of Judah and Esther," *BibInt* 23 (2015): 342–44; and Anne-Mareike Wetter, *"On Her Account": Reconfiguring Israel in Ruth, Esther, and Judith*, LHBOTS 623 (London: Bloomsbury, 2015), 97–155. For an overview of intersectionality in biblical studies, see Gale Yee,

der relations in which female autonomy is seen as threatening to male authority. The second is the realm of politics with the king at the center. And the third is the social world in which Jews face mortal danger. Interestingly, while Esther is dominated and disadvantaged in each of these categorical axes, her state of domination is not compounded by her intersectionality, as might be expected. Rather, we witness Esther "manipulate events in order to turn them into 'opportunities,'" which she seizes and turns into small advantages that she subsequently magnifies to her own ends.[9]

Gender

The book of Esther clearly calls attention to gender politics,[10] and we see the outlines of the gendered landscape take shape in the opening banquet scene of the book. On the seventh day of the extravagant feast, an inebriated King Ahasuerus commands seven eunuchs in his attendance "to bring Queen Vashti before the king, wearing the royal crown, in order to show the peoples and the officials her beauty; for she was fair to behold" (1:11).[11] Queen Vashti, host at her own banquet for female guests (1:9), refuses to abandon her post and to subject herself to objectification under the male gaze (1:12).[12] Her assertion of independence in refusing the king's command and her claim for the integrity of feminine space, circumscribed though it is by the masculine space of the king's banquet, triggers the farcical, but for all that deadly serious reactions of male actors, headed by the indecisive and buffoonish Ahasuerus. Laws are decreed that banish Vashti from King Ahasuerus's presence, ironically for refusing his audience (1:19),

---

"Thinking Intersectionally: Gender, Race, Class, and the Etceteras of Our Discipline," *JBL* 139 (2020): 7–26.

9. Kimberlé Crenshaw ("Demarginalizing the Intersection of Race and Sex: A Black Feminist Critique of Antidiscrimination Doctrine, Feminist Theory and Antiracist Politics," *University of Chicago Legal Forum* 1 [1989]: 148–49) notes that how you splice intersectional identities can have contrasting, seemingly contradictory, consequences in the court of law.

10. See, e.g., Michael Fox, *Character and Ideology in the Book of Esther*, 2nd ed. (Grand Rapids: Eerdmans, 2001), 205–11; Wetter, "Esther," 138–52.

11. On the role of the eunuchs, see Bailey, "'Interse(ct)/(x)ionality," 235–39.

12. Explanations and evaluations of Vashti's refusal are various. See Fox, *Esther*, 164–70.

and dictate nervously that "every man shall rule in his house and speak the language of his people (1:22).[13]

The opening scene introduces several themes that are important for our analysis. First, as Michael V. Fox and Jon D. Levenson have demonstrated, the theme of feasting that debuts here studs and structures the entire book, and the two central feasts that Queen Esther hosts (5:1–8; 7:1–9) mark the time and place of the major reversal of the book.[14] Second, we learn that the queen has a place proper to herself wherein she can host feasts. This (feminine) space exists within the king's house and is, therefore, vulnerable to penetrations by the king's (male) power: the king can send eunuchs to call the queen to him. Nevertheless, it is critical that the queen exercises control over a house of her own and can manage her relation to others through this space. Third, the theme of law and its relation to the king's (male) authority are introduced. The scene dramatizes the discovery of the fragility of male authority and the need to deploy imperial law as its necessary protector. Furthermore, the scene indicates that Ahasuerus has a tenuous relationship with the law, which will all but unravel toward the end of the book: himself ignorant of legal matters, Ahasuerus requires the consultation of legal scholars (1:13) and the skill of scribes to author the laws that he authorizes in name only (1:19–20). Fourth, the episode introduces the issue of multilingualism and the related issue of multiethnicity, filtered through the lens of gender politics. We learn, one, that language and so also ethnicity is a matter of male honor and, two, that a royal decree protects that honor.

Esther lives and has her being in this fraught landscape of gender relations. And while her relationships with male figures are not all of a piece, she is nevertheless always and everywhere dominated by some male figure. She is dominated by Mordecai her cousin and adopted guardian in her childhood (2:20), then by Hegai her male handler in adolescence (2:15),

---

13. On the continued importance of Vashti to the plot of Esther after her dismissal, see Timothy K. Beal, *The Book of Hiding: Gender, Ethnicity, Annihilation, and Esther* (London: Routledge, 1997).

14. Fox, *Esther*, 156–58; Jon D. Levenson, *Esther*, OTL (Louisville: Westminster John Knox, 1997), 5–6. For a different analysis of the book's structure, see Anthony Tomasino, "Interpreting Esther from the Inside Out: Hermeneutical Implications of the Chiastic Structure of the Book of Esther," *JBL* 138 (2019): 111.

and finally by Ahasuerus her husband and king in marriage. This does not mean that Esther has no agency or power over male figures.

Feminist scholars have objected that Esther appears to accept her domination without protest. Whereas Vashti refuses Ahasuerus's claim over her body and movement, Esther's coy submissiveness, it has been argued, makes her an anti-feminist hero whose rise comes at the cost of the erasure of Vashti, the true feminist hero.[15] Esther, far from challenging patriarchy, according to this view, "personif[ies] the reinstitution of patriarchal order."[16] Interpretations along this line, in my view, underappreciate Esther's heroism. And the not uncommon claim that Esther is passive, submits to the will of male authority, and acts as Mordecai's agent also misses the subtle and powerful ways in which Esther exercises agency. Let us examine, in this regard, the critical role favor/grace ($ḥēn$)[17] plays in Esther's rise to royalty.

The narrator repeatedly says that Esther "wins favor ($nāśa'$ $ḥēn$) in the eyes of all who see her" (2:15; cf. 2:9) and, pivotally, that she "won [Ahasuerus's] favor and devotion" above the other adolescent girls, with the result that she attains Vashti's throne (2:17). At first glance, the narrator appears to ascribe Esther's ability to win favor solely to her physical beauty. Esther is of "pleasant shape and beautiful appearance ($yəpat$-$tō'ar$ $wəṭôbat$ $mar'eh$)" (2:7)[18] and she undergoes a yearlong beautification (and reeducation) process (2:8–9, 12–14).[19] The narrator's emphasis on Esther's natural beauty (2:7) enhanced by the technology of cosmetics, diet, and accessorizing (2:9, 15) has led many readers to misattribute her ability to win favor to what turns out to be a red herring, the shimmering surface that obfuscates the hidden reality beneath.

But the narrator has left a trail of clues that leads to the real source of Esther's favor. The first clue is the difference between the standard Hebrew phrase for describing one's favored status in relation to another ($māṣa'$ $ḥēn$

---

15. Esther Fuchs, "Status and Role of Female Heroines in the Biblical Narrative," *Mankind Quarterly* 23 (1982): 156–57.

16. Fuchs, "Female Heroines," 158.

17. BDB, s.v. "חֵן."

18. Wetter ("Esther," 139) notes that the "portrayals of Rachel and Joseph are almost literally the same as that of Esther: both are described as יפת־תאר ויפת מראה."

19. Wetter, "Esther," 99–110.

beʿênê, "find favor in the eyes of")²⁰ and the one used by the narrator of Esther. Eschewing the standard passive expression, our narrator consistently uses the awkward but more active construction, *nāśaʾ ḥēn* (lit., "lift, carry favor"; 2:15, 17; 5:2).²¹ The active construction, which appears only in Esther and whose oddity draws attention to itself, suggests that Esther does not passively find favor but actively wins, herself pulls and lifts it out of others. That is, the phrase *nāśaʾ ḥēn* suggests that Esther, in some mysterious way, exercises agency to win favor from others and does not passively receive it on account of her outward beauty alone.²²

It is possible to interpret Esther's agency as sexual²³ and, as some have done, to condemn it on moral (because the [mis]use of one's sexuality is a moral evil) and ethical (because manipulation is ethically suspect) grounds.²⁴ But to so condemn Esther would be to fail to carry out a thorough analysis of gender and to miss the subtle language of grace that points to the (hidden) divine in the book.

Let us first turn to the issue of gender performance. Anne-Mareike Wetter, borrowing language from Judith Butler, says that Esther "engage[s] in gender performance" as the perfect "object of male desire" and that she does so as a "strategy of survival."²⁵ Esther is *being* feminine to avoid the fate of her predecessor but not, I would argue, to supplant her. Rather, Esther supplements (in the Derridean sense) Vashti's heroic but unsuccessful

---

20. BDB, s.v. "חֵן", "מָצָא," and "עַיִן."

21. Beal, *Book of Hiding*, 35–39. BDB, s.v. "נָשָׂא" and "חֵן."

22. For a general discussion of Esther's agency, see Fox, *Character and Ideology*, 199–202; Kevin McGeough, "Esther the Hero: Going beyond 'Wisdom' in Heroic Narratives," *CBQ* 70 (2008): 55–56; Sydnie White Crawford, "Esther: A Feminine Model for Jewish Diaspora," in *Gender and Difference in Ancient Israel*, ed. P. L. Day (Minneapolis: Fortress, 1989), 161–77.

23. For example, Bailey ("Interse(ct)/(x)ionality," 240) writes that Esther "*wattiśśā-ḥen*, she aroused (lit., she raised up favor in) him" and, in this way, "the narrator lets the reader know that Esther has 'unusual sexual abilities and process.'"

24. A feminist critique might underline that Esther conforms to patriarchal norms and desires for a woman. Fuchs ("Female Heroines," 159), for example, condemns Esther as a story "of female role models determined and fostered by the strongly developed patriarchal ideology so characteristic of the society in which they lived."

25. Wetter, "Esther," 141. See Judith Butler, *Gender Trouble: Feminism and the Subversion of Identity* (New York: Routledge, 1990).

resistance against patriarchy. Esther survives the gendered violence which Vashti exposed and to which she succumbed with the goal of dismantling it. Furthermore, as others have argued, Vashti does not in fact disappear from the book: Mordecai's struggle analogically mirrors Vashti's.[26] Vashti, while exscripted from the narrative, continues to shape the Esther story in a nontrivial manner.

Going further, Wetter argues that the book of Esther, far from reinstating patriarchy, works to undermine its authority by exposing the human origin of the rules that are supposed to govern gender relations. Note, in this regard, that it is claimed in the Vashti episode that Persian imperial laws are effective forever and everywhere. Memucan, one of the officials, declares that "a royal order," like all "the laws of the Persians and the Medes," "may not be altered" (1:19; cf. 8:8). And the specific law in question, that "every man should be master in his own house," is published in "all the royal provinces, to every province in its own script and to every people in its own language" (1:22). Imperials laws, in this view, are comparable to natural laws in their unalterable eternity and effective omnipresence; and the Persian king rivals, if not displaces, God as the maker of such laws.[27] However, in emphasizing precisely the human origin of these laws, the author of Esther undermines the claim for their eternity and omnipresence. Wetter, this time building on Pierre Bourdieu, insightfully writes:

> Irrevocable as Persian law may be, the fact that it is the king who decides that every man should rule in his household pulls this issue from the self-evident cosmic ordering of things into the arbitrariness of human affairs.... [M]ale power over women ... is now recognized as an arbitrary human ordinance ... [and] unmasked as an accident of history rather than a divinely decreed cosmic order.[28]

26. Beal, *Book of Hiding*, 50–59.

27. The authors of Esther critique Persian (possibly also Hellenistic) self-presentation as law makers, not unlike the Danielic authors. On Daniel as resistance literature, see Anathea Portier-Young, *Apocalypse against Empire: Theologies of Resistance in Early Judaism* (Grand Rapids: Eerdmans, 2011), esp. 245–46.

28. Wetter, "Esther," 141, 142, citing Pierre Bourdieu, *Sociology in Question*, trans. Richard Nice (London: Sage, 1993), 25.

In summary, an Esther who plays by the rules and performs her gender does so as a survival tactic; and the author of Esther who unmasks gender rules as established by human and, to wit, buffoonish authorities brings to light the fact that such rules, contrary to the claims of the king and his male advisors, are neither eternal nor omnipresent. Ahasuerus may not be able to revoke laws published in his name (8:8) and the rules may be published everywhere for everyone (1:20), but the claim to both eternality and omnipresence proves false. In fact, the prestige of Persian law, tied as it is to Ahasuerus, is satirized throughout the book until, by the end of the story, it is emptied of all substance. As we shall see, Esther, with Mordecai, siphons off the core, if there ever was anything inside, and leaves behind only the shell of the Persian court. Esther performs her gender in accordance with the established rules, while at the same time dismantling the authority behind the rules in cooperation with the narrator.

Let us turn next to the issue of grace and divine presence in relation to Esther's agency. It is helpful, at this stage, to recall the well-established intertextual connections between the Esther story and the Joseph story.[29] Without repeating all the observations of others, we note that Joseph, like Esther, finds favor in the eyes of others. Joseph is loved by a father figure, Jacob (Gen. 37:3), as Esther apparently is by Mordecai. And like Esther, Joseph is physically beautiful, of "pleasant shape and pleasant appearance" (39:6; cf. Esth. 2:7), and attracts sexual attention (Gen. 39:7–12). More to the point, it is said repeatedly that Joseph "finds favor (מצא חן)" in the eyes of his superiors (39:4) or that he is "given favor (נתן חן)"[30] by superiors (39:21), ultimately winning even Pharaoh's favor and trust (41:37–43), just as Esther wins the favor of Hegai and the favor and devotion of Ahasuerus.

There is, however, an important difference between Joseph and Esther. Whereas God is named both by the narrator (Gen. 39:2–3, 21) and the characters (41:38–39, 51–52) as the power behind Joseph's favor and thus his rise in the Egyptian court, God is famously not mentioned anywhere

---

29. Fox, *Esther*, 76–77; Levenson, *Esther*, 21, 54–55; and Goering, "Intersecting Identities," 346–47n19.

30. BDB, s.v. "נָתַן."

CHAPTER 7

in the book of Esther.[31] Indeed, how Esther has "obtained royalty at such a time" (Esth. 4:14) is left shrouded in the mysterious language of grace. This difference between the two stories invites interpretation. On the one hand, the refusal to inscribe God in the text on the part of the author of Esther, coupled with the emphasis on Esther's own active role in winning favor, may signify a cynical denial of the need for God or, more strongly, God's agency in the world: "God may have been active then, in the time of Joseph, but is no longer; and we don't need God anyway. We can save ourselves!" may be the hidden message. On the other, and I think this is more likely, the intertextual relation to the Joseph story serves as a signifier to the hidden signified.[32] That is to say, the refusal to give God the definiteness of inscription leaves room for doubt; at the same time, the intertextual allusions to the Joseph story where God is clearly active, along with other narrative clues, pushes the reader to look for signs of divine presence and activity behind and beyond the written words of the Esther story and the visible events of history.[33] It teaches the practice of what Fox aptly calls faith:

> The author of Esther wishes us to hold to faith even when lacking certitude and an understanding of details. To act in such circumstances demands special courage, but the demand is not a rare one. Many people are called upon to act on a faith that is hope more than conviction.
>
> When we scrutinize the text of Esther for traces of God's activity, we are doing what the author made us do . . . He is teaching a theology of possibility. The willingness to face history with an openness to the possibility of providence—even when history seems to weigh against

---

31. Two different versions of the book of Esther are in circulation. The Hebrew Masoretic Text (MT) preserves the version familiar to Jews and Protestant Christians; and the Greek Septuagint (LXX) preserves the text familiar to the Eastern Orthodox and Roman Catholics. The MT of Esther contains no explicit mention of God. In contrast, the LXX, which contains six passages with no parallel in the MT, explicitly mentions God. For a fuller discussion of the versions of Esther, see Levenson, *Esther*, 27–34.

32. See Gabriel F. Hornung, "The Theological Import of MT Esther's Relationship to the Joseph Story," *CBQ* 82 (2020): 567–81.

33. For other narrative clues that point to the hidden divine, see Fox, *Esther*, 240–44.

its likelihood, as it did in the dark days after the issuance of Haman's decree—this is a stance of profound faith.[34]

To summarize, Esther's ability to win favor, despite the narrative misdirection, should not be ascribed solely to her physical beauty, enhanced by cosmetic technique. Esther's favor has something to do with the exercise of her own agency, as the odd locution *nāśaʾ ḥēn* indicates. And it also has something to do with the hidden "logic in history beyond natural causality," what Mordecai obliquely refers to as "deliverance ... from a different place" and what we might more bluntly call God (4:14).[35] To put the matter in the order of descending importance, Esther is able to win favor from others because God favors her and because she knows how to exercise her power over others, which is partly derived from natural endowment and human technology. In short, Esther does not receive but wins—herself pulls and lifts out—the king's love and devotion and, as a consequence, obtains the exalted station of queen.

Politics

That Esther becomes queen brings us to the realm of politics and to the heart of our analysis of space. The spatial organization of power and power relations in the book of Esther comes into clear view in chapter 4. The king occupies the center of the power structure, for it is his name and his ring that authorize laws, the primary way in which power is made manifest in the book; and surrounding the king are two concentric circles that control access to the king.

The outer circle coincides with the palace gate and the fortification around the palace. It comes into view soon after Haman's decree "to destroy and kill and annihilate all Jews" (3:13). Upon learning about the decree, Mordecai puts on sackcloth and presents himself in front of the palace gate (4:1–2). We learn subsequently that Jews throughout the empire likewise engage in "a great mourning ... with fasting and weeping and lamenting" and put on sackcloth (4:3). Mordecai, in whom the lamenting

34. Fox, *Esther*, 247.
35. Fox, *Esther*, 246.

CHAPTER 7

Jews are symbolically present at the king's gate, does not enter the palace to plead with the king. What bars Mordecai from entering the palace, more than the physical barrier or the spear of the gatekeepers, is the legal custom that forbids anyone "clothed with sackcloth" from entering the king's gate (4:2). The legal custom does not explicitly address issues of ethnicity or justice; it prescribes proper dress for an audience with the king. Nevertheless, it has the (un)intended effect of denying access to those who need access to power in times of crisis, in this case the mourning Jews under threat of total annihilation.

The second, inner circle around the king is internal to the palace and coincides with the wall that surrounds the inner court where the king sits enthroned. Esther's response to Mordecai's command that she "go to the king to plead with him and to entreat before him concerning her people" (4:8) makes the second boundary visible to the readers. She responds:

> All the servants of the king and the people of the provinces of the king know that if any man or woman who approaches the king in the inner court without being called, there is one law for him: to be put to death. Only if the king extends to him the golden staff may he live. (4:11)

Esther's response has been interpreted negatively by some as cowardly and, therefore, as marking her belated decision to venture into the inner court as motivated more by Mordecai's prodding than by her own volition. She is, as Fuchs argues, "the obedient agent of Mordecai."[36]

I disagree with this assessment for two reasons. First, Esther's response fulfills the primary narrative role of relaying vital information to the reader. Esther states that everyone in the kingdom, both inside and outside the palace, knows the mortal danger of entering the king's presence unbidden. This means that the information being relayed is not actually intended for anyone in the world of the story, including Mordecai, but for the readers who need to be brought up to speed. Second, Esther's response does not so much contrast "Esther's trepidity at breaking court etiquette" and "Mordecai's temerity" as it juxtaposes her knowledge of the mortal danger of entering the king's presence unbidden and the bravery of her resolving to do

---

36. Fuchs, "Female Heroines," 153.

so anyway.[37] Furthermore, Esther's temerity in deciding to go to the king puts Mordecai's trepidation in relief, not the other way around. For Mordecai could have doffed his sackcloth, entered the palace, and presented himself before the king unbidden just as easily as Esther eventually does. If Mordecai wishes Esther to plead with the king, it is because he recognizes that she is better positioned for the task, not because she alone has access to the king. He also has access, if only he is willing to play *with/in* the rules. And Esther decides to go, not because she is shamed into doing so by Mordecai, but because she has a masterful plan. Esther enters the inner court to confront Ahasuerus with a plan of her own devising, not Mordecai's, and asks only that Mordecai and the Jews "hold a fast on [her] behalf" (4:16).

To summarize, the picture of the political power structure that emerges in the book of Esther and which Esther must navigate is a circular labyrinth. The king sits at the center, and two concentric barriers control access to the king: the palace wall and the walls of the king's inner court. Guarding the points of entry are physical barriers bolstered by the social technology of law and custom. Within this labyrinth, Queen Esther occupies an in-between space, neither in the inner court with the king nor outside the palace walls with Mordecai; she has a house of her own within the king's house. And deliverance for the Jews will look something like transgressive border crossings and the emptying out of the center.

Ethnicity

The third matrix of power relations that comprises Esther's intersectional identity is ethnicity.[38] Two issues remain to be discussed under this heading: the relationship between knowledge and power and the relationship between authority and authorship.

The central conflict that animates the drama of Esther is set in motion by enmity between two men, "Haman son of Hammedatha the Agagite" (3:1) and "Mordecai son of Jair son of Shimei son of Kish, a Benjamite" (2:5). These two men reprise, as their genealogies indicate, the distant memory

---

37. Fuchs, "Female Heroines," 153.

38. For other aspects of Esther's intersectionality, see Bailey, "Interse(ct)/(x)ionality."

CHAPTER 7

of the Benjamite King Saul's failure to annihilate Agag King of Amalek (1 Samuel 15) and the more distant memory of the ancient enmity between Israel and Amalek (Exod. 17:8–16; 1 Sam. 15:2).[39] The conflict internal to the book of Esther begins with Ahasuerus's unexplained promotion of Haman to a position "above all the officials who were with him" (Esth. 3:1) and the accompanying decree that "all the king's servants who [are] at the king's gate [bow] down and [do] obeisance to Haman" (3:2). Mordecai, however, refuses to honor Haman. While the only explicit and somewhat puzzling explanation for Mordecai's refusal is that he is a Jew (3:4), the possible reasons are multiple and include religious and ethnic considerations.[40] Whatever Mordecai's reasons, Haman's response to the slight is an outsized determination "to destroy all the Jews, the people of Mordecai, throughout the whole kingdom of Ahasuerus" (3:6). Toward this goal, Haman corrupts Ahasuerus with bribery and falsehoods against "a certain people" (3:8, 11); and Ahasuerus, without knowing the target of Haman's destructive wish, "[takes] his signet ring from his hand and [gives] it to Haman son of Hammedatha the Agagite, the enemy of the Jews" (3:10). Then, Haman authors a royal decree and authorizes it "in the name of King Ahasuerus and [seals it] with the king's ring" (3:12). The decree gives "orders to destroy, to kill, and to annihilate all Jews, young and old, women and children, in one day, the thirteenth day of the twelfth month, which is the month of Adar, and to plunder their goods" (3:13).

The first thing to note is that, as a Jew living in the Persian empire after Haman's genocidal decree, Esther is potentially dominated by all non-Jews. Mordecai reminds her, "Do not think that in the king's palace you will escape any more than all the other Jews . . . [Y]ou and your father's family will perish" (4:13, 14). That is, Esther's royalty cannot provide protection from the violent hatred against Jews that Haman's decree has unleashed.

---

39. See Fox, *Esther*, 28–29, 42; Levenson, *Esther*, 56–57; Beal, *Book of Hiding*, 33, 53–54, 58; and Machinist, "Spectacle," 116–17.

40. The religious conflict may be encoded in Mordecai's refusal to "bow down or do obeisance (יכרע וישתחוה)." Machinist ("Spectacle," 116) explains, "it would appear that the verbs otherwise used in the Bible for bowing—*hištaḥăweh* or *nāpal*, each alone, or the combinations *nāqad wə-hištaḥăweh* or *hištaḥăweh wə-nāšaq*—can indicate bowing down out of respect but *hištaḥăweh* with *kāraʿ* carries a sense of worship. Levenson and Ego note as well that *kāraʿ* alone almost always applies to bowing before God."

Queen Esther's Gambit

There is a crucial difference, however, between Esther and other Jews. The possibility that Esther might escape, to which Mordecai alludes, rests on the fact that, in obedience to Mordecai, Esther did not reveal "her people or her kindred" (2:10; cf. 2:20). By withholding knowledge of her Jewishness, Esther withholds from her would-be enemies not only knowledge but also power, for they cannot attack whom they do not know to be a Jew. Furthermore, Esther more than withholds power from others; she holds on to power. That her Jewishness is hidden gives her control over if, when, and how she reveals that knowledge. As we shall see, Esther transforms her Jewishness, which Haman's decree has made a social vulnerability, into a devastating weapon by its tactical revelation from a position of strategic strength. That is, Esther deploys the knowledge of her Jewishness as a form of offensive power.[41]

The need to attribute the genocidal decree to both Haman and Ahasuerus brings us to the second issue, namely the relationship between authorship and authority. Power, in the book of Esther, predominantly takes the form of law. The royal decrees in particular are represented as eternally valid (since they cannot be revoked) and in force everywhere (they are published). What requires further analysis is the precise nature of the king's relationship to the laws his name and seal authorize.

First, authoring and authorizing laws are distinct and separate events to which the king enjoys only a tenuous relationship. As concerns authorship, the king not once authors the laws in Esther. Memucan (1:16–22), Haman (3:8–15), Mordecai (8:7–10), and Esther (9:13) are the actual authors of laws, never the king. It is only once a law has been authored that the king authorizes the law. That is, the author of Esther inserts a space between the king and the royal decrees that bear his name. While the laws make the king's power manifest, they are not manifestations necessarily of his will.

---

41. See Michel Foucault, *The History of Sexuality*, in *The Critical Tradition: Classic Texts and Contemporary Trends*, 3rd ed., ed. David H. Richter (Boston: Bedford, 2007), 1627–36. Foucault (*History of Sexuality*, 1632, emphasis added) writes concerning silence, "Discourse transmits and produces power; it reinforces it, but also undermines and exposes it, renders it fragile and makes it possible to thwart it. In like manner, silence and secrecy are a shelter for power, anchoring its prohibitions; *but they also loosen its holds and provide for relatively obscure areas of tolerance.*"

Furthermore, the king does not fully control the process of authorizing laws. The issue is not only that Ahasuerus is liable to corruption (3:7–11). Ahasuerus's authority, embodied symbolically and metonymically in his name and his seal, is transferable to others and thus can be stolen from him. For example, we are told that Ahasuerus "took his signet ring from his hand and gave it to Haman," who is then permitted "to do with [the certain people] as it seems good to [Haman]" (3:10, 11). Because the power to authorize laws is not coterminous with the person of the king but is metonymically invested in his name and signet ring, it is not actually the king but whoever possesses the king's name and ring that has the power to authorize laws. In short, the king neither authors nor truly authorizes the laws that bear his name. To look forward to our analysis below, the king's non-identity with the laws sealed and published in his name comes to comic, and tragic, relief when Ahasuerus does not realize that he has authorized the killing of his queen and her people and asks, "Who is he, and where is he, who has presumed to do this?" (7:5). The answer given in the story is, "A foe and enemy, this wicked Haman!" (7:6). The hidden, ironic answer is, "You, O king, are the man."

To summarize, Esther is dominated as to gender, political power, and ethnicity. However, as we shall see shortly, she creates fissures within the overlapping and entangled systems of domination and exploits them to turn the table, quite literally, against the enemy of "her kindred and her people": Haman, of course, but also Ahasuerus and the gender, political, and social structures of her world.

The Tactical Deployment of Strategy

Esther's Tactics in the House of the King

Esther begins to implement her plan, whose brilliance shines all the more brightly when seen through the lens of de Certeau's concepts of strategy and tactics, soon after she reminds Mordecai (and informs the reader) that, "if any man or woman approaches the king in the inner court without being called, there is one law for him: to be put to death." The "one law" teaches us that power resides at the center of the political structure behind trap doors. It also teaches us that there is a way to break in: One can at any point open the gate into the interior from the outside, from a place of weakness into the seat of power, and transgress the boundary, if one is willing to risk death. That is, one must be willing to die possibly to access power that can give life.

And that, to be willing to die, is precisely the resolve with which Esther decides "to go to the king to plead with him and to entreat him concerning her people" (4:8). In a moment of generational reversal when a child grows larger than the parent, Esther commands Mordecai:

> Go, gather all the Jews to be found in Susa, and fast for me, and neither eat nor drink for three days, night and day. I also, with my maids, will likewise fast. Then I will go to the king, though it is against the law. And if I perish, I perish. (4:16)

With those famous words, rife with intertextual significance (cf. Gen. 43:14), Esther enters the king's presence, a place fraught with danger for anyone who appears unbidden. Esther does not wait for an opportune moment to enter, no such opportunity having presented itself over the past thirty days (Esth. 4:11). Rather, she decides to create her own opportunity, even if it should cost her life, and transgresses the boundary into the seat of power. It is the crux of the entire story when the fate of the Jewish people, thus far marked for death, begins to rise.

What happens once Esther opens the door into the inner court appears to be the king extending mercy to Esther. Esther is, after all, in a space not her own and one ostensibly controlled absolutely by the absolute monarch. However, those with ears to hear will recognize in the oddity of the phrase, "she won favor" (*nāśa' ḥēn*), Esther's near magical agency and power over others and even the mysterious presence of God: "When the king saw Esther the Queen standing in the court, she won favor in his eyes, and the king extended the golden staff that was in his hand to Esther" (5:2). The golden staff is in the king's hand, but it would not be a mistake to say that it is Esther who lifts up (*nāśa'*) his arm. With extreme subtlety and art, the author of Esther denies the king even the small privilege of showing favor to his queen. Ahasuerus does not give favor; Esther wins it, lifts and pulls it out of the king. And it is Esther who exercises control in the scene, however subtly, with God's help, be it invisible.

CHAPTER 7

Having created an opportunity to address the king at great personal risk, Esther must find some way to turn this small, personal favor into grace that can protect all the Jews of the vast empire from death. She begins to do this by first transforming the tactical opportunity into a strategic advantage, wherefrom she can execute her redemptive plan. That is, she finds a way to seize control over a space in and through which she can manage her relations with both the king, the symbolic source of all authority, and Haman, the enemy of the Jews.

To this end, once the king extends the golden staff, Esther approaches the king and touches his scepter. The king says, "What is it, Queen Esther? What is your request? Up to half of the kingdom will be given you" (5:3). Esther wisely ignores the king's initial offer as rhetorical hyperbole. Instead, she uses the opportunity to change the scene of their interaction and invites the king and Haman to a banquet, which she will prepare in her own house, the same space where Vashti had hosted a feast for her female guests (1:9).[42] To be sure, her house is a space within the king's house; but it is critically a space she can organize according to her plan.

Esther's Strategy in a House of Her Own

Esther's invitation to a feast likely struck the king as inconsequential. This explains why he asks the queen again to state her (real) request during the first feast (5:6; see also 7:2). However, from Esther's perspective, the request to host a feast for the king and Haman is neither a squandered opportunity nor a delay tactic. It is a tactical deployment of her momentary access to power to redefine and manipulate the power relations among the king, Haman, and herself in and through a space over which she exercises control. That is, she transforms a tactical opportunity into a strategic advantage.

In this regard, we should remember that a feast requires the (re)organization of space for an event of political, judicial, and religious significance, to be distinguished from a daily meal, however elaborate. A feast is, in a sense, a diplomat's battlefield where the host (re)organizes structures of power and not infrequently issues judgment around a table.[43] On the one

---

42. Note the ironic reversals.
43. Nathan MacDonald, *Not Bread Alone: The Uses of Food in the Old Testament* (Oxford: Oxford University Press, 2008); Janling Fu and Peter Altmann, "Feasting:

hand, you invite allies and potential allies and assign them seats of honor befitting their relative status in the political world (re)drawn around a dining table as a means of maintaining as well as disrupting the status quo. On the other, you invite enemies and potential enemies to judge and to execute judgment on them in demonstration of power and authority.[44] At a feast, you strengthen bonds of fealty and sever the heads of enemies.

Given the political significance of feasts, it is no surprise that Haman leaves the first of the two feasts Esther prepares for him and the king "happy and delighted" (5:9). Ever hungry for honor, Haman interprets the fact that the queen has invited him to join the king twice as evidence of prestige even above what he already enjoys (5:11–12). Haman begins to believe that he stands not only above all the other officials and ministers of the king but also on equal footing with the king. His boast to his wife and friends is telling: "Did not even Queen Esther welcome none but me *with the king* to the feast that she prepared? And tomorrow also I am invited by her *with the king*" (5:12, emphasis added). Haman does not realize that, since a feast is equally a place of honor and a place of judgment, he occupies a particularly ambiguous seat at the table as neither the host nor the king. Blinded by hatred and self-interest, he fails to consider that the seat that Esther has prepared for him at the table may be equally a seat of judgment as it is one of honor.

The Tactical Weaponization of Strategic Weaknesses

Having successfully moved the scene from the king's inner court to a house of her own, Esther begins to execute her plan to save her people at the extraordinary second feast.

The second feast is part farce and part tragedy in which Esther weaponizes her strategic weaknesses of being an ethnic minority and female against

---

Backgrounds, Theoretical Perspectives, and Introductions," in *Feasting in the Archaeology and Texts of the Bible and the Ancient Near East*, ed. Peter Altmann and Janling Fu (Winona Lake: Eisenbrauns, 2014), 1–31.

44. On the theme of judgment within a feasting context, see MacDonald, *Not Bread Alone*, 166–95, and Paul K.-K. Cho and Janling Fu, "Death and Feasting in the Isaiah Apocalypse (Isaiah 25:6–8)," in *Intertextuality and Formation of Isaiah 24–27*, ed. Todd Hibbard and Paul Kim, SBLAIL 17 (Atlanta: Society of Biblical Literature, 2013), 139–42, esp. footnote 43.

CHAPTER 7

Haman.[45] The beginning is a virtual repetition of the first feast up to the moment the king asks Esther to state her "request" and "petition." In response, Esther begins, "If I have found favor in your eyes, O king" (7:3a). Esther does not say that she "won" (*nāśa'*) the king's favor but uses the unmarked phrase, "to find favor (*māṣa' ḥēn*) in your eyes," as if to flatter the king with agency he does not quite possess. In any case, with her opening statement, Esther underlines what she has already confirmed twice by asking to host a feast for the king, that she has the king's favor. And more than courtly rhetoric, the reminder of her favored status sets up the following request, which is rife with dramatic irony.[46] She continues, "if it seems good to the king, let my life be given to me as my request" (7:3bα). "If it seems good to the king"! We can almost hear the king shout with flabbergasted and ignorant shock, "You have my devotion and favor. Of course, you may have your life!"

Esther's next move is critical. In a bold act of metonymic transfer, Esther transforms the personal favor she won from the king into a shield for all Jews. To "let my life be given to me as my request," she adds, "and my people as my petition" (7:3b). With this entreaty, Esther begins to deploy her closely guarded secret, that she is a Jew whose annihilation the king has authorized, as power. Her first move is to use her power to shield all Jews. By binding her fate with that of her people, "my life" to "my people," she forces the king to save the whole if he means to save the part, to save all Jews if he wants to save his queen.

Next, having taken the people under her wings, Esther turns the shield of favor into a sword of revenge. She says, "For we have been sold, I and my people, to be destroyed, to be killed, and to be annihilated" (7:4a). Ever the dimwit, the king does not immediately recognize that Esther has drawn the sword and is pointing it at Haman and asks for clarification: "Who is he, and where is he, who has presumed to do this?" (7:5). Then, Esther thrusts the sword at Haman's neck: "The foe and enemy. This wicked Haman" (7:6a). She beats a strategic disadvantage, that she is a Jew, into a weapon by its tactical revelation at an opportune time. That is, she deploys the knowledge of her Jewishness in the form of offensive power. Haman's response is appropriately one of terror: "Haman was terrified before the king and the queen" (7:6).

---

45. On the genre of Esther, see Berlin, *Esther*, xvi–xxxvi; Fox, *Esther*, 141–52.
46. Goering, "Intersecting Identities," 358.

In addition to her ethnicity, Esther also weaponizes her gender. After the revelation that Haman, in pursuing to annihilate all Jews, had marked Queen Esther for death, King Ahasuerus inexplicably leaves the feast, leaving his wife alone with her mortal enemy (7:7). Then, Haman makes a tactical mistake. Esther—host, queen, and master of the house—places herself on her bed, and Haman approaches, then falls on the bed in an attempt to plead for his life. When the king returns, whatever Haman's intentions, what the king sees is Haman on the queen's bed in her and, importantly, also his house. As one scholar dismissively put it, this "pivotal moment occurs within the framework of a bedroom scene."[47] What Esther's detractors miss, however, is that this is "a bedroom scene" as staged, cast, and directed by the queen. Whatever gender role she performs (for her survival and the deliverance of her people) and whatever gender role she has Ahasuerus perform (as the titular master of the house), the scene is an example of Esther managing her relation to others in and through the place over which she wields control. She performs the role of vulnerable wife, casts Haman in the role of the sexual aggressor, and directs Ahasuerus to play the role of the protective husband. Thus, as if on cue, the king (mis)reads the situation as Esther has scripted it and says, "Will he even ravish the queen with me in the house?" (7:8aβ). Esther has made Haman appear to threaten the king's own decree that "every man should be master in his own house" (1:22). The consequence is swift and exactly what Esther had strategized to bring about: Haman's death.

> And Horbana, one of the eunuchs who serve the king, said, "Look, the stake which Haman made for Mordecai, who spoke to the king's benefit, stands in the house of Haman, fifty cubits high." And the king said, "Hang him on it." And they hung Haman on the stake, which he prepared for Mordecai. And the anger of the king abated. (7:9–10)

Through a combination of tactics and strategies, Esther transforms her disadvantage as a woman into power. She performs her gender to transform Haman into a rival of her husband and thereby manipulates her husband to execute the enemy of the Jews. She pits phallocentric power against itself and turns to her own ends forces alien to her.

---

47. Fuchs, "Female Heroines," 155.

To summarize, Esther hosts two feasts in her own house to take hold of a momentary strategic advantage over her enemies. Then, in acts of reversal (in a book of reversals), she weaponizes presumed weaknesses and liabilities to judge, condemn, and execute her enemy. Honor and judgment are equally parts of a feast, and Haman came to the table and presumed to sit at the seat of honor. To his unfortunate surprise, Esther turns the table and seats Haman in the dock, then executes him.

So Haman dies, and "the anger of the king abated."

The Theft

Haman is dead. But who died? That is, did Ahasuerus kill Haman because he planned to murder Esther and her people or because Haman appeared to ravish his wife?

In a real sense, both the enemy of the Jews and the king's sexual rival died. Nevertheless, it is important to note that the proximate reason that Ahasuerus kills Haman is that he appeared to Ahasuerus to be a sexual rival, not because he legislated the killing of Jews, whatever Ahasuerus says in 8:7 notwithstanding. That is why the king's anger can subside when Haman dies, even though Esther's life and the lives of Jews remain under threat. Hatred, it turns out, is not only a matter of personal animus but can be encoded in the political and legal systems that organize social relations. Haman the Agagite may be dead, but his murderous decree lives on to empower untold numbers to destroy, to kill, and to annihilate all Jews. Thus, Haman's death does not ensure redemption for Jews, and the solution to the problem of prejudicial hatred must be sought at the legal, political, and social levels, well beyond the personal relationships among individuals.

To that end, sometime after the second feast, Esther again opens the door into the inner court of the king unbidden; and, again, Ahasuerus holds out the golden scepter (8:4). That the scene advances quickly, almost as a matter of fact, should not blind us to the fact that death still lurks behind the door. In entering the inner court, Esther again risks her life and demonstrates her willingness to die for the sake of her people. The unremarkable statement, "The king held out the golden scepter to Esther" (8:4), underlines not the nonexistence of danger but the triviality of violence in empire. Had the king not raised his scepter, the result would have been a swift and altogether lawful execution for Esther.

Once in the king's presence, Esther asks that Ahasuerus revoke Haman's decree. However, the king responds that "an edict written in the name of the king and sealed with the king's ring cannot be revoked" (8:8b). This statement deserves closer analysis. Ahasuerus repeats the propaganda that decrees written in his name and sealed by his ring enjoy eternal authority. We discussed above that the king himself authors no laws and that others can seal laws with his ring. Furthermore, with the declaration that he cannot revoke his own decrees, Ahasuerus confirms that he enjoys no actual power over laws once they are unleashed into the world. He has neither the ability to give birth to laws nor to kill them.

The king's admission of his powerlessness to revoke royal decrees (ironically stated as a consequence of his powerfulness) creates an existential conundrum for Esther and her people. The solution, the king himself suggests, is to write counter-decrees, and the king authorizes Esther and Mordecai to "write as you please with regard to the Jews, in the name of the king, and seal it with the king's ring" (8:8; cf. 3:11). We should recall that the king had already given his signet ring to Mordecai (8:2; cf. 3:10). Ahasuerus now also hands over the authority of his name (cf. 3:11–12). The result is that what Haman once possessed by bribery (3:10), Esther and Mordecai together possess as a gift from the king. Thus, when Esther and Mordecai walk out of the king's inner court, they walk out with the ability and the authority to publish laws and leave behind a room emptied of all actual power. They rob the king, with the king's blessing.

As we come to a conclusion, let us summarize what we have learned about the relationship between King Ahasuerus and laws.

1. The king is not versed in matters of law and relies on legal experts (1:13).
2. The king does not author laws (1:16–22; 3:8–15; 8:7–10; 9:13).
3. The king can and habitually authorizes others to write laws in his name (3:11–12; 8:8).
4. The king can and habitually gives his signet ring to others (3:10; 8:2).
5. The king cannot alter or revoke published laws (8:8).

The overall picture is of a king who has no actual connection with the law and who exercises no actual authority over laws; and what we have are laws that, far from expressing the will of the king, reflect a decentralized matrix of competing interests.

If the spatial analysis above found that the king occupies the center within a series of concentric rings, we have also discovered that power does not actually reside at the center with the king but elsewhere with whoever has stolen the king's name and ring. What is at the center is a guarded secret: the myth of an all-powerful king whose laws are eternally valid everywhere. The book of Esther uncovers this myth but does not dismantle it. Within the world of the story, the myth is left hidden because the myth is useful to the work of saving Jews under threat of annihilation. Esther and Mordecai tactically employ the myth, which is constitutive of the spatial strategy of empire, to resolve the acute crisis at hand. This should not be taken as the author's capitulation to imperial claims to legitimacy, no more than the fact that Esther performs her gender should be taken as a reinstitution of patriarchal ideology. For the book of Esther, in the world outside the story, exposes and ridicules the empty center of Persian imperial power, caricatured in Ahasuerus, and the fiction of male dominance encoded in the laws of the empire. The emperor really has no clothes.

Willingness to Die in Esther

Esther risks her life twice. She first risks death to initiate her plan to kill Haman, the enemy of the Jews who decreed the mass murder of her people (5:1), then a second time to counter the genocidal decree (8:3). In short, it is because she is willing to die that Esther can lead her people through threatened death to life, to be defended and celebrated during the feast of Purim. Moreover, the tactical and strategic importance of Esther's willingness to die receives thematic and structural emphasis in the book.

Eminent biblical scholar Jon D. Levenson argues concerning the date on which Esther first approaches the king unbidden: "If Esther's intercession occurs immediately at the conclusion of the three-day fast (4:16), and if the fast immediately followed the issuance of the genocidal decree on the thirteenth of the first month (3:12), then she approaches Ahasuerus during Passover (Lev. 23:5–6)—a most auspicious date for the Jews."[48] In

---

48. Levenson, *Esther*, 89.

this regard, Levenson notes that just as God "had disposed the Egyptians favorably (*ḥēn*) toward the people" of Israel during the time of the Passover (Exod. 12:36), so Esther wins Ahasuerus's favor on the fateful day (Esth. 5:2).

Additional support for the centrality of Esther's willingness to die comes from a structural analysis of the book. Scholars have long appreciated the structural artistry of the book of Esther, noting its impressive chiasm and especially the way scenes of feasting punctuate the book.[49] In a recent article, Anthony Tomasino argues that a shortcoming with earlier reconstructions is that they typically locate the turning point of the structure in chapter 6.[50] He argues that "[t]he 'hinge' of the chiasmus should possess true *cruciality*, being essential to the narrative or thematic development of the text," and that Esther 6, in which Haman is made to honor Mordecai, does not. He makes an alternate proposal in which Esther 5:1–8 is the pivot:

A Introduction: The glory of Xerxes (1:1–2)
  B The two feasts of the king; Vashti's downfall (1:3–22)
    C Esther triumphs over her rivals; triumph celebrated with a feast (2:1–18)
      D Mordecai foils the plot against the king (2:19–23)
        E Conflict between Haman and Mordecai is initiated (3:1–6)
          F Haman petitions the king for the death of the Jews (3:7–15)
            G Esther and Mordecai plot against Haman (ch. 4)
              H Esther invites the king to a feast (5:1–8)
            G' Zeresh and Haman plot against Mordecai (5:9–14)
          F' Haman goes to petition the king for Mordecai's death (ch. 6)
        E' Conflict between Haman and Mordecai is concluded (ch. 7)
      D' Mordecai foils the plot against the Jews (ch. 8)
    C' The Jews triumph over their rivals; triumph celebrated with a feast (9:1–17)
  B' The two feasts of the Jews; Haman's downfall (9:18–32)
A' Conclusion: The glory of Xerxes and Mordecai (10:1–3)[51]

---

49. Fox, *Esther*, 156–58; Levenson, *Esther*, 5–6.
50. Tomasino, "Interpreting Esther," 102
51. Tomasino, "Interpreting Esther," 111

Tomasino's reconstruction is open to critique. For example, does he capture the essence of chapter 6? What I appreciate about the proposal, however, is that he correctly identifies the scene of Esther's first entrance into Ahasuerus's presence unbidden, thus risking death, as the pivotal moment when the fate of the Jews, thus far marked for death, begins to rise toward life. The proposal also correctly places Esther at the dramatic center of the book and names her as the main character of the story, who "displays . . . 'personal growth' through the course of the narrative" and who serves as "a model of how to navigate the treacherous waters of diasporal existence."[52]

Conclusion

Esther willingly embraces the possibility of death to save her people. Her appearance before Ahasuerus unbidden is her opening move in an elaborate strategy, in fact, a calculated risk to transform her dominated position in a space not her own to one of strategic advantage by inviting her enemies into a house of her own. As such, it is quite simply a brilliant move and the decisive moment in the book when the fate of Jews pivots from death toward life. The death that Esther risks, similar to the death that Judah and Moses risk, has no moral value. Should she have died, her death would have accomplished little except an expression of her love for her people. The risked death makes a way for redemption, but the death itself works no benefit either for herself or others.

The value of risked death as a strategic tool changes dramatically with the advent of martyrdom. Martyrdom, as we shall see in the following chapters, infuses death with power, so that it becomes possible to work benefit for others even in the event of death. In martyrdom, the dead can give life and also come back to life.

---

52. Tomasino, "Interpreting Esther," 117, 118.

CHAPTER 8

From Suicide to Martyrdom

μάρτυς, ὁ, ἡ: *witness*[1]

μάρτυς, μάρτυρος, dat. pl. μάρτυσιν m.: *a person who has been deprived of life as the result of bearing witness to his beliefs*[2]

THE GREEK WORD *martys*, from which the English word "martyr" ultimately derives, refers to a "witness" in a legal setting. But around the middle of the second century CE, *martys* came also to have a more specialized meaning, indicating an executed Christian. The seemingly radical change in meaning was not comprehensive in scope—*martys* continued to mean "witness" in normal usage, as it does in modern Greek—and was the result of an accumulation of discursive practices. If there is a singular historical impetus for the change, it would be the manner of Roman persecution of Christians: Christians, during their trials, were asked to testify against themselves, and when they bore truthful witness (*martys*), declaring, "I am a Christian," they were, as a result, executed.[3] Because bearing true witness in a court of law became an act of embracing death for Christians, Christian communities in the Roman empire began to call executed Christians *martyres*,

---

1. LSJ, s.v. "μάρτυς."
2. Louw-Nida, s.v. "μάρτυς."
3. On the question of the prevalence of martyrdom in early Christianity, see Candida Moss, *The Myth of Persecution: How Early Christians Invented a Story of Martyrdom* (New York: HarperCollins, 2013).

CHAPTER 8

martyrs. In this way, a legal act came to be infused with religious meaning: to bear witness became an act of imitating Christ in his death;[4] and the act of voluntarily choosing death made it possible for Christian apologists to portray Christian martyrs as gladiatorial warriors who, by fighting bravely in the face of almost certain death, could win honor, admiration, and sometimes even their lives.[5] Martyrdom, in other words, became for Christians a means of participating in Christ's suffering and death, so also in his glory and triumph, and was presented to Roman society as proof of Christianity's superiority in the honor and sacrifice language of Roman culture.[6]

The Christian origin of the use of the word "martyr" to refer to those executed for religious reasons led some scholars to argue that martyrdom did not exist before Christianity.[7] So to equate the word with the concept and phenomenon, however, is to confuse the signifier for the signified; for things can and do exist independent of and prior to corresponding lexica.[8] In this regard, consider the above discussion on suicide and terrorism. A more fruitful question, and the one we shall take up below in light of the Christian provenance of the word "martyr," is whether we have martyrs in the Hebrew Bible, even if we do not have a corresponding biblical

---

4. Carole Straw, "'A Very Special Death': Christian Martyrdom in Its Classical Context," in *Sacrificing the Self: Perspectives on Martyrdom and Religion*, ed. Margaret Cormack (Oxford: Oxford University Press, 2002), 39–57; Candida Moss, *The Other Christs: Imitating Jesus in Ancient Christian Ideologies of Martyrdom* (Oxford: Oxford University Press, 2010).

5. Carlin Barton, "Honor and Sacredness in the Roman and Christian Worlds," in *Sacrificing the Self: Perspectives on Martyrdom and Religion*, ed. Margaret Cormack (Oxford: Oxford University Press, 2002), 23–38.

6. For an analysis of the ways in which Christian martyrdom appropriates Roman social roles and ethical standards for oppositional purposes, see Karen L. King, "Willing to Die for God: Individualization and Instrumental Agency in Ancient Christian Martyr Literature," in *The Individual in the Religions of the Ancient Mediterranean*, ed. Jörg Rüpke (Oxford; Oxford University Press, 2013), 342–84.

7. Marc Brettler, "Is There Martyrdom in the Hebrew Bible?," in *Sacrificing the Self: Perspectives on Martyrdom and Religion*, ed. Margaret Cormack (Oxford: Oxford University Press, 2002), 3–22.

8. See Moss, *Myth of Persecution*, 24–25. I agree with Marc Brettler ("Martyrdom in the Hebrew Bible," 4) and Moss (*Myth of Persecution*, 27–29) that the concept and phenomenon of martyrdom predate Christianity.

From Suicide to Martyrdom

Hebrew word or phrase.[9] In answering the question, we shall first define martyrdom, then revisit previously discussed alloforms of voluntary death, before we turn our attention to two examples of martyrdom in the Hebrew Bible in the next two chapters.

Defining Martyrdom

The definition of martyrdom is contested, as would be expected of a complex and powerful concept.[10] The etymology of the term already alerts us to the dramatic shifts in meaning a word may undergo in history: a word denoting a legal witness coming to refer also to an executed Christian. Compounding the difficulty of definition are the wide range of popular usages that have developed over time, from its analogical use to refer to political "martyrs" to its sarcastic use to refer to those with an exaggerated sense of victimhood.[11] But perhaps the greatest challenge comes from the issue of perspective. For one group's martyr may be another's terrorist, not unlike Samson who was an Israelite hero in certain time periods but, as some have argued, "a terrorist . . . if you were a Philistine." Standing on either side of the perspectival divide, the other's definition appears clearly and indefensibly wrong. Given these difficulties, one scholar of martyrology observes, "A history of martyrdom becomes a history of ideas, and the definition of martyrdom starts to lack definition."[12]

The difficulty of definition makes me hesitate to offer one, but a definition is helpful, especially in a concise treatment of the topic. Thus, I will offer a proposal, however provisional. Fortunately for our purposes, the work of Arthur Droge and James Tabor provides a good starting point.

---

9. The Hebrew term קידוש השם ("sanctification of the name") comes to have a meaning proximate to martyrdom in post-biblical Hebrew; it is especially associated with the Jewish victims of the Crusades; Brettler, "Martyrdom in the Hebrew Bible," 3.

10. For an insightful treatment of the problem, see Candida R. Moss, *Ancient Christian Martyrdom: Diverse Practices, Theologies, and Traditions* (New Haven: Yale University Press, 2012), in particular the "Introduction" on pp. 1–22.

11. Moss, *Myth of Persecution*, 25–26.

12. Moss, *Ancient Christian Martyrdom*, 5.

CHAPTER 8

According to Droge and Tabor, martyrs (and martyrdom in general) reflect the following characteristics:

> First, they reflect situations of opposition and persecution. Second, the choice to die, which these individuals make, is viewed by the authors as necessary, noble, and heroic. Third, these individuals are often eager to die; indeed, in several cases they end up directly *killing themselves*. Fourth, there is often the idea of vicarious benefit resulting from their suffering and death. And finally, the expectation of vindication and reward beyond death, more often than not, is a prime motivation for their choice of death.[13]

We should note that Droge and Tabor derive the above five characteristics of martyrdom from examples of voluntary death found primarily in the Apocrypha. The number of examples being limited, however, there is room and a need to modify these characteristics before applying them to an analysis of the Hebrew Bible.

The first characteristic, that martyrdom reflects "situations of opposition and persecution," establishes the necessary condition for martyrdom and should be retained.[14]

The second characteristic addresses the thorny issue of perspective and identifies the author of the martyr story as the evaluating subject of the choice to die. It is the author, and not necessarily the dead, who views the chosen death as "necessary, noble, and heroic," and presents it as such for purposes that may or may not align with the reason that the martyr himself or herself chose death. That is to say, all martyrologies begin with an act of theft on the part of the living and involve the manipulation of the stolen story and deployment of the prestige won at the price of death to an end

---

13. Arthur J. Droge and James D. Tabor, *A Noble Death: Suicide and Martyrdom among Christians and Jews in Antiquity* (New York: HarperCollins, 1992), 75.

14. Moss has questioned, if not the reality, then the prevalence of persecution in early Christianity in her insightful book *The Myth of Persecution*. Moss's book helpfully underlines the constructed nature of the martyrologies and correctly characterizes them as discursive events that both represent and create what they recount. We do well to keep in mind the issues of narrative ethics, identity politics, and ideological contest, even if they cannot be discussed adequately in the present work.

not necessarily shared with the dead. In this way, the second characteristic illustrates the illusiveness of the subject of martyrology (conceived either as the martyr or the event of martyrdom) and reveals the study of martyrdom as a study not necessarily of historical figures or events but of their representation (in narrative or in other media) and deployment for a range of social and theological ends. While we cannot attend to all the artistic, ethical, and theological issues involved in the study of martyrdom, we do well to keep these complicating issues in mind as we proceed.

The third characteristic of martyrdom, that martyrs are "often eager to die," should be modified. While Droge and Tabor's observation holds true for the few examples they examine, an eagerness to die is not a necessary characteristic of a martyr. In fact, in early Christianity the matter of enthusiasm for martyrdom became an acute controversy. For example, Augustine spoke decisively against it, "If we loved death it would be nothing to bear it for the faith.... We praise the martyrs precisely because they bear what they do not love: suffering."[15] It is admitted that enthusiasm for martyrdom, which should be differentiated from an enthusiasm for death, can arise from certainty about "vindication and reward beyond death," which is Droge and Tabor's fifth characteristic of martyrdom. And it is also admitted that enthusiasm may be related to the belief that a martyr's death, seen as an imitation of Christ, participates in Christ's victory over death and Satan.[16] But that an eagerness to die is not an essential or necessary characteristic of martyrdom may be deduced from the logic of Christian martyrdom as *imitatio Christi*, for the Synoptic Gospels portray Christ, far from being eager to die, as praying that he might escape death, saying: "My Father, if it is possible, let this cup pass from me; yet not what I want but what you want" (Matt. 26:39; cf. Mark 14:36; Luke 22:42).[17] The apologetic and motivational goals of martyr stories, more than the actual enthusiasm of the martyrs themselves, likely led to portrayals of martyrs as enthusiastic to die. Portraying martyrs as eager to die bolstered the author's claim

---

15. Augustine, *Sermon 299*, 8; cited in Paul Middleton, *Martyrdom: A Guide for the Perplexed* (London: T&T Clark, 2011), 83.

16. Middleton, *Martyrdom*, 71-74.

17. The Johannine conceptualization differs significantly from the Synoptic Gospels on this point, as noted in chapter 1.

for the certainty of reward beyond death, which encouraged persecuted coreligionists and countered the intended effect of persecution to discourage the religious group. Thus, as with the third characteristic, we need to differentiate between the author and the martyr and say that the martyr demonstrates, or is portrayed as demonstrating, a willingness to die.

The fourth characteristic of martyrdom according to Droge and Tabor, "the idea of vicarious benefit resulting from [the martyr's] suffering and death," is related to the second, since it also involves the author's imputation of meaning and value to the death. If the idea of vicarious benefit was already established before the martyr's death, it is possible that the idea informed or even motivated the martyr's choice to die; but it is the living whom we would expect and not surprisingly find indeed to emphasize the benefit the death suffered by the martyr has for the living. In this light, we should also note that the author of the martyr story is likely to emphasize that the choice to suffer death rather than renounce one's belief marks the belief as something worth dying for—thus to live for—which is a significance the martyr himself or herself would also have been aware of and which most benefits the living, including presumably the author of the martyr story. As one historian of martyrdom notes, "The Chosen Death was (and is) the chief means of affirming existing values or of sanctifying new ones."[18] The desire to attribute meaning and value to death, especially death unjustly dealt out, is a timeless human impulse and should be retained for our purposes.

The fifth and final characteristic of martyrdom, "the expectation of vindication and reward beyond death," is related to the third and should be likewise modified in two ways. First, an expectation assumes the prior knowledge of the thing expected, which means that the thing expected must first be discovered and articulated. In the case of martyrdom in the Hebrew Bible, we are dealing with that prior stage of discovery and not with the logically dependent stage of expectation. Furthermore, we have to distinguish, once again, the martyr from the authors of the martyr story.

---

18. Barton, "Honor and Sacredness," 34n17. Barton elsewhere states that, for the Romans, like the Greeks, "In the absence of the Chosen Death nothing was sacred, including life" (p. 17). The economy of the chosen death applies more generally, as Barton notes, for to have found something worth dying for is to have found something to live for.

For example, in Deutero-Isaiah, we have to speak of the authors of Isaiah 53 as discovering and articulating an expectation for vindication and reward beyond death and not of the Suffering Servant. This brings us to the second modification. While an expectation for vindication or reward can be one or even the main motivation for choosing death for some, it cannot be said to be the "prime motivation" or even a motivation for all martyrs. Martyrs can choose death without any expectation of vindication or reward beyond death.

In conclusion, we have a modified list of Droge and Tabor's characterizations of martyrdom:

1. Martyrdom reflects situations of opposition and persecution.
2. Authors of martyr stories view the choice to die that the martyrs make as necessary, noble, and heroic.
3. The martyr demonstrates or is portrayed as demonstrating a willingness to die.
4. The martyr, the author, or both impute to martyrdom the idea of vicarious benefit from a martyr's suffering and death.
5. An expectation of vindication and reward beyond death develops in relation to a martyr's death and may motivate the choice to die.

We shall adopt these characteristics first to reevaluate previously discussed alloforms of voluntary death, then, in the next two chapters, to argue that the Suffering Servant in Deutero-Isaiah and the Danielic Wise are examples of martyrs in the Hebrew Bible who, in choosing to die, give life.

From Suicide to Martyr

The idea of martyrdom did not arise *de novo*. And thanks to more recent work on martyrdom, we now have a better understanding especially of the Hellenistic and Roman cultural and historical contexts in which Jewish and Christian forms of martyrdom developed. To date, however, no work has sought to clarify the various ways in which earlier traditions about voluntary death in the Hebrew Bible have contributed to the development of or, put more modestly, illuminate the broad cultural framework within which

CHAPTER 8

martyrdom later developed in the Hebrew Bible.[19] To address this issue, we will reexamine the previously discussed figures and ideas, including those who express a willingness to die but do not in fact die voluntarily, through the lens of martyrdom. What we shall find are reflections of the five characteristics of martyrdom, though never all five of them together, in various portrayals of those who express a willingness to die, from would-be suicides to sacrificial leaders.

Suicide in the Deuteronomistic History

The suicides in the Deuteronomistic History we examined in chapter 1 (Abimelech, Saul, Saul's armor-bearer, Ahithophel, and Zimri) are not martyrs. For example, none can be said to expect vindication and reward beyond death (characteristic 5). The accounts of their deaths, however, do exhibit other characteristics of martyrdom. All the figures, for example, kill themselves or seek to kill themselves (characteristic 3) in situations of opposition (characteristic 1). Furthermore, the deaths of two, Saul and Ahithophel, may be argued to be honorable (characteristic 2) and to benefit others (characteristic 4). Let us begin with Saul.

The Deuteronomistic Historians, far from condemning Saul's suicide, portray Saul's death as necessary, noble, and heroic. Saul's death by his own hands is portrayed as an attempt to deny the Philistines the opportunity to abuse him, which would have brought shame on Saul and also on the Israelites. Furthermore, David does not condemn but commemorates

---

19. Previous work on martyrdom in the Hebrew Bible demonstrates well that the late development of the idea of martyrdom shares characteristics with biblical and other traditions. No studies, however, offer a detailed analysis of the continuities between other forms of voluntary death and martyrdom in the Hebrew Bible. Droge and Tabor (*Noble Death*, 56), for example, argue that voluntary death, "within Israelite society, as early as the period of the united monarchy . . . given the proper circumstances, was understood as honorable and even routine" but do not see a link between Ahithophel's chosen death and the Danielic martyrdom. Brettler ("Martyrdom in the Hebrew Bible"), who also treats martyrdom in the Hebrew Bible, is interested in a negative thesis, namely that there is no martyrdom in the Hebrew Bible, save for the book of Daniel. My interest here is to see the various ways in which voluntary death or those who demonstrate a willingness to die that we previously discussed may have contributed to the late examples of full-blown martyrdom we find in Deutero-Isaiah and Daniel.

From Suicide to Martyrdom

Saul's and his sons' deaths in a lament song (2 Sam. 1:17–27), which begins, "Your glory, O Israel, lies slain upon your high places!" (1:19). According to this construction, Saul is a manifestation of divine glory even in his death. Droge and Tabor thus correctly write that Saul's death "demonstrates that a voluntary death, given the appropriate circumstances, was seen as an *honorable* act," indistinguishable from other combat deaths (1 Sam. 31:6).[20]

Not only do the Deuteronomistic Historians portray Saul's death as honorable, they leave space for reading Saul's death as having vicarious benefit for the Israelites. News of Saul's death has a depressive effect on the Israelites: "When the men of Israel who were on the other side of the valley and those beyond the Jordan saw that the men of Israel had fled and that Saul and his sons were dead, they forsook their towns and fled; and the Philistines came and occupied them" (1 Sam. 31:7). While Israel's military retreat cannot be attributed solely to Saul's death, news of his demise directly contributes to Israel's flight before the Philistines. Saul's defeat is symptomatic or even, one is tempted to say, symbolic of Israel's defeat. We can extrapolate from the correlation between Saul and Israel in this instance that Saul's torture and abuse would have caused not only personal shame but also national shame. Thus, while the Philistines retrieve Saul's corpse and impale it on the wall of Beth-shan to Philistine glory and Israelite shame (1 Sam. 31:8–10), Saul voluntarily killing himself deprives the Philistines an opportunity to inflict even greater shame by torturing him alive. Saul's death, it may be argued, has the vicarious benefit of sparing the Israelites the greater shame of having their king tortured and humiliated by the enemy.

The account of Ahithophel's suicide by hanging is brief but exhibits an austere dignity befitting a wise royal counselor (2 Sam. 17:23). Droge and Tabor write that Ahithophel's death demonstrates the "routinization" of voluntary death.[21] I disagree. If there is an example of a routine voluntary death in the Hebrew Bible, it is the death of Saul's armor-bearer (1 Sam. 31:5). The reason that Droge and Tabor mischaracterize Ahithophel's death as routine is twofold. First, Ahithophel's death occurs as part of an inclusio to the core narrative of Absalom's rise and fall, a narrative

---

20. Droge and Tabor, *Noble Death*, 54.
21. Droge and Tabor, *Noble Death*, 56.

that is on the whole structured chiastically: Ahithophel leaves his hometown of Giloh to join Absalom as his counselor (2 Sam. 15:12); and, when Absalom does not follow his counsel, he returns home to die (17:23). The structural balance of the narrative lends to each element of the narrative, especially its beginning and ending, a sense of inevitability that Droge and Tabor misread as routine. Second, the death is presented as the result of the thoughtful premeditation of a preternaturally wise man. Ahithophel does not destroy himself in response to an immediate, desperate situation, as is the case with every other instance of suicide in the Deuteronomistic History, but in anticipation of future events. By choosing to die, he avoids certain eventualities and prevents others he, in his wisdom, could foresee. The calm thoughtfulness and foresight leading to the act of self-destruction contribute to Droge and Tabor's mischaracterization of Ahithophel's suicide as routine. In my opinion, the biblical authors portray Ahithophel's suicide as a noble expression of his wisdom and as a heroic act with the preservation of his honor and the safety of his household in mind.

This brings us to the vicarious benefit of Ahithophel's suicide. An important detail of Ahithophel's suicide is that he returns home to Giloh, the text explains, to "set his house in order" before hanging himself (2 Sam. 17:23). While the exact meaning of the notice eludes us, we can surmise that Ahithophel had in mind the future survival of his household after his death. In dying, he spared his household the shame and ruin of a traitor's family when David should return to power, an eventuality Ahithophel uniquely could foresee. It might be added that Ahithophel's killing himself in direct response to the rejection of his counsel indicates his firm conviction concerning the wisdom of his advice and correspondingly the (intentional) foolishness of Hushai's opposing advice. Ahithophel's suicide affirms his faith in his own wisdom. To summarize, Ahithophel's suicide is not a death of despair but a deed calculated to benefit others precisely by his death. In choosing to die, Ahithophel gives his household the possibility of survival and life. It also confirms Ahithophel's faith in his own wisdom, which in retrospect proves to have been equal to its high esteem.

To conclude, among the various forms of voluntary death, suicide may appear to be the farthest removed from martyrdom. However, we can see that within the honor and shame cultural matrix of ancient Israel there are continuities between even suicide and martyrdom.[22] In addition to the obvious commonality of the existence of opposition, certain acts of self-destruction are portrayed as necessary, noble, and heroic in the Hebrew Bible and, what more, as potentially working vicarious benefit for others. In addition, we learned that suicide, like martyrdom, can confer prestige on the reason that the suicide chooses death, such as faith in God for a Christian martyr and faith in his wisdom for Ahithophel. If scholars have missed these connections between suicide and martyrdom in the past, it is because of the Western and modern judgment that suicide is to be condemned as an irredeemable act of desperation and despair. Suicide, however, was understood in biblical Israel as potentially honorable and possibly salutary.

Wishing and Willing to Die in Job

Job does not commit suicide. He dies a natural death, "old and full of days" (Job 42:17). So, there is no possibility of his being a martyr. This is not to say, however, that there are no connections between Job and martyrdom as it develops in the Hebrew Bible. In fact, there are rich developmental connections between Job and martyrdom arising from the ways in which Job relates to death. Toward the beginning of the book, Job expresses a desire for death, which we argued is characteristic of suicide ideation. Recall his words early in the dialogue: "I would choose strangling / and death rather than this body" (7:15). However, this is not the only or the most consequential way in which Job relates to death. While Job does look to death as an escape from life's ills, especially during the first half of the book, he begins to imagine death as a portal to another, more palatable mode of existence. For example, at the conclusion of his dialogue with his friends (Job 3–31) and at the beginning of his encounter with God (Job 38–41), Job expresses a willingness to die for the possibility of vindication and of living with his dignity and honor restored (27:2–6; 31:1–40). It is this later development in Job's relationship to death in which we see connections to the characteristics of martyrdom we identified above.

The exact nature of opposition and persecution that Job suffers is complex, more so than it may first appear, and constitutes a major subject of

---

22. In agreement with Droge and Tabor, *Noble Death*.

discussion among Job and his friends. It is, in certain respects, the animating question of the entire book: What is the reason for human suffering? On the one hand, Job believes that God opposes him and persecutes him "for no reason (*ḥinnām*)." Job declares, "For [God] bruises me with tempest / and multiplies my wound for no reason (*ḥinnām*)" (9:17). The book of Job, therefore, may be read as Job's attempt to find the (real) reason that God torments him against other (false) explanations, such as the ones offered by his friends. Important to remember, however, is that the readers know the reason that Job suffers: Job is made to suffer because he is pious. Job's piety—to discover whether it is genuine and free of ulterior motives—is the known reason (to the reader) that the Satan proposes, and God permits, that Job be stripped of his blessings (Job 1), then inflicted with bodily and social pain (Job 2). That is, if martyrs suffer death precisely because of their pious faith in God, so too does Job.

Answering the question of whether the Joban authors view Job's relation to death as necessary, noble, and heroic requires that we differentiate Job's wish for death from his willingness to die. In giving full articulation to Job's despair and his consequent desire to die so that his suffering might end, the authors of Job infuse lament and even complaint in the face of loss and tragedy with pious dignity, for it is God who describes what Job has said throughout his conversation with his friends, including, presumably, his complaints and laments, as "what is right" (Job 42:7, 8). The anatomy of a righteous and pious soul, the Joban authors declare, includes parts capable of experiencing "griefs, sorrows, fears, doubts, hopes, cares, perplexities," and other negative emotions that Calvin says agitate human hearts.[23] A pious man in his piety may despair of life and even wish for death.

If the Joban authors transpose a wish for death to within the pale of piety, they elevate Job's willingness to die to the level of the heroic. As discussed in chapter 2, Job's willingness to die develops throughout the book of Job and comes into full view in Job 31. Toward the end of Job's dialogue with his friends, Job expresses a willingness to die precisely as a means to demonstrate his righteousness and force an encounter with God

---

23. John Calvin, "The Author's Preface," in his *Commentary on the Book of Psalms*, trans. James Anderson, repr. (Grand Rapids: Baker, 1998), xli–xliii.

(Job 31, 38–42). With oaths of innocence (Job 31), Job obligates God either to punish him should he have committed a sin, be it a peccadillo of deed or thought, or otherwise to declare him righteous. That is, Job wagers his life and limb (see 31:22) on the conviction that he has not sinned and is wholly righteous for an opportunity to see God.

The first thing to note is that Job's risking death in this way is necessary to the plot of the book. The Satan and God make Job suffer as a means to see whether Job is capable of pure piety that is motivated by neither the carrot of blessings nor the rod of punishment. Given this premise, for Job either to agree with his friends that his present suffering is the result of past sins (22:21–22) or to do as his wife seems to advise and curse God and die (2:9) would be to prove the Satan right, that human beings act piously only to avoid suffering and to receive blessings. For Job to prove God right and the Satan wrong, Job must hold onto his integrity, his life, and God against the advice of his wife and friends. That is precisely what he does in the pivotal final speech to his friends: "As God lives," Job begins,

> who has taken away my right
> and the Almighty, who has made my soul bitter,
> ³ as long as my breath is in me
> and the spirit of God is in my nostrils,
> ⁴ my lips will not speak falsehood,
> and my tongue will not utter deceit.
> ⁵ Far be it from me to say that you are right;
> until I die I will not put away my integrity from me.
> ⁶ I hold fast my righteousness, and I will not let it go;
> my heart does not reproach me for any of my days. (27:2–6)

In this remarkable passage, Job makes life the middle term between God and his integrity. Job affirms God as the source both of his life and its bitterness: "the Almighty, who has made my soul bitter . . . as long as . . . the spirit of God is in my nostrils." This realization does not lead Job to despair at this stage in the book, however, as it did toward the beginning. While acknowledging the bitterness of life, Job makes life coequal and coeval with his integrity: "until I die I will not put away my integrity from me . . . my heart does not reproach me for any of my days." The equation of his

CHAPTER 8

life with his integrity means that to choose to die would be tantamount to declaring himself guilty and deserving of punishment.

There is, however, a tension among the three terms: God, life, and integrity. God, in making Job's life bitter, has also placed a question mark on Job's integrity. The friends, for example, see in Job a life made bitter by God and a life without integrity. It is in order to resolve this tension that Job will wager his life in Job 31: If Job is wrong that he is without sin, he would that God kill him that his bitterness might end; but if Job is right, he would that his integrity be made known and his honor restored. In short, Job's wagering his life is the necessary event as the plot turns toward its still enigmatic and awesome conclusion.

More than merely necessary, the Joban authors present Job's willingness to die as heroic. The drama of the book of Job does not consist in outward events, save the events of the prologue, but in transformations that take place in the internal orientation of the characters. The friends are rather flat characters and do not experience any meaningful change from beginning to end. Job, on the other hand, undergoes numerous such reorientations throughout the book, and the stance Job assumes at the climax of the drama is to stand before God, holding fast to his integrity, and to demand that God prove him right or else execute him. Job standing before God in this way is heroic for a number of reasons and is related to the implications it has for him and humanity.

The reason Job embraces the possibility of death in Job 31 may appear, at first glance, to be self-centered. His desire for a confrontation with God constitutes a rejection of the counsel of his friends and the traditions they advocate and has as its sole goal, it would appear, the restoration of personal honor. Whatever Job's individual hopes, however, we can be certain that the Joban authors viewed Job's actions as having global implications, for the dignity of humanity falls and rises with Job in the book. In this regard, recall that, in the prologue, God singles out Job from among all of humanity, declaring, "There is no one like him on the earth" (1:8; cf. 2:3). The implication is that Job exemplifies and, to God and in the drama that unfolds, represents (the best of) humanity. The dialogue between Job and his friends, with frequent references to the human condition at large, bears this out. Consider, for example, Job's question: "What are human beings, that you make so much of them, that you set your mind on them?" (7:17), a question that echoes God's question to the Satan in the prologue concerning Job: "Have you set your mind on my servant Job?" (1:8; cf. 2:3).[24] At issue is not Job's predicament alone but a matter that concerns all of humanity. In his closing speeches, Job reinforces the analogy between himself and humanity by comparing himself to Adam: "If I covered my transgressions like Adam" (31:33). Job conjures up Adam, the first human being God created according to Genesis 2, and declares himself better than him. Where Adam failed, by sinning and covering it up, Job says he has succeeded. He has not sinned, so has nothing to cover up. If Job's self-comparison with Adam seems hubristic (which it is),[25] we should remember that God appears to agree that at issue in the problem of Job is nothing short of all creation. If Job was mistaken about the importance of his situation, it is that he thought too little of himself. Judging from the scope of God's response, which touches on cosmogony and the wild and mythical creatures that populate creation, the Joban problem has to do not only with humanity but also with creation and the cosmos. To summarize, when Job stands before God and demands that God respond, he does so for himself personally but, in the view of the authors, also as a champion of humanity and, beyond that, creation.

But what does Job achieve by wagering his life? Are his efforts heroic or quixotic? Recent scholarship has tended to claim that Job failed to elicit the response he desired from God or, more accurately, that God failed to provide the kind of response that would satisfy Job. According to this view, rather than address Job's concerns, God browbeats Job into humiliated submission with an inordinate display of divine knowledge and power. The divine speeches are yet another instance of divine abuse.[26] While there are important insights to be garnered from these readings, to read the divine speeches as such is to miss three clear indications that Job wins a valuable victory for himself and humanity.

24. My translation.
25. See Paul K.-K. Cho, "Job the Penitent: Whether and Why Job Repents (Job 42:6)," in *Landscapes of Korean/Korean-American Biblical Interpretation*, ed. John Ahn, IVBS 10 (Atlanta: Society of Biblical Literature, 2019), 145–74.
26. See, for example, John Briggs Curtis, "On Job's Response to Yahweh," *JBL* 89 (1979): 497–511. For a contrarian reading, see Cho, "Evolutionary Psychology and Suicide in the Book of Job."

CHAPTER 8

First, God shows up. God's appearance before Job is the direct result of Job's oath of innocence and is the first and necessary step in God's response to Job's request that he be declared righteous or else executed. Second, God does not address the question of Job's righteousness. The non-response is significant. In not responding, that is, in not condemning Job for sin as required by Job's self-imprecations, God in effect declares Job to be as righteous as he claims to be. Job says, "My heart does not reproach me for any of my days"—and neither does God. In fact, and this is the third point, God twice declares that what Job said in dialogue with his friends is "right" (42:7, 8).

The implications of the above three observations are subtle but monumental. The most obvious implication, the vindication of Job, quells the friends' insistence that Job's suffering is either warning against sin or retribution for sin. Job's suffering is not the result of sin but rather suffering despite righteousness. Furthermore, Job's vindication means that Job, against the Satan's prediction that Job would surely "curse you [God] to your face" (1:11; 2:5), has demonstrated piety that is motivated by neither the carrot of blessings nor the rod of punishment. Job proves himself capable of piety without reason in the face of suffering without reason. These personal victories have more global implications: Job's triumph enacts a paradigm shift in regard to suffering and restores humanity's standing before God. First, Job teaches us that suffering is not necessarily the result of sin. In fact, suffering may happen despite or, as is the case with Job, precisely because of piety. Job infuses suffering with honor and expels the shame usually associated with suffering.[27] Second, Job's victory elevates human standing in the cosmic order as beings capable of pure piety. In fact, Job's piety without reason ambiguates all forms of piety so that it cannot be said with certainty that any piety is externally motivated by either a desire to avoid pain or gain blessing. Job's victory, in sum, radiates out to benefit all humanity by dignifying those who suffer and those who act with piety. And this constitutes Job's heroism in the eyes of the Joban authors. To quote Michael V. Fox, the book of Job, thanks to Job's willingness to die for his dignity, "asserts the transcendent importance of human righteousness and the exalted meaning of human life even in—or especially in—suffering."[28]

---

27. On this point, I agree with Fox, "Job the Pious," 363.
28. Fox, "Job the Pious," 364.

From Suicide to Martyrdom

The issue of an expectation of vindication and reward beyond death in Job is complex. As we discussed in chapter 2, Job explicitly considers the possibility of resurrection, asking, "If mortals die, will they live again?" (14:14), and beyond that even of vindication beyond death. Recall the well-known and perplexing passage:

> ^{25} For I know that my Redeemer lives,
> and that at the last he will stand upon the earth;
> ^{26} and after my skin has been thus destroyed,
> then in my flesh I shall see God,
> ^{27} whom I shall see on my side,
> and my eyes shall behold, and not another.
> My heart faints within me! (19:25–27)

Whether the redeemer is God, Job, or a third neutral figure is not as important as the fact that Job imagines the possibility of redemption "after [his] skin has been thus destroyed," that is, after death. He does not, in the context of the book, pursue such a vindication, but rather seeks and receives vindication in life, as we discussed above. However, it is remarkable that Job broaches, then explores the theme of vindication beyond death, a theme so central to martyrology.

To summarize, Job is not a martyr. But we see in Job themes crucial to martyrdom as it develops elsewhere in biblical literature. Job is, for starters, persecuted because of his righteousness, a most challenging aspect of the book that will lead to the demonization of the Satan figure who, yet in the book of Job, is a functionary in the divine court. We have inchoate in the book of Job the relational structure necessary for religious persecution that will give rise to martyrdom: God, the faithful people of God, and their opponent. Beyond the situation of opposition, the authors of Job portray Job's willingness to die, though he does not indeed die, as necessary, noble, and heroic, achieving vicarious benefit for all of humanity in the face of the Satan's challenge to the purity of human piety. Job struggles mightily to restore dignity to the innocent sufferer and faith in the human capacity for righteousness. Perhaps most surprisingly, Job also opens the door onto a landscape beyond death and to the possibility that vindication and reward might be found there for those who suffer an unjust death. The book of Job,

CHAPTER 8

then, reflects a framework of thematic relations out of which martyrdom will eventually arise.

Samson

Samson, more than any other figure under discussion, showcases the perspectival divide that attends discussions of martyrdom. To be clear, Samson is not a martyr, since there is no expectation of vindication and reward beyond death. "Samson's vindication is the death of many Philistines, not some otherworldly reward."[29] But not unlike martyrs, he is a hero to some and a murderer or worse to others. Be that as it may, however, the story of Samson features other characteristics of martyrdom and so participates in the cultural and intellectual tradition that gives rise to biblical martyrdom.

Samson clearly lives in a situation of opposition and persecution. While Samson's immediate motivation for acting, including his decision to undertake a suicide attack, is consistently personal, his personal conflict with the Philistines exists within the larger situation of Philistine domination over Israel (Judg. 15:11). That is, Samson may be read as an analogue for Israel in his relation to the Philistines.[30] Thus, whatever Samson's conscious awareness, his personal conflicts reflect Israel's agonistic relationship with the Philistines, and his attacks on the Philistines participate in Israel's struggle against Philistine rule. This uneasy, quasi-allegorical relationship between the personal and the collective contributes to the perspectival complications of the story. Samson, as an individual, is in many respects distasteful and offensive but, as a representative of the group, enacts heroic actions against the enemy, chief among them being his suicide attack.

Samson's suicide attack in the Dagon temple, as discussed in chapters 3 and 4, appears only in the exilic edition of the Samson story (Judges 13–16). We need not again attend to the troubling aspects of the episode for the purposes of the present discussion, only note that Samson's suicide attack, by means of intertextual allusions and connections, participates in a canon-wide message of hope and redemption for an exilic audience: Samson is a proleptic

---

29. Brettler, "Martyrdom in the Hebrew Bible," 5.
30. Edward Greenstein, "The Riddle of Samson," *Prooftexts* 1 (1981): 237–60.

Zedekiah and looks forward to a new Davidic leader in Jehoiachin who, like Joseph, rises up out of prison onto a seat of honor and so anticipates not only survival in a foreign land, but flourishing and an eventual return home to Zion. According to the exilic Deuteronomistic Historians, Samson's death does not accomplish the hoped-for redemption and only begins to redeem Israel (Judg. 13:5), but it nevertheless participates in the long arc of events that will eventuate in Israel's redemption out of Babylon. In short, Samson's chosen death is heroic and has vicarious benefits for others.

To summarize, "Samson's death . . . approaches martyrdom."[31] Samson dies willingly in a situation of persecution and opposition, and the authors portray his death as heroic and as achieving vicarious benefit for Israel. Samson is not a martyr because there is no belief that he will receive vindication or reward beyond death.

Judah

There is no question of Judah being a martyr, since he dies a natural death and there is no expectation of postmortem vindication or reward. Judah, however, does express a willingness to die for the other that the authors of the Joseph story portray as necessary, noble, and heroic and, to boot, as having vicarious benefits. These connections among Judah's embrace of death, nobility, and vicarious benefit contribute to a fuller understanding of the developmental background of martyrdom in the Hebrew Bible.

Judah expresses a willingness to die twice. In the first instance, there is an ongoing famine throughout the region, and Jacob's family needs to travel back to Egypt to buy more grain. However, Joseph as Egyptian governor has demanded that his brothers bring Benjamin the next time they come to Egypt. This would constitute no obstacle, save Jacob's refusal to entrust Benjamin to his brothers for the journey. Reuben, the eldest son, had tried earlier to convince Jacob to entrust Benjamin to his care, offering Reuben's children as collateral, but to no avail (Gen. 42:37–38). Judah, however, succeeds by offering himself as surety: "I myself will be surety for him; you can hold me accountable for him. If I do not bring him back to you and set him before you, then let me bear the blame forever" (43:9). Judah's taking

---

31. Brettler, "Martyrdom in the Hebrew Bible," 5.

CHAPTER 8

on the responsibility for Benjamin's safe return is necessary to the survival of the family and, in contrast to Reuben's grotesque offer of his two sons, "You may kill my two sons if I do not bring [Benjamin] back to you" (42:37), demonstrates both tact and nobility. Survival has not been achieved, but, as Judah clearly articulates, his willing embrace of responsibility, even if it should mean death, opens the door for life: "Send the boy with me ... so that we may live and not die—you and we and also our little ones" (43:8).

The second instance of Judah's willing embrace of death occurs in Egypt. In Egypt, Joseph frames Benjamin for theft and thus places Benjamin's safety, if not his life, in jeopardy. In response to this situation, Judah entreats Joseph that he be permitted to keep his promise to Jacob and take Benjamin's place in punishment. The immediate result of Judah's taking Benjamin's place is Benjamin's safety. More important is the indirect consequence of the survival of Jacob, whose "life is bound up in the boy's life" (44:30). The authors of the Joseph story infuse Judah's unusually long speech to Joseph (44:18–34) with noble pathos. Judah pleading that he might "remain as a slave to my lord in place of the boy" resolves numerous narrative complications, from the survival of Jacob's family through famine and the reconciliation of the sons of Israel, that is, the eponymous ancestors of the tribes of Israel, and is the climax of the Joseph story. That is, Judah's embrace of the symbolic death of Egyptian slavery is necessary, noble, and heroic. To boot, it also delivers Jacob (= Israel) from death and reunites his sons (= the tribes of Israel) in one fell swoop.

Though there is no "beyond death" for Judah per se, the Joseph story makes several gestures toward a notion of vindication and reward beyond death. Joseph, as we noted, symbolically descends into the realm of death, first into a pit, then down to Egypt, and finally into prison, ultimately to rise therefrom. In addition, Joseph commands that his bones be carried out of Egypt to Canaan, when God should come to bring the Israelites out of Egypt to the promised land (Gen. 50:24–26); and, indeed, Joseph's bones participate in Israel's redemptive journey out of Egypt (Exod. 13:19) into the promised land (Josh. 24:32) in a kind of postmortem resurrection. If we take the character of Judah as symbolic of the tribe of Judah, he too receives a reward beyond death in the form of kingship (Gen. 49:8–12). Though this is not explicitly stated, Judah's willingness to die for the benefit of the group wins him the honor and privilege of royalty.

To summarize, Judah is not a martyr, but we nevertheless see in him the development of an economy of chosen death. In willingly choosing death for the sake of the group, Judah gives life to the group and, what more, purchases immense prestige and honor for himself. In so doing, Judah anticipates the ways in which the dynamic relationship among death, life, and power and the potential to negotiate that relationship will develop into martyrdom's triumph over death.

Moses at Mount Sinai

Moses at Mount Sinai during the golden calf incident would appear to be an odd figure to discuss in relation to martyrdom. The situation that Moses and Israel face, to begin, is quite different from the "situations of opposition and persecution" that martyrs might face. The Israelites stand under the threat of annihilation at the hand of God for the sin of idolatrous unfaithfulness, not faithfulness; and Moses himself is not in immediate or obvious danger. Nevertheless, Moses does express a willingness to die, and the authors portray Moses's willingness to die as heroic and as bringing about vicarious benefits. Furthermore, though there is no mention of vindication or reward beyond death, the mention of a mysterious "book that [God has] written" (Exod. 32:32) introduces the possibility of reward or punishment beyond death.

The situation of opposition in which Moses finds himself in Exodus 32 is complex. The people have committed idolatry in making and worshipping a golden calf, which they implicitly see as replacing Moses, who has long replaced God in their eyes. In response, God threatens to destroy the people and entertains the possibility of making a people for himself anew with Moses. "Of you," God says to Moses, "I will make a great nation" (32:10). In other words, Moses initially does not face opposition or persecution but rather the possibility of exaltation as a second Abraham.

Moses's curious and altogether heroic response to God is to identify with the people in punishment and, consequently, in opposition to God who wishes to punish them: "Alas, this people has sinned a great sin; they have made for themselves gods of gold," Moses acknowledges, then goes on to say, "But now, if you will only forgive their sin—but if not, blot me out of the book that you have written" (32:32). We are not dealing here with vicarious suffering, since Moses does not expect that his death (if that is what being blotted out of the book means) will bring about forgiveness. In view, nevertheless, is "atonement for . . . sin," since that is the stated reason that Moses approaches God. Before climbing Sinai once again to confront God, Moses says to the people, "You have sinned a great sin. But now I will go up to the Lord; perhaps I can make atonement for your sin" (32:30). Moses uses his life, whose value to God was confirmed by the divine wish to start anew with Moses, as a negotiating tool. Moses risks his life for the sake of the people, though God refuses to allow Moses to die.

Moses arguably risks his life a second time for the sake of the people in asking God, "Show me your glory, I pray" (33:18). The narrative thus far has established the danger God's holy presence poses to the rebellious people. God says it succinctly and forcefully, "You are a stiff-necked people [Israel]; if for a single moment I should go up among you, I would consume you" (33:5). But Moses successfully convinces God to promise to accompany the people (33:14). The danger of divine holiness remains, however, and Moses must also negotiate a change in the mode of God's presence among the people to mitigate the danger of God's presence. It is to precipitate this change that Moses risks his life again. He asks that God reveal himself to him in an encounter God says poses mortal danger to Moses (33:20). The result is that God shows his glory to Moses in the mode of grace and mercy. In touching anthropomorphism, God places Moses in a protective location, in the since proverbial "cleft of the rock," and covers Moses with God's hands (33:21). God accommodates for Moses's frailty and demonstrates that to show Moses God's glory necessitates a divine gesture of grace and mercy. That is, grace and mercy become an integral part of the economy of God's self-revelation to human beings and result in the awesome proclamation: "The Lord, the Lord, a God merciful and gracious, slow to anger, and abounding in steadfast love and faithfulness" (34:6). Though Moses failed to atone for Israel's sin, he succeeds in transforming the manner of God's dealing with Israel by again risking his life to do so. God in his relationship with his people is first and foremost merciful and gracious, and grace and mercy become the foundation of God's covenantal relationship with Israel.

Moses does not die in the golden calf incident, so there can be no talk of vindication or reward beyond death. Nevertheless, Moses mentions a mysterious book that he says God wrote (32:32) and God calls "my book" (32:33). It is unclear whether the book is "the register of the house of Israel" (Ezek. 13:9), a "book of remembrance" (Mal. 3:16), or something different. What is clear is that to be expunged therefrom is akin to, if not worse than, death. Stated negatively, Moses's willingness to be expunged from the book for the sake of Israel points to the possibility of postmortem reward and vindication. In this regard, the book no doubt has some relationship with "the book" that appears in Daniel 12: "But at that time your people shall be delivered, everyone who is found written in the book" (12:1).

To summarize, Moses adumbrates the atoning potential of sacrificial death, risks his life so that God might change for the benefit of the people, and hints at the possibility of punishment, and so also reward, beyond death. Moses is no martyr, but the ways in which he relates to death in the golden calf incident reveal interesting ways in which the embrace of death can release life-giving power that will develop more fully in later biblical tradition.

Esther

Esther lived in a situation of opposition and persecution, and she heroically risked her life to confront and dismantle the murderous hatred that threatened Jewish life. Despite sharing these important characteristics with martyrdom, however, the book of Esther is "ultimately anti-martyrdom."[32]

Haman's hatred for Mordecai's people, the Jews, which hurtles Persia toward genocide, is an outworking of a convoluted and evil logic that ranges from the personal to the legendary. In the book of Esther, Haman's hatred has its birth in a personal grudge against a political rival: Haman takes umbrage at Mordecai's refusal—because he is a Jew (Esth. 3:4)—to "bow down and do obeisance" to him, as decreed by King Ahasuerus (3:2). Out of an exaggerated sense of self-importance, Haman ascribes the personal offense to all Jews (3:6) and justifies his generalized loathing with an "ideological opposition to difference" as such.[33] He explains to Ahasuerus, "There is a certain people scattered and separated among the peoples in all the provinces of your kingdom; their laws are different from those of

---

32. Brettler, "Martyrdom in the Hebrew Bible," 13.
33. Brettler, "Martyrdom in the Hebrew Bible," 12.

CHAPTER 8

every other people, and they do not keep the king's laws, so that it is not appropriate for the king to tolerate them" (3:8). The authors of Esther deepen the significance of Haman's prejudicial hatred with allusion to the memory of Amalek's unmotivated assault on the Israelites when they came up out of Egypt (1 Sam. 15:2; cf. Exod. 17:8–16). Haman's hatred, in sum, wells up from a near mythic source and percolates onto the historical plane through the sluices of personal animus, then insidiously floods a world empire. Such are the ways of prejudicial hatred.

Haman's hatred establishes the kind of situation of opposition and persecution that will give rise to martyrdom in the book of Daniel, which we will examine in chapter 10. The book of Esther, however, does not even gesture toward martyrdom and may be described as "anti-martyrdom." Esther does express a willingness to die (4:16), as discussed, but she risks death as a tactic to achieve a strategic end dynamically opposed to death. Should she in fact be killed for entering the king's presence unbidden, then her plan to deliver Jews from death would fail. That is, in contrast to martyrdom where the martyr's death itself is seen to have positive effects, such as vicarious benefits and vindication and reward beyond death, Esther's death would be purely negative, resulting in a strategic failure. Redemption, in Esther, is a this-worldly reality, not to be deferred to a life or world to come.

This observation alone does not render Esther anti-martyrdom. Martyrdom is at heart a nonviolent form of resistance that refuses to compromise, whatever the demands of the persecutors. Esther and the Jews in the book, in contrast, carry out strategic and military resistance and are willing to assimilate to non-Jewish life. This is not to say that Esther condones all forms of violence or espouses total assimilation. The physical resistance the Jews carry out against their enemies is limited by the typical biblical principle of measure-for-measure and fits the artistic principle of doubling that structures the book. And there are limits to the assimilationist spirit in Esther. While Esther withholds her Jewishness and marries a non-Jew, suggesting a high level of assimilation, Mordecai refuses to "bow down and do obeisance" to Haman arguably because of the religious conviction that a Jew should bow down and do obeisance only to God. In the book of Esther, there are limits to assimilation and the principles for which one rightly risks death. Having said that, it is important to underline that the book of Esther espouses tactics and strategies for survival and flourishing as a minority population in a non-Jewish world at odds with martyrdom.

In summary, Esther reflects the reality of, or at minimum the growing apprehension about, persecution for Jews. Esther's strategic and assimilationist resistance, especially along with the forms of resistance we will find in Daniel, demonstrates the biblical instinct to protect and embrace life and the wide range of resistance options available to Jews who would remain faithful to the God of Israel. One can embrace death as a principled commitment to faith in the God of creation and of history, as the Wise advise. Or, as Esther demonstrates, one can engage in tactics and strategies in defense of a Jew's right to life and to her understanding of faithful living.

Conclusion

Martyrdom, whatever else it does, transforms the usual relationship between life and death. It renders the martyr an active participant in the event of dying in such a way that the martyr can gather the power inherent in life, concentrate and amplify it, and transform death into a means of unleashing that power. Martyrdom, as it comes to be known in the Christian era, is rare in the Hebrew Bible. However, throughout the Hebrew Scriptures, we have glimpses of a cultural and theological framework that will give birth to full-blown martyrdom toward the end of the biblical period centuries prior to the birth of Christianity. We have, in this chapter, briefly examined glimpses of that larger framework and turn in the next two chapters to Deutero-Isaiah and Daniel where we arguably find two examples of martyrdom in the Hebrew Bible.

CHAPTER 9

The Suffering Servant Exalted and Lifted Up and Very High

They did not believe in him.

John 12:37

WITH THE FIGURE OF THE MARTYR, we approach the conclusion of our investigation of the transformation that the relationship between death and life undergoes in the Hebrew Bible. Our study began with the examination of suicide and found that biblical tradition, while affirming the high value of life and counseling endurance in the face of adversity, sees the choice to kill oneself under certain extreme circumstances as potentially honorable and even capable of benefiting others. Along the way, we also discovered that the willing embrace of death can unleash a mysterious and life-giving power. From Samson to Moses, a willingness to die undoes the opaque tyranny of death over life and places in the hand of the dead—and the living who are willing to die—an immense power that death can uniquely unlock: the power to comfort and encourage a despondent population; the power to move vicegerents, kings, and even God; and the power to transform deathly situations into springs of life. With martyrdom, we see the full maturation of the power the willing embrace of death can unleash into life.

In this and the next chapter, we shall see that the two martyrs in the Hebrew Bible, in continuity with and significant departure from trends

The Suffering Servant Exalted and Lifted Up and Very High

observed in other alloforms of chosen death, reconfigure the normal relationship between life and death so that death becomes a portal to new, more abundant life. Death does not lose its deathliness in martyrdom. But the willing embrace of death to uphold a vision of reality with faith more resolute than the ferocity of the opposition undoes the threat of death and, what is more, transforms death itself into a life-affirming and life-giving symbolic. Martyrdom can transform death into its very opposite, a beginning and not an end, a source of life and not its demise. The birth of the martyr, then, marks not only an event in language, the transformation of *martys* from a legal witness to a faithful believer, but also an event in being: the birth of the dead that gives life.

Deutero-Isaiah

The first example of martyrdom in the Hebrew Bible comes from the section of the book of Isaiah scholars have come to call Deutero-Isaiah (Isaiah 40–55). More precisely, the so-called Suffering Servant of Isaiah 52:13–53:12—whom we shall argue is none other than the prophetic figure responsible for the core message of Deutero-Isaiah—dies a martyr's death, and his martyrdom marks a critical node in the development of the idea that death can work benefit for others and the self.

Let us first set the scene.

Deutero-Isaiah is a scholarly construct and identifies the middle section of the book of Isaiah, chapters 40–55, that stems from a sixth-century context sometime after the destruction of the Jerusalem temple in 587 BCE but before 515 BCE when the second Jerusalem temple was dedicated. Deutero-Isaiah can be further divided into two subsections. Isaiah 40–48 clearly reflects a Babylonian context; these chapters assume that the Babylonian exile has already occurred and proclaim the return to Jerusalem as an imminent hope for the exilic community (e.g., 40:1–2; 43:27–28; 44:26, 28). Furthermore, these chapters should be dated to the years immediately prior to the Persian king Cyrus's conquest of Babylon in 539 BCE: the text mentions Cyrus both explicitly and indirectly and calls him God's shepherd (44:28) and, even more shockingly, God's anointed (45:1) in anticipation of the Persian conquest of Babylon. In contrast, Isaiah 49–55 reflects a Jerusalem context. While there are calls to depart "from there" (52:11) and to return to Jerusalem (51:11), seemingly addressing Jews in Babylonian and other diasporic communities, the focus of these chapters is overwhelmingly on the restoration of Zion (e.g., 49:14-21; 52:1-2; 54:1-3) and suggests a Jerusalem context before the dedication of the second temple in 515 BCE.[1]

Isaiah 52:13–53:12, which belongs to the latter half of Deutero-Isaiah, speaks of a figure God calls "my servant" (52:13; 53:11) and whom an anonymous group describes as "a man of suffering and acquainted with infirmity" (53:3). This figure, whom tradition has come to call the Suffering Servant, is arguably the first martyr in the Hebrew Bible. The task of identifying the Suffering Servant is complex; we have no clear answers to a range of questions, from the basic question of whether the Suffering Servant refers to an individual or a collective group, to the vexed question of his death. The complexity places even a review of the principal issues and scholarship outside the scope of the present argument.[2] Thus, we limit our discussion to issues relevant to the argument that the Suffering Servant, at one level of tradition, refers to the prophet of Deutero-Isaiah who preached a message of imminent redemption from Babylon, initially to positive attention, but then increasingly to ridicule and persecution. His suffering retrospectively came to be understood as an expression of positive divine will and his death as a martyr's death that gives life.

The Suffering Servant in Isaiah 53

Let us begin with the admission that what we know of the Suffering Servant and the prophet of Deutero-Isaiah comes from the book of Isaiah

---

1. For a detailed discussion of one reconstruction of the history of composition of Deutero-Isaiah, see Ulrich F. Berges, *The Book of Isaiah: Its Composition and Final Form*, trans. Millard C. Lind, HBM 46 (Sheffield: Sheffield Phoenix, 2012), 315–77.

2. See, among others, C. R. North, *The Suffering Servant in Deutero-Isaiah*, 2nd ed. (Oxford: Oxford University Press, 1956); David J. A. Clines, *I, He, We and They: A Literary Approach to Isaiah 53*, JSOTSup 51 (Sheffield: JSOT Press, 1976); and Bernd Janowski and Peter Stuhlmacher, eds., *The Suffering Servant: Isaiah 53 in Jewish and Christian Sources*, trans. Daniel P. Bailey (Grand Rapids: Eerdmans, 2004).

itself. That is, the argument below cannot escape the inevitable circularity of textual interpretation. Thus, when I argue that the prophet was active during the Babylonian exile or that he experienced support, then persecution, the argument is based on an interpretation of the text; and that interpretation feeds into and frames further interpretation in the same vein. The lack of extrabiblical information about the prophet and the Suffering Servant makes the circularity inevitable. However, this is not to say that I am engaged in an act of willful fabrication. The text allows for multiple, even divergent readings that may not be (easily) reconciled. But the givenness of the text nevertheless exerts meaningful pressure on interpretive creativity. What I purpose, within the creative freedom permitted by the text, is to demonstrate the reasonableness of the claim that the Suffering Servant of Isaiah 53 is the prophet of Deutero-Isaiah.

The first issue to clarify about the "Suffering Servant" is that the epithet is composite and reflects the composite nature of the text of Isaiah 53. In this regard, note that there are two distinct voices in Isaiah 53. God speaks in the first-person singular in the framing sections (52:13–15 and 53:11aβ–12) and twice calls the figure "my servant" (52:13; 53:11). In the middle core (53:1–11aα), a "we-group" speaks in the first-person plural. The we-group does not refer to the figure as a "servant of Yhwh" or the like. Rather, the we-group provides a brief biographical sketch in which the suffering of the anonymous figure predominates: he "grew up ... like a young plant ... out of dry ground" and "had no form or majesty that we should look at him" (53:2); he "was despised and rejected by others" and, what more, was "a man of suffering and acquainted with infirmity" (53:3); and he appeared to others to be "struck down by God, and afflicted" (53:4) until he was "cut off from the land of the living" (53:8). In sum, the epithet "Suffering Servant" fuses the testimony of the two distinct—though thematically intertwined[3]—sections. We know that the figure suffers from the testimony of the we-group in the middle core, and we call him the servant of Yhwh because God calls him "my servant" in the frame.

---

3. The motif of the servant's despicable appearance (52:14; 53:2), the unbelievable nature of his ministry (52:14, 15; 53:1), his vicarious suffering (53:12b; 53:4–5, 10), and the divine approval of the servant's mission (52:13; 53:12; 53:1, 10) thematically connect the framing divine speeches and the we-group's confession in the core of Isaiah 53.

CHAPTER 9

The distinction between the frame and core suggests that the two sections belong to different compositional layers and, furthermore, that the core came first. In this regard, consider that, while the core can stand alone, the frame cannot. The core recounts a coherent story about the pitiable figure and dramatizes the changing attitude of the we-group toward the man of suffering in what we might characterize as a confessional mode. In contrast, the frame is dependent on the core for its narrative content and is incoherent without it. Not an independent unit, the frame plays an essentially bridging function to integrate the we-group's confessional account into the larger Isaianic corpus. This compositional history suggests that the frame is a later interpretive addition to the older core.[4] Thus, we begin our investigation into the identity of the Suffering Servant with the core of Isaiah 53 and understand the frame as a reinterpretation and recasting of the identity of the Suffering Servant to reflect the wider theological and literary framework of the Isaianic corpus.

The Three Mysteries of the Suffering Servant

Isaiah 53:1 provides a fitting introduction to the core of Isaiah 53:

> Who has believed what we have heard (*šəmuʿātēnû*)?
> And to whom (*ʾal-mî*) has the arm of the LORD (*zərôʿa yhwh*) been revealed? (53:1)

The verse identifies the dramatic pivot of the entire passage: the change in the attitude of the we-group regarding the man of suffering from disbelief to shocked realization that "it was the will (*ḥāpēṣ*) of the LORD to crush [the man of suffering] with pain" (53:10). That is, the goal of the we-group's confessional account of the man of suffering is not to identify the Suffering Servant or to tell his life story, which was well known to them, but rather to account for the transformation of their belief about him and the meaning of his suffering. That is, there is a frustrating mismatch between our desire to know the identity of the Suffering Servant and the goal of the

---

4. Berges, *Isaiah*, 378.

we-group to offer a testimony concerning their own conversion regarding the Suffering Servant.

This is not to say that the passage does not contain clues concerning the identity of the Suffering Servant. While the text is not interested in our exact question, it nevertheless raises and provides answers to three mysteries that are of interest to us: the mystery of the message of the Suffering Servant, the mystery of the person of the Suffering Servant, and the mystery of the person as message.

In this regard, note first that Isaiah 53:1 identifies the object of disbelief as "what we have heard" (*šəmuʿātēnû*). The referent is ambiguous and could be either what the suffering man had said in the past or the explanation concerning the man's suffering, which the we-group is about to supply. In other words, what is declared to be incredible may be, on the one hand, the mystery of the message of the Suffering Servant or, on the other, the mystery of the person of the Suffering Servant. The second half of the verse mirrors the split referent of "what we have heard." The reference to the revelation of "the arm of Yhwh" (*zərôʿa yhwh*) points to the message that the suffering man had proclaimed in the past. This is the first mystery of the message of the person. Furthermore, the focus placed on the person "to whom it was revealed" (*ʿal-mî niglātāh*) emphasizes the mystery of the Suffering Servant in two senses and gives us the second and third mysteries. The second mystery is the more straightforward question of identity: Who is the person to whom it was revealed? The third mystery is the more complex question of meaning: Why was the arm of Yhwh revealed to him?

Let us now turn to solving the three mysteries that Isaiah 53:1 lays out in turn: the mystery of the message of the Suffering Servant, the mystery of the person of the Suffering Servant, and the mystery of the person as message.

The Mystery of the Message of the Suffering Servant

The message of the Suffering Servant, much like the identity of the Suffering Servant, was likely not a mystery to the we-group. The we-group unproblematically refers to the message as "what we have heard" (*šəmuʿātēnû*) and provides almost no other clue to help us identify the message. But there is, thankfully, one clue: the incredible report is related to "the arm of Yhwh" (*zərôʿa yhwh*).

CHAPTER 9

The parallel between "the arm of Yhwh" and "what we have heard" indicates that the we-group came to understand what they once found incredible to be of divine origin. In the course of history, the content of the message that the we-group seems to testify came to pass. Since, as we shall argue, the message upholds Cyrus as an important agent of God's redemptive plan for Israel, we locate the composition of Isaiah 53 sometime after Cyrus's conquest of Babylon in 538 BCE and either just before the Jewish return migration to Jerusalem or soon afterward. More importantly for our immediate purposes, the motif of Yhwh's arm connects directly to the message of Deutero-Isaiah, and the link gives us reason to identify the Suffering Servant with the prophet of Deutero-Isaiah.

The figure of Yhwh's arm appears in Deutero-Isaiah in three ways. First, consonant with the common figurative meaning of "arm" (*zərôʻa*), Yhwh's arm in Deutero-Isaiah refers generally to God's power and rule (40:10, 11; 51:5).[5] Second, Deutero-Isaiah associates the figure to God's redemptive plan for Israel from Babylon (51:9; 52:10).[6] Third, Deutero-Isaiah relates Yhwh's arm to the mission of Cyrus (48:14–16). Foregoing the discussion of the common meaning of the motif, let us turn to the second and third more specific cases.

Let us turn first to the remarkable prayer directed to the arm of Yhwh in Isaiah 51:9–11:

> [9] Awake, awake, put on strength, O arm of the Lord!
> Awake as in days of old, generations long ago.
> Is it not you, the Hewer of Rahab, the Piercer of Dragon?
> [10] Is it not you, the Drier of Sea, the waters of the Great Deep,
> The One who makes a path in the depths of the sea for the redeemed to cross over?
> [11] And the ransomed of the Lord shall return and enter Zion with singing,
> And everlasting joy shall be upon their heads.

---

5. BDB, s.v., "זְרוֹעַ."

6. It is interesting that the motif of Yhwh's arm appears only twice in Proto-Isaiah, in sections closely related to Deutero-Isaiah (30:30; 33:2), and appears four times in Trito-Isaiah (59:16; 62:8; 63:5, 12).

The Suffering Servant Exalted and Lifted Up and Very High

> They will obtain joy and gladness,
> And sorrow and sighing will flee away. (51:9–11,
>   my translation)[7]

The prophet directs the prayers to the arm of Yhwh and identifies Yhwh's arm as the agent of both the remembered and hoped-for mighty acts. The prophet presents the past as having two layers. In the cosmic past of myth, the prophet portrays the arm as the Hewer and Piercer of mythical monsters, Rahab and Dragon, and references a cosmic battle between Yhwh and the watery monsters of disorder. Recalled and remembered is Yhwh the conquering creator God over opposing cosmic forces.

From there, the prophet moves on to recount the deeds of Yhwh's arm during the time of the exodus in 51:10. The referents of "Drier of Sea" and "the waters of the Great Deep" are ambiguous and may be either mythical personalities or this-worldly geography, and, as such, the two phrases play a bridging function between the realm of myth and the realm of historical geography. But we can be certain that we are dealing with historical memory when the prophet prays to "the One who make a path in the depths of the sea for the redeemed to cross over (*'ābar*)." The prayer references events recounted in Exodus 14–15 and echoes language found therein:

> [21] Then Moses stretched out his hand over the sea. The Lord drove the sea back by a strong east wind all night, and turned the sea into dry land; and the waters were divided. [22] The Israelites went into the sea on dry ground, the waters forming a wall for them on their right and their left.... [29] But the Israelites walked on dry ground through the sea, the waters forming a wall for them on their right and their left. (Exod. 14:21–22, 29)

> [16] Terror and dread fell upon them;
> By the might of your arm (*zərô'ăkā*), they became still
>   as a stone
> Until your people, O Lord, passed by (*'ābar*),

---

7. For further discussion of the passage and its translation, see Cho, *Myth, History, and Metaphor*, 157–60.

CHAPTER 9

> Until the people whom you acquired passed by (*'ābar*).
> (Exod. 15:16)

The Isaianic prayer recalls the miracles of the exodus, identifies Yhwh's arm as the seat of power, and attempts to reactivate the divine arm to act in like manner to deliver Israel from the exile.

Finally, the prophet calls on the arm of Yhwh, as the creative power behind the *Chaoskampf* of creation and the liberative power of the exodus, to awaken in the exilic present to enact a comparable act of creative redemption so that—note the verbal tense—"the ransomed of the LORD shall return and enter Zion with singing" and so that "they shall obtain joy and gladness" (Isa. 51:11).[8] The prophet awakens Yhwh's arm not only because it is the seat of divine power but also because it is the seat of power that, in the mythic and historical past, redeemed creation and Israel from cosmic disorder and tyrannical destruction. In demonstration of considerable poetic athleticism, he moves from the world of mythic battle, through historical memory, to the prophetic future in which the arm of Yhwh shall redeem Israel, all in the compact space of three verses.

To summarize, the arm of the Yhwh motif in Isaiah 53, read within its larger literary context, is not a generic reference to divine might. The motif refers specifically to hope for redemption in the imminent future based on a memory of the past that the prophet believes can be reactivated in the present. The arm of Yhwh is what destroyed mythic monsters and historical oppressors in the past and, as such, is the hoped-for power that can redeem the faithful out of the present predicament into a glorious future.

Further insight regarding the fraught background to the arm of Yhwh motif in Isaiah 53 comes from another, more proximate text. In Isaiah 52:11-12, the prophet pleads with the exilic community: "Depart, depart, go out from there," and promises that they "shall not go out in haste (*ḥippāzôn*)." The Hebrew word for "haste" (*ḥippāzôn*) appears two other times in all of the Hebrew Bible, both times directly related to the exodus event. In Exod. 12:11, the Israelites are commanded to eat the Passover meal "in haste" (*ḥippāzôn*); and, in Deut. 16:3, they are described as departing Egypt "in

---

8. Carroll Stuhlmueller, *Creation Redemption in Deutero-Isaiah* (Rome: Pontifical Biblical Institute, 1970).

haste" (*ḥippāzôn*). Thus, the rare word *ḥippāzôn* in Isa. 52:12 is no doubt an explicit allusion to the exodus tradition. If we take seriously this and other allusions to the exodus tradition (51:9–11, etc.), then according to the prophet Israel shall experience a second exodus out of Babylon and deliverance that resembles, but is better than, the first exodus out of Egypt.

Now, according to the prophet, what makes the second exodus possible? The answer is found in Isaiah 52:7–10. The passage begins:

> ⁷ How beautiful upon the mountains
> are the feet of the messenger who announces peace,
> who brings good news, who announces salvation,
> who says to Zion, "Your God reigns." (52:7; cf. 40:6–11)

The prophet goes on to announce that, as in Isa. 51:9–11, YHWH's arm is the agent of salvation and manifestation of divine royal power:

> ¹⁰ The LORD has bared his holy arm
> Before the eyes of all the nations;
> And all the ends of the earth shall see
> the salvation of our God. (52:10)

It would appear that YHWH has heard the prophet's prayer in Isaiah 51:9–11 and, in response, has revealed his holy arm. YHWH's arm is both the outward sign that salvation on a grand scale is about to unfold and the reason that Israel can depart at leisure, not in haste, from Babylon. We see once again that the arm of YHWH does not refer to power generally but refers specifically to God's redemptive plan for Israel out of Babylon that is a better repetition of the first exodus.

Before we turn to the final reference to YHWH's arm in 48:14–16, it will be helpful to make one more observation concerning the passage immediately preceding Isaiah 53. As noted above, Isaiah 52:7 references a "messenger who announces peace" (*məbaśśēr mašmîʿa šalôm*) and a "messenger who brings good news" (*məbaśśēr ṭôb*). These epithets recall the opening passages of Deutero-Isaiah, in which debuted a "messenger of good tidings to Zion" (*məbaśśeret ṣîyôn*) (40:9), and another early passage in which God promises to send the same "messenger of good tidings" (*məbaśśēr*) to

Jerusalem (41:27). These three references to the messenger of good tidings in Deutero-Isaiah paint a picture that may be summarized in this way: God sent the messenger to proclaim the coming salvation to the Jewish community in Babylon, with emphasis on the return to Zion, from at least before the advent of Cyrus (40:9; 41:27); and the "arm of Yhwh" will accomplish the announced salvation in repetition of the exodus pattern (52:7–12). The arm of Yhwh will destroy Babylon and all other forces that stand in the way of Israel's return to Zion, just as God had destroyed the Pharaoh of history and the Dragon of myth—just as the messenger has been declaring from the beginning. Living in the eve of these world-historical events, the messenger raises his voice once more to encourage the people to live into the reality that he has proclaimed from before: Yhwh's arm has awakened to redeem Israel from Babylon so that they may cross over to Zion, rebuild the Temple, and celebrate the return of Yhwh the king.

With the theocentric dimension of the prophet in mind, let us now turn to Isaiah 48:14–16. The question that the text answers is how Yhwh's arm is to become manifest in history. The provided answer is not without ambiguity because the text does not explicitly name Cyrus. However, the contextual evidence points to the Persian king as God's chosen manifestation of Yhwh's arm.

Isaiah 48:14–16 reads:

> [14] Assemble, all of you, and hear!
> Who among them has declared these things?
> The Lord loves him;
> He shall perform his purpose on Babylon,
> And his arm shall be against the Chaldeans.
> [15] I, even I, have spoken and called him,
> I have brought him, and he will prosper in his way.
> [16] Draw near to me, hear this!
> From the beginning I have not spoken in secret,
> From the time it came to be I have been there.
> And now the Lord God has sent me and his spirit.

Who is it that Yhwh loves? Who will perform God's purpose against Babylon and act as God's arm against the Chaldeans? Whom has God called and empowered to prosper? Frustratingly, the text does not tell us directly. At the same time, the text declares that his identity is not a secret and has been spoken out loud from the beginning. If that is the case, the one whom Yhwh loves has to be Cyrus.

Cyrus is mentioned only twice by name in Deutero-Isaiah, in 44:28 and 45:1. However, many scholars agree that he is the subject of several other oracles throughout Isaiah 40–48, the Babylonian section of Deutero-Isaiah: 41:1–4, 25–29; 45:9–13; 46:9–11; and 48:12–16.[9] Taken together, the centrality of Cyrus to Deutero-Isaiah's message becomes clear.

The middle Cyrus passage (44:24–45:7) provides the hermeneutical key for reading the other passages: it explicitly names Cyrus twice (44:28; 45:1) and declares Yhwh's election of Cyrus as his shepherd (44:28) and anointed one (45:1). There can be no doubt that Yhwh has empowered Cyrus to deliver Israel from Babylon and to restore Zion. In the first half of the passage (44:24–28), Yhwh declares that he created Cyrus (44:24) and, calling him "my shepherd," commissions him to rebuild and restore Jerusalem and the temple (44:28). In the second half (45:1–7), Yhwh calls Cyrus "my anointed" (45:1) and declares that, though Cyrus does not yet know or worship Yhwh (45:4, 5), Yhwh will empower Cyrus's conquest of nations, presumably including Babylon (45:1–2). Central to Deutero-Isaiah's message is that Cyrus will free Israel from Babylon and initiate the restoration of Jerusalem.

Given the hermeneutical key, the references to Cyrus in the other passages that punctuate the beginning, middle, and end of Isaiah 40–48 come readily into view. To review the passage from the beginning to the end, Cyrus is the "victor from the east" (41:2); the "one from the north" who comes from "the rising of the sun . . . summoned by name" (41:25); the one whom God, against the protests of many (45:9–12), has aroused in righteousness (45:13); the "bird of prey from the east, the man for [God's] purpose from a far country" (46:11); and the one who "shall perform [God's] purpose on Babylon" and make manifest "[Yhwh's] arm . . . against the Chaldeans" (48:14).

If the above interpretation is correct, there can be no doubt concerning the centrality of Cyrus to Deutero-Isaiah's message of redemption. From

---

9. Berges, *Isaiah*, 312.

an early stage in his ministry, the prophet proclaimed that Cyrus is God's chosen instrument and dared to bestow on a non-Jew, whom the prophet acknowledges is not a Y<small>HWH</small>-worshipper, the august titles of Y<small>HWH</small>'s shepherd and anointed. What more? Isaiah 48:14 more directly associates Cyrus and God, making Cyrus the very embodiment of Y<small>HWH</small>'s saving arm: "his arm shall be against the Chaldeans."

To return to Isaiah 53, Isaiah 53:1 expresses consternation about what the we-group has heard (*šəmuʻātēnû*), about the message of the Suffering Servant that in part is described further as the revealed "arm of Y<small>HWH</small>." If the above discussion is correct, we can attach three levels of meaning to "the arm of Y<small>HWH</small>" as a means of solving the mystery of the message of the Suffering Servant. First, the arm of Y<small>HWH</small> refers to the power and reign of God, consonant with the common, figurative meaning of "arm." Second, the arm of Y<small>HWH</small> refers to the full shape of salvation God has planned for exiled Israel: The arm of Y<small>HWH</small>—who defeated chaos monsters in creation and led Israel out of Egypt across the Red Sea in the exodus—has now awakened and will soon lead exiled Israel out of Babylon back to Jerusalem, where the temple will be rebuilt and from which Y<small>HWH</small> will once again reign as king. Third, the arm of Y<small>HWH</small> will make God's power and rule manifest in and through a pagan king, Cyrus. Cyrus will be the one who conquers Babylon, sets Israel free, and rebuilds Jerusalem and the temple. While the first two are expected, if bold, understandings of the arm of Y<small>HWH</small> motif, the third—that Cyrus is God's anointed shepherd—likely shocked the prophet's Jewish audience and became a source of controversy and even scandal. As we shall argue, the prophet's endorsement of Cyrus partially explains the opposition and persecution the prophet, thus the Suffering Servant, experienced.

To summarize, the "arm of Y<small>HWH</small>" motif helps us solve the mystery of the message of the Suffering Servant. It was, on the whole, unbelievably good news for Zion as proclaimed by the messenger of peace and good news (52:7). However, on account of its endorsement of Cyrus, it was also the cause of acerbic opposition for the prophet, that is, the Suffering Servant. With that, let us turn to the mystery of the person of the Suffering Servant, an issue that is intimately related to the mystery of the message.

The Suffering Servant Exalted and Lifted Up and Very High

The Mystery of the Person of the Suffering Servant

Isaiah 53:1 registers disbelief not only about the message of the Suffering Servant but also about the person of the Suffering Servant. More precisely, the we-group expresses disbelief that God chose to reveal "the arm of Yhwh" to a person like the Suffering Servant, whose biography and constitution, in their view, could cast doubt on the message itself: "And to whom has the arm of Yhwh been revealed?" In calling the message of the Suffering Servant "the arm of Yhwh," the we-group acknowledges that what they had initially found incredible is in fact the work of God. Thus, more than the message, what shocked the we-group is the chosen messenger for the message: Why would God entrust the momentous message of Israel's salvation to a man who "had no form or majesty," who possessed "nothing in his appearance that we should desire him" (53:2), "a man of suffering and acquainted with infirmity," and who "was despised" and disregarded (53:3)? That is, at the center of the mystery of God's election of the person of the Suffering Servant are the nature of his suffering, his physical deformity, and his social ostracization.

Explanations for the nature of the Servant's suffering are numerous. I would like to discuss two that demonstrate the wide range of possible interpretations the textual evidence establishes. The first explanation is that the Suffering Servant was persecuted for his message, and the second is that he was ostracized on account of his skin anomaly.

The explanation that the Suffering Servant was persecuted due to the content of his message stems largely from his elevation of Cyrus, a foreign ruler, as Israel's redeemer. A central feature of the prophet/Suffering Servant's message is that Cyrus will enact God's plan for Israel's deliverance from Babylon and the restoration of Jerusalem. Given that the audience for this message would have been the prophet's fellow Yahwists, it is not difficult to imagine that granting such eminence to a non-Yahwist and foreign king would have irked and possibly angered some among the prophet's coreligionists. In fact, the negative reaction can be inferred from the defensiveness on display in Isaiah 45:9–17.

The central argument of Isaiah 45:9–17 is that God, as the creator, has the freedom to do as he wishes with his creatures and offers the analogy of

CHAPTER 9

a potter with his earthen jars (45:9) and a parent with her children (45:10). The general discussion about divine freedom culminates with the pointed defense of Yʜᴡʜ's choice presumably of Cyrus as Israel's redeemer. I say "presumably" because Cyrus is not actually named in the passage—though certain English translations (NRSV, NIV) supply the name. In any case, context makes it relatively certain that Cyrus is in view. Isaiah 45:13 reads:

> [13] I have aroused him in righteousness,
> And I will make all his paths straight (*yāšar*);
> He shall build my city
> And set my exiles free,
> Not for price or reward,
> Says the Lᴏʀᴅ of hosts.

The description of him whom God has aroused in righteousness matches what was previously said about Cyrus. In Isaiah 44:28, God explicitly names Cyrus as the one who is to rebuild Jerusalem, and God promises to go before Cyrus and "level (*yāšar*) the mountains" in 45:2.

That the prophet feels the need to defend God's election of Cyrus and, furthermore, to base that defense on the theological claim that Yʜᴡʜ is creator points to the existence of strong opposition to the message. It is but a small interpretive leap to imagine that the opposition took verbal and even physical form directed at the prophet.

Direct evidence that the prophet suffered opposition and persecution is slight but not nonexistent. The divine speeches that frame Isaiah 53 connect the Suffering Servant to the servant of Yʜᴡʜ mentioned elsewhere in Deutero-Isaiah. While the connection between the first three so-called servant of Yʜᴡʜ songs (42:1–4, 49:1–6, 50:4–9) and Isaiah 53, the fourth song, has been debated, it is reasonable to assume a connection among the texts.[10] The four passages, while they should not be read in isolation as has sometimes been done, share enough thematic and imagistic com-

---

10. Bernhard Duhm (*Das Buch Jesaia: Übersetzt und erklärt* [Göttingen: Vandenhoeck & Ruprecht, 1922], 311) first isolated the so-called servant of Yʜᴡʜ songs. For the opposing view, see Tryggve Mettinger, *A Farewell to the Servant Songs: A Critical Examination of an Exegetical Axiom* (Lund: Gleerup, 1983).

monalities to warrant being read together. If so read, what we find is an episodic portrayal of the ministry of the prophet in which opposition and then persecutions seem to become a reality.

We can detect the presence of opposition in the second song (49:1–6). The Servant, who is identified as Israel in 49:3, possibly by a later redactor, complains:

> ⁴ I have labored in vain,
> I have spent my strength for nothing and vanity. (49:4a)

The nature of the Servant's labor is not detailed, but the reference to his "mouth [which is] like a sharp sword" indicates that his work concerned proclaiming an unpopular message. There is, in short, a general match between the experience of the servant of Yhwh in the song and what we have reconstructed about the Suffering Servant/prophet: At God's bidding they speak a message that brings them hardship.

The theme of speaking at God's bidding continues in the third song (50:4–9). So too does the theme of persecution. However, the persecution in the passage takes on physical form:

> ⁶ I gave my back to those who struck me,
> and my cheek to those who pulled out my beard;
> I did not hide my face from insult and spitting. (50:6)

What might have been neglect and dismissal in the second song has turned decidedly more hostile by the time of the third song. Lament about rejection and disbelief becomes testimony about physical abuse.

The fourth servant of Yhwh song (Isa. 52:13–53:12) provides a kind of culmination to the story. The Servant not only experiences verbal and physical abuse but possibly also death:

> ⁷ He was oppressed, and he was afflicted,
> yet he did not open his mouth;
> like a lamb that is led to the slaughter,
> and like a sheep that before its shearers is silent,
> so he did not open his mouth.

> ⁸ By a perversion of justice he was taken away.
> Who could have imagined his future?
> For he was cut off from the land of the living,
> stricken for the transgression of my people.
> ⁹ They made his grave with the wicked
> and his tomb with the rich,
> although he had done no violence,
> and there was no deceit in his mouth. (53:7–9).

There is debate concerning whether the Suffering Servant is represented as dying in the passage. Despite what strikes me as clear indication of death—the slaughter image, the statement that he was "cut off from the land of the living," the reference to "his tomb"—it is possible to interpret these images metaphorically to refer to extreme sickness. The statement that the servant "shall see his offspring, and shall prolong his days" in Isaiah 53:10 provides further ground for the metaphorical interpretation. Even given this contrastive interpretive possibility, what is important is that it is reasonable to take the above passage as referring to the Servant's death, a death that the we-group once thought was a just punishment from God: "we accounted him stricken, struck down by God, and afflicted" (53:4b).

To summarize, the Suffering Servant, who is to be identified with both the prophet of Deutero-Isaiah and the servant of Yʜᴡʜ of the servant songs, experienced opposition, persecution, and finally death in part for his message that God chose and empowered Cyrus to enact Israel's deliverance out of Babylon. The episodic and gapped nature of the textual evidence makes it impossible to claim certainty, but the givens of the text allow for the reconstructed scenario in which the Suffering Servant was persecuted for his message.

One difficulty to the above interpretation that the Suffering Servant endured persecution and ultimately death for his message of imminent redemption at the hand of other human beings arises from the observation that, in Isaiah 53, God alone is named as the responsible party for the Servant's suffering. According to the second and third servant songs, other people are the source of the prophet's ills (49:4, 50:6), and God is consistently named as a source of strength and vindication (49:4–5, 50:7–9).

The Suffering Servant Exalted and Lifted Up and Very High

However, the fourth song throughout says that God struck and afflicted and crushed the Suffering Servant (53:4-10). If the people participate in causing the Servant's pain, it is through social ostracization: "He was despised and rejected by others . . . he was despised, and we held him of no account" (53:3).

On account of these observations, Bernhard Duhm, who first isolated the four so-called servant songs and proposed that they should be read together, suggested that the Suffering Servant had a skin anomaly.[11] The usual Hebrew word to indicate skin disease, ṣāra'at, does not appear in Isaiah 53, which uses the generic word for illness, ḥŏlî (53:3, 4; cf. v. 10). However, auxiliary vocabulary often associated with skin disease elsewhere in the Hebrew Bible, including Leviticus (e.g., nāga' [53:4, 8], ḥālal [53:5], and pāga' [53:10]), describes the experience of the Suffering Servant. This suggests that the Suffering Servant had a skin anomaly.[12]

Jeremy Schipper has recently built on Duhm's thesis to argue more forcefully that the Suffering Servant was a person with a skin anomaly and who, as a result, experienced social isolation.[13] Schipper observes that ancient Near Easter traditions, including the Hebrew Bible, thought of deities as the controlling source of skin disease and other diseases.[14] In the Hebrew Bible, for example, God afflicts the Pharaoh (Gen. 12:17), the Philistines (1 Sam. 5:9; 6:9), and King Uzziah (2 Kgs. 15:5) with various diseases. Perhaps most revealing is Exodus 4, in which God causes then heals a skin anomaly on Moses's hand (4:4-8). The consequence of this theological explanation was in part social and resulted in social isolation. As one Babylonian omen says of a person with a skin anomaly, "rejected by his God . . . he is rejected by humanity."[15] Schipper argues that this pattern (a deity strikes a person with skin disease, then the person experiences social isolation) provides a reasonable analogy to the experience of the

---

11. Duhm, *Das Buch Jesaia*, 368; cited in Jeremy Schipper, *Disability and Isaiah's Suffering Servant* (Oxford: Oxford University Press, 2011), 32.
12. See Schipper, *Disability and Isaiah*, 32-33.
13. Schipper, *Disability and Isaiah*, 35-42.
14. Schipper, *Disability and Isaiah*, 35-36.
15. On this omen, see Hector Avalos, *Illness and Health Care in the Ancient Near East: The Role of the Temple in Greece, Mesopotamia, and Israel*, HSM 54 (Atlanta: Scholars, 1995), 180-81; cited in Schipper, *Disability and Isaiah*, 37.

CHAPTER 9

Suffering Servant: He was understood to be stricken by God (plausibly with a skin anomaly) and so was rejected and despised by others.

Schipper, given his focus on demonstrating that the Suffering Servant may reasonably be thought of as a figure with disabilities, does not attempt to relate the Servant's skin condition and the resulting social experience to solving the mysteries of his message, person, and suffering.[16] Schipper's proposal nevertheless contributes meaningfully to unraveling the mystery of the shock the we-group expresses concerning the person of the Suffering Servant.

If the Suffering Servant was a person with disabilities, which the we-group and others understood to have been afflicted upon him by God, then he is likely to have experienced social isolation, including shame:

> He was despised and rejected by others;
> a man of suffering and acquainted with infirmity;
> and as one from whom others hide their faces
> he was despised, and we held him of no account. (53:3)

The claim that a person who was believed to be stricken, smitten, and afflicted by God with disease had, from the same God, received a revelation concerning Israel's redemption—and this through the hand of a faraway pagan king—would have been met with dismissal and disbelief: "And to whom has the arm of the LORD been revealed?" (53:1). But when the Suffering Servant insisted, perhaps having won over a small group of believers, ridicule and persecution may have followed:

> I gave my back to those who struck me,
> and my cheeks to those who pulled out the beard;
> I did not hide my face from insult and spitting. (50:6)

It is not possible to ascertain the cause of the Servant's death (if indeed he died), but it is not unimaginable that he died from his underlying physical condition, exacerbated by social isolation and abuse: "like a lamb that is

---

16. Schipper, *Disability and Isaiah*, 31–32.

The Suffering Servant Exalted and Lifted Up and Very High

led to the slaughter . . . he did not open his mouth. . . . For he was cut off from the land of the living" (53:7, 8).

The Servant's detractors and persecutors, including the we-group, may have thought little about the Suffering Servant and his message. They may have pitied him, lamented his suffering even, but they likely did not ponder what the man had said and, when they did, considered it the ramblings of a diseased mind. Until, that is, what they had heard came to pass and was retrospectively revealed to have been the work of Yhwh's arm. The realization would have occurred after the advent of Cyrus, his conquest of Babylon and his decree releasing Jews to return to Jerusalem. At that time, the we-group would have turned their attention to the once maligned figure with wonder: How is it that God chose to reveal Israel's redemption to such a person? What is the meaning of his suffering, if it was not a sign of divine opprobrium?

This brings us to the mystery of the person of the Suffering Servant as message.

The Mystery of the Person of the Suffering Servant as Message

The message of the Suffering Servant and the person of the Suffering Servant, including his possible skin anomaly and experience of social isolation, were not mysteries to the we-group who composed Isaiah 53. The content of the message and the identity of the Servant were known to the we-group. This has meant that, for us, the message and identity of the Suffering Servant remain genuine mysteries. The one mystery that we as readers of Isaiah 53 share with its authors is the mystery of the person as message, namely the meaning of the Servant's suffering, which the we-group retrospectively realized could not be a sign of divine disfavor and did not disqualify the Servant's message. The we-group in their confession in the core of Isaiah 53 offers a novel understanding of the suffering; they write that the figure suffered vicariously and worked vicarious benefit for the we-group.[17] God in the frame of Isaiah 53 goes beyond the claims of the we-group in the core.

---

17. For a discussion of the prehistory of the idea of vicarious suffering, see Hermann Spiekermann, "The Conception and Prehistory of the Idea of Vicarious Suffering in the Old Testament," in *The Suffering Servant: Isaiah 53 in Jewish and Christian Sources*, ed. Bernd Janowski and Peter Stuhlmacher, trans. Daniel P. Bailey (Grand Rapids: Eerdmans, 2004), 1–15.

In a truly remarkable development, God elevates the Suffering Servant to a position of glory above any other human being. The Servant's inhuman suffering marks him, not as subhuman, but superhuman—almost divine.

Debate continues concerning the precise meaning of the Suffering Servant's vicarious suffering, about the details of vicariousness in Isaiah 53 and the history of development. For our purposes, it suffices to understand the basic contours of the explanation the we-group offers concerning the mystery of the person as message.

The we-group holds on to the theological explanation of disease and maintains that God caused the Servant's suffering. The quality of the causation, however, has changed: What was once thought to be evidence of having been stricken, smitten, and afflicted by the divine (53:3), the we-group ultimately characterizes as an expression of positive divine volition: "Yet it was the will of the LORD (*yhwh ḥāpēṣ*) to crush him with pain" (53:10). The dramatic change in perspective stems from the belated recognition that the message of the Suffering Servant, which the we-group had dismissed as the product of a sickened imagination, was trustworthy and of divine origin. With this reevaluation, one fundamental enigma remained: Why did God make the Servant, whom God chose as the messenger for the momentous message, suffer?

The we-group did not arrive at the radical possibility that suffering at times may not have any meaning, that one might suffer for nothing (*ḥinnām*), but instead retained the traditional explanation that suffering was due to sin. The innovation came, not in breaking the causal link between sin and punishment, but in locating the sin outside the suffering body.[18] The we-group came to believe that the Servant suffered on account of their sin and not for his own sin. The Servant suffered vicariously the punishment the we-group believed they and others who dismissed and despised the Servant justly deserved:

> [4] Surely he has borne our infirmities
> And carried our diseases . . .

---

18. The portrayal of Moses as being denied entry into the promised land on account of the people's sin in Deut. 1:37 as well as the sacrificial practices may anticipate this development. I thank Jon D. Levenson for this insight.

> ⁵ But he was wounded for our transgressions,
> Crushed for our iniquities;
> Upon him was the punishment that made us whole,
> And by his bruises we are healed
> ⁶ All we like sheep have gone astray;
> We have all turned to our own way,
> And the LORD has laid on him the iniquity of us all. . . .
> ⁸ By a perversion of justice he was taken away.
> Who could have imagined his future?
> For he was cut off from the land of the living,
> Stricken for the transgression of my people.
> ⁹ They made his grave with the wicked
> And his tomb with the rich,
> Although he had done no violence,
> And there was no deceit in his mouth.
> ¹⁰ Yet it was the will of the LORD to crush him with pain.
> When you make his life an offering for sin. (53:4, 5-6, 8-10)

Understandably, the we-group devotes the majority of their confession to their novel understanding that the Suffering Servant bore the punishment due to them and others who had committed the sin of not believing the Servant's message from God. The we-group also alludes to more nefarious misdeeds when they accuse a third party of making the Servant's "grave with the wicked and his tomb with the rich." It is likely that some who opposed the Suffering Servant went beyond dismissal and verbal abuse and contributed to his physical suffering and possibly death.

The notice that the Servant's life was made into "an offering for sin" (*'āšām*) has led to speculations whether the Servant's death may be thought of as an atoning sacrifice. The image of the Servant being led away like a lamb has suggested for some that the we-group is portraying the Servant's death as a ritual sacrifice, comparable to the guilt offering (*'āšām*) in Leviticus 5:14-16 or the "scapegoat" from Leviticus 16:10, 20-22.[19] While these significances, in particular that of the guilt offering, cannot be dismissed

---

19. See Bernd Janowski, "He Bore Our Sin: Isaiah 53 and the Drama of Taking Another's Place," in *The Suffering Servant: Isaiah 53 in Jewish and Christian Sources*,

completely, lack of auxiliary lexica and concepts associated with ritual atonement caution against overstatement. Bernd Janowski, in my opinion, arrives at as precise a definition as the textual evidence permits. He agrees with Knierim that *'āšām* means "the obligation to discharge guilt that arises from a situation of guilt" and writes concerning its use in Isaiah 53:

> Israel, which is in no position to take over the obligation arising from its guilt, must be released from this obligation in order to have any future. This liberation comes from an innocent one who surrenders his life according to Yahweh's 'plan' (v. 10a, b) and as a consequence of his own ministry (vv. 7–9).[20]

In this way, the Suffering Servant "[takes] over the consequences of *others' actions*."[21]

In this light, the core of Isaiah 53 is confessional in two ways. First, the we-group admits that they were mistaken about the message and person of the Suffering Servant. His message was no fanciful madness but the proclamation of YHWH's plan for Israel's redemption, and the Servant did not suffer punishment for his own sins but suffered at the will of God to fulfill the obligation of others. Second, their reinterpretation of the Servant's suffering forces them to recognize that they are guilty of sin, including unbelief and unjust persecution. The Suffering Servant's unwavering commitment to proclaiming "the arm of YHWH" despite the persecution, that is, his willing embrace of death for his faith in the revealed will of God, take away the guilt the we-group and Israel incur. The Suffering Servant proclaims a redemptive future for Israel and, in willingly dying in its service, paves a path for Israel to live into that future.

The frame of Isaiah 53, in which God speaks of the Suffering Servant, elevates the figure even further and places him high above any other human being. God ascribes to the Suffering Servant a near divine status. Here is the text:

---

ed. Bernd Janowski and Peter Stuhlmacher, trans. Daniel P. Bailey (Grand Rapids: Eerdmans, 2004), 67.

20. Janowski, "He Bore Our Sin," 69.
21. Janowski, "He Bore Our Sin," 69.

The Suffering Servant Exalted and Lifted Up and Very High

> ^{52:13} See, my servant shall prosper;
> he shall be exalted and lifted up,
> and shall be very high.
> ¹⁴ Just as [the many] were astonished at him—
> so marred was his appearance, beyond human semblance,
> and his form beyond that of mortals—
> ¹⁵ so he shall startle many nations;
> kings shall shut their mouths because of him;
> for that which had not been told them they shall see,
> and that which they had not heard they shall contemplate.
> . . .
> ^{53:11aβ} The righteous one, my servant, shall make
> [the many] righteous,
> and he shall bear their iniquities.
> ¹² Therefore I will allot him a portion with [the many],
> and he shall divide the spoil with the strong;
> because he poured out himself to death,
> and was numbered with the transgressors;
> yet he bore the sin of many,
> and made intercession for the transgressors.
> (52:13–15, 53:11aβ–12)[22]

As we noted above, the Suffering Servant is called God's servant—both times in the first-person possessive "my servant" (52:13; 52:11)—only in the divine speeches. In the core of Isaiah 53, the figure remains anonymous and without a title. The function of this nomenclature is to connect the Suffering Servant to the servant figure that appears in other parts of Deutero-Isaiah, which we discussed above. Another function of God's speeches concerning the Servant, to which we turn now, is to glorify and elevate him. Important in this regard is that God says that the Servant "shall be exalted (*rûm*) and lifted up (*nāśaʾ*), and shall be very high (*gābah*)" (52:13). These thematic words find important intertexts in Isaiah 2 and 6.

In Isaiah 2 and 6 taken together, we find that both human pride and haughtiness and divine glory and exaltation are described in the same

---

22. Following the NRSV except to translate הרבים consistently as "the many."

terms God uses to describe "my servant." Furthermore, these passages mark human elevation for punishment and divine height for worship. Let us turn first to Isaiah 2:

> [11] The haughty (*gābah*) eyes of people shall be brought low,
> and the pride (*rûm*) of everyone shall be humbled;
> and the LORD alone will be exalted in that day.
> [12] For the LORD of hosts has a day
> against all that is proud and lofty (*rûm*),
> against all that is lifted up (*nāśa'*) and high;
> [13] against all the cedars of Lebanon,
> lofty (*rûm*) and lifted up (*nāśa'*);
> and against all the oaks of Bashan;
> [14] against all the high (*rûm*) mountains,
> and against all the lofty (*nāśa'*) hills;
> [16] against all the ships of Tarshish,
> and against all the beautiful craft.
> [17] The haughtiness (*gābah*) of people shall be humbled,
> and the pride (*rûm*) of everyone shall be brought low;
> and the LORD alone will be exalted on that day. (2:11–17)

This passage emphasizes that human self-exaltation, described in the language of physical elevation (*rûm, nāśa', gābah*), is marked for punishment and is to be "brought low" and "humbled." In contrast, the passage says that God "alone will be exalted" (2:11, 17). The theme of divine exaltation is further developed in the temple vision of Isaiah 6, in which divine glory is described in the exact terms used to describe the servant in Isaiah 53:

> In the year that King Uzziah died, I saw the Lord sitting on a throne, high (*rûm*) and lofty (*nāśa'*); and the hem of his robe filled the temple. (6:1)

A contrastive and antagonistic picture emerges: Human self-elevation is pitted against divine glory, and divine exaltation requires the dismantling of human pride.[23] There is room for only one in the heights.

---

23. Berges, *Isaiah*, 379.

The Suffering Servant Exalted and Lifted Up and Very High

The antagonistic relationship between divine height and glory and human elevation and pride frames the interpretation of God's description of his Servant as "exalted and lifted up [and] . . . very high" in Isaiah 53. That human elevation and pride is relentlessly marked for divine punishment suggests that the Servant, whom God elevates, should not be regarded as other human beings are. Rather, the Servant is to be regarded as more akin to God. The servant of Yhwh is "high and lifted up" unlike how other human beings are, but very much like how God is. This vertical and qualitative proximity of the servant of Yhwh to God invites a counterintuitive interpretation of God's statement that the servant's "appearance [was marred] beyond human semblance, and his form beyond that of mortals" (52:14). His non-participation in human likeness does not mark him as subhuman or as rejected by God, as it was unsurprisingly interpreted (53:4). No, the divine speeches reinterpret the Servant's physical deformation and suffering as marks of divine glory. The servant of Yhwh—not despite his appearances but as his outer nonhuman form accurately indicates—approaches divinity more than humanity, is more godlike than humanlike.

This is the oxymoronic meaning of the person of the Suffering Servant—whose human deformation signifies divine glory—that in part renders the kings of many nations mute with shock and forces them to consider what was previously unimaginable (52:15). What is unimaginable in part is the theological meaning and function of the Servant's deformation and suffering. Adding to this shock is the claim that the Servant's deformations are also evidence of vicarious suffering that makes others righteous: "The righteous one, my servant," God says in the closing frame, "shall make [the many] righteous, and he shall bear their iniquities" (53:11). Furthermore, so as to give material evidence for the Servant's theological significance, that is, to make visible what is invisible, God promises to give his servant "a portion with [the many]" and "spoil with the strong" (53:12). The mystery of the Servant—of his identity, ministerial horizon, and promised exaltation—deepens with this indication of his world-historical significance. He is a figure whose humiliation and glorification, which cannot be distinguished but are in fact one and the same, reverberate on the world stage among "many nations" and their astounded kings. They thought themselves to be high, lifted up, and exalted but find that the servant of Yhwh,

CHAPTER 9

marred and deformed as he appears, shares in God's glory and accomplishes God's mission for the many nations.

To summarize, upon their belated recognition that the man of suffering, who is the prophet of Deutero-Isaiah, delivered God's message of redemption for Israel, the we-group struggles to understand the reason for the prophet's suffering. Why would God allow an innocent man, his own chosen prophet, to suffer? They arrive at the novel understanding that "the Lord has laid on him the iniquity of us all" (53:6). The prophet vicariously suffered the we-group's punishment and, thereby, fulfilled the obligation incurred by their sin. A later redactor, who sought to integrate the confession of the we-group (Isa. 53:1–11aα) into the book of Isaiah, composed the frame, in which God honors the prophet with the title "my servant." The title identifies the prophet with "the servant of Yhwh" in the servant of Yhwh songs in Deutero-Isaiah and, even more shockingly, elevates him to a position of glory denied other human beings, glory that in Proto-Isaiah appeared to be the exclusive possession of Yhwh alone. Like Yhwh who sits "on a throne, high and lofty" (6:1), so too does God say that the Suffering Servant is "exalted and lifted up, and shall be very high" (52:13). This is not deification. But it is close.

The Suffering Servant as Martyr

We are now able to answer the question: Was the Suffering Servant a martyr? We can do this by checking the evidence against the five characteristics of martyrdom we established in chapter 8.

1. Martyrdom reflects situations of opposition and persecution.

The Suffering Servant faced opposition and persecution on multiple fronts. His skin anomaly, if we are correct that he experienced this particular disability, would have meant that he experienced social isolation and antagonism. The prophet's message of imminent redemption, which emphasized the agency of the Persian king Cyrus, also faced opposition and incited some to persecute him. Either because of persecution alone or due to a combination of social isolation and physical persecution, the Suffering Servant ultimately died.

2. Authors of martyr stories view the choice to die that the martyr makes as necessary, noble, and heroic.

Isaiah 53 makes clear that the Servant's suffering, including his death, was necessary, for it was divine will that he suffered (53:10). That the Servant did not protest his death but was silent points to the dignity and nobility of his choice to die (53:7). And the divine speech speaks to the high heroism of the Suffering Servant.

3. The martyr demonstrates or is portrayed as demonstrating a willingness to die.

The Suffering Servant's silent acceptance of his death in the we-group's confession ambiguously points to his willingness to die. God ascribes to the Servant a more active embrace and participation in his death in stating that "he poured out himself to death . . . and made intercession for the transgressors" (53:12). According to the divine speech, the Suffering Servant did not merely accept his death passively but, with full comprehension of his role in the economy of debt and forgiveness, participated in his suffering to fulfill vicariously the guilty obligation incurred by the we-group.

4. The martyr, the author, or both impute to the martyrdom the idea of vicarious benefit from a martyr's suffering and death.

In the core of Isaiah 53, the we-group confesses to their belated understanding of the vicariousness of the servant's suffering and death:

> [5] But he was wounded for our transgressions,
> Crushed for our iniquities;
> Upon him was the punishment that made us whole,
> And by his bruises we are healed. (53:5)

Furthermore, God seems to suggest that the Suffering Servant himself was aware of the vicarious benefit he was to bestow in stating that he actively "poured out himself to death" in order to make "intercession for the transgressors."

CHAPTER 9

5. An expectation of vindication and reward beyond death develops in relation to a martyr's death and may motivate the choice to die.

We cannot say for certain that the Suffering Servant expected to be vindicated or rewarded after death. However, the we-group, upon contemplating the mystery of the Servant's suffering and death, came to believe that the Servant would be vindicated and rewarded after death. They write:

> ¹⁰ He shall see his offspring, and shall prolong his days;
> Through him the will of the Lord shall prosper.
> ¹¹ Out of anguish he shall see light;
> He shall find satisfaction through his knowledge. (53:10b–11aα)

As noted above, the language is ambiguous. Some scholars interpret the talk of the Servant's offspring and the prolongation of his days literally and, therefore, understand the previous verses that speak of the Servant's death figuratively. Those who interpret references to the Servant's death literally understand verses 53:10–11 figuratively as referring to a state of being beyond death. Without claiming certainly either way, I propose to read these verses as referring to a postmortem state of affairs. The offspring may speak to the prophet's disciples who, having come to believe in the prophet's message after he suffered death, carry on the mission of the Servant. In this way, they prolong the Servant's days and contribute to the success of God's will.

The framing divine speech, written with knowledge of the Servant's death, takes the further step of exalting the Servant and claims for him both material reward, in that the servant is to find "a portion with the great" and share in the "spoil of the many," and honor, in that he is to be exalted above other human beings and seated, as it were, next to God.

Conclusion

A wide range of interpretations concerning the Suffering Servant of Isaiah 53 are both possible and defensible.[24] What I have tried to accomplish

---

24. See Marc Brettler and Amy-Jill Levine, "Isaiah's Suffering Servant: Before and After Christianity," *Interpretation* 73 (2019): 158–73.

The Suffering Servant Exalted and Lifted Up and Very High

in this chapter is to argue for the reasonableness of identifying the enigmatic figure with both the prophet of Deutero-Isaiah and the servant of the servant of Yhwh songs. When we allow for this identification, it becomes possible to reconstruct, provisionally and with caveats, that the Suffering Servant died a martyr's death and that his death, along with his suffering more generally, came to be understood as working vicarious benefit for others. He bears and satisfies the guilty obligation of others, the we-group minimally and of Israel maximally, and makes it possible for them to live into the redemptive reality that was the subject of his message. Furthermore, the Suffering Servant's willing embrace of death wins for him glory and honor far above other human beings and comparable to what Yhwh enjoys. God says of the Suffering Servant, as the prophet Isaiah had said of Yhwh: "He shall be exalted and lifted up, and shall be very high" (52:13; cf. 6:1).

CHAPTER 10

The Wise Shall Live Again

The reality of [a human being] . . . is not abolished in death, but rather is transposed into another mode of existence.

Karl Rahner[1]

THE FINAL INNOVATION REGARDING the relationship between death and life that we shall examine occurs in the book of Daniel. A group called the Wise (*maśkilîm*), who likely composed the latter half of the book of Daniel (Daniel 7–12) and was responsible for the final form of the book, built on the conceptual developments of Isaiah 53 to advocate for nonviolent resistance against persecution, even to the point of death. They taught that those who stand in faith and wait, should they "fall by sword and flame" (Dan. 11:33), shall rise again "to everlasting life" (12:2). This is the first unambiguous reference to the doctrine of resurrection in the Hebrew Bible, and the celebrated innovation occurred during a time of extreme turmoil for Jews. It was persecution that demanded a willingness to die from the faithful, and martyrdom inspired the belief in everlasting life beyond death.

---

1. Karl Rahner, *Foundations of Christian Faith: An Introduction to the Idea of Christianity*, trans. William V. Dych (New York: Crossroad, 1978), 436.

The Wise Shall Live Again

The Wise and Martyrdom

The Wise lived in Judea during the reign of the Seleucid King Antiochus IV (175-164 BCE). Antiochus, for still unclear reasons, began to persecute Jews in 169 BCE.[2] According to the book of Daniel, Antiochus "[spoke] arrogantly" and more importantly attempted "to change the times and the law"; he issued edicts that outlawed the practice of Judaism in an attempt to disrupt the cultic calendar, including sabbath observance, and to erase Jewish identity and way of life (7:8, 11, 25; cf. 1 Macc. 1:45; 2 Macc. 6:6). The oppressive policies culminated in the erection of a desolating sacrilege in the Jerusalem temple on Chislev 15, 145 (= December 6, 167 BCE; 1 Macc. 1:54; cf. Dan. 8:11-13). Those who resisted the edicts through noncompliance were met with threats, torture, and execution.[3]

A variety of responses to the persecutory program was possible and practiced by Jews. The Maccabees, at one end of the spectrum, led a successful military revolt against the Seleucids and won for the Jews self-governance. They founded the Hasmonean dynasty (167-37 BCE). In contrast, the Wise practiced and taught nonviolent resistance. Like the Maccabees, the Wise chose to fight the Antiochian attempt at religious and cultural erasure and continued to hold on to faith in the God of Israel. But unlike the Maccabees, even when persecution became violent, the Wise refused to take up arms against their oppressors. Rather, they resisted through "prayer, fasting, and penitence, teaching and preaching, and covenant fidelity even in the face of death."[4] They resolutely held on to their faith in God and, in this way, actively witnessed to their faith in

---

2. See Cho, *Myth, History, and Metaphor*, 199-203. For a review of scholarly proposals, see John J. Collins, *Daniel: A Commentary on the Book of Daniel*, Hermeneia (Minneapolis: Fortress, 1993), 63-65. For a recent suggestion, see Anathea Portier-Young, *Apocalypse against Empire: Theologies of Resistance in Early Judaism* (Grand Rapids: Eerdmans, 2011), 115-39.

3. Portier-Young, *Resistance*, 176; Collins, *Daniel*, 323-24; Rainer Albertz, "The Social Setting of the Aramaic and Hebrew Book of Daniel," in *The Book of Daniel: Composition and Reception*, ed. John J. Collins and Peter W. Flint, 2 vols. (Leiden: Brill, 2001), 1:187.

4. Portier-Young, *Resistance*, 229.

God. They knew the violent intent of Antiochus IV and that some would die "by sword and flame, and suffer captivity and plunder" (Dan. 11:33). Nevertheless, the Wise advocated for what we have defined as martyrdom. They are the one undisputed group who clearly articulated a defense of martyrdom and became martyrs. So let us turn to the demonstration that the Wise experienced martyrdom.

1. Martyrdom reflects situations of opposition and persecution.

Daniel 7–12 is apocalyptic literature. It is "a genre of revelatory literature with a narrative framework, in which a revelation is mediated by an otherworldly being to a human recipient, disclosing a transcendent reality that is both temporal, insofar as it envisages eschatological salvation, and spatial insofar as it involves another, supernatural world."[5] As such, to the extent that they speak about historical events, these chapters employ symbolic and often cryptic language that retard, if not obfuscate, comprehension. This has meant that debate continues about many details of the historical background of Daniel, but scholars have successfully identified key historical markers that help us understand the historical situation in which the Wise lived and died.

We can say with confidence, for example, that the fourth beast of the apocalyptic vision in Daniel 7 refers to the Greek empire (7:7, 19) and that the eleventh, little horn is Antiochus IV Epiphanes (7:8, 20). This historical touchstone makes it possible to identify the war that the eleventh horn is said to wage against the "holy ones" as Antiochus's programmatic persecution of Jews that began with his first direct military action against Jerusalem and the plundering of the temple in 169 BCE (7:21; cf. 1 Macc. 1:20–28; 2 Macc. 5:11–21). Furthermore, the emphasis on the little horn's "arrogant words" (Dan. 7:8, 20)—words that are spoken "against the Most High," "wear out the holy ones of the Most High," and "attempt to change the sacred seasons and the law" (7:25)—meaningfully characterizes Antiochus's edicts against the practice of Judaism. These would include the laws that forced Jews "to profane Sabbaths and feasts" (1 Macc. 1:44–50;

---

5. John J. Collins, "Introduction: Towards the Morphology of a Genre," *Semeia* 14 (1979): 9.

2 Macc. 6:6) and ordered the execution of Jews in possession of the Torah or engaged in Jewish practices (1 Macc. 1:57).

Daniel 8 continues to use the symbolic language of the "little horn" to refer to Antiochus IV and furthermore refers to the profanation of the temple cult:

> [11] Even against the prince of host [the little horn] acted arrogantly; it took the regular burnt offering away from him and overthrew the place of his sanctuary. [12] Because of wickedness, the host was given over to it together with the regular burnt offering; it cast truth to the ground, and kept prospering in what it did. [13] Then I heard a holy one speaking, and another holy one said to the one that spoke, "For how long is this vision concerning the regular burnt offering, the transgression that makes desolate, and the giving over of the sanctuary and host to be trampled?" (8:11–13)

The vision refers to the desecration of the temple, which took place on December 6, 167 BCE (1 Macc. 1:54; Dan. 11:31), and an interpreting angel goes on to clarify that the little horn is "a king of bold countenance" who "shall cause fearful destruction . . . destroy the powerful and the people of the holy ones . . . and shall even rise up against the Prince of princes," that is, the archangel Michael (Dan. 8:23–25). Daniel 8 acknowledges that the persecution under Antiochus will include violence to "the holy ones" who decide to remain faithful to the God of Israel in defiance of edicts decreed against Judaism.

Daniel 11 presents a review of key historical events in coded language, beginning with the career of Alexander the Great who is referred to as a "warrior king" (11:3). Toward the end of the chapter, Daniel 11 speaks directly about the violent death that the Wise and their adherents will experience under Antiochus IV, the "contemptible one" (11:21):

> [30] He shall be enraged and take action against the holy covenant . . .
> [31] Forces sent by him shall occupy and profane the temple and fortress. They shall abolish the regular burnt offering and set up the abomination that makes desolate. [32] He shall seduce with intrigue those who violate the covenant; but the people who are loyal to their God shall stand firm

> and take action. ³³ The wise among the people shall give understanding to many; for some days, however, they shall fall by sword and flame, and suffer captivity and plunder. (11:30b–33)

The passage overlaps with previous visions concerning Antiochus's war against the Jews and desecration of the temple. New are details about those who are "seduced" by Antiochus to "violate the covenant," Jews who capitulate or even collaborate with Antiochus. In contrast, the Wise and others who choose to remain "loyal to their God," the passage makes clear, will face opposition and persecution. And while capitulation as well as military action were possible responses, the Wise chose nonviolent resistance as a means of expressing their faith that their God will fight on their behalf and be victorious. Their pacifist response to opposition and persecution insured that some would die "by sword and flame." In advocating and practicing nonviolent resistance, the Wise were choosing to die.

2. Authors of martyr stories view the choice to die that the martyr makes as necessary, noble, and heroic.

The Wise are the likely authors of the apocalyptic portion of Daniel. They are, in other words, both the authors and heroes of the martyr stories, and they view the willing embrace of death as necessary, noble, and heroic. Of course, it is important to remember that the Wise did not choose to die per se. Their choice was to remain "loyal to their God," that is, to continue to live in faithful commitment to Judaism and the Jewish way of life, despite serious pressure to do otherwise. The persecutorial edicts of Antiochus's reign made their commitment to faithfulness a proxy for a willingness to die. And to the extent that the Wise taught and believed that faithfulness to God is good and that faith in God required a commitment to nonviolence, they lived in willing embrace of death. This means that the Wise are heroes quite apart from their choice to die, and this is the way they are presented. Their nobility and prestige exist prior to the choice to die, for they "give understanding to [the] many" (11:33) and "lead [the] many to righteousness" (12:3). The choice to die for the Wise, therefore, is an extension of their choice to live in faithfulness. That is, their willingness to die is the strongest endorsement possible of their chosen way of life.

3. The martyr demonstrates or is portrayed as demonstrating a willingness to die.

Given the murderous persecution of Jews and Judaism, the commitment of the Wise to nonviolent resistance constituted a willingness to die. We cannot and should not ascribe to them a desire to die. They came to believe a martyr's death to be purifying (11:35), but glorification (12:3) appears to have been the result of faithful living, including dying in faithfulness, if necessary, but not reserved for those who are martyred. The willingness to die of the Wise was a commitment to faithful living.

4. The martyr, the author, or both impute to the martyrdom the idea of vicarious benefit from a martyr's suffering and death.

We cannot say with any certainty whether the Suffering Servant of Isaiah 53 believed that his death would vicariously benefit others. What we can say is that the authors of Isaiah 53, including the we-group, came to believe that the Servant's suffering and death fulfilled the obligation their sin had incurred (Isa. 53:10) and contributed to making "the many righteous" (53:11). The Wise of Daniel pick up these themes and apply them to their own situation. Note, in this regard, that the Wise refer to themselves as "those who lead [the] many to righteousness" (Dan. 12:3), an unmistakable allusion to the Suffering Servant of whom God says, "The righteous one, my servant, shall make the many righteous" (Isa. 53:11). The Wise thought of themselves as carrying on the legacy and ministry of the Suffering Servant. Thus, the Wise came to believe that their chosen death would have similar vicarious benefits as the Suffering Servant's death. They posited a causal link between their death and purification: "Some of the wise shall fall, so that they may be refined, purified, and cleansed" (Dan. 11:35). Furthermore, the Wise would "shine like the brightness of the sky ... [and] like the stars forever and ever" (12:3). This brings us to the idea of vindication and reward beyond death.

CHAPTER 10

5. An expectation of vindication and reward beyond death develops in relation to a martyr's death and may motivate the choice to die.

The authors of Daniel clearly express an expectation that those who die in faithfulness will be vindicated and rewarded beyond death.

> [1] But at that time your people shall be delivered, everyone who is found written in the book. [2] Many of those who sleep in the dust of the earth shall awake, some to everlasting life, and some to shame and everlasting contempt. [3] Those who are wise shall shine like the brightness of the sky, and those who lead [the] many to righteousness, like the stars forever and ever. (12:1b–3)

The passage articulates a doctrine of resurrection. Moreover, a postmortem judgment is announced, which leads to condemnation for some and vindication, in the form of everlasting life, for others. Further set apart among the vindicated are "those who are wise" and "those who lead the many to righteousness," whom we have called the Wise. This subgroup is marked for greater glorification and likened to "the brightness of the sky" and "the stars." The stars refer to the host of heaven (cf. Dan. 8:10), that is, angels. This means that the risen Wise, while they are not said to become angels, are associated with angels in glory and also in function. They are elevated and made to shine gloriously like the angels of heaven; and the Wise will fight God's battles against the cosmic forces of evil and protect the people, much like Michael and his host of angels (12:1). This is not angelification nor deification, but it is close.

The doctrine of resurrection, which is here given its clearest and, some have argued, only articulation in the Hebrew Bible, provides a rationale for martyrdom. It also comforts and emboldens the faithful to live in commitment to covenant faithfulness and to embrace death, should that prove necessary for faithfulness. There is no reason to believe that belief in resurrection encouraged Jews to seek out martyrdom during the Antiochian persecution. But it no doubt gave them the necessary courage to walk faithfully through death in expectation that they shall walk into eternal life, and glory.

Conclusion

The resurrection of individuals from the dead appears in the final chapter of the latest book of the Hebrew Bible with exceptional clarity. No other passage in the Hebrew Bible speaks so unambiguously of resurrection.[6] Explanations for its emergence have emphasized multiple factors, including possible Persian influence from Zoroastrianism, prior Jewish references to resurrection in *1 Enoch*, or the conceptual framework of the restoration of the people of Israel in the Hebrew Bible as seen in, for example, Ezekiel 37.[7] Whatever the influences that led to the emergence of the idea of resurrection, which are likely to be multiple and more complex than we can reconstruct, we note that it is the dire circumstances surrounding martyrdom that gave birth to arguably the greatest innovation concerning the relationship between life and death: that those who willingly embrace death in faithful and nonviolent commitment to the God of Israel shall rise from the dead to eternal life.

---

6. See Collins, *Daniel*, 394-95.

7. Collins, *Daniel*, 394-98; Jon D. Levenson, *Resurrection and the Restoration of Israel: The Ultimate Victory of the God of Life* (New Haven: Yale University Press, 2008).

EPILOGUE

No one takes it from me, but I lay it down of my own accord. I have the power to lay it down, and I have power to take it up again.

John 10:18

AT THE END OF OUR JOURNEY (which began in the middle of my life's journey), we are now able to offer several summary comments and observations about the willingness-to-die tradition in the Hebrew Bible.

1. The Hebrew Bible is not blind to the sorrow and despair caused by the experience of tragic loss and inexplicable suffering. Job, a person of paradigmatic piety and blessedness, gives expression to unbelievable piety (Job 1:21), but also to strong and deeply felt lament. His suffering is such that, at one point in his motley and plaintive dialogue, he says, "I would choose strangling and death rather than this body" (7:15). What more, God affirms Job's speeches as "what is right." Neither the book of Job nor any other part of the Hebrew Bible characterizes deaths of despair as right or good. But the book of Job in particular affirms the value of honest talk and dialogue among friends about the heavens and the earth and everything in between, which includes experiences of evil.

EPILOGUE

2. From suicide to martyrdom, those who express a willingness to die or die willingly in the Hebrew Bible enjoy a positive relationship to life in several respects. First, voluntary death may be understood to protect and preserve the honor the willing dead enjoyed in life and to affirm and sanctify values and beliefs by which the dead had lived. This retrospective effect pertains not only to martyrdom, as may be expected, but also to suicide. The honor and shame culture of ancient Israel, in which one might be permitted or even expected to suicide to avoid the shame of social death, in part explains this observation. The retrospective valorization that martyrdom performs on the values and beliefs by which the martyr had lived, therefore, shares an explanation with suicide. Ahithophel and Saul, in other words, share commonalities with the Suffering Servant and the Wise. There is a difference, however, in directionality. A suicide by dying voluntarily curtails the loss of honor he earned in life, but a martyr bestows honor on his life he may not have enjoyed in life. A suicide death does not add to one's honor. But a martyr's death generates new honor. This generative quality of martyrdom is one important difference between martyrdom and suicide.

3. Another positive relationship between voluntary death and life is that those who are willing to die or die willingly can confer a variety of benefits on the living. Ahithophel arguably delivers his household from financial ruin and social shame by voluntarily killing himself (2 Sam. 17:23). Saul's suicide may also be understood as saving him and Israel from further shame.

Judah's, Moses's, and Esther's willingness to die for the people in their assumed leadership roles is generative. Judah's assumption and execution of the responsibility for Benjamin's safety from Jacob and before Joseph keep many alive, including Jacob/Israel and the little ones (Gen. 43:9). At the risk of his life, Moses brokers a new basis for Israel's covenantal relationship, which proved mortally dangerous for Israel on account of the violent incompatibility between the holiness of God and the sinfulness of the people, by asking God to reveal more fully what it means to be YHWH. In arguably the most consequential event of divine self-revelation in the Hebrew Bible, God confirms that—in addition to God's gracious liberation of Israel from slavery in Egypt, which

Epilogue

forms the foundation for the covenantal relationship (Exod. 20:2)—God's freedom to be merciful and show mercy apart from the dictates of justice, without abandoning justice, ensures the endurance of the covenant between God and Israel (33:19; 34:6–7).

Esther risks her life as the gambit to her ingenious tactical strategy to save Jews throughout the Persian empire from genocide.

Martyrs also confer benefit on the living. The we-group who composed Isaiah 53 comes to understand the Suffering Servant's death and his suffering more generally as satisfying the guilty obligation that the we-group minimally or Israel maximally has incurred, first, by their disbelief in the message of the Suffering Servant and, second, by their persecution of the person of the Suffering Servant. The Suffering Servant's death and suffering make it possible for the we-group and Israel to live into the redemptive future he had proclaimed from the beginning of his ministry. The Wise, in resolutely practicing Judaism and holding fast to a principle of non-violence in the face of the deadly persecution of Antiochus IV, encourage other Jews to stand fast in their faith in the God of Israel and to wait on God's deliverance, even if it should mean death and even if vindication should come after death.

4. A final positive relationship between voluntary death and life is the doctrine of resurrection. The belief in the resurrection of individuals in the Hebrew Bible, early Judaism, the New Testament, and early Christianity blossomed in soil fertilized by multiple sources and influences both internal and external to the Bible. One of them is the willingness-to-die tradition. Job reasons that "there is hope for a tree" to come back to life after death (Job 14:7) but reasons that "mortals lie down and do not rise again" (14:12). However, he leaves open the possibility of resurrection for human beings when he asks, "If mortals die, will they live again?" (14:14). Centuries after the composition of Job (and Isaiah 53), the authors of Daniel clearly articulate a belief in the resurrection of individuals, eschatological judgment, and postmortem vindication and glorification for those who lived and died in faithful commitment to the God of Israel (Dan. 12:2–3). The promise of resurrection and vindication after death was an encouragement to live faithfully, even if it should bring death, and likely reflects diverse influences from both

EPILOGUE

Jewish and non-Jewish traditions, as well as biblical and extrabiblical sources. It was a powerful idea that has exerted considerable influence in religious history.

5. The relationship between God and several figures who express a willingness to die or die willingly has been a topic of examination. First, in discussing Samson, we considered the theological implication of God's reasons for empowering Samson to carry out acts of violence against the Philistines. We wondered whether divine empowerment meant divine approval and if that makes Judges 13–16 a text in praise of terrorism. Second, in discussing Judah, we considered the theological implication of the repeated notice that God was with Joseph in Egypt, including in the Egyptian prison (Gen. 39:2, 3, 21, 23). We wondered whether divine accompaniment in situations of human suffering, which literally and symbolically signify death and deathliness, means that God suffers with the human being as a compassionate companion. Third, in discussing Moses, we considered the theological implication of God's declared freedom to be merciful and gracious against the strict requirements of justice (Exod. 33:19; 34:6–7). We wondered whether the practice of divine mercy and graciousness accounts for the deadly consequences of sin by absorption and what that absorption might mean. Does God experience deathliness or even death when God chooses to dwell among a stiff-necked people? Is God's exercise of divine freedom to be gracious and merciful a willing embrace of deathliness or death?

I raise these questions about the relationship between God and the willingness-to-die tradition but cannot provide a full answer. However, as I bring the book to a conclusion, I would like to provide an indication of how we might answer these questions from a Christian perspective in the hope of spurring further thinking and reading.

That God can die is the necessary condition on the basis of which we can say that God is willing to die. Thus, the logically prior question is: Can God die according to the Hebrew Bible? It should be stated at the outset that the Hebrew Bible does not entertain the question of whether the God of Israel can die. The question, to be forthcoming, arises for me from my Trinitarian and christological interests. Yet, when we look at the Hebrew

Epilogue

Bible from this perspective, the question of divine death does not appear as distant as it may first appear.

To begin in the thought-world of the ancient Near East of which the Hebrew Bible was a part, gods can and do die in its mythologies. A well-known example is the death of the Canaanite storm god Baal in the Baal Cycle:

> [One lip to He]ll, one lip to Heaven,
> [a to]ngue to the Stars.
> [Ba]al will enter his innards,
> Into his mouth he will descend like a dried olive,
> Produce of the earth, and fruit of the trees. (*KTU* 1.5 II 2–6)[1]

The passage foretells when Baal will descend the throat of Mot, the deity of death, and into his belly. Incidentally, Baal comes back to life in the Cycle at the request of the high god El. The resurrected Baal sends rain to the parched and dying land, and life returns on earth.

Not unlike in the wider ancient Near Eastern literatures, gods can also die in the Hebrew Bible. A key passage in this regard is Psalm 82.[2] Without going into the finer details, the psalm recounts the deicide of the "gods" (*'ĕlōhîm*) by God (also *'ĕlōhîm*) on account of their injustice and lack of knowledge. The judicial execution of the unjust and ignorant gods occurs in verses 6–7. God is speaking to the gods:

> [6] I say, "You are gods,
> children of the Most High, all of you;
> [7] nevertheless, you shall die like mortals,
> and fall like any prince."

God declares that the unjust and ignorant gods shall die like human beings and effectively executes them.

---

1. From Mark S. Smith, trans., "The Baal Cycle," in *Ugaritic Narrative Poetry*, ed. Simon B. Parker, SBLWAW 9 (Atlanta: Scholars, 1997), 81–180.

2. For a thorough treatment of Psalm 82 on the question of divine death, see Peter Machinist, "How Gods Die, Biblically and Otherwise: A Problem of Cosmic Restructuring," in *Reconsidering the Concept of Revolutionary Monotheism*, ed. Beate Pongratz-Leisten (Winona Lake: Eisenbrauns, 2011), 189–240.

EPILOGUE

That the biblical tradition thought that gods could die does not prove that it was thought that the God of Israel could also die. In fact, the possibility of God dying is never broached. However, if it were possible or even imaginable that God might die in biblical thought, there are two potential scenarios where this could occur. First, as in Baal's death, God might die in cosmic combat against forces of death and disorder. Second, as in Psalm 82, God might die due to a judicial judgment for injustice and lack of knowledge.

The combat scenario is not uncommon in the Hebrew Bible and arguably undergirds biblical conceptualizations of every major time period, including creation, exodus, exile, and eschaton.[3] Most relevant for our discussion is the eschatological battle God is to enter against forces of evil and disorder according to Daniel 7–12. While God's defeat is a categorical impossibility for the authors of Daniel, it is ecologically consistent with the worldview of myth on which Daniel's apocalypse is built. If Baal can die in battle, it is at least imaginable that Yhwh can too. Thus, even if God's death is quite distant from the thought-world of Daniel, it is possible for us to imagine God dying in battle against the cosmic monsters that rise from the sea (Dan. 7:3). To boot, for God to be defeated in eschatological battle would mean that God will have failed to uphold justice, in particular for those who lived and died in faithful commitment to God, since God's death would foreclose the possibility of resurrection and postmortem vindication. God's defeat in cosmic combat would equal divine death and the reign of injustice.

The judicial scenario of God being in the dock is rare but not absent in the Hebrew Bible. The most relevant instance in which God is put on trial for possible injustice and lack of knowledge also comes from within the willingness-to-die tradition. Job, at the same time he steps into the dock to be declared righteous or to be executed for sin (Job 29–31), puts God on trial as well. Has God committed injustice by submitting Job to undeserved suffering? Does God have the knowledge of good and evil needed to judge between what is right and what is wrong?[4] The outcome

---

3. See Paul K.-K. Cho, *Myth, History, and Metaphor in the Hebrew Bible* (Cambridge: Cambridge University Press, 2019).

4. On the importance of the legal metaphor to the book of Job, see Norman C. Habel, *The Book of Job*, OTL (Philadelphia: Westminster, 1985).

Epilogue

of the trial is ambiguous, to say the least, and the book in part questions the legitimacy of putting God on trial. But the challenge to God is clear from Job's opening soliloquy in which Job counters God's first creative act, "Let there be light," with his own, "Let there be darkness." There is more than rhetorical danger that, should God be proven to be unjust and to lack knowledge, judgment could be pronounced against God: "You shall die like a mortal."

Noteworthy in the two above scenarios is the convergence of four themes: creation, combat, justice, and the trial. First, cosmic combat in ancient Near Eastern and biblical traditions coincides reliably with the theme of creation. Baal engages in cosmic combat in order to create, as does the Babylonian deity Marduk. And, according to numerous attestations in the Hebrew Bible, YHWH engages in cosmic combat in order to create as well—with the important exception of Genesis 1 and others. Therefore, it may be argued that, in the book of Daniel, God who battles the cosmic beasts does so in order to re-create, that is, to restore order to, the cosmos. And, here is the second convergence, to re-create and restore order is to reestablish justice. Creation and order are, in a sense, synonymous with justice. Thus, God in Daniel engages in cosmic battle both to re-create the cosmos and to reestablish justice. The same convergence can be seen in Job. If Job's experience of injustice results in Job's attempt to uncreate the cosmos, God must demonstrate that the cosmos God created is just or at least not unjust. This is the reason that we find the language of creation and cosmic combat peppered throughout the book of Job, especially in the divine speeches (Job 38–41). Justice on a grand scale is concomitant with creation. The final convergence is with the trial scene. Just as God puts the unjust and ignorant gods on trial in Psalm 82, so the book of Job puts God on trial on suspicion of acting unjustly. So too does God put individuals who are brought back to life (and the four monstrous beasts in Dan. 7:7–9, 13–14) on trial in the eschaton (12:2).

In the convergence of justice, the trial, creation, and combat as they animate the books of Job and Daniel, injustice is always the reason that God enters into scenarios in which, if it were possible, God could die. Either God enters direct combat against forces of injustice, as in Daniel, or God takes the stand in the dock against charges of injustice, as in Job. In both cases, we may wonder whether God is risking divine death in order to address the problem of injustice. That is, does God demonstrate a willingness to die, if indeed God can die, to address and combat injustices that cause suffering to God's creatures, especially God's special possession, Israel? If so, it might be said that God too participates in the willingness-to-die tradition as a just, compassionate, and loving deity who for the sake of God's people just might be willing to die.

With such a God at the helm, one might disembark, on whichever bank.

SELECTED BIBLIOGRAPHY

Ahn, John. *Exile as Forced Migrations: A Sociological, Literary, and Theological Approach on the Displacement and Resettlement of the Southern Kingdom of Judah.* BZAW 417. Berlin: de Gruyter, 2011.

Albertz, Rainer. *Israel in Exile: The History and Literature of the Sixth Century B.C.E.* Translated by David Green. SBLStBL 3. Atlanta: Society of Biblical Literature, 2003.

———. "The Social Setting of the Aramaic and Hebrew Book of Daniel." Pages 1:171–204 in *The Book of Daniel: Composition and Reception.* Edited by John J. Collins and Peter W. Flint. 2 vols. Leiden: Brill, 2001.

Augustine. *The City of God.* Translated by Henry Bettenson. London: Penguin, 1984.

———. "Sermon 364." Pages 276–81 in *Sermons 341–400.* Translated with notes by Edmund Hill. Edited by John E. Rotelle. Vol. III/10 of *The Works of Saint Augustine: A Translation for the 21st Century.* Brooklyn: New City, 2017.

Avalos, Hector. *Illness and Health Care in the Ancient Near East: The Role of the Temple in Greece, Mesopotamia, and Israel.* HSM 54. Atlanta: Scholars, 1995.

Avioz, Michael. "Divine Intervention and Human Error in the Absalom Narrative." *JSOT* 37 (2013): 339–47.

Bailey, Randall. "'That's Why They Didn't Call the Book Hadassah!': The Interse(ct)/(x)ionality of Race/Ethnicity, Gender, and Sexuality in the Book of Esther." Pages 227–50 in *They Were All Together in One Place: Toward Minority Biblical Criticism.* Edited by Randall C. Bailey, Tat-siong Benny Liew, and Fernando F. Segovia. SemeiaSt 57. Atlanta: Society of Biblical Literature, 2009.

Balla, Angela. "Wars of Evidence and Religious Toleration in Milton's *Samson Agonistes*." *Milton Quarterly* 46 (2012): 65–85.

Barthes, Roland. "Myth Today." Pages 107–64 in *Mythologies*. Translated by Annette Lavers. New York: Hill and Wang, 1972.

Barton, Carlin. "Honor and Sacredness in the Roman and Christian Worlds." Pages 23–38 in *Sacrificing the Self: Perspectives on Martyrdom and Religion*. Edited by Margaret Cormack. Oxford: Oxford University Press, 2002.

Bayet, Albert. *Le suicide et la morale*. Paris: Librarie Felix Alcan, 1922.

Beal, Timothy K. *The Book of Hiding: Gender, Ethnicity, Annihilation, and Esther*. London: Routledge, 1997.

Berges, Ulrich F. *The Book of Isaiah: Its Composition and Final Form*. HBM 46. Translated by Millard C. Lind. Sheffield: Sheffield Phoenix, 2012.

Berlin, Adele. *Esther*. Philadelphia: Jewish Publication Society, 2001.

Berlyn, Patricia. "The Rise of the House of Omri." *JBQ* 33 (2005): 223–30.

Birch, Bruce C. "1 and 2 Samuel." Pages 2:947–1383 in *New Interpreter's Bible*. Nashville: Abingdon, 1998.

Bird, Phyllis. *Missing Persons and Mistaken Identities: Women and Gender in Ancient Israel*. Minneapolis: Fortress, 1997.

Bloom, Harold. *Genius: A Mosaic of One Hundred Exemplary Creative Minds*. New York: Warner Books, 2002.

Blumenthal, Fred. "Samson and Samuel, Two Styles of Leadership." *JBQ* 33 (2005): 108–12.

Boling, Robert G. *Judges*. AB 6A. Garden City, NY: Doubleday, 1975.

Bourdieu, Pierre. *Sociology in Question*. Translated by Richard Nice. London: Sage, 1993.

Brettler, Marc Zvi. *The Book of Judges*. London: Routledge, 2002.

———. "Is There Martyrdom in the Hebrew Bible?" Pages 3–22 in *Sacrificing the Self: Perspectives on Martyrdom and Religion*. Edited by Margaret Cormack. Oxford: Oxford University Press, 2002.

Brice, Lee L. "Insurgency and Terrorism in the Ancient World." Pages 3–30 in *Brill's Companion to Insurgency and Terrorism in the Ancient Mediterranean*. Edited by Timothy Howe and Lee L. Brice. Leiden: Brill, 2016.

Brown, Dennis. "Moral Dilemma and Tragic Affect in Samson Agonistes." *Literature and Theology* 20 (2006): 91–106.

Selected Bibliography

Butler, Judith. *Gender Trouble: Feminism and the Subversion of Identity*. New York: Routledge, 1990.

Calvin, John, "The Author's Preface to the *Commentary on the Book of Psalms*." Pages xli–xliii in *John Calvin: Selections from His Writings*. Translated by James Anderson. Grand Rapids: Baker, 1998.

Camus, Albert. *Le myth de Sisyphe: Essai sur l'absurde*. Paris: Édition Gallimard, 1942.

Carey, John. "A Work in Praise of Terrorism? September 11 and *Samson Agonistes*." *Times Literary Supplement* (6 September 2002): 15–16.

Certeau, Michel de. *The Practice of Everyday Life*. Translated by Steven Rendall. Berkeley: University of California Press, 1984.

Chan, Michael J. "Joseph and Jehoiachin: On the Edge of Exodus." *ZAW* 125 (2013): 566–77.

Chapman, Stephen B. *1 Samuel as Christian Scripture: A Theological Commentary*. Grand Rapids: Eerdmans, 2016.

Chernaik, Warren. "Tragic Freedom in *Samson Agonistes*." *The European Legacy* 17 (2012): 197–211.

Cho, Paul K.-K. "'I Have Become a Brother of Jackals': Evolutionary Psychology and Suicide in the Book of Job." *BibInt* 27 (2019): 208–34.

———. "The Integrity of Job 1 and 42:11–17." *CBQ* 76 (2014): 230–51.

———. "Job 2 and 42:7–10 as Narrative Bridge and Theological Pivot." *JBL* 136 (2017): 857–77.

———. "Job the Penitent: Whether and Why Job Repents (Job 42:6)." Pages 145–74 in *Landscapes of Korean/Korean-American Biblical Interpretation*. IVBS 10. Edited by John Ahn. Atlanta: Society of Biblical Literature, 2019.

———. *Myth, History, and Metaphor in the Hebrew Bible*. Cambridge: Cambridge University Press, 2019.

Cho, Paul K.-K., and Janling Fu. "Death and Feasting in the Isaiah Apocalypse (Isaiah 25:6–8)." Pages 117–42 in *Intertextuality and Formation of Isaiah 24–27*. Edited by Todd Hibbard and Hyun Chul Paul Kim. SBLAIL 17. Atlanta: Society of Biblical Literature, 2013.

Clemons, James T. *What Does the Bible Say About Suicide?* Minneapolis: Fortress, 1989.

Clines, David J. A. *I, He, We and They: A Literary Approach to Isaiah 53*. JSOTSup 51. Sheffield: JSOT Press, 1976.

———. *Job 1–20*. WBC 17. Nashville: Thomas Nelson, 1989.

———. *Job 21–37*. WBC 18A. Nashville: Thomas Nelson, 2006.
Collins, John J. *Daniel: A Commentary on the Book of Daniel*. Hermeneia. Minneapolis: Fortress, 1993.
———. "Introduction: Towards the Morphology of a Genre." *Semeia* 14 (1979): 1–20.
Crawford, Sydnie White. "Esther: A Feminine Model for Jewish Diaspora." Pages 161–77 in *Gender and Difference in Ancient Israel*. Edited by P. L. Day. Minneapolis: Fortress, 1989.
Crenshaw, Kimberlé. "Demarginalizing the Intersection of Race and Sex: A Black Feminist Critique of Antidiscrimination Doctrine, Feminist Theory and Antiracist Politics." *University of Chicago Legal Forum* 1 (1989): 139–67.
Cross, Frank M. *Canaanite Myth, Hebrew Epic: Essays in the History of the Religion of Israel*. Cambridge: Harvard University Press, 1973.
Cruveilhier, P. "Le lévirat chez les Hébreux et chez les Assyriens." *Revue Biblique* 34 (1925): 524–46.
Curtis, John Briggs. "On Job's Response to Yahweh." *JBL* 89 (1979): 497–511.
Daube, David. "Absalom and the Ideal King." *VT* 48 (1998): 315–25.
———. "Linguistics of Suicide." *Philosophy & Public Life* 1 (1972): 387–437.
Dietrich, Jan. *Der Tod von eigener Hand: Studien zum Suizid im Alten Testament, alten Ägypten und alten Orient*. ORA 19. Tübingen: Mohr Siebeck, 2017.
Doak, Brian R. *The Last of the Rephaim: Conquest and Cataclysm in the Heroic Ages of Ancient Israel*. Cambridge: Harvard University Press, 2012.
Dozeman, Thomas B. *Exodus*. ECC. Grand Rapids: Eerdmans, 2009.
Droge, Arthur J. "Suicide." *ABD* 4:225–31.
Droge, Arthur J., and James D. Tabor. *A Noble Death: Suicide & Martyrdom among Christians and Jews in Antiquity*. New York: HarperCollins, 1992.
Duhm, Bernhard. *Das Buch Jesaia: Übersetzt und erklärt*. 4th ed. HKAT 3.1. Göttingen: Vandenhoeck & Ruprecht, 1922.
Durkheim, Émile. *Suicide: A Study in Sociology*. Translated by John A. Spaulding and George Simpson. Edited with an introduction by George Simpson. London: Routledge, 2005.
Edelman, Diana V. *King Saul in the Historiography of Judah*. JSOTSup 121. Sheffield: JSOT Press, 1991.

Exum, J. Cheryl. "Aspects of Symmetry and Balance in the Samson Saga." *JSOT* 19 (1981): 3–29.

———. "The Many Faces of Samson." Pages 13–32 in *Samson: Hero or Fool? The Many Faces of Samson*. Edited by Erik Eynikel and Tobias Nicklas. TBN 17. Leiden: Brill, 2014.

Fish, Stanley. *How Milton Works*. Cambridge: Harvard University Press, 2001.

Fishbane, Michael. "Jeremiah IV 23–26 and Job III 3–13: A Recovered Use of the Creation Pattern." *VT* 21 (1971): 151–67.

Fohrer, Georg. "The Righteous Man in Job 31." Pages 3–22 in *Essays in Old Testament Ethics (J. Philip Hyatt, In Memoriam)*. Edited by James L. Crenshaw and John T. Willis. New York: Ktav, 1974.

Fokkelman, Jan P. *The Crossing Fates (I Sam. 13–31 & II Sam. 1)*. Vol. 2 of *Narrative Art and Poetry in the Books of Samuel: A Full Interpretation Based on Stylistic and Structural Analysis*. Assen: Van Gorcum, 1986.

Fox, Michael V. *Character and Ideology in the Book of Esther*. 2nd ed. Grand Rapids: Eerdmans, 2001.

———. "Job the Pious." *ZAW* 117 (2005): 351–66.

Fretheim, Terence E. *The Suffering of God: An Old Testament Perspective*. Philadelphia: Fortress, 1984.

Frolov, Serge. "Judah Comes to Shiloh. Genesis 49.10bα, One More Time." *JBL* 131 (2012): 417–22.

———. *Judges*. FOTL. Grand Rapids: Eerdmans, 2013.

Fu, Janling, and Peter Altmann. "Feasting: Backgrounds, Theoretical Perspectives, and Introductions." Pages 1–31 in *Feasting in the Archaeology and Texts of the Bible and the Ancient Near East*. Edited by Peter Altmann and Janling Fu. Winona Lake: Eisenbrauns, 2014.

Fuchs, Esther. "Status and Role of Female Heroines in the Biblical Narrative." *Mankind Quarterly* 23 (1982): 149–60.

Galpaz-Feller, Pnina. "Let My Soul Die with the Philistines (Judges 16.30)." *JSOT* 30 (2006): 315–25.

Ginzberg, Louis. *The Legends of the Jews*. Vol. 4. Philadelphia: Jewish Publication Society, 1928.

Girard, René. "'The Ancient Trail Trodden by the Wicked': Job as Scapegoat." *Semeia* 33 (1985): 12–41.

Goering, Greg. "Intersecting Identities and Persuasive Speech: The Cases of Judah and Esther." *BibInt* 23 (2015): 340–68.

Good, Edwin M. "The 'Blessing' on Judah, Gen 49.8–12." *JBL* 82 (1963): 427–32.

———. *In Turns of Tempest: A Reading of Job*. Stanford: Stanford University Press, 1990.

Greenstein, Edward. "The Riddle of Samson." *Prooftexts* 1 (1981): 237–60.

Gregory, Tobias. "The Political Messages of *Samson Agonistes*." *Studies in English Literature, 1500–1900* 50 (2010): 175–203.

Guillaume, Philippe. *Waiting for Josiah: The Judges*. LHBOTS 385. New York: Bloomsbury, 2004.

Gunkel, Hermann. *Genesis*. Translated by Mark E. Biddle. Macon, GA: Mercer University Press, 1997.

Gunn, David M. *Judges Through the Centuries*. Oxford: Blackwell, 2005.

Gutiérrez, Gustavo. *On Job: God-Talk and the Suffering of the Innocent*. Translated by Matthew J. O'Connell. Maryknoll, NY: Orbis Books, 1987.

Habel, Norman C. *The Book of Job: A Commentary*. OTL. Philadelphia: Westminster, 1985.

Hacking, Ian. "The Suicide Weapon." *Critical Inquiry* 35 (2008): 1–32.

Hecht, Jennifer Michael. *Stay: A History of Suicide and the Philosophies Against It*. New Haven: Yale University Press, 2013.

Heffelfinger, Katie M. "'My Father Is King': Chiefly Politics and the Rise and Fall of Abimelech." *JSOT* 33 (2009): 277–92.

Henshke, David. "'The Lord Brought Us Forth from Egypt': On the Absence of Moses in the Passover Haggadah." *AJS Review* 31 (2007): 61–73.

Herman, Judith Lewis. *Trauma and Recovery: The Aftermath of Violence from Domestic Abuse to Political Terror*. Rev. ed. New York: Basic Books, 1997.

Hertzberg, Hans Wilhelm. *I and II Samuel: A Commentary*. OTL. Philadelphia: Fortress, 1964.

Hornung, Gabriel F. "The Theological Import of MT Esther's Relationship to the Joseph Story." *CBQ* 82 (2020): 567–81.

Houtman, Cornelis. "Who Cut Samson's Hair? The Interpretation of Judges 16:19a Reconsidered." Pages 67–86 in *Samson: Hero or Fool? The Many Faces of Samson*. Edited by Erik Eynikel and Tobias Nicklas. TBN 17. Leiden: Brill, 2014.

Irwin, Brian P. "Not Just Any King: Abimelech, the Northern Monarchy, and the Final Form of Judges." *JBL* 131 (2012): 443–54.

Selected Bibliography

Janoff-Bulman, Ronnie. *Shattered Assumptions: Towards a New Psychology of Trauma.* New York: Free Press, 1992.

Janowski, Bernd. "He Bore Our Sin: Isaiah 53 and the Drama of Taking Another's Place." Pages 48–74 in *The Suffering Servant: Isaiah 53 in Jewish and Christian Sources.* Edited by Bernd Janowski and Peter Stuhlmacher. Translated by Daniel P. Bailey. Grand Rapids: Eerdmans, 2004.

Janowski, Bernd, and Peter Stuhlmacher, eds. *The Suffering Servant: Isaiah 53 in Jewish and Christian Sources.* Translated by Daniel P. Bailey. Grand Rapids: Eerdmans, 2004.

Jensen, Hans J. L. "Desire, Rivalry and Collective Violence in the 'Succession Narrative'." *JSOT* 55 (1992): 39–59.

Jeter, Joseph R., Jr. *Preaching Judges.* St. Louis: Chalice, 2003.

Johnstone, William. *Exodus 20–40.* SHBC 2B. Macon, GA: Smyth & Helwys, 2018.

Junior, Nyasha, and Jeremy Schipper. *Black Samson: The Untold Story of an American Icon.* New York: Oxford University Press, 2020.

Kaplan, Kalman J., and Matthew Schwartz. "Suicide and Suicide Prevention in the Hebrew Bible." *Journal of Psychology and Judaism* 24 (2000): 99–109.

Kim, Jichan. *The Structure of the Samson Cycle.* Kampen: Kok Pharos, 1993.

King, Karen L. "Willing to Die for God: Individualization and Instrumental Agency in Ancient Christian Martyr Literature." Pages 342–84 in *The Individual in the Religions of the Ancient Mediterranean.* Edited by Jörg Rüpke. Oxford: Oxford University Press, 2013.

Krouse, Michael. *Milton's Samson and the Christian Tradition.* Princeton: Princeton University Press, 1949.

Kwon, JiSeong James. *Scribal Culture and Intertextuality: Literary and Historical Relationships between Job and Deutero-Isaiah.* FAT 2.85. Tübingen: Mohr Siebeck, 2016.

Levenson, Jon D. *The Death and Resurrection of the Beloved Son: The Transformation of Child Sacrifice in Judaism and Christianity.* New Haven: Yale University Press, 1993.

———. *Esther: A Commentary.* OTL. Louisville: Westminster John Knox, 1997.

———. "The Last Four Verses in Kings." *JBL* 103 (1984): 353–61.

———. *The Love of God: Divine Gift, Human Gratitude, and Mutual Faithfulness in Judaism.* Princeton: Princeton University Press, 2016.

———. *Resurrection and the Restoration of Israel: The Ultimate Victory of the God of Life*. New Haven: Yale University Press, 2008.

———. *Sinai and Zion: An Entry into the Jewish Bible*. New Voices in Biblical Studies. New York: HarperCollins, 1985.

Liess, Kathrin. "Todessehnsucht." Pages 402–6 in *Wörterbuch alttestamentlicher Motive*. Edited by Michael Fieger, Jutta Krispenz, and Jörg Lanckau. Darmstadt: Wissenschaftliche Buchgesellschaft, 2013.

MacDonald, Michael, and Terence R. Murphy. *Sleepless Souls: Suicide in Early Modern England*. Oxford: Oxford University Press, 1990.

MacDonald, Nathan. *Not Bread Alone: The Uses of Food in the Old Testament*. Oxford: Oxford University Press, 2008.

Machinist, Peter. "Achaemenid Persia as Spectacle. Reactions from Two Peripheral Voices: Aeschylus, *The Persians* and the Biblical Book of Esther." *Eretz-Israel* 30 (2018): 109–23.

———. "Biblical Traditions: The Philistines and Israelite History." Pages 53–69 in *The Sea Peoples and Their World: A Reassessment*. Edited by Eliezer D. Oren. Philadelphia: University of Pennsylvania Press, 2000.

———. "How Gods Die, Biblically and Otherwise: A Problem of Cosmic Restructuring." Pages 189–240 in *Reconsidering the Concept of Revolutionary Monotheism*. Edited by Beate Pongratz-Leisten. Winona Lake: Eisenbrauns, 2011.

Mailer, Norman. *Why We Are at War?* New York: Random House, 2003.

Mathewson, Dan. *Death and Survival in the Book of Job: Desymbolization and Traumatic Experience*. LHBOTS 450. New York: T&T Clark, 2006.

McGeough, Kevin. "Esther the Hero: Going beyond 'Wisdom' in Heroic Narratives." *CBQ* 70 (2008): 44–65.

Middleton, Paul. *Martyrdom: A Guide for the Perplexed*. London: T&T Clark, 2011.

Milton, John. *Complete Poems and Major Prose*. Edited by Merritt Y. Hughes. Upper Saddle River, NJ: Prenctice Hall, 1957.

———. *Complete Prose Works of John Milton*. Edited by Don M. Wolfe. 8 vols. New Haven: Yale University Press, 1953–82.

Minois, George. *History of Suicide: Voluntary Death in Western Culture*. Translated by Lydia G. Cochrane. Baltimore: Johns Hopkins University Press, 1999.

Selected Bibliography

Moberly, R. W. L. *At the Mountain of God: Story and Theology in Exodus 32–34.* JSOTSup 22. Sheffield: JSOT Press, 1983.

Mobley, Gregory. *Samson and the Liminal Hero in the Ancient Near East.* LHBOTS. New York: T&T Clark, 2006.

———. "The Wild Man in the Bible and the Ancient Near East." *JBL* 116 (1997): 217–33.

Mohamed, Feisel G. "Confronting Religious Violence: Milton's *Samson Agonistes*." *Publications of the Modern Language Association* 120 (2005): 327–40.

Moss, Candida R. *Ancient Christian Martyrdom: Diverse Practices, Theologies, and Traditions.* New Haven: Yale University Press, 2012.

———. *The Myth of Persecution: How Early Christians Invented a Story of Martyrdom.* New York: HarperCollins, 2013.

———. *The Other Christs: Imitating Jesus in Ancient Christian Ideologies of Martyrdom.* Oxford: Oxford University Press, 2010.

Na'aman, Nadav. "Ḫabiru and Hebrews: The Transfer of a Social Term to the Literary Sphere," *JNES* 45 (1986): 271–88.

Nemoy, Leon. "A Tenth Century Disquisition on Suicide According to Old Testament Law." *JBL* 57 (1938): 411–20.

Netzley, Ryan. "Reading Events: The Value of Reading and the Possibilities of Political Action and Criticism in *Samson Agonistes*." *Criticism* 48 (2006): 509–33.

Newsom, Carol A. *The Book of Job: A Contest of Moral Imagination.* New York: Oxford University Press, 2003.

Niditch, Susan. *Judges: A Commentary.* OTL. Louisville: Westminster John Knox, 2008.

———. *The Responsive Self: Personal Religion in Biblical Literature of the Neo-Babylonian and Persian Periods.* New Haven: Yale University Press, 2015.

———. "Samson as Culture Hero, Trickster, and Bandit: The Empowerment of the Weak." *CBQ* 52 (1990): 608–24.

———. "The Wronged Woman Righted: An Analysis of Genesis 38." *HTR* 72 (1979): 143–49.

North, C. R. *The Suffering Servant in Deutero-Isaiah.* 2nd ed. Oxford: Oxford University Press, 1956.

Ogden, G. S. "Idem per Idem: Its Use and Meaning." *JSOT* 53 (1992): 107–20.
Oldman, Elizabeth. "Milton, Grotius, and the Law of War. A Reading of Paradise Regained and Samson Agonistes." *Studies in Philology* 104 (2007): 540–75.
Olyan, Saul M. *Friendship in the Hebrew Bible*. New Haven: Yale University Press, 2017.
Park, Song-Mi Suzie. "The Frustration of Wisdom: Wisdom, Counsel, and Divine Will in 2 Samuel 17:1–21." *JBL* 128 (2009): 453–67.
———. "Left-Handed Benjamites and the Shadow of Saul." *JBL* 134 (2015): 701–20.
Paynter, Helen. "'Revenge for My Two Eyes': Talion and Mimesis in the Samson Narrative." *BibInt* 26 (2018): 133–57.
Petty, Valerie Fortsman. "Let There Be Darkness: Continuity and Discontinuity in the 'Curse' of Job 3." *JSOT* 98 (2002): 89–104.
Pope, Marvin H. *Job*. AB 15. Garden City, NY: Doubleday, 1965.
Portier-Young, Anathea. *Apocalypse against Empire: Theologies of Resistance in Early Judaism*. Grand Rapids: Eerdmans, 2011.
Price, J. H. "The Conceptual Transfer of Human Agency to the Divine in the Second Temple Period: The Case of Saul's Suicide." *Shofar* 34 (2015): 107–30.
Rahner, Karl. *Foundations of Christian Faith: An Introduction to the Idea of Christianity*. Translated by William V. Dych. New York: Crossroad, 1978.
Rendsburg, Gary A. "David and His Circle in Genesis XXXVIII." *VT* 36 (1986): 438–46.
Rosner, Fred. "Suicide in Biblical, Talmudic and Rabbinic Writings." *Tradition: A Journal of Orthodox Jewish Thought* 11 (1970): 25–40.
Roth, Martha. "The Middle Assyrian Laws." Pages 353–60 in *Monumental Inscriptions from the Biblical World*. Vol. 2 of *The Context of Scripture*. Edited by William W. Hallo. Leiden: Brill, 2003.
Rudd, M. David, Alan L. Berman, Thomas E. Joiner Jr., Matthew K. Nock, Morton M. Silverman, Michael Mandrusiak, Kimbery Van Odren, and Tracy Witte. "Warning Signs for Suicide: Theory, Research, and Clinical Applications." *Suicide & Life-Threatening Behavior* 36 (2006): 255–62.
Rudrum, Alan. "Milton Scholarship and the *Agon* over *Samson Agonistes*." *Huntington Library Quarterly* 65 (2002): 465–88.
Sarna, Nahum M. *Exodus*. Philadelphia: Jewish Publication Society, 1991.

Selected Bibliography

Schifferdecker, Kathryn. *Out of the Whirlwind: Creation Theology in the Book of Job*. HTS 61. Cambridge: Harvard University Press, 2008.

Schipper, Jeremy. *Disability and Isaiah's Suffering Servant*. Oxford: Oxford University Press, 2011.

Schley, D. G. "Ahithophel." *ABD* 1:121–22.

Scott, James. *Weapons of the Weak: Everyday Forms of Peasant Resistance*. New Haven: Yale University Press, 1985.

Seitz, Christopher R. "The Patience of Job in the Epistle of James." Pages 373–82 in *Konsequente Traditionsgeschichte: Festschrift für Klaus Baltzer zum 65. Geburtstag*. Edited by Rüdiger Bartelmus, Thomas Krüger, and Helmut Utzschneider. OBO 126. Göttingen: Vandenhoeck & Ruprecht, 1993.

Seow, C. L. *Job 1–21: Interpretation and Commentary*. Grand Rapids: Eerdmans, 2013.

Shear, Michael D. "Trump Says He Would Have Rushed in Unarmed to Stop School Shooting." *New York Times*. February 26, 2018.

Shemesh, Yael. "Suicide in the Bible." *JBQ* 37 (2009): 157–68.

Slivniak, Dmitri. "The Golden Calf Story: Constructively and Deconstructively." *JSOT* 33 (2008): 19–38.

Smith, Mark S., trans. "The Baal Cycle." Pages 81–180 in *Ugaritic Narrative Poetry*. Edited by Simon B. Parker. SBLWAW 9. Atlanta: Scholars, 1997.

Speiser, E. A. *Genesis*. AB 1. Garden City, NY: Doubleday, 1964.

Spiekermann, Hermann. "The Conception and Prehistory of the Idea of Vicarious Suffering in the Old Testament." Pages 1–15 in *The Suffering Servant: Isaiah 53 in Jewish and Christian Sources*. Edited by Bernd Janowski and Peter Stuhlmacher. Translated by Daniel P. Bailey. Grand Rapids: Eerdmans, 2004.

Stager, Lawrence E. "Port Power in Early and the Middle Bronze Age: The Organization of Maritime Trade and Hinterland Production." Pages 625–38 in *Studies in the Archaeology of Israel and Neighboring Lands: In Memory of Douglas L. Esse*. Edited by S. R. Wolff. SAOC 59. Chicago: Oriental Institute, 2001.

Steiner, Richard C. "Poetic Forms in the Masoretic Vocalization and Three Difficult Phrases in Jacob's Blessings: יֶתֶר שְׂאֵת (Gen 49:3), יְצוּעִי עָלָה (49:4), and יָבֹא שִׁילֹה (49:10)." *JBL* 129 (2010): 209–35.

Stokes, Ryan. "Satan, Yhwh's Executioner." *JBL* 133 (2014): 251–70.

Straw, Carole. "'A Very Special Death': Christian Martyrdom in Its Classical Context." Pages 39–57 in *Sacrificing the Self: Perspectives on Martyrdom and Religion*. Edited by Margaret Cormack. Oxford: Oxford University Press, 2002.

Strawn, Brent A. *What Is Stronger Than a Lion? Leonine Image and Metaphor in the Hebrew Bible and the Ancient Near East*. OBO 212. Göttingen: Vandenhoeck & Ruprecht, 2005.

Stuhlmueller, Carroll. *Creation Redemption in Deutero-Isaiah*. Biblical Institute, 1970.

Tarlin, Jan William. "Tamar's Veil: Ideology at the Entrance to Enaim." Pages 174–81 in *Culture, Entertainment and the Bible*. Edited by George Aichele. JSOTSup 309. Sheffield Academic, 2000.

Tomasino, Anthony. "Interpreting Esther from the Inside Out: Hermeneutical Implications of the Chiastic Structure of the Book of Esther." *JBL* 138 (2019): 101–20.

Westermann, Claus. *Genesis 37–50*. Translated by John J. Scullion. Minneapolis: Fortress, 1982.

Wetter, Anne-Mareike. *"On Her Account": Reconfiguring Israel in Ruth, Esther, and Judith*. LHBOTS 623. London: Bloomsbury, 2015.

Yee, Gale. "Thinking Intersectionally: Gender, Race, Class, and the Etceteras of Our Discipline." *JBL* 139 (2020): 7–26.

Zalewski, Saul. "The Purpose of the Story of the Death of Saul in 1 Chronicles X." *VT* 39 (1989): 449–67.

Zee, Lara van der, "Samson and Samuel: Two Examples of Leadership." Pages 53–65 in *Samson: Hero or Fool? The Many Faces of Samson*. Edited by Erik Eynikel and Tobias Nicklas. TBN 17. Leiden: Brill, 2014.

INDEX OF NAMES AND SUBJECTS

Aaron, 157–59, 164
Abel, 51
Abimelech, 5–9, 10, 65–66
Abraham, 124, 160–62
Absalom, 14–21, 22, 23
Ackerman, Susan, 97n59
Adam, 29, 35, 57–58, 213
Ahithophel: and Absalom, 15–19, 22, 23; and concubines, 16–17; counsel of, 15, 16, 19, 20–21; and David, 17–18, 208; and God, 22, 23–24; and honor, 21, 22, 24, 26; and Hushai, 17n36, 18–21, 208; retirement, 15n32; suicide, 14–15, 19, 21–22, 24, 207–8; vicarious benefit, 208; wisdom, 15
Alexander the Great, 257
Amalekites, 12–13, 186
Ambrose, 122
angel, 166–67
Antiochus IV, 255, 256–58
apocalyptic, 256
artistry, literary, 23
Assyria, 139n10

atonement, 162–63, 220
Augustine, 4, 122–29, 203
Baal, 267, 268, 269
Baasha, 24–25
Babylon, 114, 116–18, 225–26
Barton, Carlin, 204n18
Bayet, Albert, 5n13
Benjamin, 110, 112, 114, 148, 149–51, 217–18
Bird, Phyllis, 142–43
Blind Willie Johnson, 120–21
Bourdieu, Pierre, 180
Brettler, Marc Zvi, 206n19
Brice, Lee L., 76, 80, 92, 94
Butler, Judith, 179
Cain, 51, 138
Caleb, 112
Canaan, 136
Carey, John, 72, 73, 75, 77, 94
Certeau, Michel de, 173–75, 188
Charles I, 82, 96
Charleton, Walter, 1, 2n5
City of God, The (Augustine), 122–25

INDEX OF NAMES AND SUBJECTS

Clines, David J. A., 35n16, 41n27, 50–52
consciousness, human, 125–26
Cruiveilheir, P., 139n10
Cyrus, 225, 230, 234–36, 237–38, 240
Dan, 105, 109
Daniel, book of, 254
David: Absalom's rebellion, 14n29, 17–21; and Ahithophel, 17–18, 19; Deuteronomistic History, 105, 106, 111; and Hushai, 18–21; and Israel, 113; and Jehoiachin, 117; and Judah, 112; lineage of, 146; and Philistines, 113; prayer, 23; and Samson, 106, 114, 117; Samuel, books of, 113; and Saul, 12–13, 114; and Zedekiah, 117
despair, 263
Deutero-Isaiah, 225–27, 230–32, 234, 235, 236, 238, 247, 250, 253. *See also* Isaiah; Suffering Servant
Deuteronomistic History: Abimelech, 6, 8; Ahithophel and Absalom, 23; David, 105, 106, 111; deaths of kings, 116; Delilah, 95–98, 109; and exile, 114–15, 132; heroism, 132; historiography, 105; honor and shame, 65–66; intermarriage, 108–9; Israel, 105, 106, 117, 132; Josiah, 105, 114; Judah, 105, 114; Judges, book of, 109; and martyrdom, 206–9; redeemer, 117; Samson, 9, 65–66, 101, 105–9, 113–17, 132; Samuel, 114; Saul, 9–13, 114, 206–7; suicide, 4, 28, 206–8; Zedekiah, 114–17

Dietrich, Jan, 2n4, 5n14, 10n20, 11n23
disability, 124
Donne, John, 2n5
Droge, Arthur, 201–5, 207
Duhm, Bernhard, 241
Durkheim, Émile, 14

Edelman, Diana V., 7n16
Eglon, 83
Egypt, 118, 135, 136, 147–50, 155, 157, 217–18
Ehud, 82–83, 96, 109, 112
Elah, 25
England, 1n3, 22n46
Er, 139, 140, 146
Esther: agency, 178–79, 181, 183; and Ahasuerus, 176, 178, 181, 183–85, 186, 187–96, 198, 221–22; beauty, 178, 181, 183; ethnicity, 185–88, 191–92; faith, 182; favor, 178–79, 183, 189, 192; feasting, 177, 190–91, 194; and feminism, 179; gender, 176–83, 191, 192, 194; genocide, 187, 196; and God, 181–82, 189; grace, 182; Haman, 183, 185–86, 187–88, 190–95, 221–22; Hegai, 177; intersectionality, 175–76; and Jews, 183–84, 186–87, 189–90, 192, 194, 221, 222–23; and Joseph, 181; law, 177, 180, 187–88, 195–96; life, 192, 196; male authority, 177; and martyrdom, 221–23; Mordecai, 173, 177, 178, 181, 183–87, 188–89, 192, 195, 221, 222; Passover, 196–97; and patriarchy, 178, 180; performance,

284

Index of Names and Subjects

gender, 179–80; and Persia, 173; politics, 183–85; revenge, 192; savior, 172–73; space, 183–85, 190–91, 196; strategy, 175, 190–91, 192–93; structural analysis, 197–98; tactics, 175, 181, 188–90, 191–94, 222–23; and Vashti, 179–80; versions, 182n31; violence, 222; willingness to die, 173, 196–98, 222
exile, 36, 39, 114–18, 132–33, 135, 225
exodus, 117–18, 155, 232–33
Exum, J. Cheryl, 67–68, 77, 80, 81, 89–90

Fish, Stanley, 73–75, 88
flowers, 44–46
Foucault, Michel, 187n41
Fox, Michael V., 177, 182, 214
Fuchs, Esther, 184

Gibeah, 112–13, 114
Gideon, 5, 106–7
God: and Aaron, 158–59; and Abimelech, 6, 8; and Absalom, 21, 23; accommodation, 168; and Ahithophel, 22, 23–24; arm of YHWH, 229–34, 236, 237, 243, 246; Augustine, 125; book, 163–64, 221; and Cain, 51; cosmic combat, 269; covenant, 157, 165, 170, 265; creation, 269; and Cyrus, 234–36, 237–38; death, capability of, 266–70; Deutero-Isaiah, 230–32, 234–35; and Eliphaz, 50; Er, 139; eschatological battle, 268; and Esther, 181–82, 189; exile, 117–18, 135; forgiveness, 163, 170; freedom, 237–38; glory, 167–68, 220, 248–49; and golden calf, 159–60; grace, 156, 157, 164, 168–71, 220; I AM WHO I AM, 156, 168–69; and Israel, 90, 91–92, 94, 117–18, 136, 155–67, 170, 219–20, 236, 265; and Job, 31, 33, 39, 40–42, 47, 49–50, 53, 55, 56–58, 59, 210–14; and Joseph, 135, 138, 154, 182, 266; justice, 169–70, 269; liberation, 90; Maccabees, 255–56; and martyrdom, 215; mediating figure, 158–59; Milton, 95; monsters, 39, 231–32; and Moses, 156, 158, 159–65, 167–69, 171, 219–20, 266; Onan, 139–40; and Philistines, 90–92, 94, 104–5; presence, 158, 165–66; punishment, 6, 8, 12, 164–65, 169–70; redeemer, 49–50; revenge, 90; revolutionary ideology, 94; and Samson, 69, 74, 86–87, 77, 89, 90–93, 95, 104–5, 125, 266; and Saul, 129; servant, 247–49; and sin, 170–71; and Suffering Servant, 240–42, 243–44, 246–50; tactical opportunity, 91, 104–5; terrorism, 69, 92; on trial, 268–69; will, 74; willingness to die, 266; the Wise (Daniel), 258
gods, 267–68
golden calf. *See* Israel: golden calf
grace, 156, 157, 164, 168–71, 182, 220
Greek empire, 256

Haggadah, 155n1, 166
harlotry. *See* prostitution

INDEX OF NAMES AND SUBJECTS

Hasmondean Dynasty, 255
Heber, 96
honor: Ahithophel, 21–22, 24, 26; Deuteronomistic History, 65–66; Israel, 208–9, 264; Job, 56, 57; and martyrdom, 264; Samson, 65–66; Saul, 10–11; and suicide, 264. *See also* shame
House of Baasha, 24–25
House of Jeroboam, 25
Howe, Timothy, 76
Hushai, 17n36, 18–21, 208

Immanuel, 63
Isaac, Rabbi, 119–20
Isaiah, 226–27. *See also* Deutero-Isaiah; Suffering Servant
Israel: and Amalek, 186; covenant, 157, 165, 170; and David, 113; Deutero-Isaiah, 236; Deuteronomistic History, 105, 106, 117, 132; exile, 132–33; exodus, 155; and God, 90, 91–92, 94, 117–18, 136, 155–67, 170, 219–20, 236, 265; golden calf, 156, 158, 170, 219; grace, 157, 164; honor and shame, 208–9, 264; Jehoiachin, 17; Joseph, 117, 135–36; Judges, 109–10, 112–13; leadership, 132–33, 135–36; levirate law, 139n10; and martyrdom, 208–9; and Moses, 156–58, 160–62, 219; Mount Sinai, 156, 219; presence of God, 165–66; punishment, 164; redeemer, 117; Samson, 102–3, 106, 107, 109–10, 132; and Saul, 207; sin, 164, 170, 219–20; Suffering

Servant, 239; and suicide, 208–9; weaker, 103

Jacob, 136–37, 147–50, 151–53, 181
Jael, 96–98, 109
Janoff, Bulman Ronnie, 30n5
Janowski, Bernd, 246
Jehoiachin, 116, 117–18, 133, 217
Jephthah, 124–25
Jerubbaal, 5
Jerusalem, 113, 225
Jesus Christ: and Augustine, 126–28; death, 127–28, 200; and the Jews, 127–28; leadership, 153–54; and martyrs, 200, 203; Milton, 70–71, 84; and Samson, 100, 122, 126–29; and Satan, 70–71, 84; voluntary death, 3; whole Christ, 127; wilderness temptations, 70–71; willingness to die, 153–54
Jeter, Joseph, 66–67
Jews, 119–21, 127–28, 183–84, 186–87, 189–90, 192, 194, 221, 222–23, 255, 256–57
Job: and Adam, 29, 35, 57–58, 213; agency, 50–51; and Bildad, 41, 42; and common folk, 44, 58; and cosmos, 35; and creation, 34–35, 57–58; curses birth/conception, 33–35, 41–42; date of book, 29n4; and death, 29–30, 36–38, 40–41, 42–43, 52–53, 57, 209–11; disasters, 31; and Eliphaz, 37, 38, 50; and exile, 36; flowers, 44–46; and friends, 53–55, 209–10, 212, 214; future, 58; and God, 31, 33, 39, 40–42, 47,

Index of Names and Subjects

49–50, 53, 55, 56–58, 59, 210–14; hell, 59; heroism, 59, 210–13; historical events, 35–36; honor, 56, 57; hope, 46–47; and human beings, 212–13; innocence, 38, 49, 51, 54, 57, 211; integrity, 211–12; and life, 43–45, 59, 211–12; life after death, 43–45, 47–48, 215; and martyrdom, 209, 215–16; past, 55; patience, 30n6; piety, 30–32, 210, 214; present, 55–56; redeemer, 47–52, 215; righteousness, 53, 214; and the Satan, 31, 211, 214; and Sea and Dragon, 38–39; self-imprecation, 56–57; shame, 56; Sheol, 47; and sin, 53–54, 214; sleep, 40; sociality, 54, 55–56; suffering, 29–30, 32, 36, 37, 39–40, 209–10, 214, 264; and suicide, 33, 37–38, 58–59; tradition, 54–55; trauma, 30n5, 36, 54–55; trees, 46–47; vindication, 215; wife, 32–33; willingness to die, 36–37, 209–12, 214; witness in heaven, 51–52

Johnson, Samuel, 73

Joseph: and Benjamin, 149; blessings, 153; brothers, 134–35, 137–38, 147–48, 152; and Esther, 181; and exodus, 117–18; and God, 135, 138, 154, 182, 266; and Israel, 117, 135–36; and Jacob, 147–48, 153, 181; and Jehoiachin, 117–18; journey, 134–36; and Judah, 134, 136–38, 146, 150, 152–53, 217–18; leadership, 134, 136; status, 152–53; and Tamar, 150

Josiah, 105, 114

Judah: and Benjamin, 149–51; group survival, 148–49; hypocrisy, 144–45; and Jacob, 148–50, 151–52; and Joseph, 134, 136–38, 146, 150, 152–53, 217–18; leadership, 136–39, 146, 147, 151; and levirate law, 139, 145n20; and martyrdom, 217–19; monarchy, 153; patriarchy, 139–43, 144–45; and prostitute, 142, 144; slavery, 149–50; Southern Kingdom, 151, 153; status, 152–53; and Tamar, 139–43, 144–45; tribe, 105, 109, 112, 114–15, 118; willingness to die, 149, 151, 217–19, 264, 266

judges, 106, 107, 109–10, 132

Judges, book of, 109, 110, 111–12

Kenaz, 112

kingship, 111–12. *See also individual kings*

lament, 12

leadership: Christ, 153–54; Hebrew Bible, 131; Joseph, 134, 136; Judah, 136–39, 146, 147, 151; Moses, 156; Samson, 131–33; willingness to die, 132–33, 153

Levenson, Jon D., 177, 196–97

Levi, 151–52

levirate law, 139, 145n20

Levite's concubine, 112–13

little horn (Daniel), 256–57

LORD. *See* God

Loscocco, Paula, 97n58

Lucretia, 123

INDEX OF NAMES AND SUBJECTS

Maccabees, 255
Mailer, Norman, 66
martyrdom: benefits, 265; Christians, 199–200; Daniel, 254–56, 258–61; death, 224–25; definition, 201–5; Deutero-Isaiah, 225–27; Deuteronomistic History, 206–9; and Esther, 221–23; everlasting life, 254; and God, 215; Hebrew Bible, 200–201, 204–6, 223, 224–25, 260; heroic, 202–3, 251, 258–59; honor, 264; imitation of Christ, 200, 203; Israel, 208–9; Job, 209, 215–16; Judah, 217–19; and life, 264; Moses, 219–21; opposition/persecution, 202, 250, 254, 256–58; resurrection, 260, 261; reward, 203, 204–5, 252, 260; Samson, 216–17; Suffering Servant, 205, 225, 226, 250–53, 259, 265; and suicide, 206–9, 264; vicarious benefit, 204, 251, 259; willingness to die, 203–4, 251, 259; Wise (Daniel), 258, 259; witness, 199–200
Memucan, 180
mercy killing, 7
Milton, John. *See* Samson: suicide attack
Minois, George, 28n2
Mordecai, 173
Moses: and Aaron, 157–58; and Abraham, 160–62; atonement, 162–63, 220; death, 171, 220; forgiveness, 163; and God, 156, 158, 159–65, 167–69, 171, 219–20, 266; grace, 156, 164, 168–70; and Israel, 156–58, 160–62, 219; and Joseph, 136; leadership, 156; and martyrdom, 219–21; Mount Sinai, 157, 219–21; and promised land, 244n18; punishment, 164–65; sacrifice, 162–63; skin disease, 241; status, 167–68; test, 160; willingness to die, 163, 219, 264
Moss, Candida, 202n14
murder, 122–23, 124

Nebuchadnezzar, 115
Nemoy, Leon, 3n10
Newsom, Carol A., 53n46
Niditch, Susan, 139n10, 140
Northern Kingdom, 105, 153

Omri, 24, 25
Onan, 139–40, 146
On Reformation (Milton), 83
Othniel, 109, 112

pacifism, 70, 71
Paradise Regained (Milton), 70–71, 72, 84, 88
Park, Song-Mi Suzie, 15n30, 17n36
patriarchy, 139–46, 178, 180
Paul, 3
Perez, 146
Persian empire, 173, 225
Philistines: and David, 113; and God, 90–92, 94, 104–5; and Samson, 64–66, 68–69, 77, 78, 79, 80–81, 83, 85–86, 89, 90–93, 96–99, 102–4, 107, 119–20, 216; and Samuel, 110–11; and Saul, 9–10, 113, 207

Index of Names and Subjects

promised land, 105, 158, 166, 218, 244n18
property, 21–22
prostitution, 129, 142–44

Rahab, 143n16
rape, 62n5, 112–13, 123–24
responsibility, 164
resurrection, 260, 261, 265–66
Reuben, 136–38, 147–49, 151, 217
robbery, 8n18
Roh Moo-Hyum, 26
Rudd, M. David, 38n20

sacrifice, 132, 162–63, 245
salvation, 233–34
Samson: allegory, 126–29; angel, 61–63, 107; Augustine, 124–29; binding, 115, 116–17, 132; birth and parentage, 61–64, 101, 106–7; Black Samson, 121n39; blind, 70, 80, 87; burning of fields, 67–68; and Christ, 100, 122, 126–29; common folk, 78, 81–82, 83, 84; consciousness, 125–26; core narrative, 90, 94–95, 101; Dan, tribe of, 102; and David, 106, 114; death, 61, 65–66, 115, 132, 133; and Delilah (Dalila), 63, 64–65, 68, 95–98, 109, 120; and Deuteronomistic History, 9, 66, 101, 105–9, 113–17, 132; disproportionality, 67–68; and exile, 114–18, 132–33; failure, 108; frame narratives, 90, 92, 93, 94, 107; and Gideon, 106–7; and God, 69, 74, 86–87, 88, 89, 90–93, 95, 104–5, 125, 266; and Goliath, 119, 120; hair, 126; and harlot, 129; Hebrew text, 97–98; heroism, 74, 88, 96, 97, 100–103, 104, 105, 106, 108, 113, 119–21, 130, 132, 217; honor, 65–66; and Israel, 102–3, 106, 107, 109–10, 132; jawbone of donkey, 68; and Jehoiachin, 217; judge, 106, 107, 109–10, 132; Judges, book of, 109, 110, 111; leadership, 131–33; and Manoah, 61–63, 106; marriage, 86, 90–91, 95–96; martyrdom, 216–17; middle of story, 73–74, 75; Milton, 69, 72, 73–75, 77, 81–89, 94, 95–99, 125, 126; motivation, 68–69; mystery, 95; narrative, biblical, 78–79, 101, 107; Nazirite, 61, 63, 64, 68; nobles, Philistine, 78, 79–80, 82, 84; peg/pin, 97–98; and Philistines, 64–66, 68–69, 77, 78, 79, 80–81, 83, 85–86, 89, 90–93, 96–99, 102–4, 107, 119–20, 216; praised for suicide, 3; prayer, 89, 93, 95; proportionality, 80–81, 89; rabbinic interpreters, 119–21; redeemer, 100, 101–2, 122–29; refrains, 107; revenge, 89–90, 93, 103, 120–21; revisionist interpretation, 87–88; sacrifice, 132; *Samson Agonistes*, 69, 71–72, 73–75, 77, 81–88, 94, 95–97; and Samuel, 110–11, 114; Scripture, 125; sexual transgressiveness, 102, 103–4, 108–9, 119–20; shame, 65–66; shaving, 64, 68, 93; Sisera, 96, 98, 109; strength, 63–64, 64, 87, 92, 93–94; suicide attack, 66, 67, 78,

289

116, 125, 216–17; tactical, 91, 103–4; temple of Dagon, 65, 67, 68, 72, 78, 79–80, 84–85, 87, 89, 104; terrorism, 61, 66–69, 72, 75–77, 80–81, 84, 89–90, 92, 94, 98, 100, 128–29; traditional interpretation, 87, 88; traditions, biblical, 66, 90, 93, 101, 102, 132; tyrannicide, 84, 94; vicarious benefit, 217; victim, 79; violence, 83–84, 89–90, 93, 108; voluntary act, 85–86, 133; and the weak, 103, 104; wedding feast, 67; will of God, 74; YHWH's spirit, 64; and Zedekiah, 115–18, 132, 216–17

Samson Agonistes. See Samson: *Samson Agonistes*

Samuel, 110–11, 114

Satan, 31, 70–71, 84, 211, 214

Saul: accounts of death, 9–13; and Amalekites, 12, 186; and armor-bearer, 7, 10, 12, 13–14; and Benjamin, 112; Chronicler, 12; and David, 12–13, 114; and Deuteronomistic History, 9–13, 114, 206–7; Gibeah, 113; honor, 10–11; and Israel, 207; and Philistines, 9–10, 113, 207; Samuel, first book of, 113; shame, 10–11; suicide, 9, 10, 13, 113, 206–7; vicarious benefit, 207

Schipper, Jeremy, 241–42

Scott, James C., 175

Sea and Dragon, 38–39

Seleucids, 255

Seneca, 2n4

Seow, C. L., 49–50

September 11, 2001, 66, 69, 72

shame, 10–11, 56, 65–66, 208–9, 264. *See also* honor

Shechem, 5–6, 8

Shelah, 140–41, 146

Shemesh, Yael, 3n10, 24n50

Shua, 139

Simeon, 147, 151–52

sin, 53–54, 164, 168, 170–71, 214, 219–20, 244–45, 246

Sisyphus, 40

Solomon, 151

Sonnet XIX (Milton), 70, 71

Southern Kingdom, 151, 153

strategy, 174

Suffering Servant: arm of YHWH, 229–34, 236, 237, 243, 246; benefits, 265; circularity, textual, 227; composite, 227–28; core, 227–28; and Cyrus, 237, 240; death, 239–40, 242–43, 253; deformation, 249; and Deutero-Isaiah, 225, 226, 227, 253; elevated by God, 244, 246–47, 250; frame, 227–28, 252; and God, 240–42, 243–44, 246–50; heroic, 251; identity, 228–29; Israel, 239; martyrdom, 205, 225, 226, 250–53, 265; mystery of message, 229–36; mystery of person, 237–43; mystery of person as message, 243–50; persecution, 237, 238–39, 243, 250; and pride, 247–49; reward, 252; sacrifice, 245; servant, 247–49; and sin, 244–45, 246; skin disease, 241–42, 243; social isolation, 241, 242–43; songs, 238–40; suffering, 244–47, 250; vicarious benefit,

Index of Names and Subjects

244–45, 251, 259; we-group, 227–31, 236, 237, 242, 243–46, 259, 265; willingness to die, 251, 253; and the Wise (Daniel), 259

suicide: altruistic, 14; assisted, 5; condemnation of, 3–4; social dimension of, 28–29; warning signs of, 38. *See also* Deuteronomistic History; honor; Israel; martyrdom; and *names of individuals*

Tabor, James, 201–5, 207
tactics, 91, 103–5, 174–75, 181, 188–90, 191–94, 222–23
Tamar: alternate reality, 144; David, ancestor of, 141; death, agent of, 146; and Er, 139, 164; harlot, 142–44; and Joseph, 150; and Judah, 139–42, 144–45, 147; and levirate law, 139, 145n20; and Onan, 139–40; and patriarchy, 140–41, 142–46; Perez, 146; pregnancy, 144–45; and Shelah, 140, 142; veil, 141–42, 144; widow, 140–42, 144

Temple, Jerusalem, 39, 257
Ten Commandments, 122–23
terrorism. *See* Samson: terrorism
Thebez, 5, 7
Tomasino, Anthony, 197–98
trauma, 30n5, 36

Uzziah, 241, 248

Vasthi, 176, 178, 179–80
violence, 83–84

Wetter, Anne-Mareike, 180
Wise (Daniel), 254, 255–56, 258, 259, 260, 265
women, 7–8, 123–24, 125, 140, 143

Zedekiah, 114–18, 216–17
Zimri, 24–26

INDEX OF SCRIPTURE AND OTHER ANCIENT TEXTS

OLD TESTAMENT

Genesis

Ref	Page
1	34
1:3a	34
2	213
2:18–20	56
2:23–24	35
3:8	57
4:10	51
6:1–5	62n4
6:4	64
12:2	160
12:17	241
12:36	197
15:13–16	136
34	151
35:22	151
37	152
37–50	134
37:3	181
37:12–13	137
37:18–19	137
37:22	137
37:26	137
37:27	137
37:28	137n6, 138
37:32	145n19
38	138, 139, 140n10, 147, 150
38:2–5	139
38:7	139
38:10	139
38:11	140
38:12	139
38:14	141, 142
38:15–18	144
38:24	144
38:25	145n19
38:26	145
39:2	135, 266
39:3	135, 266
39:4	181
39:6	181
39:7–12	181
39:21	135, 181, 266
39:23	135, 266
41:37–43	181
41:38–39	181
41:51–52	181
42:21	137
42:22	137
42:24	135
42:26	147
42:30–34	147
42:35	147
42:37	147, 218
42:37–38	217
42:38	148
43:8	218
43:8–10	148
43:9	217, 264
43:12	149
43:13–14	149
43:14	189
43:16–17	149
43:30	135
44:1–12	149
44:18–34	218
44:30	149, 218
44:31	149
44:32–34	149–50

Index of Scripture and Other Ancient Texts

45:1	150	14:29	231	33	165
45:1–3	150	15:16	231–32	33:1–3	165
45:2	150	17:8–16	186, 222	33:2	166
45:3	135	19	77	33:3	166
46:3	135	19–24	157	33:4	159, 166
49	151	20:2	155, 157, 265	33:5	165, 166, 220
49:1	151	20:13	4	33:7–11	167
49:4	151	21:24	80	33:11	167
49:5–7	152	25–31	157	33:12	167
49:8	152	25:2–7	158	33:12–13	167
49:8–12	136, 152, 218	25:8	157, 158	33:14	167, 220
49:9	153	29	162	33:15	167
49:10ba	152	29–30	162, 163	33:17	167–68
49:11–12	152, 152n26, 153	29:36–37	162	33:18	156, 168, 220
49:25	153	30:10	162	33:18–23	165
50:6–14	136	30:12	162	33:19	156, 168, 170, 265, 266
50:16–17	135	31:18	157	33:20	168, 220
50:17	135	32	152, 157	33:21	220
50:20	117, 135, 138, 154	32–34	156, 159, 171	33:21–23	168
50:24–26	218	32:1	157	34	169
50:25	136	32:2–3	158	34:6	220
		32:4	158	34:6–7	156, 169, 265, 266
Exodus		32:5	159	34:7	171
1:7	135	32:7–10	160	34:9	166, 170
1:21	143n16	32:9–10	159	35–40	157
3:13–16	168	32:10	161, 163, 165, 219		
3:14	156, 168	32:11–13	161	**Leviticus**	
4	241	32:14	161, 162	5:14–16	245
4:4–8	241	32:19	163	16:10	245
6:7	157	32:30	162	16:20–22	245
10:2	11	32:31–32	162	23:5–6	196
10:7–11	136n4	32:32	219, 221	24	80
10:21–29	136n4	32:33	164, 165, 221	24:19–20	80, 90
13:19	136, 218	32:34	164		
14–15	231	32:34a	165		
14:21–22	231	32:35	164, 165		

INDEX OF SCRIPTURE AND OTHER ANCIENT TEXTS

Numbers		4:17	96	13:25	64, 93
14:18	169n15	4:21	98	14–15	63, 78, 79, 90,
		5:24	96		92, 93, 101, 102,
Deuteronomy		6:1	107		104, 106, 132
1:37	244n18	6:11–24	107	14:3	104, 108, 110, 132
4:20	155	8:28	93	14:4	90, 104n11, 105
6:4–5	105	9	5, 111	14:5–18	63
7:3–4	108	9:6	111	14:6	64, 92, 93
16:3	232–33	9:7–15	111	14:12	67
19:21	80	9:23	8n18	14:12–14	104
22:25–27	62n5	9:23–24	6	14:14	67, 128
25:5–10	139, 140n10	9:25	8n18	14:18	67
26:8	155n1	9:45–49	8n18	14:19	63, 64, 92, 93
28:27	32, 54	9:51	6	15	83
28:35	32, 54	9:53	6	15:1–5	67, 104
28:37	33	9:54	5, 6, 66	15:3	89
		9:56	6	15:4–6	63
Joshua		9:56–57	6	15:9–13	104n11
2:1	143n16	9:57	6	15:9–17	63, 68
13:3	103	10:6	107	15:11	216
14:6–14	112	13	61, 63, 90, 92,	15:14	64, 92, 93
15–19	102		101, 106, 132	15:14–17	92, 104
24:32	136, 218	13–15	105, 115	15:18	92
		13–16	9, 60, 94, 95,	15:20	78, 92, 93, 106,
Judges			114, 216, 266		107, 108
1:27–34	102	13:1	106, 107, 108	16	63, 64, 78, 79, 81,
2:11	107	13:2–25	108		90, 92, 101, 115
2:17	112	13:3	63	16:1	62
3–16	132	13:3–5	61	16:1–3	63, 64
3:7	107	13:5	61, 63, 66, 92,	16:4	95
3:7–11	107		107, 132, 217	16:4–22	64
3:9	112	13:6	62	16:5	79
3:11	93	13:7	63	16:6	63
3:12	107	13:9	62	16:8	79
4	7n17	13:15–23	62	16:9	79
4:1	107	13:15–25	107	16:10	63
4:9	96	13:24	62	16:12	79

Index of Scripture and Other Ancient Texts

16:13	63	**1 Samuel**		**2 Samuel**	
16:14	79, 97–98	1	110	1	9, 12, 27
16:15	63	1:22	110	1:6	12
16:17	63, 93	3	111n22	1:9	12
16:18	79	4–7	110	1:10	13
16:20	64, 79	5:9	241	1:12	12
16:21	10n20, 79, 115, 132	6:9	241	1:14	13
		6:17	103	1:17–27	207
16:22	65, 93	7:13–14	111	1:19	207
16:23	79, 98	7:15	110, 111n22	3:10	20
16:23–30	68, 104	8:1	111n22	3:34	115n28
16:23b	65	9	111n22	5:6–9	113
16:24	77, 79–80, 81, 98	9:2	114	5:17–25	113
		10	111n22	11	6
16:24b	65	10:26	113	11:3	16n32
16:25	10n20, 104, 128	12	111n22	11:21	6, 66
16:26	104	13:19–20	101n3	12:7–12	14
16:27	78	15	186	12:11	16
16:28	9, 64, 65, 68, 80, 89, 93	15–16	111n22	15–17	23
		15:2	186, 222	15:12	15, 23, 208
16:30	9, 78, 80, 132	17	113	15:12–16:14	23
16:30b	3, 132	24	13	15:31	17, 23
16:31	93	26	13	15:31–17:14	23
17–21	106, 110, 111, 132	27:1–28:2	113	15:32	18
17:6	110, 112, 132	31	9, 11, 12, 13, 27, 113	15:33	18
18:1	110, 112	31:1–7	9, 65	15:34	18
19	11	31:2	10n19	15:34–36	18
19:1	110, 112	31:3	7	15:37	18, 23
19:12	113	31:4	6, 7, 10, 12	16:14	23
19:14	112	31:4a	10	16:15	23
19:25	11	31:4b–5	10	16:15–17:23	23
19:30	112	31:5	12, 207	16:16	18, 23
21:3	112	31:6	207	16:17	18
21:25	110, 112	31:7	11, 207	16:20–23	14
		31:8	10n19	16:21	16
Ruth		31:8–10	10, 207	16:23	15, 16
4:18–22	146	31:8–13	9n19	17	14

17:1–3	15n32, 17	25:7	115, 132	2:12–14	178
17:4	19, 20	25:27–30	116, 117	2:15	178, 179
17:7	19			2:17	178, 179
17:8	19, 20	**1 Chronicles**		2:19–23	197
17:10	19, 20	2:1–16	146	2:20	177, 187
17:11	19	2:3	139	3:1	185, 186
17:12	19	10	9, 11, 27	3:1–16	197
17:13	19	10:13–14	11	3:2	186, 221
17:14	20, 21			3:4	221
17:14bα	17	**2 Chronicles**		3:6	186, 221
17:14b	23	30:9	169n15	3:7–11	188
17:14bβ	17n37	33:11	115n28	3:7–15	197
17:23	15, 22, 23, 207, 208, 264	36:6	115n28	3:8	186, 222
				3:8–15	187, 195
18:10	24n50	**Nehemiah**		3:10	186, 188, 195
18:33	18n37	9:17	169n15	3:11	186, 188, 195
19:4	18n37	9:31	169n15	3:11–12	195
21:22	73			3:12	186, 196
23:24	16n32	**Esther**		3:13	183, 186
24:2	20	1:1–2	197	4	197
		1:3–22	197	4:1–2	183
1 Kings		1:9	176, 190	4:2	174, 184
12:28	159	1:11	176	4:3	183
16	24	1:12	176	4:8	184, 189
16:1–3	25	1:13	177, 195	4:11	173, 174, 184, 189
16:1–7	24	1:16–22	187, 195	4:13	186
16:8–14	25	1:19	180	4:14	182, 183, 186
16:12	25	1:19–20	177	4:16	173, 185, 189, 196, 222
16:18–19	25	1:20	181		
21:15–16	22	1:22	177, 180, 193	5:1	196
22:8–28	19	2:1–18	197	5:1–8	177, 197
		2:5	185	5:2	179, 189, 197
2 Kings		2:7	178, 181	5:3	190
15:5	241	2:8–9	178	5:6	190
22–23	105	2:9	178	5:9	191
23:25	105	2:10	187	5:9–14	197

Index of Scripture and Other Ancient Texts

5:11–12	191	1:8	31, 212, 213	3:17–19	43–44
5:12	191	1:9	31	3:18–19	44
6	197, 198	1:10–11	31	3:25–26	43
7	197	1:11	214	4–5	37
7:1–9	177	1:13–19	31	6:2–3	37
7:2	190	1:14–19	31	6:3	38
7:3a	192	1:20–31	31	6:4	37, 40n25, 41
7:3b	192	1:21	263	6:8–9	37, 42
7:3bα	192	2	210	7	38
7:4a	192	2:1–6	31	7:1	38
7:5	188, 192	2:3	212, 213	7:1–2	45
7:6	188, 192	2:3a	31	7:1–4	38
7:6a	192	2:3b	32	7:6a	38
7:7	193	2:4	48	7:7a	38
7:8aβ	193	2:4–5	32, 48	7:9a	38
7:9–10	193	2:5	214	7:11	38n20
8	197	2:7	32, 54	7:12	38
8:2	195	2:9	32, 53, 211	7:13–14	40
8:3	196	2:9b	33, 36	7:15	40, 42, 58, 209, 263
8:4	194	2:10a	33		
8:7	194	3	33, 36, 37, 52, 57	7:16	41, 42
8:7–10	187, 195	3–31	209	7:17	212–13
8:8	180, 181, 195	3:1	34	7:20	40n25
8:8b	195	3:3–7	34	8	41
9:1–17	197	3:3–10	35	9:17	210
9:13	187, 195	3:3b	35	9:33	50
9:18–32	197	3:4	58	10:1	41n27
10:1–3	197	3:4aα	34	10:1–22	47
		3:7	58	10:1aα	41
Job		3:7a	35	10:8a	41
1	210	3:7b	35	10:11a	41
1–2	42	3:11	42	10:16	40n25
1:1	30	3:12	42	10:16–17	41
1:2–3	30	3:13–14	42n29	10:16a	41
1:4–5	30	3:13–15	43–44	10:18–19	42
1:6–12	31	3:14	44	12:2–3	265

13:4	53	30	55, 58	114:5	156
14:1–2	44	30:8	55	116:5	169n15
14:6	45	30:9	55	119:154	4
14:7	265	30:29	55–56	145:8	169n15
14:7–9	46	31	38, 56, 58, 210, 211, 212	**Proverbs**	
14:10–12	46				
14:12	265	31:1–40	209	20:25	38
14:13	49	31:13	56		
14:13–14a	47	31:16–17	56	**Song of Songs**	
14:14	215, 265	31:22	211	1:14	45
14:19b	47	31:24–25	56	2:1–2	45
16:2	53	31:29	56	5:13	45
16:6–17	42n29	31:33	213		
16:7–17	40n25, 51	31:33–34	56, 57, 58	**Isaiah**	
16:18	51	38–41	209, 269	2	247, 248
16:19	50, 51, 52	38–42	211	2:11	248
16:21	50, 51	42:7	59, 210, 214	2:11–17	248
19:23–24	48	42:7–8	50	2:17	248
19:25	49, 50, 51, 52	42:7–10	50n41	6	247, 248
19:25–27	47–48, 215	42:8	59, 210, 214	6:1	248, 250, 253
19:26b	48	42:14	143n16	7:14	63
20:5	35n16	42:17	59, 209	28:1	45
22	54			28:4	45
22:21	53	**Psalms**		30:30	230n6
22:21–22	21	19:14	49	33:2	230n6
27:2–6	53, 209, 211	19:15	49	40–48	225, 235
27:2–7	52	74	38, 39	40–55	225
27:6	53	74:12–14	39	40:1–2	225
29	55, 58	82	267, 268, 269	40:6–8	45
29–31	36, 55, 268	82:6–7	267	40:6–11	233
29:2	55	86:15	169n15	40:9	233, 234
29:2–6	55	103:8	169n15	40:10	230
29:8	55	103:15–16	45	40:11	230
29:9	55	111:4	169n15	41:1–4	235
29:11–17	55	112:4	169n15	41:2	235
29:25	55	114:3	156	41:14	49

41:25	235	49:4a	239	53:4	227, 241, 244–45, 249
41:25–29	235	49:7	49		
41:27	233–34	49:14–21	226	53:4–5	227n3
42:1–4	238	50:4–9	238, 239	53:4–10	241
43:27–28	225	50:6	239, 240, 242	53:4b	240
44:6	49	50:7–9	240	53:5	241, 251
44:24	49	51:5	230	53:5–6	244–45
44:24–28	235	51:9	230	53:6	250
44:24–45:7	235	51:9–11	230–31, 233	53:7	242–43, 251
44:26	225	51:10	231	53:7–9	239–40, 246
44:28	225, 235, 238	51:11	226, 232	53:8	227, 241, 242–43
45:1	225, 235	52:1–2	226	53:8–10	244–45
45:1–2	235	52:7	233, 236	53:10	227n3, 228, 241, 244, 251, 259
45:1–7	235	52:7–10	233		
45:2	238	52:7–12	234	53:10–11	252
45:4	235	52:10	230, 233	53:10a	246
45:5	235	52:11	226, 247	53:10b	246
45:9	238	52:11–12	232	53:10b–11aα	252
45:9–12	235	52:12	233	53:11	226, 227, 249, 259
45:9–13	235	52:13	226, 227, 227n3, 247, 250, 253		
45:9–17	237			53:11aβ–12	227, 247
45:10	238	52:13–15	227, 247	53:12	227n3, 249, 251
45:13	238	52:13–53:12	225, 226, 239	53:12b	227n3
46:9–11	235			54:1–3	226
46:11	235	52:14	227n3, 249	54:5	49
47:4	49	52:15	249	54:8	49
48:12	49	53	226, 227, 227n3, 228, 236, 238, 240, 243, 246, 247, 248, 251, 252, 259	59:16	230n6
48:12–16	235			62:8	230n6
48:14	235, 236			63:5	230n6
48:14–16	230, 233, 234			63:12	230n6
48:17	49	53:1	227n3, 228, 229, 236, 237, 242	**Jeremiah**	
49–55	225				
49:1–6	238, 239	53:1–11aα	227, 250	32:18	169n15
49:3	239	53:2	227, 227n3, 237	37–38	19
49:4	240	53:3	226, 227, 237, 241, 242, 244	39:7	115n28
49:4–5	240			52:11	115n28

Ezekiel

11:16	135n3
13:9	221
34	153
37	261

Daniel

7	256
7–12	254, 256, 268
7:3	268
7:7	256
7:7–9	269
7:8	255, 256
7:11	255
7:13–14	269
7:19	256
7:20	256
7:21	256
7:25	255, 256
8	257
8:10	260
8:11–13	255, 257
8:23–25	257
11	257
11:3	257
11:21	257
11:30b–33	257–58
11:31	257
11:33	254, 256, 258
11:35	259
12	221
12:1	221, 260
12:1b–3	260
12:2	254, 269
12:3	258, 259

Joel

2:13	169n15

Jonah

4:2	169n15

Nahum

1:3	169n15

Malachi

3:16	163–64, 221
3:17	164
4:1	164

DEUTERO-CANONICAL BOOKS

1 Maccabees

1:20–28	256
1:44–50	256
1:45	255
1:54	255, 257
1:57	256

2 Maccabees

5:11–21	256
6:6	255, 256

PSEUDEPIGRAPHA

Pseudo-Philo

Liber Antiquitatum Biblicarum

42	62n4

ANCIENT JEWISH WRITERS

Josephus

Jewish Antiquities

5.124–27	62n4

NEW TESTAMENT

Matthew

26:15	138
26:39	203

Mark

3:27	8n18
14:36	203

Luke

22:42	203

John

6:41	128
10:11	131, 153
10:18	263
10:18a	3
12:37	224

1 Corinthians

2:11	125

Philippians

1:21–24	3

Hebrews

11:1	71
11:32–34	122

Index of Scripture and Other Ancient Texts

Rabbinic Works

Ecclesiasticus Rabbah
1.18   119

Leviticus Rabbah
5.3   119

Numbers Rabbah
9:24   119

Early Christian Writings

Augustine

The City of God
1.17	122
1.18	123
1.19	123, 124
1.20	122
1.21	124, 125
1.26	125
27	4n12
31	4n12

Sermon 364
2	127
3	127, 128
5	129
6	126, 127–28